HOOKING ON POUCH" FOR DELIVERY.

RECEIVING "POUCHES."

STARLAND R.I.

ADE UP. PARCELS POST VAN.

ROYAL MAIL
THE POST OFFICE SINCE 1840

ROYAL

THE POST OFFICE SINCE 1840

FOREWORD BY ASA BRIGGS

LONDON AND DOVER, NEW HAMPSHIRE

MAIL

M.J. DAUNTON

THE ATHLONE PRESS

First published in Great Britain in 1985
by the Athlone Press
44 Bedford Row, London WC1R 4LY and
51 Washington Street, Dover, New Hampshire

British Library Cataloguing Publication Data
Daunton, M.J.
    Royal mail: the Post Office since 1840
    1. Great Britain. *Post Office* – History
    I. Title
    383'.4941   HE6935
    ISBN 0–485–11280–9

Library of Congress Cataloging in Publication Data
    Daunton, M. J. (Martin J.)
    Royal mail.
    Includes index.
    1. Great Britain.   Post Office – History.
    2. Postal service – Great Britain – History.
    I. Title.
    HE6935.D38   1985   383'.4941   85–13510
    ISBN 0–485–1280–9

Typesetting by The Word Factory Limited, Rossendale, Lancashire
Printed in Great Britain by St Edmundsbury Press, Bury St Edmunds
Bound by Norton Bridge, Hitchin, Herts.

Contents

Illustrations

ILLUSTRATIONS

Between pages 238 and 239

Foreword

The Post Office is an old institution. There was a 'Master of the Posts' from the reign of Henry VIII. It is also one of the best-known national institutions which has directly affected people's daily lives. It was radically transformed in the nineteenth century and has been just as radically transformed in the twentieth. Less emphasis is now placed on its role as an institution and more on its role as a business. Rowland Hill, one of the best-known names in the country for his association with the new penny post, would have approved.

This important new history, which starts with Rowland Hill – and reassesses his career – traces the development of the Post Office as an institution and as a business and the widening range of activities in which it engaged during the nineteenth and twentieth centuries. It ends with the demise of the Post Office as a government department in 1969 – and with it the office of Postmaster-General – and the subsequent separation of postal services and telecommunications. Because the history has been commissioned by the Post Office, it leaves telecommunications out of the picture before the separation. They deserve a full study in themselves.

It is a mistake to consider that the history of the Post Office is exclusively of interest to readers fascinated by stamps, although one great historian, Marc Bloch, was particularly drawn to that aspect of the subject. As this new history shows, there are many points of entry into the subject and many important general issues are raised as the history unfolds. Some of the issues have a bearing on major policy decisions being taken today in other fields. One of the great merits of this history is that it not only takes those issues into account, but that it also takes into full account other issues raised by historians. History is an old study, but in recent years it has changed just as much as the Post Office itself.

Asa Briggs

Worcester College, Oxford

Acknowledgements

Any historian is in debt to the archivists who supply the material for his research, but even more is this the case when their service is so friendly and helpful as at the Post Office Archives. Jean Farrugia and her staff were unfailingly generous and eased my task in many ways; Celia Constantinides above all made it a pleasure to visit the search room at St Martin's le Grand to face the intimidating mass of files. One of the least welcome aspects of authorship is the isolation it normally entails and here again I was fortunate in reporting to a group of managers of the Post Office who took a positive and enthusiastic interest in my work, showing remarkable patience in reading early drafts. If the completed book has any virtues, it must be in some part the result of their endeavours. At various times Jerry Baxter, Nigel Walmsley, Ian Barr, Henry Tilling, John Mackay and Sam Haskett commented on chapters and showed that the concerns of an academic historian and the administrators of a major nationalised industry are not so far removed. Retired members of the Post Office also gave advice, particularly John Newton and George Downes.

At University College London, my colleagues Robin Craig, David Tierney and Maldwyn Jones supplied references and advice, and I am grateful to members of the graduate seminars at the Institute of Historical Research in London, the University of Sussex, and the University of Southampton for listening to my early thoughts with forbearance. Theo Barker of the London School of Economics placed me in his debt once more by reading the text and putting at my disposal his wide experience of writing commissioned histories. Michael Wagner, the historian of the Austrian Postsparkasse, opened up many new approaches for me. I was fortunate to meet, on my first visit to the Post Office Archives, Charles Perry of the University of the South, who guided the faltering steps of a novice by sharing the wide knowledge he had acquired in writing his doctoral thesis on the Post Office. I am deeply grateful to him. I learned much from other researchers at the Post Office Archives, and I would thank in general terms everyone who has helped me with remarks and references over the past three years as we read our voluminous files. I must also acknowledge the assistance of librarians and archivists at the RAF Museum, Hendon; Public Record Office, Kew; National Maritime Museum, Greenwich; the British

Library; University College Library; and the London Library. The illustrations of Cunard ships come from N.R.P. Bonsor, *North Atlantic Seaway*, and I wish to thank Mr Bonsor's executors for permission to reproduce these drawings. The plates have been supplied by the Post Office's photographic library. Nazneen Razwi yet again transformed my poor typing and worse handwriting into an immaculate typescript, and I wish to thank her also for helping me to snatch time from administration to complete this book. Above all, I must thank my wife for her support as I have struggled to finish this project; she cannot have realised that she was marrying St Martin's le Grand.

M.J. Daunton
November 1984

Preface

Why write a history of the Post Office? Historians normally select a topic because it has grown out of their past work or from a continuing scholarly debate, and it appears as a natural progression. But in the present case, the normal process was reversed: here was a topic in search of an author. The Board of the Post Office had decided, at the prompting of The Athlone Press, to commission an official history to replace Howard Robinson's *Britain's Post Office*, which had appeared in 1953.[1] It seemed to the Board to be a propitious moment for a fresh consideration of the development of the Post Office, for much had changed since Robinson wrote. In the early 1950s, the Post Office was still a government department under the Postmaster General, responsible for both posts and telecommunications; it was in serious financial difficulties and had yet to adjust to the changes of the postwar world. By the early 1980s, the Post Office had become a public corporation, the Postmaster General was a memory and British Telecom had been formed as a separate enterprise; the Post Office was profitable, adopting an aggressive marketing policy and pressing through a major programme of modernisation. There were, therefore, perfectly understandable reasons why the Board should commission a history, for our view of the past is formed by the vantage point of the present. It would, however, be wrong to stress the purely internal motives for producing a new history for, after all, other nationalised industries were already active in this particular field. Leslie Hannah has produced a two-volume study of the electricity industry, Terry Gourvish is considering the development of British Rail since nationalisation and, most ambitiously, the National Coal Board has sponsored a five-volume history of the coal industry since the middle ages.[2] In comparison with these grandiose projects, with their teams of research assistants, the present history has a distinct modesty.

By a process which has something in common with Anthony Trollope's appointment to the Post Office through the power of patronage rather than the assessment of merit, an official historian was found. My initial reaction to the project was one of defensive embarrassment, for an academic career which had been largely spent in the consideration of nineteenth-century towns did not provide an obvious lead into the history of the Post Office. The project did not grow out of my own past work, and neither did it appear to connect with any current scholarly controversies. In retrospect, it now appears to be very surprising that historians have devoted so little attention to a major British institution. The standard text-books on the social, economic or political history of modern Britain scarcely mention the Department, with the possible exception of a passing nod in the direction of Rowland Hill and the introduction of the Penny Post. This is all the more surprising in view of the wealth of information in the Post Office archives, which must rank as one of the major collections on a modern institution. Why should the history of the Post Office have been so relatively neglected at a time when nineteenth- and twentieth-century history has attracted the attention of so many historians? In part, it is in response to the organisation of the archives, which have been retained at the Post Office rather than transferred to the Public Record Office. Until recently, the archive was all but unknown to academic historians, and the facilities in the old headquarters at St Martin's le Grand were not such as to encourage extensive use of the material. This is no longer the case, and it is possible to detect already a growing use of the archives by historians interested in a wide variety of topics, whether the employment of women or the development of the shipping industry or the changing structure of labour relations. There has also been a tendency to think of the history of the Post Office in terms of philately, and there was certainly some puzzlement amongst other readers in the archives who interpreted postal history in terms of post marks, stamps and the reconstruction of mail routes. The Post Office, to most professional historians, had an unfortunate reputation for being worthy and dull. They might recall that Anthony Trollope and Flora Thompson were employees, and then turn to draw upon their accounts of nineteenth-century society. The most obvious reason, however, for the neglect of the history of the Post Office was a sense that it had already been done. The work of Howard Robinson, starting with *The British Post Office: A History* in 1948, continuing with his more popular history of 1953, and culminating in 1964 with *Carrying British Mails Overseas*, created a definite sense that whatever needed to be said had been.[3] In the first stages of the research, the most frequent response from colleagues was that Robinson's books provided a definitive treatment, and this book would certainly be the poorer if it had not built on the foundations he laid. It must also be said that the approach followed here is very different, for a few visits to the Post Office archives soon suggested that the history of the Department connects with many of the new areas of concern which have been brought into the scope of historical enquiry since Robinson's early work. It is not only the Post Office which has changed since the early 1950s but also the questions asked by historians.

How, then, have the concerns of historians changed since the last history of the Post Office? One of the most buoyant areas of the subject at present must be business history, and funds may still be found to finance large-scale company histories.[4] Although old-fashioned commemorative celebrations of firms do still appear, there has been a general transformation of the quality of business history which now has its own journal, research institute and professor. [5] Serious historical attention is given to themes which in Robinson's day had scarcely penetrated an academic world where business schools and their concerns were alien to the British tradition. Historians were still dominated by traditional accounts of high politics and diplomacy, and while there had been a separate development of economic history this had in turn been dominated by the current framework of economics with its emphasis upon growth in the aggregate. This tradition of economic history does still continue in some quarters, with its treatment of the past in somewhat abstract and theoretical terms, but there has also been a new concern for the institutions of economic life. Decisions were made within firms and it is important to understand how they operated. The creation of a coherent management structure to control a business might in itself be as important as the famous machines of the industrial revolution.[6] This recent work in business history has informed my approach to the Post Office at many points and I would argue that the Department deserves a central role in accounts of the development of modern business structures. By the First World War, it had a workforce of 250,000 and a revenue of £32.6m which placed it amongst the largest concerns of the time. Professor Hannah has shown that the merger wave of the turn of the century foundered in part because British businessmen had been unable to devise managerial techniques for the efficient operation of large combines,[7] yet the Post Office continued to expand into new areas such as financial services, telegraphs and telephones. How successful was this public enterprise in controlling its rambling empire when so many of the large private companies were failing?

This at once raises another question. What should be the proper boundary between private and public enterprise? The rise of the modern business corporation is one theme which historians must face and related to this is the emergence of a 'mixed' economy, for one of the major political debates of the twentieth century has been the proper relationship between private and public enterprise. This can hardly be ignored at a time when the privatisation of British Telecom in 1984 casts a new light on the nationalisation of the private telegraph companies in 1870 and the telephone companies in 1912. A theme which runs through the history of the Department is precisely the nature of public enterprise. Should the Post Office have a monopoly on its letter services and, if it should, was it permissible to move from this secure base to compete with private concerns in the carriage of parcels, the sale of insurance policies, or the provision of financial services? The cast has changed but many of the arguments remain the same; the present critic of public monopolies can seek support from the unlikely quarter of Rowland Hill, the originator of the Penny Post. Even if the need for public enterprise was accepted, another crucial issue remained. Was the role of a public business to maximise its profit or to stress social benefit? This question was to trouble the Post Office throughout its history.

The developments in business history certainly assist the writing of a new history of the Post Office, so long as it is remembered that the Post Office was not really a business: it was until 1969 a government department, under a political head, and staffed by civil servants. The concerns of political historians with the nineteenth-century 'revolution in government' here became relevant. The traditional view of A.V. Dicey's pioneer study was that the mid-Victorian period was pre-eminently an age of individualism and *laissez-faire*, which was to be replaced towards the end of the nineteenth century and in the twentieth century by collectivism and state intervention.[8] However, historians subsequently noted that the distinction was overdrawn and a major controversy developed over the nature of the government's role and its determinants. In particular, a difference of opinion arose between those who stressed the significance of the ideas associated with Jeremy Bentham and the utilitarian reformers, and those who minimised the role of ideas and instead stressed the incremental growth of new powers through the dynamic of administration.[9] It is surprising that the Post Office has been neglected in these controversies, for it certainly does cast new light on these issues.[10] Rowland Hill was associated with Bentham and the utilitarians, which gives some support to those who insist on the relevance of ideas, but some other explanation must be found for the subsequent broadening of the scope of the Department. Here was a branch of government which was expanding its role throughout the nineteenth century and which was also, apparently against the tenets of *laissez-faire*, providing subsidies to private shipping companies. The debates which took place within the Post Office over its proper sphere produced a particularly clear statement of many of the issues of *laissez-faire* versus state intervention which have fuelled historical controversy over the past twenty or thirty years.

The debate over the nature of nineteenth-century government had already started when Robinson was writing *Britain's Post Office*, for J.B. Brebner's classic article on the subject was published in 1948. There was, however, scarcely any sign in the historical literature of the concerns which were to come to the fore in the 1960s and 1970s: social history, with its ambition of rescuing the mass of society from anonymity. History from below became a major growth area in the radical days of the 1960s, and it has persisted into the more conservative 1980s in a different guise. It would not be too much of an exaggeration to distinguish two phases. The initial response was to find the voice of the previously inarticulate, charting their resistance to economic and social change, and celebrating their positive achievements.[11] More recently, the emphasis has been upon the ability of the established order to contain and limit opposition, and this connects with recent work in economics and business history. The concern is often the internal world of the business or workplace, stressing the division of the workforce into separate segments and the maintenance of the power of the employer by the development of new techniques of discipline and hierarchy, which might in part involve the incorporation of unions into a formal system of labour relations.[12] Howard Robinson clearly could not take account of such approaches to the past which have only developed since he wrote, but they do form a major concern in the present study. The Post Office was, after all, the largest employer in the country for most of the period and it had to face in a peculiarly acute way the problems of ordering and controlling a massive workforce. A study of the changing stratagems which were adopted illuminates one of the central themes in modern British history.

These are the major concerns which have shaped the writing of this book, and the aim has been to integrate the history of the Post Office with wider trends in the economy, society and politics of modern Britain. Of course, it has been necessary to provide a great deal of detail on the operation of the Department, so that it is hoped that anyone who wishes to discover, say, the postage rate in 1875 or the name of the Postmaster General in 1928, will not be disappointed. However, in order to treat the major issues with any coherence the book had to be organised on a thematic basis rather than according to strict chronology. Readers might be puzzled by two other features of the book. One is that the telegraph and telephone services have been excluded, for the project was sponsored by the Board of the present Post Office after the separation of posts from telecommunications. It cannot be denied that this does distort the history of the Department at a time when the services were combined in one institution, and there have been times when it has been impossible to avoid discussion of telegraphs and telephones. Nevertheless, the history of telecommunications does raise a new set of concerns, such as the nature of the market, the relation with suppliers, the development of technology and patterns of investment. These themes could usefully form the subject of another book, and perhaps the newly privatised British Telecom will commission a historian to reflect upon the way in which services developed under the control of a public body; it would certainly be an interesting and relevant exercise. The other point which must be emphasised is the period covered by this book. The starting point is 1840 with the introduction of the Penny Post, which coincided with the switch from road to rail transport, the development of steam navigation, and the reform of the political system. Although it is of course necessary to provide some brief details about the earlier era, there is no pretence to add any new interpretations or material. The sway of Howard Robinson in the earlier period remains undisputed. At the other end of the time scale, the analysis moves to a different level after the Second World War. The Post Office is now a nationalised industry but access to its records remains limited by the thirty-year rule which governs the release of material to the public. The developments since the Second World War cannot be considered in detail, and the final chapter is merely an epilogue which attempts to suggest some of the major changes which have occurred. It will remain for another historian in the next generation to provide a full account of the introduction of mechanised sorting, the strike of 1971, and the change in the status of the Post Office – and by the time the records are available for the recent past it will certainly be time to take a fresh look at the years up to the Second World War.

'Having so steeped myself, as it were, in postal waters,' Anthony Trollope reflected after thirty-three years of service in the Department, 'I could not go out from them without a regret.' Although the research and writing of this book did not take quite so long, it did produce something of the same obsession with the work of the Post Office which Trollope noted in his autobiography, where he remarked on his desire to allow the public in little villages to buy postage stamps, to receive their letters early and to have pillar boxes. But no obsession with postal concerns could rival Rowland Hill's total absorption in the affairs of the Department from 1837 until his death, and any history of the modern Post Office must start with the forbidding figure of the 'king of postal reform'. 'I was always an anti-Hillite,' remarked Trollope, 'it was a pleasure to me to differ from him on all occasions.'[13] The sentiment is, as we shall see, easily understood.

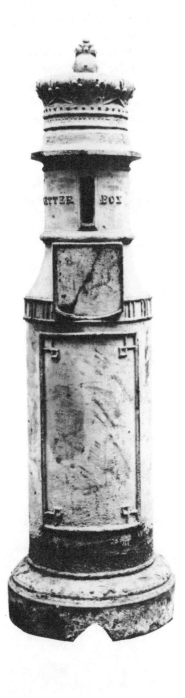

PART I
Improvement
and
Expansion

Thirty years ago the arrangements . . . were . . . of the most primitive kind. . . . The public required little attention, and got but little. Being prior to the time of postage stamps, and we may almost add of money orders, not to speak of savings' bank business, few applications were ever made to the officers – consisting of a postmaster, his wife, and another clerk – for anything but stray scraps of information relative to the despatch of mails. The communication with the public was anything but close, being conducted . . . through a trap-door in a wooden pane in the office-window . . . .Now this is changed, and almost all postal arrangements, prior to the days of Sir Rowland Hill, are as so many things of the past.

W. Lewins, *Her Majesty's Mails : A History of the Post Office and an Industrial Account of its Present Condition* (2nd edn, 1865), pp. 289-90, 292.

1 Rowland Hill: From Radical to Administrator

> Certainly he is a king of postal reform and I felt myself a very small subject in waiting upon him.
> Lyon Playfair to Edwin Chadwick after a visit to Sir Rowland Hill in 1873.[1]

Rowland Hill died in 1879, but his presence still haunts the Post Office. His statue stands outside the chief office in the City, sternly confronting the former Postal Headquarters at St Martin's le Grand. He lies buried in Westminster Abbey as a benefactor of the nation, and he has appeared on commemorative issues of postage stamps throughout the world. No other Secretary of the Post Office has achieved such fame and popular recognition, and his successors at St Martin's le Grand who formulated policy and controlled the whole vast business remain by contrast hidden in anonymity. The human face of the Post Office is more usually the postman on his walk and the clerk at the counter; only one other senior postal official, Anthony Trollope, has attained such fame, but he is remembered as the creator of the fictional world of Barchester rather than for his labours as a Surveyor of the Post Office. Rowland Hill is an exception, because his fame rests securely upon his involvement with the Department, without which he might have been no more than a minor figure in the radical world of the 1830s. The historian of the Post Office becomes all too conscious that the initial conception of his task is reduced to a single individual, a solitary event, and one date: Rowland Hill and the introduction of the Penny Post in 1840.

This is to take Rowland Hill and his penny postal achievements at his own valuation. The truth is that the development of the Post Office is now viewed almost entirely through the distortions of Hill's own voluminous writings, works of self-justification which do not provide

3

SIR ROWLAND LE GRAND.

Rowland Hill retired as Secretary of the Post Office in 1864, and Tenniel's cartoon indicates the esteem in which he was held by the public, if not by his subordinates at St Martin's le Grand.

an objective view of the reforms introduced in 1840.[2] In fact, the arguments against penny postage did not rest merely on benighted ignorance as he insisted, but were firmly grounded in the realities of the postal service. And it was not only the entrenched officials at St Martin's le Grand who were hostile to Hill, for the new generation which had a firm commitment to penny postage also found it impossible by the 1860s to work with him or to accept his interpretation of the Post Office's principal purpose. Trollope himself remarked upon the pleasures of a career involving 'feuds – such delicious feuds! I was always an anti-Hillite . . . believing him to be entirely unfit to manage men or to arrange labour. It was a pleasure to me to differ from him on all occasions; – and looking back now, I think that in all such differences I was right.'[3] There was, for all of his bluff tone, a considerable element of truth in Trollope's remarks and there must be serious reservations about the traditonal view of Hill as the father of the modern Post Office. He had fundamentally miscalculated the economics of his scheme for a Penny Post, and by the end of his career he was unfitted for the management of a large civil service department. Hill was obsessive about 'my plan', and his diaries present a picture of a man who considered himself to be misunderstood and unappreciated, facing malicious attacks from all quarters. He quarrelled with successive Postmasters General and with competent subordinates as a result of his peremptory and high-handed behaviour. Indeed, he seemed incapable of working with anyone outside his own family and he brought so many relatives into the Department that a wit who enquired why Sir Rowland was like the sun could expect the reply, 'because he touches the little Hills with gold'.[4] Edmund Yates, who commenced his career in the Post Office in 1847, was no enemy of Hill but remarked that he 'had a peculiarly effective way of saying a caustic and unpleasant thing: voice and manner lent their aid to send the shaft rankling home'.[5]

Rowland Hill and postal reform

Rowland Hill emerged from relative obscurity in 1837 with the publication of *Post Office Reform: Its Importance and Practicability*, a pamphlet with aimed to sweep aside the complex arrangements which existed at that time. In London, there were three offices: the Twopenny Post Office handled mail within London and its environs; the Inland Office had general charge of the whole postal system for the country; and the Foreign Office dealt with the overseas correspondence. These offices had their own separate staffs, so that a Londoner might receive his mail from three letter-carriers. The charge for local letters within the central area of London was twopence, and

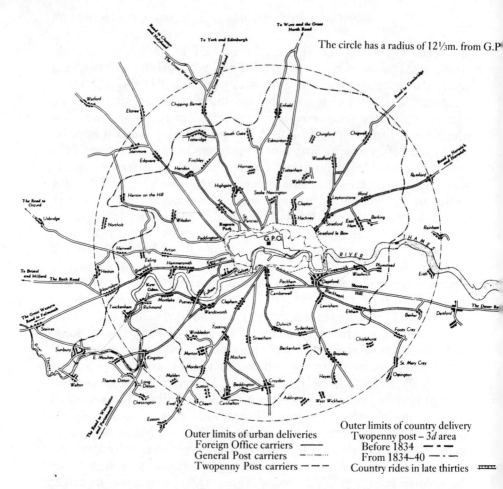

The circle has a radius of 12⅓m. from G.P

Outer limits of urban deliveries
Foreign Office carriers ⎯⎯
General Post carriers ⎯⎯⎯
Twopenny Post carriers ⎯ ⎯ ⎯

Outer limits of country delivery
Twopenny post – 3d area
Before 1834 ⎯ ⎯
From 1834–40 ⎯ · ⎯
Country rides in late thirties ▮▮▮

Before the introduction of the Penny Post, letters posted and delivered within central London paid 2d, and in outer London 3d. These local letters were delivered by the Twopenny Post Carriers; there were also separate carriers, with their own limits, for the General Post from the rest of the country, and the Foreign Office

there was also an outer area in which there was a charge of an extra penny. Cheap local posts also existed in other towns: by the mid-1830s there were 295 Penny Posts in Ireland, 81 in Scotland and 356 in England and Wales. The postage on letters which were sent beyond their limits through the 'General Post' varied according to distance and the number of sheets of paper. The lowest rate for a letter of a single sheet was fourpence for up to 15 miles, rising to one shilling for a distance up to 300 miles. Beyond that, one penny was charged for each additional 100 miles. A double letter of two sheets paid twice these rates, and a treble letter three times; 'heavy' letters were charged by the quarter ounce. This scale meant that a single letter from London to Brighton cost eightpence, to Birmingham ninepence, to Liverpool

TwoPyPo/t
· Unpaid ·
Brompton

Aldgate
2py P·Paid

ABERGAVENNY
Unpaid
Penny Post

AYLSHAM
Penny Post

Brompton and Aldgate:
Mail sent through the Twopenny Post in London could be paid by the sender who handled the money over at the receiving house, where the letter would be stamped as paid. Alternatively, the postage was paid by the recipient, in which case the letter was stamped as unpaid.

Abergavenny and Aylsham:
Letters posted in the local penny posts were stamped with the name of the town; in most cases the recipient paid the postage.

elevenpence. The postage was generally paid by the recipient of the letter. Although the London local post had started on the basis of payment by the sender, in 1794 this was made optional so that letters in the Twopenny Post were in consequence stamped as 'Paid' or 'Unpaid'. In local posts, the penny was in general paid on delivery; in the General Post, the sender could pay in theory but the vast majority of letters were in practice sent without prepayment. Since the rate for General Post letters was not uniform, they had to be 'taxed' by writing the postage on the outside. This 'taxing' of letters and the collection of postage from the recipient were time-consuming: a letter-carrier in London, for example, could deliver, on average, only seventy letters in a 'walk' of an hour and a half. The system also produced highly complex and confused internal accounts. It must not be assumed, however, that letters were generally delivered to the recipients' house. Although this was the case in London and within recognised 'free delivery' areas of towns, elsewhere it was usual to collect mail from the post office. Neither were letters posted in road-side letter boxes, for it was necessary to take them to a post office or 'receiving house' or, in London and some provincial towns, to hand them to a 'bellman' who collected letters in the street, attracting attention by ringing a bell.

The postmen, before the general introduction of prepayment, collected the postage from the recipients of letters, which made the task of delivery slow, and their visit not always welcome.

This, in very broad terms, was the system which existed before the introduction of the uniform Penny Post in 1840: rates were high and the system complex.[6]

Hill's pamphlet proposed the reshaping of the postal system, to a considerable extent by developing elements which already existed, such as the low local rates and the system of prepayment. His starting point was that the revenue of the country exceeded the expenditure, so that some reduction in taxation might be anticipated. Hill argued that in selecting which tax to cut, the government should take care to give the maximum of relief to the public with the minimum of injury to the revenue. This led him to the high rates of postage. The argument was not original, for Hill was adopting the same approach as Sir Henry Parnell's *On Financial Reform*, which he cited in his pamphlet. Parnell claimed that 'when a tax has been carried to an excessively high point, the reducing of it is not necessarily followed by a reduction of revenue, but may lead to an increase'. Parnell indeed mentioned the Post Office to illustrate his contention, and Hill's pamphlet should be seen as part of the general debate on the level of indirect taxes and tariffs which was one of the major political issues of the 1830s.[7] Hill observed that the revenue from the Post Office was not rising with the population. In 1815, the net postal revenue had been £1.6m and in 1833 it had fallen slightly to £1.5m, whereas if the revenue had increased in step with the population it should by then have reached £2m. The high level of postage rates was, he argued, acting as a barrier to growth. The net revenue was more than twice the cost of management, so that 'the tax is about 200 per cent on the natural or untaxed cost of postage'. The loss to the revenue caused by the excessive postage charges was, claimed Hill, even more serious when the injuries inflicted on society were taken into account. Religious, moral and intellectual progress were checked, and trade was hindered. The Post Office, he asserted, was a monopoly which was 'uninfluenced by the ordinary motives to enterprise and good management'.

The issue, as Hill saw it, was how to determine the correct level of tax on the transmission of letters. He proceeded by establishing the 'natural cost' of conveying a letter, which he defined as the cost of the service if the Post Office was run on ordinary commercial principles. He then added to the 'natural cost' the duty which would produce the revenue required by the government. The apparent cost of each item of mail was calculated to be $1\frac{1}{8}d$ (1.13d), but if various extraneous charges were removed the actual cost came down to 0.84d. The cost of carriage alone was O.28d, but this was an aggregate figure including bulky newspapers; for an ordinary letter the average cost of conveyance was only 0.009d. The letter might, of course, be sent to the next street or the whole length of the country, and the next stage in Hill's argument was to calculate the actual cost of carriage for a letter between London and Edinburgh. He found this to be only $\frac{1}{36}d$ (0.03d), and he concluded that postage 'must be made uniformly the same from every post-town to every other post-town in the United

Kingdom, unless it can be shown how we are to collect so small a sum as the thirty-sixth part of a penny'. Postage rates should, he concluded, not vary with distance. Administrative costs were, he felt, unnecessarily inflated both by the complexity of charges under the existing system and by the collection of postage from the recipient of a letter. Hill asserted that uniform rates and prepaid postage would allow the existing staff of clerks and letter-carriers to handle at least a four-fold increase in business. On the assumption that the traffic would quadruple from 126m to 500m items, he estimated that the average cost would fall from $0.84d$ to $0.32d$. The rate to be charged to the public should, in Hill's view, be set at a level which would be sufficiently low both 'to neutralise the objection' to prepayment and to produce the revenue required by the government. A rate of $1d$ would, he believed, remove hostility to prepayment and generate a considerable increase in the traffic, especially if the service was improved at the same time.

These calculations were complicated by the fact that two classes of traffic would not be affected by lower rates: newspapers, which already paid stamp duty giving the right to free transmission through the post; and letters sent free under the franks of Members of Parliament. A four-fold increase in the total traffic would therefore, Hill calculated, require an increase of five and a quarter times in the number of 'chargeable letters', from 89m to 167m. Hill was confident that such a growth of traffic was well within the bounds of possibility. The demand for postal services was, argued Hill, responsive to price and a cheap rate would both bring 'contraband' letters into the official Post Office service and also increase the total number of letters written. The illegal conveyance of letters by stage coach, carriers and ships in defiance of the Postmaster General's monopoly would be unnecessary if a cheap rate was charged by the Post Office. His belief that the total number of letters would increase rested upon an analogy with the higher consumption of tea, soap, coffee and cotton when prices fell. Hill formulated a law, whose meaning is admittedly opaque, that 'the increase in consumption is inversely as the squares of the prices'; more specifically, a reduction in postage charges from sixpence to one penny would produce a 36-fold increase in traffic, far surpassing the increase which was necessary to protect the revenue from serious erosion.[8]

The scheme of 1837 was, it should be noted, confined to the 'primary distribution' between and within post-towns; the 'secondary distribution' from the post-towns 'to places of inferior importance' was not covered. Hill believed that 'any branch of the Post Office ought, in my opinion, to defray its own expenses' so that letters should not be delivered for one penny to districts where this would impose a loss, unless it would be made good by the local authority or an extra charge levied by the Post Office. Hill rejected the principle of cross-subsidisation between profitable and unprofitable services. 'What he advocated', remarked R.H. Coase, 'was not uniformity, but uniformity in so far as it was justified by costs.' However, in the desire to secure support for his plan, Hill was to abandon this refinement and to propose that the Penny Post should be extended to all places with a delivery, a change he was later to regret as 'a great aggravation of the immediate loss of revenue'.[9]

How did it come about that these notions of a little-known pamphleteer already in his forties found their way on to the statute book by 1839? Even Rowland's brother Matthew expressed surprise at the rapidity with which the theories of *Post Office Reform* had become reality:

> This bold project did not obtain authority from the name of its author, who was little known to the world. . . . Its boldness was . . . likely to be quietly contemned as empirical rashness by a busy population like our own. . . . No scheme, therefore, was ever promulgated with less probability of success from adventitious causes; and yet no scheme ever made its way in so short a time to the convictions of mankind, not only in this country, but wherever a post-office is to be found.[10]

The explanation for the speed with which the scheme for penny postage was implemented is to be found in the manner in which it meshed with other aspects of 'economical reform' in the 1830s. Reform of the Post Office, far from being an isolated event, was a relatively minor aspect of a wider programme with which not only Rowland Hill but also his brothers were involved. The Hill family was not in the front rank of the wider reform movement, and Rowland's fame resulted from his single-minded concentration after 1837 upon one policy and one Department. Even his family felt that his obsession with postal reform was carried too far. When he met Garibaldi at a banquet in 1864, for instance, his sole topic of conversation was the state of the Italian post office. 'When you go to heaven', his brother remarked, 'I foresee that you will stop at the gate to inquire of St Peter how many deliveries they have per day, and how the expense of postal communication between heaven and the other place is defrayed.'[11]

The ambitious Hills

The family background of Rowland Hill explains not only his route to the publication of *Post Office Reform*, but also his association with the radical reform movement of the 1830s. Robert Owen in his auto-biography reminisced about a meeting in London with 'several members of a very remarkable family, possessing, I think more practical ability, administrative and deliberative, than I have ever since found united in any one household'.[12] A recent writer has suggested that 'the Hill brothers combined an interest in reform with an enlightened self-interest in their own advancement, and . . . as a cohesive family unit they were able to use the personal contacts of individual members of the family to benefit the careers of other family members'.[13] Their father, Thomas Wright Hill (1763-1851), came from a Dissenting background of small traders and had, despite a desire to become an attorney, been apprenticed to a brass founder in Birmingham. There he was influenced by Joseph Priestley, the Unitarian minister, radical and scientist. Hill became a Unitarian, engaged throughout his life in eccentric scientific projects, and took an active role in radical politics in Birmingham. Priestley secured him a post in a charity school and he remained a teacher until 1795 when he joined his elderly father in an ill-fated venture in the manufacture of ponchos. The business soon failed and after a period superintending a workshop he opened a private school, 'Hill Top', at Birmingham in 1803. He had married Sarah Lea in 1791. She had worked as a nursery governess and although her father was a working man, she was proud of the fact that her mother was the daughter of a gentleman. They were to have six sons and two daughters: Matthew Davenport (1792-1872), Edwin (1793-1876), Rowland (1795-1879), Arthur (1798-1885), Caroline (1800-77), Frederic (1803-90), William (1805-30) and Sarah (1807-40). Hill's children agreed that their father was lacking in business acumen and ambition, with an inability to complete any project. But they also accepted that he was an 'admirable father' who was approachable and warm-hearted. Matthew remarked that 'from infancy, he would reason with us. Arguments were taken at their just weight. The sword of authority was not thrown into the scale.' It was from Sarah, according to Frederic, that the brothers 'inherited our ambition to conquer difficulties and to improve our position in the world'. She introduced thrift, practical common sense and organisation into the family, so that they 'retained their position in the middle class of society'. The school was a family enterprise in which the brothers became teachers in their early teens, and it was Matthew and Rowland who were to transform Thomas Wright Hill's conventional institution into an educational experiment which appealed to the competitive business spirit of early nineteenth-century Britain and attracted national attention. They were, in short, educational entrepreneurs.[14]

Matthew and Rowland introduced changes from about 1816 which were to become famous as the 'Hazelwood system', named after a new school they opened at Edgbaston in 1819. The principles were outlined in *Public Education*, published anonymously in 1822 and revised in 1825.[15] The school aimed to teach the forms of public business so that pupils would be, prepared to fill their future places in society without the trouble and pain of initiation'. Although it had a democratic system of government, it was not permissive or libertarian; rather it was a plan 'for an ideal community, governed by the values of representative government and of *laissez-faire* capitalism'.[16] By the time *Public Education* appeared, Matthew had already moved to London to become a barrister. He entered Lincoln's Inn in 1814, taking up permanent residence in London in 1818, and he was actively involved in radical politics, becoming acquainted with Henry Brougham, the Whig politician. It was, however, the publication of *Public Education* which brought him into close connection with Jeremy Bentham and the utilitarian reformers. There were, indeed, marked similarities between the Hills' system and Bentham's *Chrestomathia* of 1817, which outlined the curriculum and teaching methods for a secondary school for the 'middling and higher ranks'. The Hills denied plagiarism, but lost no time in presenting their book to Bentham, which resulted in the patronage of Hazelwood by the utilitarians. When Brougham, James Mill and others planned to establish their own 'chrestomathic' school in London, the Hills responded in 1827 by opening a school at Bruce Castle, Tottenham. Although Hazelwood continued for several years longer, London was now the family's main base.[17] The hopes which Rowland had expressed in his diary in 1821 seemed nearer to realisation:

> The more I mix with the world, the more insight I have into the proceedings and opinions of other men, the conviction is forced upon me that our family possesses talents and energy and devotedness to one object seldom to be met with; and that we only want full scope for our powers to operate, to convince the world of our superiority.[18]

The move to London allowed Rowland to join Matthew in public affairs for the first time. They were both founder members of the Society for the Diffusion of Useful Knowledge (SDUK), which was sponsored by Brougham and supported by James Mill and the publisher Charles Knight. Matthew's political career was furthered by his involvement in the Newark elections of 1830 and his defence of the men accused of attacking Nottingham castle in the Reform Bill riots of 1831. The family also decided to release one of their number from the school to take part in the campaign for the Bill, and Frederic was deputed to work with the Birmingham Political Union. In the first election after the Reform Act was implemented, Matthew became member for Hull. The extension of the franchise which had been sought by father and sons promised to give full scope to their ambitions.[19]

Matthew's political career, however, ended with his defeat in the election of 1834, and he subsequently held posts as Recorder of Birmingham and Commissioner in Bankruptcies for Bristol.[20] Frederic also secured a government post, for in 1835 he was appointed Inspector of Prisons in Scotland.[21] Rowland for a time considered communitarian schemes which would bring the family together now that the partnership of the school was dissolving. Five brothers were to survive into the 1840s, of whom four abandoned school-teaching for government posts – Frederic was to leave the prison service to join Rowland at the Post Office in 1851, while Edwin was installed at the Stamp Office in 1840 to supervise the manufacture of postage stamps. Arthur alone remained loyal to education, continuing as headmaster at Bruce Castle into the 1860s. Although the involvement of the Hill brothers with the school was considerably reduced, a 'Family Fund' was set up in 1832 into which each branch of the family paid half the surplus income which remained after necessary expenses had been met. This fund would be used to assist any member in need and to give security against poverty. The brothers remained remarkably close despite their separate careers, and 'Family Councils' were held to discuss all major decisions. When the fund was eventually dissolved in 1856, the brothers remarked that 'we attribute such success as has attended our family very much to the spirit of co-operation'.[22] Although communitarianism was only a brief phase in Rowland Hill's interests, reliance upon family co-operation was crucial, and this explains how he came to make St Martin's le Grand into a family concern.

Rowland's communitarian ideas turned in a different direction, for in 1832 he published *Home Colonies* with the explicit intention of obtaining a government post.[23] Reform of the poor law was a major concern and, his eye always on the main chance, Hill's contribution to the debate was to propose the creation of pauper agricultural communites. The inmates would be insulated from vice, given a 'useful' education and required to work hard. When habits of industry had been learned, they would be restored to society where they would no longer be a charge on the community. The 'Hazelwood system' was brought to bear on the poor, who would be taught the virtues of work and discipline. *Home Colonies* marked the next stage of reform. The Reform Act had removed the electoral disabilites of men like himself, and political power had now to be used to dismantle the barriers which impeded the play of competition and ambition so that the newly enfranchised could fully participate in the social and political system. Privilege and restrictions of trade should be destroyed, imperfections in existing institutions removed, and respect for private property instilled. The correct reponse to riots and rick-burning was not, in his view, draconian punishment and intimidation, which would only increase hostility to property, but the removal of the barriers of privilege which brought property into disrepute. Once these faults had been rectified, the poor should be taught that, whatever their poverty, any further change in property institutions would only increase distress. 'The utility of the institutions of property, the importance and absolute necessity to the labourers themselves of accumulations of capital, – must be taught as an essential part of popular education; and, above all, the working classes must be made familiar with the circumstances which regulate the price of their labour.'[24] Reform of the Post Office was part of this general approach: the imperfection of an existing institution would be removed in order to allow wider access to its benefits; and it should thereafter be run according to the strict laws of political economy.

Home Colonies did not result in the hoped-for government appointment, but Hill became involved with another Benthamite, Gibbon Wakefield, in his scheme to establish colonies of self-supporting paupers abroad. Hill helped to steer the South Australia Act through Parliament and from 1834 to 1839 he held an official appointment as Secretary of the South Australian Commission at a salary of £500.[25] It was during this period that he made another bid for power and influence by developing his scheme to change the Post Office, clearly part of the campaign of the Benthamites to reform existing institutions. These radical reformers were not critics of private property, but of the political and legal impediments to full participation in its benefits. The self-elective municipal corporations, the monopoly rights of trading companies and the corn laws were examples of such injustices which benefited some at the expense of others. High postage rates were yet another example of the injustice of limited access or unfair distribution to which he had drawn attention in *Home Colonies*. Pupils at Hazelwood were taught to succeed in a world in which artificial impediments to achievement had been removed; they were not to challenge the institutions of property but to work within the laws of political economy which gave all an equal chance. This theme united the 'Hazelwood System', the Society for the Diffusion of Useful Knowledge, the argument of *Home Colonies*, and the Hills' own careers. Postal reform was closely related to educational purposes. Lower

15

postage rates would encourage education, giving the Post Office 'the new and important character of a powerful engine of civilisation; capable of performing a distinguished part in the great work of national education, but rendered feeble and inefficient by erroneous financial arrangements'.[26] A grievance against property institutions would be removed, and the application of the laws of political economy extended. In Hill's view, financial success and the wider social or educational benefits were indistinguishable. Social benefit should not be obtained at the expense of financial success, for the aim of reform was precisely to show the equity of the laws of political economy when unfettered by the constraints of privilege. This perception goes far to explain the policy pursued by Hill when he was responsible for the administration of the Post Office.[27]

Rowland Hill's pamphlet of 1837 was not an isolated criticism of the management of the Post Office. The intitiative had already been taken by Robert Wallace, who was elected to Parliament as the member for Greenock in 1832, representing the same ideology of 'economical reform' as Matthew Davenport Hill. In 1833 Wallace launched 'a general attack on the [Post Office], its personnel, its conservatism, the methods of distributing letters and its complicated and confusing mechanism'.[28] Free trade, he urged, should be applied to the Post Office, which 'ought to be conducted on more liberal principles'.[29] The pressure he exerted on the government led in 1835 to the appointment of a Commission 'to inquire into the management of the Post-Office Department'. It issued ten reports during the next three years, recommending competitive tenders for mail-coach contracts; the transfer of packet services to private contractors or the Admiralty; the end of the Money Order Office as a semi-private concern within the Department and the introduction of the registered letter as an alternative means of transmitting money; and the establishment of a low postage rate for price lists. These reforms were accepted, but the suggestion that a Board of Commissioners should replace the Postmaster General did not find favour.[30] No radical changes were proposed in postage rates, although Howard Robinson has suggested that 'throughout the reports made by the Commissioners of 1835 runs the idea of lessening the cost of postage, and a belief that the cheapening of rates would actually increase the revenue'.[31] Robert Wallace anticipated Rowland Hill when he assured the Commissioners that 'the cheapening of postage rates would increase the revenue', and that the cost of handling a greater volume of traffic 'ought not with good management to be increased at all'.[32] In 1837, no fewer than five Acts were passed but these merely consolidated the legislation concerning the Post Office: they did not alter postage rates. 'These Acts of 1837', Robinson concludes, 'did not bring a reform in the Post Office: they simply brought order into the regulations.'[33] The Commissioners in their ninth and tenth reports, which appeared after Hill's pamphlet, did, indeed, move in the direction of lower rates. When *Post Office Reform* appeared the Commission was examining the London Twopenny Post where Hill suggested the first instalment of reform should start; he was invited to give evidence and his suggestion that the rate for prepaid letters should be reduced to one penny was supported.[34] When the tenth and final report of the Commissioners appeared in 1838, they pointed out that their brief had been the general management of the Post Office rather than postage rates, but they did propound a general principle which contradicted the existing practice of treating the Post Office as a source of taxation:

> The safe and speedy conveyance of letters, for the benefit of trade and commerce, was the primary consideration with the Government on the first establishment of a General Post Office.
> The revenue, which it was expected would arise from the exclusive privilege conferred on the Postmaster General, was held to be of minor importance. . . . The Postage duties must, therefore, be looked upon not merely as a source of Revenue, but as the price paid by the public for the performance of a particular service, which it has been found expedient to have executed under the control and supervision of the Government.[35]

This claim was historically unfounded but did indicate the new approach which was emerging. Indeed, the debate had moved on a stage by the time this report appeared in 1838.

In May 1837 Wallace moved for the appointment of a Select Committee 'to report on the present rates of postage, and especially to examine the improvements recommended, and the mode of charging postage proposed, in a pamphlet by Mr. Rowland Hill, with a view to the general reduction of postage duties'. He withdrew this motion when the government claimed to have the plan under consideration, but the auguries were not good. Lichfield, the Postmaster General, derided Hill's plan in the Lords: 'Of all the wild and visionary schemes which he had ever heard or read of, it was the most extraordinary.' However, the return of the Whigs to power later in 1837 gave Wallace his chance, and a Select Committee was appointed under his chairmanship.[36] 'Mr. Rowland Hill's plan', remarked one cynic, 'was certainly worthy of parliamentary consideration, and we only complain that the tribunal was so very *select*.'[37] Select Committees and Royal Commissions were not in the 1830s intended to provide dispassionate enquiries, but were rather seen as a means of making the case for a preconceived change. The bulky volumes of evidence produced by the

17

UNIFORM PENNY POSTAGE.

A Public Meeting

Of the Bankers, Merchants, & Traders, of the City of London,

WILL BE HELD AT THE

EGYPTIAN HALL OF THE MANSION HOUSE,

ON

Wednesday Next, July 10,

To Petition Parliament for the Adoption of Mr. ROWLAND HILL'S *Plan of a* UNIFORM PENNY POSTAGE,

AS RECOMMENDED BY THE SELECT

Committee of the House of Commons.

THE RIGHT HON. THE LORD MAYOR,

Will take the Chair at TWO o'Clock precisely.

The Metropolitan Members are expected to attend.

PRINTED BY T. BRETTELL, RUPERT STREET, HAYMARKET.

The Mercantile Committee organised an effective campaign in support of the introduction of Penny Postage. This meeting at the Mansion House was held in 1839.

Select Committee were supplemented by the work of pressure groups in the country. The most significant was the Mercantile Committee formed in February 1838, which collected evidence for the Select Committee, submitted petitions to parliament and published appeals to public opinion. Its newspaper, the *Post Circular*, included a play in which Queen Victoria, after exclaiming, 'Mothers pawning their clothes to pay the postage of a child's letter!', summoned Hill and commended his scheme to the Prime Minister. This edition was bound into 40,000 copies of a part of *Nicholas Nickleby* and a further 100,000 were printed. A total of 2,007 petitions with 262,809 signatures were submitted to Parliament, including one from the Lord Mayor of London and 12,500 City merchants. The appearance of popular backing was fostered by the summoning of working-class leaders such as Gravenor Henson to give evidence to the Select Committee, but critics of Hill could argue that his support came largely from

18

merchants and bankers who paid considerable sums in postage. The chairman of the Mercantile Committee was Joshua Bates of Baring Brothers, and the treasurer George Moffatt, a tea merchant. Hill's critics saw cheap postage as a means of increasing the profits of such men. In order to 'make up for that defalcation in the Post-office revenue, the people of England must be taxed to exactly the amount that shall be conveyed by this reform into the private purses of Messrs *This* or *That*'. But the attempt to deride the campaign as merely for '*mercantile* convenience and advantage' did not succeed,[38] not least because the scheme also had the support of such as Charles Knight the publisher, the SDUK, and leading politicians like Brougham and Richard Cobden. The attack upon high postage charges was part of the general work of radical reform, and the welcome given to the appearance of the Wallace Report 'almost took the form of an assault on one of the remaining strongholds of the old regime'.[39]

The Wallace Committee in its final report in 1838 did not, in fact, fully endorse Hill's plan, largely because of concern for the state of the revenue. Although the government had a surplus in 1836 and 1837, there was a deficit in 1838 and 1839. Uniform rates and payment by weight were accepted, but compulsory prepayment was not recommended and the rate which was proposed was twopence for the first half ounce and one penny for each additional half ounce. Since local rates might already be lower, the Committee proposed that a penny rate should apply to prepaid letters within a limit of 15 miles, and the principle of uniformity was therefore contradicted.[40] However, the caution of the Select Committee and the government's fear of a loss of revenue were swept aside during the energetic campaign mounted by the proponents of penny postage in 1839. The Whig government was pressured into introducing a Bill to permit penny postage, and although many Tories were sceptical their opposition was perfunctory. The Duke of Wellington accepted the measure 'with great reluctance and pain', and advised others to follow his lead. The Act reached the statute book in August 1839. In December a transitional rate was introduced, set at one penny in London and fourpence for a letter of half an ounce in the rest of the country. Pressure continued and on 10 January 1840, uniform penny postage was implemented: a letter of half an ounce could be carried anywhere in the United Kingdom for one penny.[41]

The economics of the Penny Post

Rowland Hill's scheme depended upon low postage rates, prepayment to reduce the burden of administration, and better distribution to

GREAT WEIGHT AND NO PRICE! LITTLE WEIGHT AND ALL PRICE!!

This caricature of an Edinburgh mail coach appeared in the *Post Circular*. It was the inspiration of Henry Cole who was to become director of the Victoria and Albert Museum.

attract more traffic. The entire proposal was based upon two major assumptions about the economics of the postal service. The first was that the demand for the letter post was responsive to the rate charged, so that the reduction in the postage rate would induce an increase of five and a quarter times in the volume of traffic. The second was that there would be a considerable reduction in the cost of handling each item at higher volumes, so that the existing establishment would suffice for the increased traffic. Both assumptions were, argued the Departmental officials, seriously flawed.

In 1837, Hill was an outsider with no administrative experience in the Post Office, eager to overturn the whole method of business of the entrenched bureaucracy at St Martin's le Grand. The permanent head was Lt-Col. W. L. Maberly (1798–1885) who had been appointed in 1836 after a career in the army and Parliament. He was to stress that he was engaged specifically to improve the services of the Post Office and that 'we were in a state of improvement and reform long before we heard of Mr Hill or his pamphlet'. The reforms advocated by the Commission were implemented and, argued Maberly, 'the first revolution in the Post-office, if it had gone on, would, I have no doubt, have been followed by a reduction of the rate'.[42] This vision of Maberly as a dynamic administrator is not totally convincing. Edmund Yates, writing in 1884, painted a graphic picture:

> his chief characteristic was, I think, indifference. He liked his status at the Post Office, he liked the salary which it gave him, he was fond of money, and he went through the work; but he was an Irish landlord . . . and his mind was running on whether Tim Mooney would pay his rent, or Mick Reilly the bailiff would get a good price for the heifer. He was married to a beautiful and brilliant lady, who wrote fashionable novels and went into society, so he had much besides the Post Office to occupy his thoughts.

Maberly would arrive at the office at eleven in the morning and ring for breakfast. A clerk would then read out the correspondence whilst Maberly engaged in his private business:

> 'Well, my good fellow, what have you got there – very important papers, eh?' 'I don't know, sir; some of them are perhaps.' 'Yes, yes, my good fellow; no doubt *you* think they're very important: *I* call them damned twopenny-ha'penny! Now, read, my good fellow, read!'. . . . The Colonel, still half engaged with his private correspondence, would hear enough to make him keep up a running commentary of disparaging grunts, 'Pooh! stuff! upon my soul!' etc. Then the clerk, having come to the end of the manuscript, would stop, waiting for orders; and there would ensue a dead silence, broken by the Colonel who, having finished his private letters, would look up and say, 'Well, my good fellow, well?' 'That's all sir.' 'And quite enough too. Go on to the next.' 'But what shall I say to this applicant, sir?' 'Say to him? Tell him to go and be damned, my good fellow!'

Despite this eccentric approach to business, Yates felt that 'Colonel Maberly was a clear-headed man of business, old-fashioned, inclined to let matters run in their ordinary groove, detesting all projects of reform, and having an abiding horror of Rowland Hill'.[43] There is certainly evidence that the 'gallant Colonel' had a better grasp of the economics of the postal service than the 'man from Birmingham', and it is not accurate to dismiss him as the *Dictionary of National Biography* later did, as an incompetent who wasted 'some millions of public money' and 'declined to encourage any schemes of postal reform'.[44] His case against Hill did have a sound basis in fact.

Hill had assumed that the demand for postal services was responsive to price, so that the postage rate could be reduced without threatening the net revenue. The Post Office took a very different view. A reduction in duty, it was claimed, did not necessarily maintain the revenue, as had been shown when lower duties were introduced on wool, advertisements and newspapers. It was also argued from actual experience that reduced rates did not have a great impact on postal traffic. A cut in the postage rate to France by 29 per cent in 1836 had resulted in an increase of only 5.3 per cent in the traffic, and this and other adjustments to postage rates led to the conclusion that 'the augmentation in the number of letters on the whole is gradual'.[45] The significance of illegal conveyance had, in the Department's view, been exaggerated, though it was nevertheless considerable. Maberly believed it amounted to between 25 and 50 per cent of the country's correspondence. The Post Office also took a cynical view of the public's response to lower rates. People, it was argued, would not sit down and write letters simply because it had become cheaper, and demand was not responsive to price so much as to increases in population and business. 'I think there are quite as many letters written now,' declared the Assistant Secretary of the Post Office, 'as there would be even if the postage were reduced. I do not think any man would write four times the number of letters he does now merely because he could send them for a penny a piece.' Maberly refused to believe that the working classes would write a large number of letters; this was, he felt, a mere figment of the reformers' imagination.[46] Indeed, one critic went so far as to argue that:

> the benefit which this class derives from cheap postage amounts to nothing, when compared with the benefit derived from it by mercantile firms, the class of bankers, London and provincial, and by the rich generally. . . . Indeed, the point is too plain for argument, that Penny Postage is a boon to the rich instead of to the poor, and is a sacrifice of national revenue to swell the coffers of a class which do not require it.[47]

Maberly put his position in his usual assertive manner. Hill's scheme, he claimed, 'appears to me a most preposterous plan, utterly un-supported by facts, and resting entirely on assumption'. He warned of serious financial consequences, for 'with a small reduction the revenue will recover itself, but if it were reduced to $1d$ I think it would not recover itself for 40 or 50 years'.[48]

The second assumption made by Hill was that the cost of handling an item of mail would fall as the traffic increased. This was also disputed by Maberly, who took the view that 'the expenses of Mr. Hill's plan must increase in a much larger proportion than he assumes they would increase'.[49] Maberly felt that this was particularly likely in view of Hill's desire to extend facilities, which 'will be so costly, when compared with the new rate of postage, as seriously to diminish the net revenue which he anticipates as the result of his plan'.[50] Hill, it was felt, had failed to grasp the complicated nature of the organisation of the Department. Of course, there was a certain element of inertia in the response of the Post Office and, as one advocate of reform noted in 1838, the officials of the Department were simply the agents who collected the high rates of postage which it was not for them to question. Whereas a private business would increase its establishment to meet rising demand, the Post Office view, this critic argued, was that 'the business should be cut down to the standard of his department':

> An official, particularly if he happens to be an aged official, is a creature of habit; if he is one whose duties confine him pretty closely to his office, that office becomes the world to him, and to propose to enlarge its boundaries shocks him like an earthquake.
>
> If, too, he enjoys his place under an establishment which is a monopoly, his notion is, that the business of the 'barbarians' without should be cut down to the measure of his office within.[51]

The conservatism of experienced officialdom met the radicalism of an enthusiastic amateur expounding the fashionable theories of the day.

1.1 TRAFFIC AND FINANCIAL PERFORMANCE OF THE POST OFFICE, 1839–53

	Chargeable letters (m)	Gross revenue (£)	Cost of management (£)	Net revenue (£)	Cost per 100 letters (£)
1839	75.9	2,390,763	756,999	1,633,764	1.0
1840	168.8	1,359,466	858,677	500,789	0.5
1845	271.4	1,887,576	1,125,594	761,982	0.4
1850	347.1	2,264,684	1,460,785	803,899	0.4
1853	410.8	2,574,407	1,400,679	1,173,728	0.3

Source: PP 1857 IV, *Return showing the number of chargeable letters delivered in the United Kingdom*, p. 332 and PP 1867–8 XLI, *Comparative Statement of the Gross Revenue, Cost of Management and Net Revenue of the Post Office...*, p. 315.

Note: The Post Office was at this time operating on the basis of a year ending 5 January. The figures given for 1839 strictly refer to the year ending 5 January 1840, and so on. The cost of packet services and stationery, and the revenue from impressed newspaper stamps are excluded.

Political support meant that the demand for reform did carry the day against the advocates of caution. But Maberly and his subordinates, arguing from experience rather than theory, reached conclusions which proved nearer the mark. The table shows that Hill was wrong on both main counts: traffic grew less rapidly than he expected, and management costs were not unaffected even by this more moderate growth.

Hill would not, of course, so readily have assumed that his scheme had failed. The cost of management had been inflated, he claimed, by the high cost of railway services and the general lack of attention to economy. Reforms which he had advised to reduce costs, such as the amalgamation of the separate forces of London letter-carriers, had not been effected. The growth of traffic had been checked, he argued, by the failure of the Post Office to make improvements in the service. Quite simply, argued Hill, his plan had not been given a fair trial. A measure of the extent to which performance fell short of expectations is also complicated by the failure of Hill to specify how long it would take the number of chargeable letters to rise five and a quarter times. Critics were certainly alarmed, for it was only in 1853 that his expectations were fulfilled. The unit cost of handling a letter did fall by a considerable margin, but the expectations of Hill that the sacrifice of the revenue would be slight proved to be mistaken. Maberly's pessimism was justified, for in the first year of Penny Post the net revenue fell by £1,132,975, or 69.3 per cent, and it was only in 1863 that it was to regain the level of 1839. Hill in 1841 had promised that the gross revenue of 1839 would be regained 'in something less than five years from the reduction in the rates'.[52] Even this scaled-down promise, which did not take costs into account, was not fulfilled until 1851. Although the cost of handling a letter did fall by a large margin, it was unreasonable to expect an establishment of the same size to handle five and a quarter times the traffic. In fact, in 1853 the cost of management was 85 per cent above the level of 1839 to deal with an increase in traffic of just under 400 per cent. These figures would suggest, on any realistic assumptions, a considerable measure of success by the Post Office in adjusting to its changed circumstances. Hill's assumptions of 1837 had been at once proved wrong by experience, and the prognostications of the 'practical men' of the Post Office had been vindicated. Hill was derided by his critics for 'tenaciously adhering to fallacies so amply detected and exposed', and the survival of the penny rate was under threat. 'Whilst *Mesmerism*, and the other attractive novelties of the day, have had their hour,' wrote a critic in 1844, 'the quackery of Penny Postage ought surely now to follow the same course.'[53] Of course, Hill had an obvious response to the failure of his forecasts and the fulfilment of Maberly's gloomy expectations. Matthew Hill wrote to Rowland in September 1839:

> You have excited great hostility at the Post Office. . . . It is not in human nature that the gentlemen of the Post Office should view your plan with friendly eyes. . . . That a stranger should attempt to understand the arcana of our system of postage better than those whose duty it was to attain to such knowledge, was bad enough; that he should succeed, was still worse; but that he should persuade the country and the Parliament that he had succeeded is an offence very difficult to pardon. Now, you are called upon to undertake the task of carrying into action, through the agency of these gentlemen, what they have pronounced preposterous, wild, visionary, absurd, clumsy and impracticable. They have thus pledged themselves, by a distinct prophecy, repeated over and over again, that the plan cannot succeed. I confess I hold in great awe prophets who may have the means of assisting in the fulfilment of their own predictions.[54]

The family view was that Hill's economic analysis was beyond reproach, but that his plan had been subverted by a conspiracy of opponents at St Martin's le Grand who were eager to prove him wrong. Attention must therefore turn from the economics of penny postage to the administrative tussles of its implementation. There could be no doubt that Hill, an ambitious and inexperienced amateur, was to be in for a rough ride, especially while the old guard remained in charge at Post Office Headquarters.

The administration of the Penny Post[55]

In 1839, Hill was offered a short-term appointment for two years at a salary of £500 a year which was raised, after he expressed outrage at the undervaluation of his services, to £1,500. He was to be based at the Treasury rather than at St Martin's le Grand. F. T. Baring, the Chancellor of the Exchequer, explained:

> You will have access to the Post Office, and every facility given you of inquiring both previously to the arrangements being settled and during their working. Your communications will be to the Treasury, from whom any directions to the Post Office will be issued; and you will not exercise any direct authority, or give any immediate orders to the officers of the Post Office.[56]

This position would have been difficult even for a person more tactful and less dogmatic than Hill. The first meeting with Maberly was not auspicious. According to Hill, 'I was received with great apparent

25

civility, but little things were said and done, I firmly believe, with the intention of annoying me. The less I have to do with the gallant Colonel the better.' Hill's journals were subsequently scattered with reports of Maberley's 'boasting at the Travellers Club of the fulfilment of his prophecies', and assertions that 'the government made a great mistake in continuing him at the head of the Department'.

The procedure to be followed was that Hill drew up a minute recommending a particular course of action, which was approved by the Chancellor and sent to Maberly at the Post Office for implementation. This reversed the normal pattern of business, in which the Post Office decided on a policy and submitted it to the Treasury for approval. The independent role of the Postmaster General and his officials was eroded, a change which had started in 1837. Previously, the Treasury had little information concerning the Post Office, and there were only one or two communications a month between them. Maberly, not surprisingly, preferred the independence of action which had existed before 1837 and he commented in 1843:

> If the Government have confidence in the Postmaster General, they may just as well entrust him with doing the business as they entrust the Secretary of State for the Home Department, or the Secretary of State for the Colonies, or the other great departments. They may perhaps keep a check over him as regards the more important communications; but certainly as to the minor ones, in the extent to which we have latterly pushed it, I think there is a great deal of inconvenience.[57]

Maberly had identified a tension between the Department's desire for autonomy and the Treasury's claim to control, which continued as a dominant theme in the Post Office's history. In the short term, the appointment of Hill to the Treasury in 1839 exacerbated the hostility already felt by the Post Office at attacks upon its independence. Maberly was placed in the difficult position of implementing schemes which he considered to be misguided, at the behest of an outsider from the Treasury. When he was pressed to explain his attitude in 1843, he remarked:

> My constant language to the heads of the Department was, 'This plan, we know, will fail. It is our duty to take care that no obstruction is placed in the way of it by the heads of the department and by the Post Office. The allegation, I have not the least doubt, will be made at a subsequent period, that this plan has failed in consequence of the unwillingness of the Government to carry it into fair execution. It is our duty as servants of the Government, to take

care that no blame eventually shall fall upon the Government through any unwillingness of ours to carry it into proper effect.'[58]

Maberly's approach was one of caution, stressing the difficulties of altering the complex patterns of work which had developed within the Department. In some cases this was clearly obstructive, as in the refusal to merge the two separate bodies of letter-carriers who delivered the Twopenny and General Post letters in London. Neither, can there be much doubt that Maberly did misuse statistical evidence to overstate the decline in the net revenue; for example, he debited the Post Office with the entire cost of the Admiralty packet service, although the West Indies packets cost £240,000 a year and yielded a postal revenue of only £40,000 to £50,000.

The failure of net revenue to accord with Hill's prophecies weakened his position at the Treasury and he reacted by seeking to influence matters in the Post Office which were strictly not his concern, in order to bring the finances of the Department into line with his expectations. 'This week', he reported in October 1840, 'has been very much occupied in disposing of numerous communications from the Post Office. Few of them have even the most remote connection with penny postage but it is probably a better and certainly a simpler rule for me to undertake the whole correspondence.' He had arrogated to himself the role of the Treasury in supervising the Post Office. 'I must', he claimed, 'act by myself or not at all.' The economic failure of the Penny Post was thus likely to exacerbate the administrative tensions created by Hill's anomalous position.

Hill argued that the Department had failed to control expenditure so that the unit cost of handling the increased traffic had not fallen as expected. He was particularly concerned at the inflated cost of the railway services. Payment to railway companies increased from £10,000 to £51,000 between 1838 and 1840, whilst the cost of mail coaches also rose. The cause was 'chiefly in the fact that the opening of the railways, by diminishing competition on parallel lines, has produced an augmentation in the charges for mail conveyance, amounting, in some instances, even to double the previous cost'.[59] Hill saw the railways as a separate issue from the Penny Post, and he was prepared to argue that the scheme could have succeeded without the new method of transport. The higher cost of rail transport was, in his view, an 'untoward coincidence' which did not invalidate his initial calculations. Maberly, he felt, had not adopted a firm line with the companies and one of Hill's main tasks was to drive down the price of contracts, a topic which is considered in chapter 4.

Mail had not only to be conveyed around the country, but it had also to be processed at each end. The Post Office was, in fact, a labour-intensive service. Hill in the 1840s was certain that there was an inclination to increase establishments and a 'disposition to advance the salaries which is unfortunately too apparent at present'. The increase in the staff could, he felt, have been avoided and the mounting costs did not, in his view, arise from mistaken assumptions about the economics of the service but rather from an administrative structure which allowed his enemies to falsify his analysis:

> These circumstances connected with the hostility towards the plan displayed by the Post Office authorities . . . , their prophecies that it would fail . . . lead inevitably to the conviction that it is the intention of the Post Office to make the measure fail apparently, in a financial point of view at least, by making the increase of expenses keep pace with that of letters.

Cost control, he also insisted, depended upon ancillary reforms such as the introduction of prepayment and the amalgamation of the separate bodies of letter-carriers. He therefore refused to admit that his scheme had failed until the entire plan was implemented, adding 'nor will I admit it in any amount of time, so long as those who have to carry it out are hostile to it'.

Nevertheless, the Post Office's view that expenses would increase was plausible and when Hill complained to Baring, he received little sympathy. Baring 'was I fear a good deal annoyed. He does not see the matter in the same light that I do, on the contrary, he thinks that the Post Office has borne the pressure upon it with great good temper and has done all that could reasonably be expected.' Maberly and the Postmaster General, the Earl of Lichfield, claimed that the whole system was close to breakdown, and implied that the fault was Hill's for proposing an impractical reform. By the middle of 1841, Hill was pressing Baring to be given Maberly's position at the Post Office. Maberly, he argued, would be pleased to leave, for the success of the Penny Post would contradict his judgement, while its failure would be put down to his opposition. His own appointment to the Post Office would, he insisted, 'put an end to a divided, unacknowledged and therefore ineffectual responsibility'. But Baring refused to move Maberly to the Poor Law Commission, and Hill's position was further weakened when the Tories came to power. His access to Post Office information was limited to papers relating directly to the Penny Post, the power of the Postmaster General was reasserted, and Hill's direct contact with the Chancellor curtailed.

Hill was thus increasingly isolated, and one indication of his weakening power was the response to his plan in 1842 to visit

Newcastle-upon-Tyne to inspect the arrangements for the day mail service. The Postmaster General, Lord Lowther, objected: 'I looked upon Mr. Hill as the adviser of the Treasury . . . and not to act in the character of a surveyor. Mr. Stow and Mr. Tilley had been in communication with the directors of the different railways, and in my own judgement and responsibility I thought them fully as competent, or more competent, to deal with the directors than Mr. Hill.'[60] The Chancellor agreed, and this marked the demise of Hill at the Treasury. He was informed that his appointment would not be renewed, and although he did offer to complete his plan without a salary, the suggestion was turned down. The Chancellor explained that the introduction of the Penny Post had been effected and while further changes would no doubt arise, 'such improvements would necessarily lead either to an entire supercession of those who are by their offices responsible for the management of the Department or to a conflict of authorities highly prejudicial to the Public Interests'. Hill left the public service and became chairman of the Brighton railway.

In 1846, with the return of the Whigs to power, Hill for the first time received an appointment within the Post Office at a salary of £1,200. The previous experience of tension between the Post Office and the Treasury would, it was confidently expected, not be repeated and Hill was instead to become Secretary to the Postmaster General. The anomaly was, however, scarcely less remarkable for Maberly continued in office as Secretary to the Post Office. Hill expressed his doubts: 'I see almost insuperable difficulty in attempting to collect information and to issue instructions otherwise than through the general secretary's office, and yet, judging from past experience, it appears hopeless to look for his [Maberly's] voluntary co-operation, while his position makes him too strong to be effectually coerced.'

It is certainly possible to sympathise with Hill, but it is also necessary to see the situation through Maberly's eyes. He explained that 'the Secretary's office is the Department in which the whole business of the Post Office centres and from which all orders are given to the different heads of offices' and no order from one officer to another could be obeyed unless it was directed through the Secretary. This gave the Secretary's office an overview of the whole Department, creating that 'unity of plan and system' and 'vigour in action' which Maberly considered to be essential. It followed that Hill should seek information only through the Secretary's office, and that all new papers should be issued to him only on the authority of the Postmaster General. Maberly also held that 'it is not intended that Mr. Hill shall interfere in the general business but only take part in such special matters as your Lordship shall think fit to refer to him'. The result was a continuing battle between the two men for supremacy within the Post Office which went on for the next eight years.[61]

The outcome at any moment rested upon the attitude of the Postmaster General. Hill was in the ascendant between 1846 and 1852 when the Marquess of Clanricarde was Postmaster General, for he was inclined to 'dexterously set aside the blarney of Maberly'. The appointment of the Earl of Hardwicke in 1852 marked a change, for he was, unlike Clanricarde, concerned with the administrative details of the Department. 'Blowhard', as he was known in the family, had been a naval officer. 'He always brought a picture of the sea before me,' remarked Lady Battersea, 'his fine healthy colour, his brilliant dark eyes with their quick glance, his language, racy, to the point, original, direct – all seeming to belong to the old seafaring world.' Edmund Yates felt that 'the Bosun' was blunt, eccentric and mannerless with an overweening sense of his importance; certainly he would stand for no insubordination.[62] 'He says (all in good temper)', commented Hill, 'that hitherto I have really been Postmaster General, but that he intends to be Postmaster General himself.' Hardwicke was also unwilling to accept the continuation of the internal feud. 'There cannot be two kings in Brentford,' was his frequent cry. In Hardwicke's view, it was essential to have a clear hierarchy and this entailed that Hill should be subordinate to Maberly. This was only a short interlude, however, and Hill's position was restored when Canning was appointed to the Post Office in 1853. When Hill had been based at the Treasury, he had raised one theme which was to run through the history of the Post Office: the tension between the Department's desire for autonomy and the Treasury's wish to impose control. The relocation of Hill at St Martin's le Grand raised another issue which will be considered at greater length: the relationship between the Postmaster General as the political head of the Department and the civil servant as the executive head. The contrast between Clanricarde and Hardwicke was to persist with a changing cast until the office of Postmaster General was abolished.

Hill did not only rely upon his internal position in the Post Office, for he also lobbied sympathetic MPs and appealed to the Chancellor and Treasury over the head of the Postmaster General. He used all the means in his power to remove Maberly and secure his own appointment as sole Secretary. Indeed, ambitious as ever, he wished to remove the control of the Postmaster General and to create a Board to run the Post Office, under his chairmanship. The Commission on the Post Office had recommended the creation of such a board in 1835,[63] but the abolition of a political head of the Department was not to occur until 1969. Hill in some ways acted as if the office of Postmaster General had already been abolished: he certainly did not accept a conventional view of the relationship between civil servant and politician. He had a proprietorial interest in the Department which would permit no interference, and he did succeed in circumventing many restrictions on his power by forming an alliance with the Treasury. He paid a weekly visit to the Treasury to assist officials in reaching decisions on Post Office papers which had been withheld from him in the Department. 'Apprehensions were expressed that Maberly would be very jealous', but Hill reported that the Treasury officials 'appear very much inclined to follow my advice'. He did admit that 'I scarcely know what to do when my opinion is against measures which have been recommended by the Postmaster General without consulting me'. Fortunately, Clanricarde was not concerned and he 'wishes me to have no scruples as to any measures but to advise against them unhesitatingly, if so inclined'. Hill was threatening to replace not only the Postmaster General, but also the Treasury which had a general responsibility for the control of the Department.

The division between Hill and Maberly inevitably led to considerable confusion within the Department. There was, as Hill admitted, 'want of proper co-operation or of a division of Departments'. This was to some extent mitigated in 1847 by assigning the Money Order Department to Hill, and in 1851 he secured the appointment of his brother Frederic as head of the railway department. Hill's journals show an obsession with Maberly, whose every action was interpreted solely in the light of its effects on his position rather than as a genuine disagreement. When Maberly recommended increased salaries, for example, this was interpreted as a device to make Hill unpopular when he advised their rejection. Hill's health started to deteriorate, and he complained of sickness, sleeplessness, and headaches. His continued complaints to the Postmaster General, MPs and Treasury alienated many, but the matter was finally resolved in his favour in 1854 when the Treasury inquiry into the administration of the Post Office recommended a single Secretaryship. Maberly was moved to the Audit Board and Hill at last entered into what he had always seen as his natural and proper position.

Hill's accession to power in 1854 came at the same time as the general reform of the civil service resulting from the Northcote – Trevelyan Report. This was, as will be shown in chapter 8, to produce important changes in the administration of the Department. Hill could also proceed to introduce his 'plan' in full by completing the ancillary changes which were expected to reduce costs and attract traffic by improving service. The Post Office did not, however, enter a phase of peace and harmony. Hill had experienced fifteen years of frustration, and for the next ten years he attempted to rule the Department in an autocratic fashion which permitted no dissension, however well founded the criticisms. Clearly, Maberly had been no friend of the Penny Post and he had not taken a firm hold on expenditure. However, Hill's actions after 1854 showed that the abstractions of his pamphlet of 1837 had a greater reality to him than the pragmatic necessities of running the Department. Costs had to be forced to fit the impractical assumptions which he had formulated before ever visiting St Martin's le Grand, despite warnings that the efficiency of the postal services would be put at risk. A renewed crisis was at hand.

Lord Stanley of Alderley was appointed Postmaster General in 1860. Hill could not accept that his role as a civil servant was to implement the decisions of his political master and he complained to the Chancellor that it was 'impossible to work with the Postmaster General – he has, intentionally or not, undermined my authority and influence'. In April 1861 Hill recorded with amazement that Stanley 'flew into a violent passion – accused me of dictating to him–of acting as though I, not he, were Postmaster General'. Hill's response was to appeal to the Prime Minister, Palmerston, to remove Stanley and to appoint a Board to run the Post Office which, he claimed, 'with myself for Chairman, would work well'. Palmerston was less impressed. The explanation was clear to Hill for he recorded in his journal with bold emphasis: '*The Postmaster General is an old friend of Col. Maberly's.*'

Hill felt that his authority was threatened not only by the Postmaster General, but also by a 'cabal' of officials. By 1861, a new generation had emerged within the Post Office which, while it no longer questioned the whole basis of the Penny Post, was nevertheless unable to accept Hill's rigid standards of economy. These civil servants were 'zealots' eager to expand their functions unfettered by the constraints of retrenchment. Hill and his generation emphasised 'economical' reform which would sweep away the obstacles to free trade and to *laissez-faire* economics, principles which should be applied with particular rigour in the operation of a State monopoly such as the Post Office. Each branch of the service should be self-supporting, he asserted, for any other policy was 'contrary to the true principles of free trade, as swerving into the unsound and dangerous practice of protection'. The existence of a monopoly and the absence of the discipline of competition meant that the officials should pursue this aim with great assiduity and Hill was even inclined to favour the demise of the Post Office monopoly in order to ease the task. This would, he argued, entail 'the removal of an offence from our statute book and the probable rise of a wholesome competition wherever the service is performed with less than the greatest efficiency and cheapness; a competition which, more perhaps than any other external circumstance, would tend to compel the department to have due regard to simple merit in its officers, and economic efficiency in all its arrangements'.[64]

The most important figures in the new generation were John Tilley who was in 1864 to succeed Hill as Secretary, and Frank Ives Scudamore who was involved both in the introduction of the Post Office Savings Bank in 1861 and the nationalisation of the telegraph companies in 1870. As will be seen in later chapters, in the 1860s they were to collide with Rowland Hill over the criteria for determining wages and with Frederic Hill over the terms of contracts with shipping companies. The Tilley–Scudamore view was to prevail in both cases against the narrower, inflexible perceptions of the Hills who stressed the primacy of financial considerations and the payment of minimum rates. Tilley and Scudamore rejected such an approach: the insistence on low wage rates was unrealistic and threatened efficiency; similarly, cheaper contracts could only be secured by using unreliable services which would threaten the regularity of the mails. By the 1860s, net revenue had been restored to the level which had existed before the Penny Post, and the extreme economy advocated by the Hills seemed to be unnecessary. Whereas Tilley and Scudamore viewed the Post Office in some senses as a social service, the Hills were to a large extent still fighting the old campaigns against Maberly and paring costs to allow the Penny Post to succeed. The new generation of officials had different concerns and came to view the Hills in much the same way as they had viewed Maberly, as opponents of change.

The tension within the Department came to a head when a commission of enquiry was appointed in 1860 to consider the letter-carriers' grievances about their wages. Rowland Hill was absent from the Department on extended sick leave, and the Assistant Secretary, John Tilley, suggested to the Postmaster General that a committee of enquiry be appointed. Frederic viewed this as an attack on his absent brother and he instructed the committee that it should not proceed to any steps which it had reason to believe would not be approved by both himself and Tilley. The committee refused to proceed on such terms and requested either that Frederic's instructions should be countermanded or that the members should be relieved of their duties. The chairman asserted 'the right and duty of exercising an independent judgement and of expressing without reserve, the opinions they may arrive at, when acting under the authority of government, without subjecting themselves to any direct or indirect animadversion from a superior Departmental officer'. The Hills were seeking to control the operations of a committee appointed by both the political and the acting permanent head of the Department in order to resolve serious discontent among the workforce. In Rowland's view, the committee 'sins against every principle of subordination. Officers under my superintendence and control were . . . elected without my concurrence, into judges of my measures; and a spirit of antagonism has thus been evoked which will probably for years go far to paralyse the authority of the executive head of this great department.' The real task of Tilley, he asserted, was to impose discipline and not to enquire into grievances. The whole basis of wage determination by the market was, argued Hill, threatened by the implication that the State 'becomes subject to some undefined, and, indeed, utterly incomprehensible duty to pay some higher price'.[65] Hill certainly had a valid point, for during the last third of the nineteenth century wages in the Post Office indeed rose faster than in comparable occupations, for reasons which are explained in chapter 6. The method by which wages should be determined in the public sector remained an area of debate in which different approaches prevailed at various times and Hill was the spokesman for one particular solution, that wages should be fixed by the market.

Hill's general approach to administration revealed his serious weaknesses. One was his inclination to favour drastic and unrealistic solutions rather than to operate within the realm of practical policy. This applied both to his own dealings with railway companies and to Frederic's handling of the shipping contracts. The second was his treatment of the Post Office as his personal dominion. It was scarcely normal practice in the civil service to treat a committee appointed by the political head of a department as insubordinate, and to submit a 57-page memorandum of criticism directly to the Treasury. It would be more accurate to view Hill's own behaviour as insubordinate and a threat to the efficient operation of the Post Office. Indeed, this was Hill's final *contretemps* after more than two decades of acrimony. His ultimatum that he would remain at the Post Office only on condition that he was appointed permanent Director answerable immediately to the Treasury was unlikely to succeed and he expressed surprise that his direct appeal to Palmerston 'appeared to put him out of temper and he spoke rather crossly of the right of the head of a Department to have his own way'. Hill was then 68 years old and his health, never good, was at last breaking under the strain. He noted in his journal that he could do no more than play two or three games of cribbage at a sitting and that he had 'mental strength for no serious exertion'. He took six months' leave at the end of 1863 to allow his strength to recover, but in 1864 he resigned, with his full salary for life and a special grant of £20,000 voted by Parliament.

Rowland Hill has achieved a mythical status in the Post Office's history, and the reverence in which he is held would surely have amazed both the Maberly and Tilley regimes at St Martin's le Grand. It can now be seen that the proposal for penny postage developed from the general debate on fiscal reform in the 1830s, and Robert Wallace was already voicing some of the ideas which Hill, unsuccessful in his attempt to take advantage of poor law reform, was later to develop. A commission had already commenced its investigation into the management of the Post Office when Hill's pamphlet appeared; change in the administrative structure of the Post Office was part of a wider movement of civil service reform which was to culminate in the 1850s. Hill's importance was as an amateur propagandist who had the support of the most powerful pressure group of the day, and who capitalised upon the obvious political attraction of much cheaper postage. But his financial arguments in favour of the Penny Post were mere guesses, far less soundly based than those who had years of experience within the Post Office itself. The nation as a whole, however, benefited from his miscalculations and the world was to follow the United Kingdom's pioneer example. Propagandists do not necessarily make good administrators and Hill created twenty years of acrimony and tension within the Post Office which probably hindered rather than helped the successful development of the Penny Post. Trollope was prone to exaggerate, but perhaps not when he remarked, 'I never came across anyone who so little understood the ways of men, – unless it was his brother Frederic.'[66]

Mail Services

... the Post Office is essentially a department of progress, and one which admits of constant improvement and expansion. The public, therefore, not only have a right to look for increased facilities, and for the removal of obstacles and faulty arrangements, but their representations may greatly aid in the accomplishment of those subjects.(PP 1854–5 XX, *First Report of the Postmaster General on the Post Office*, p. 599.)

The Post Office in 1840 had not experienced a complete transformation and the revolutionary impact of Penny Post should certainly not be exaggerated. The internal administration of the Department was not to be placed on a new basis until 1854, which was in many ways as significant a date in the history of the Post Office as 1840. The services provided by the Department in 1840 were also somewhat narrow, for while the Penny Post had reduced the cost of sending letters it had neither added new facilities nor improved the existing ones. The reduction of postage rates in 1840 was only the start of a long-term change in the character of the Post Office, as services were improved and extended. The Department in 1840 still relied upon the monopoly it had been granted in the seventeenth century to supply an inland letter service, but by the First World War it had added a wide range of new functions including a parcel post and savings bank which involved competition with private enterprise. At the same time, the letter service was improved as the number of deliveries was increased and the area covered by 'free' delivery to the recipient's house for no extra charge extended. This widening of the scope of the Department and the improvement in services characterised the period up to the First World War. The emphasis subsequently changed, as the financial problems which emerged after the war turned the attention of the Department to maintaining what had been achieved rather than pushing into new directions. This defensive stance might require major departures, such as the introduction of motor vehicles or the creation of a new administrative structure, but did not involve a major widening in the scope of the Department. The era of expansion from 1840 to 1914 gave way to a period of consolidation.

The 'completion of my plan'

'"My plan"', remarked Rowland Hill's daughter, 'was often on his lips and ever in his thoughts.'[1] The introduction of Penny Postage in 1840 did not, in Hill's opinion, complete 'my plan' and it is indeed difficult to be certain what would. 'The phrase was indefinite', Howard Robinson has commented, 'and cloaked as well an ambition to serve in the Post Office.'[2] It was a defence against accusations that his scheme had failed. In his evidence to the Select Committee on Postage in 1843 he denied, somewhat surprisingly, that he had ever claimed that the number of letters would increase five-fold, and he insisted that he 'did not calculate on sustaining the net revenue, even remotely'. The anticipation that the net revenue would be £1.3m was, he stressed, based on 'the introduction of the plan as a whole; and no one could have supposed that the plan could have been introduced as a whole in the very first week'.[3] A reader of *Post Office Reform* could be excused for not realising this. The reduction of postage rates certainly rested upon prepayment and Hill devoted considerable attention to the methods by which this could be effected. He did, it is true, refer to the need to improve the system of distribution, but he was confused and contradictory on the precise connection between this and the introduction of lower postage rates. The reduced postage was at one point in his analysis to *produce* a four-fold increase in total traffic which would permit 'greatly increased facilities of communication', but at another point lower rates and the improved services were together expected to *cause* the four-fold rise in traffic.[4] Hill was not a systematic thinker and Lord Lowther, the Postmaster General, could certainly be excused for thinking that improved facilities were to *follow* from the introduction of the Penny Post and the abolition of complicated accounts, 'which would so facilitate the business of the General Post Office that the men would have nothing to do but to run round and leave their letters in boxes at doors as fast as their legs would carry them'.[5] In *Post Office Reform* Hill did remark that the revenue could not be 'secured from all risk of suffering', but this warning could easily be overlooked in his enthusiastic calculations of the possible increase in the letter traffic, which meant that it was 'very possible' that there would be no sacrifice of the revenue and 'highly probable' that it would not suffer much. All that was necessary was that the public should spend as much on postage after the cut in the rate as before, and the experience of other commodities was 'enough to establish the high probability, and indeed almost absolute certainty of this sustained expenditure'. He scarcely admitted the possibility that the net revenue would be reduced below £1.3m, and he had even raised the prospect that the traffic might increase 36-fold in response to the lower postage rate.[6]

Hill's denials in 1843 do indeed ring very hollow, for the only measure which *Post Office Reform* had stressed as essential to the success of the scheme was prepayment; the other ancillary proposals were developed in his evidence in 1837 when the Commission was considering the London Twopenny Post. He suggested that the number of deliveries should be increased, initially to every hour or half-hour and ultimately to every 15 minutes. The number of receiving houses in London should be augmented so that they were 'more uniformly distributed with reference to the density of the letter-writing population'. There should not, he argued, be a single central office at St Martin's le Grand for the local distribution of letters, for London should be divided into eight or ten districts. 'It appears to me that one cause of the dilatoriness of the present delivery is the attempt to treat so enormous a place as London as a single town. I think it should be treated as several. Suppose there were ten of these district offices, then London would be divided into ten great districts, each of which would be treated as a distinct town.'[7] There is no doubt that these reforms would produce a better service in London, but it is not clear that they were necessary for the financial success of his 'plan'. On the contrary, the more frequent deliveries would lead to a considerable increase in costs, by as much as two-fold. Hill's 'plan' was to expand still further, and Lowther in his evidence in 1843 listed thirty-one suggestions, the most important of which were the amalgamation of the London District and General Post letter-carriers; an extension of the number of post offices to cover every registrar's district in the country; and the introduction of greater economy by revising both salaries and contracts with railway and shipping companies for the carriage of mail.[8] The plan had, in fact, extended from the few simple propositions of *Post Office Reform* to the total administration of the Department.

An essential part of Hill's scheme for reform of the Post Office was the prepayment of postage, which would reduce the time spent rating letters, collecting money from the recipients, and checking the accounts of letter-carriers and postmasters. In the first edition of *Post Office Reform*, he suggested that a letter should be handed in at a post office or receiving house with the postage, which the clerk would mark as paid

W. MULREADY, R.A.   JOHN THOMPSON.

The stamped cover designed by William Mulready was introduced in 1840. Its design, symbolising the benefits of cheap postage, produced a spate of caricatures and it was withdrawn in 1841. A simple stamped cover was introduced with an embossed circular reproduction of the queen's head.

with a 'tell-tale stamp'. An alternative method was added in the second edition: stamped covers and sheets of paper might be sold 'at such a price as to include the postage', and the letters might then be left in a box at the receiving house. But Hill accepted that a problem might arise if this second method were adopted. What would happen if stamped paper was not used and the letter was entrusted to an illiterate person to deposit at the receiving house? It would be necessary to buy a stamped cover in which the letter might be placed and the unfortunate bearer would be unable to write the address on the outside. It was to guard against such an eventuality that Hill, somewhat as an afterthought, suggested the sale of adhesive postage stamps. 'Perhaps this difficulty might be obviated by using a bit of paper just large enough to bear the stamp, and covered at the back with a glutinous wash, which the bringer might, by applying a little moisture, attach to the back of the letter, so as to avoid the necessity for redirecting it.'[9] There would, therefore, be three methods of prepayment: in cash to the clerk at the post office; by using stamped paper or envelopes; or by affixing a postage stamp. However, it might not be expedient to make prepayment compulsory and Hill recommended that unpaid letters might still be sent at double the postage to offset the cost of collection, a suggestion which was adopted.[10]

Although the Penny Post was introduced in January 1840, it was not until 6 May 1840 that stamps were on sale either as stamped paper and envelopes or as adhesive postage stamps. The Treasury had announced a competition in 1839 with prizes of £200 and £100 for ideas for stamped covers and adhesive postage stamps and it took some further time to solve the technical problems of printing and cancellation in a way which would avoid fraud.[11] Edwin Hill was installed at the Stamp Office with a salary of £500 a year to ensure that the work proceeded to Rowland's satisfaction.[12] By 1841, less than a tenth of the letters in London were posted unpaid and about half of the prepaid letters were stamped. The next stage was to abolish the costly system of prepayment by handing money to a clerk by insisting that all prepaid letters should be stamped. Prepayment in money was abolished in provincial offices in 1851, and this was extended to London, Edinburgh and Dublin in 1852, excepting the chief office in London where it continued until 1855.[13] In 1859, Hill resolved to go a stage further, by making prepayment compulsory. Letters which had been paid in part would be delivered, but the recipent was to pay the balance and a penalty of one penny; unpaid letters would be opened and returned to the sender. Although unpaid letters by this time amounted to only 2 per cent of the total, there was outrage at this loss of freedom and threat to the sanctity of correspondence. Hill was forced to abandon compulsion, and the right to send letters unpaid, at double postage, has survived.[14]

2.1 PAID, STAMPED AND UNPAID LETTERS IN LONDON, 1839–41 (PER CENT)

4 weeks ending	London General Post			London District Post		
	paid	stamped	unpaid	paid	stamped	unpaid
2 March 1839	13.6	—	86.4	n.a.	—	n.a.
29 Feb 1840	86.1	—	13.9	80.8	—	19.2
27 Feb 1841	46.7	45.2	8.1	47.5	41.4	11.1

Source: R. Hill, *Results of the New Postal Arrangements* (1841), p. 15.

The popularisation of stamps removed the necessity of visiting a post office or receiving house to prepay the postage in money and also made possible the introduction of road-side pillar boxes in which stamped prepaid letters could be deposited. Although the erection of 'strong iron boxes' in the street had been suggested in 1846, the idea was rejected as impracticable. Anthony Trollope was responsible for the first experiment in Jersey in 1852 and this successful trial was followed by the extension of the scheme to the mainland in 1853, and the provision of six pillar boxes in London in 1855.[15] By 1900 there were 32,593 in the United Kingdom,[16] and an innovation which had so alarmed Miss Jemima

Stanbury in Trollope's *He Knew He Was Right* had become an unconsidered part of everyday life. Miss Stanbury 'had not the faintest belief that any letter put into one of them would ever reach its destination. She could not understand why people should not walk with their letters to a respectable post-office instead of chucking them into an iron stump, – as she called it, – out in the middle of the street with nobody to look after it.'[17]

In 1840, it could not be taken for granted that a 'respectable post office' would be within reach. There were, indeed, large areas of the country which did not have a post office: in 1841, 400 of 2,100 registrars' districts in England and Wales, containing a population of 1.5m, had no post office. 'There are districts of great extent,' the Treasury complained, 'some measuring even from 100 to 200 square miles, and containing several thousand inhabitants, which possess no post-office whatever.' The free delivery of letters had been confined to 'post-towns' within limits somewhat arbitrarily determined by the Postmaster General. In other districts a variety of methods were used to obtain mail. A messenger might be employed to convey letters from the nearest post-town, who might be paid by a subscription raised among the residents of an area, or by a fee charged on each letter. Often such a messenger was an employee of the postmaster who was providing a delivery service as a private business; mail coaches might also arrange to leave letters along the route for a fee. The residents of country houses might keep a private bag at the post office, which they would arrange to have carried back and forth. The cost of these services varied from as little as a halfpenny to as much as a sixpence a letter, but unless the fee was paid the receipt of a letter depended upon going to the post office to collect it. The introduction of Penny Post did not immediately introduce free delivery as a right, and the question remained of how swiftly this would be extended. 'The unauthorized, and frequently excessive charges, to which a large proportion of the correspondence of the country is thus subjected, the irregularity and delay in its delivery, and the risk to which it must be exposed from the employment of irresponsible messengers are circumstances', remarked the Treasury in 1841, 'which appear . . . to require serious attention.'[18]

The introduction of the Penny Post at first slowed down the extension of free delivery, for the Department took the view that the deterioration in the financial position since 1840 did not permit such concessions. Although Hill and Maberly agreed that free delivery should not extend to the entire country, they differed over the speed with which new post-towns should be created. Hill argued that a systematic national coverage of post offices was necessary to complete his 'plan', for the revenue would not, he claimed, recover without 'increased facility of communi-

The first letter boxes erected in London followed this design. Box Number 2 was on the south side of the Strand, and opened on 11 April 1855.

cation' to encourage the growth of traffic.[19] The policy which Hill wished the Post Office to follow was incorporated in a Treasury minute in August 1841. Delivery in the country districts had, it was noted, been solved to some extent by the introduction of 'guarantee posts' by which 'responsible parties' agreed to pay the full expense of the service. But this created anomalies, for some places with a post office were less important than places without an office; what was required was 'some intelligible, well-defined principle, by which to regulate the extent to which the official conveyance of letters, without extra charge, shall be carried'. It was assumed that free delivery 'cannot be extended to every place in the kingdom, however remote and however small its correspondence . . .; any attempt of the kind would certainly entail an enormous expense on the Post-office, which could only be met by the Legislature increasing the general rate of postage, and thus pressing unnecessarily and unfairly on the larger towns, and restoring, as between them, the contraband conveyance of letters.' The Treasury ruled that the number of post-towns linked to the national mail network should be extended so that they 'should be somewhat in proportion to the amount of population and extent of service combined; that is to say, that they should be nearer to one another where the population is dense, but more numerous, as compared with the inhabitants, where the population is scattered'. In practice, this was to involve the establishment of a post office in each Registrar-General's district: the expected cost was £8,000 a year for 400 offices. Letters would be carried to the post-town at no extra expense; the introduction of a free delivery to each household within the town was to depend upon the number of letters and the density of population and should be granted 'wherever it can be established with due regard to the interests of the revenue'.[20]

The Treasury minute was in fact not implemented, for a change in government in 1841 permitted Maberly and the Postmaster General to suspend the policy on the grounds of expense. The extension of postal facilities was slowed down until 1843 when it was at length decided that 'wherever a village or hamlet, or walk through which the postman should go, should have 100 letters addressed to it, that district should be entitled to a post at the public expense'.[21] A considerable extension of free deliveries followed: 621 new posts serving 1,942 villages were established between June 1843 and January 1845 and a further 71 guarantee posts serving 82 villages were taken over by the Department. In 1850, the terms on which a delivery was granted were amended to ensure that the service was self-supporting. In future, a post was only introduced if it covered its cost on the basis of a halfpenny for each letter received; since it was believed that the number would double when free delivery was established, a revenue of one penny per letter was assumed.

A general revision began in 1851 and was largely completed by 1858. Letters were delivered free to wider areas around the large towns so that in 1854, for example, 515 post offices were opened, 1,242 free deliveries established and a further 245 extended. Indeed, by 1859 about 93 per cent of letters were delivered free of additional charge.[22]

2.2 EXTENSION OF POSTAL FACILITIES, 1839–43

	Sept 1839– Sept 1841	Sept 1841– Aug 1843
Free deliveries established	311	188
Extended	65	23
Rural posts established	91	89
Guarantee posts established	25	64

Source: PP 1843 VIII, *Select Committee on Postage*, Q 2880.

The terms for the introduction of free delivery were liberalised in 1890 when a revenue of three farthings per letter was allowed in calculating whether it would be financially viable. The Department was facing pressure to improve services, and in 1892 a resolution was introduced in the Commons by Sir E. Birkbeck, with the support of the Committee of Conservative Agricultural Members, which urged the introduction of daily deliveries in rural parishes as a first claim on the Post Office's surplus. The motion was passed and the Department, despite its scepticism that a national daily delivery was possible, decided to apply the terms of 1890 with 'utmost rigour'. The Post Office was caught between parliamentary pressure on the one hand and Treasury hostility to increased expenditure on the other, for in 1893 the Treasury expressed alarm at the expense. Extension of deliveries was checked until the late 1890s when the government's decision 'to infuse some life into the decaying rural districts' led to a change in attitude. The Post Office in 1897 decided to give a regular delivery on at least two or three days of the week to every house in the country, and by the end of 1898 free delivery had been extended to 31.8m letters at a cost of £90,939. A further 11.6m remained, of which 0.7m were in England and Wales, 5.5m in Scotland and 5.4m in Ireland. The task was substantially completed by 1900.[23]

Letters delivered in London accounted for almost a quarter of the total correspondence of the country and Hill gave high priority to improving the efficiency of the postal service in the capital by three measures: the amalgamation of the separate corps of letter-carriers who delivered the General and District posts; the creation of separate postal districts which would serve London as a number of independent

This sentimentalised view of a country letter carrier appeared in 1872.

post-towns; and the introduction of hourly deliveries of letters during twelve hours of the day. The Post Office opposed these proposals in its evidence to the Select Committee on Postage of 1843. Consolidation, it was argued, would not produce any savings of staff and would indeed cause delay since the delivery of local letters would have to await the arrival of the General Post from the country. An hourly delivery of letters was estimated to cost £26,500 without the expectation of an increase in the number of letters to cover the cost. The division of London into separate districts was considered to be impracticable, for letters would have to sorted to the separate districts which could increase the expense and lead to confusion. 'All I know is', remarked William Bokenham, 'that if a man in the Manchester Office can manage to divide London into ten districts correctly, I should be very glad to have him in my own office.'[24] There was here a mixture of good sense and obstinacy.

2.3 PERCENTAGE DISTRIBUTION OF LETTERS DELIVERED IN THE UNITED KINGDOM, 1850 AND 1910/1

	w/e 21 July *1850*	*1910/1*
London inland and foreign district	12.7 12.0 24.7	24.1
Rest of England and Wales	55.6	60.9
Ireland	9.6	5.5
Scotland	10.1	9.4
	100.0	100.0

Source: Post 19/45, Abstract of the Number of Letters Delivered in the United Kingdom in the week ended 21 July 1850; Post 19/68, Abstract of Delivered Letter Returns 1910–1911.

Consolidation of the disinct groups of letter-carriers was an obvious economy and Hill was in fact requested on a number of occasions during his period as joint Secretary to create a single force. He took the view, however, that it was 'difficult and hazardous' to make any change whilst Maberly was still in office.[25] In 1854, Hill proceeded to implement all three reforms of the London service as a combined package: the letter-carriers would be consolidated; there would be a continuous series of hourly deliveries starting at 7.30 a.m.; and ten districts or '*quasi* different towns' would be created. Local letters would in future remain in the district or be exchanged directly between districts, and 'a letter from Cavendish-square to Grosvenor-square, instead of travelling four or five miles, as at present, would go almost directly from one place to another'. Letters from the provinces could be sorted for each district before arriving in London, which reduced the pressure and speeded the delivery. The district system was, despite Bokenham's forebodings, a major improvement in efficiency. There was more ground for alarm at the cost of more frequent deliveries, although it should be remembered that the London service was profitable; the rate of return was lower in areas of dispersed population. Hill secured a major improvement in the

1   Sir Rowland Hill, 'one of the least eccentric members of a very strange family'.

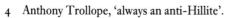
2 W. L. Maberly, 'the gallant colonel'.

4 Anthony Trollope, 'always an anti-Hillite'.

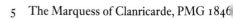
3 Frederic Hill, 'a most dangerous man'.

5 The Marquess of Clanricarde, PMG 1846

quality of the London mail service. At the beginning of 1856, only 5.0 per cent of deliveries in London were completed by 9 am, but by the beginning of 1857 this had risen to 65.2 per cent. The number of deliveries in suburban districts was also improved so that it became normal for the head office to provide twelve deliveries and the surburban offices six or seven. This established the general basis of the London mail service to the First World War.[26]

2.4 LETTER DELIVERIES IN LONDON, 1908

		Number of deliveries	First am	Last pm
East Central		12	7.15	8.30
Northern	head office	12	7.00	8.15
	East Finchley	6	7.15	8.50
North Western	head office	12	7.05	8.10
	Kentish Town	7	7.15	8.25
South Eastern	head office	11	7.10	8.15
	Blackheath	7	7.15	8.45
Western Central	head office	12	7.20	8.15

Source: Post 14/9 London Postal Service, Tables showing Times of Collections, Deliveries, and Despatches to and from Head Offices and Sub District Offices, also the Hours of Business at District Offices, Jan. 1908.

The number of deliveries in provincial towns was also increased during the second half of the century. In Birmingham, for example, there were three deliveries in the early 1850s; in 1903 there were six, starting at 7 a.m. and ending at 6.30 p.m.[27] The provision of an extra delivery was guided by the same principle as the introduction of a free delivery – that it should pay its way. In 1853 a service was considered to be financially viable if costs were covered by a revenue of one farthing for each letter; the figure was increased to a halfpenny in 1892.[28] The basis upon which the Post Office operated, whether in permitting later posting or providing improved deliveries, was explained by the Secretary, S.A. Blackwood, in 1885:

It is an established principle long recognised in this Department that if any considerable acceleration can be given to letters at an expense which shall not exceed a farthing per letter, such outlay is justifiable on the ground that increased facilities by developing correspondence will fully recoup the Revenue in the expense incurred. . . . This Rule . . . has been justified in its operation by the fact that the Post Office revenue derivable from letters has always grown in a greater ratio than the expense incurred for the improvement of mail service.[29]

This was the general principle, but its application depended upon the local postmaster. Although there were no rigidly enforced standards, generally speaking a town with 20,000 letters a week had four deliveries in 1914. There were, however, glaring anomalies so that Newark, with 40,000 letters a week, had five deliveries and Northampton, with 235,000 letters, had four.[30]

2.5 LETTER DELIVERIES, OCTOBER 1914

	letters per week	number of deliveries
Manchester (central)	2,037,653	8
Liverpool	2,013,131	7
Newcastle-on-Tyne	894,463	7
Birmingham	2,797,774	6
Bristol	905,683	6
Cardiff	488,272	6
Exeter	316,644	5
Swindon	85,483	5
Northampton	235,137	4
Monmouth	12,813	4

Source: Post 30/4056, E2671/1918, file III.

The First World War imposed strains upon the mail system. Recruitment into the army led to the restriction of services, the use of temporary staff and a reliance on overtime. At the end of 1914 a consistent policy was formulated: where there were normally fewer than four deliveries, the service should be maintained; where there were four or more deliveries, the service should be reduced in proportion to the fall in correspondence, with a maximum of six deliveries except in the London head districts where the limit was eight. This standard was conditional upon obtaining temporary staff at 'approximately the normal rates of pay', and further restrictions were to be made where labour was not available.[31] These war-time reductions in the services were not restored when peace returned, and indeed in some towns services were cut still further in the face of the postwar collapse of profitability and the need to reduce costs.[32] The standard of service in London in 1919 was seven or eight deliveries in the head districts and six to four in the sub-districts.[33] The level of deliveries which had been reached by 1914 was to be the peak of the British letter post.

By the 1930s, the financial health of the Post Office had been restored and there was pressure in 1934–5 for the Department to reintroduce at least the evening delivery. 'Just put yourself in the position of a resident in Walsall,' complained one disgruntled MP in 1934, 'if he wants to communicate with any of his friends living only half a mile away he must post the letter before 3.45p.m. otherwise it will not be delivered until the next morning.' He received little sympathy, in part because of the cost but also because of the implications for staffing. An extension in the hours to be covered by postmen would require the use of part-time staff which the Department was pledged to reduce; it must be remembered that the standard of service in 1914 was only possible given the nature of the labour market, a point which is developed in chapter 6. Emphasis in the 1930s was placed upon completing the first morning delivery by 8.30a.m., rather than on reintroducing an evening delivery.[34] Residents of Walsall would, by 1934, be well advised to install a telephone, an innovation which had, of course, changed the pattern of demand for the letter post. The City businessman who wished to inform his wife that he would be late for dinner could in 1914 send a letter; in the 1930s he could telephone.

2.6 LETTER DELIVERIES IN BIRMINGHAM

	1903	1939
am	7.00	7.00
	9.30	9.30
	11.30	11.30
pm	1.45	
	4.15	4.00
	6.30	

Source: Post Office Guide for Birmingham and District, March 1903; Birmingham and District Post Office Guide, July 1939.

Monopoly and competition

The sole reason why the Post Office has a remunerative monopoly is to enable it to include services which are unremunerative. Free competition in London or other large towns would make short work of the present Post Office rates. And if these rates are forcibly maintained the country ought to get some compensation in the shape of a reasonably good service to every corner of the kingdom. (*Pall Mall Gazette*, 28 May 1892.)

Rowland Hill did not entirely favour the monopoly granted to the Post Office. The most usual justification of the monopoly is that it enables a service to be provided across the country at a standard rate, permitting cross-subsidisation between profitable and unprofitable areas. But in Hill's view, each branch of the Post Office should be self-supporting. He complained in his autobiography that a view often

erroneously attributed to me . . . is, that so long as the department thrives as a whole, its funds may justly be applied to maintain special services which do not repay their own costs; whereas, from the first, I have held that every division of the service should be at least self-supporting, though I allowed that, for the sake of simplicity, extensions might be made where there was no immediate expectation of absolute profit. All beyond this I have always regarded as contrary to the true principles of free trade, as swerving into the unsound and dangerous practice of protection. Whenever, therefore, it is thought that the net revenue from the Post Office is too high for the interests of the public, I would advise the application of the surplus to the multiplication of facilities in those districts in which, through the extent of their correspondence, such revenue is produced.[35]

It followed that Hill saw little virtue in the Post Office's monopoly and he felt that its abandonment would be desirable to remove 'an offence from our statute-book' and to create 'wholesome competition' which would 'compel the department to have due regard to simple merit in its officers, and economic efficiency in all its arrangements'. Hill was nevertheless forced to admit that it would be harsh for the Department to provide a service in remote areas and at the same time to 'be exposed to competition in that more profitable part of its business, which alone rival establishments would undertake'.[36] Both Rowland and Frederic emphasised the principle that services should be self-supporting and minimised the scope of cross-subsidies. In comparison, other members of the Department were prepared to give more weight to non-economic factors and to use surplus revenue to support unprofitable areas of business.

The Post Office (Management) Act of 1837, which consolidated the legal powers of the Department, confirmed the long-standing exceptions to the monopoly. Letters might be delivered by a friend who was on a journey; they could be 'sent by a messenger on purpose, concerning the private Affairs of the Sender and Receiver thereof'; commissions, affidavits and writs issued by a court were excluded; and letters concerning goods might be delivered by carriers with the merchandise.[37] Great care was taken that these concession were not too liberally interpreted. Could colleges in Oxford and Cambridge employ a messenger to deliver letters for members? The system was allowed in 1871, but was discontinued at the request of the Post Office in 1885 when it was found that letters were collected on a regular basis and delivered to the general public in a manner which did not come under the concession of a 'messenger on purpose'.[38] The Post Office kept a wary eye on a variety of practices and subterfuges: the Ritz delivered letters for guests; W.H. Smith sent letters to its station book-stalls by rail; Pickford's delivered catalogues for D.H. Evans; coal-merchants had boxes at London stations to collect orders; agents in London received orders from provincial drapers for distribution to the various firms from which goods were required.[39] More important were the private firms or charities which delivered addressed circulars and the messenger companies which offered a special delivery service. In 1869, the London and Metropolitan Circular Delivery Co. was convicted of infringing the Post Office monopoly on the grounds that it did not come under the category of a 'messenger on purpose', but at the end of the century advances in advertising led to a considerable development of the business of delivering addressed circulars. The Reliable Advertising and Addressing Service in 1907 had a register of nearly 30,000 private car owners and lists of 170,000 households in London graded by rent; the firm claimed to handle over nine million envelopes for clients such as Dunlop, the Columbia Phonograph Co. and the Railway Benevolent Institution. These agencies addressed the envelopes – the Bessbrook Advertising Agency charged 5s per 1,000 – which might then be despatched by post or delivered by the firm itself at a charge varying from 3s to 12s 6d per 1,000 or 3s to 5s per man per day. The Department attempted to enforce the regulations prohibiting such a delivery service, but the warnings were not always observed.[40]

In 1887, a company – Boy Messengers Ltd – was established in London to provide a special delivery service at the rate of twopence per mile, and one penny per mile for the return journey. In 1890, a further company, the Court Bureau Ltd, was formed for use by 'the leisured or more opulent classes' in order to leave visiting cards, invitations or urgent notes which would, it was claimed, 'save one's servants no end of running about'. This was joined by the District Messenger Service and News Co. which allowed a subscriber to summon a messenger by an electric signal. The Post Office was alarmed that these companies would encroach on the profitable traffic in short-distance letters and although the Department claimed that the services did not fall within the category of messengers on purpose, its case was by no means certain. There were a number of alternatives to legal action: the companies could be licensed or appointed agents of the Post Office; or the Department could itself introduce a special or express delivery service. A departmental committee had indeed recommended the establishment of an express service in 1882, which had been postponed by more pressing business. This proposal was resurrected in 1888 and in 1891 the Post Office introduced its own service. Steps might then, it was thought, be taken to suppress the private companies, but this assertion of monopoly encountered strong opposition. In 1891 the government accepted that the private 'electric call' companies should be granted licences for 12 years, paying a royalty of £25 plus 2s 6d for each instrument and recompensing the Post Office with one penny for each letter carried. The official Express Post was introduced at ninety-one London and forty-three provincial offices at a rate of twopence for the first mile and threepence for subsequent miles in addition to the ordinary postage, and it was hoped that this would successfully compete with the private companies. It was, argued the Department, 'absolutely essential for the protection of the Revenue to stop the further development of the system of private delivery of letters'. The threat was indeed to disappear and the District Messenger Co. survived as an agency for the sale of theatre tickets rather than as a delivery service.[41]

IN THE PUBLIC INTEREST.

"How now!" cried Post Officiousness: "The Public sending a letter by hand that it may arrive without delay? Stop! It is an infringement of my rights: but I, myself, will convey the letter."

"There, now – just learn these few rules by heart; and then bring your letter to the nearest post office appointed for the purpose, and the thing's done."

The assertion of the Post Office's monopoly rights against the private messenger companies in 1891 appeared obstructive to many.

The introduction of the Express Post raised important questions about the nature of Post Office services. Robert Hunter, the Solicitor of the Post Office, in 1888 expressed serious reservations:

There would in fact if the scheme were carried out be two postal tariffs instead of one, and the principle of uniformity, the application of which to the postal service was the principal merit of Sir Rowland Hill's reforms and which has obtained in reference to this service since 1840, would be violated. . . . It seems to me that an express service is inconsistent with the principle upon which the monopoly of the Postmaster General is generally defended, viz. that in the hands of the State specially lucrative services pay for those which from their unprofitable character would not be undertaken by private enterprise except at high rates and that thus the monopoly leads to a higher general level of efficiency than could otherwise be obtained. At present we do give what are in the nature of express services in populous districts, i.e. we multiply deliveries but we do this for one uniform charge taking all things into account and for the benefit of the public generally and not of particular persons who may be able and willing to pay exceptional rates.[42]

In Hunter's opinion, monopoly was a necessary consequence of uniform postage. The Department charged the same postage to all parts of the country regardless of cost, but if the monopoly were breached private companies would take over the profitable areas, leaving the Post Office with the loss-making districts. This was the conventional wisdom at St Martin's le Grand. A private management, commented Henry Fawcett, professor of economics at Cambridge and Postmaster General, 'might probably have introduced a halfpenny post in London, and have left the country worse served than at present'.[43]

The Secretary, Sir Stevenson Arthur Blackwood, was willing to justify the introduction of an express service on the basis of pragmatic expediency. A refusal to supply a service for which there was a demand would, he argued, only lead to charges of obstructiveness and criticism for adopting a 'dog-in-the-manger policy'. An additional fee was, after all, charged for registered letters. He was sceptical about arguments put forward by opponents of the express service that the rich 'would benefit at the expense of the many', and that the emphasis should instead be placed on a general improvement in the letter post. Why, the Secretary wondered, should the rich not have advantages? 'As long as money will buy money's worth, the possessors of money must have advantages over those who possess it not. A wealthy man can send more letters than a poor man. What law is there in political economy that forbids him to use his money in sending them more speedily? If there is no advantage in possession of wealth, and the poor are to be equal to the rich, then the main incentive to the acquisition of wealth, in other words, to self-elevation in social scale, is withdrawn.'[44] Blackwood justified the imposi-

53

tion of higher charges for special services, but there was certainly no question that the rate for, say, profitable local letters within London might be reduced. This was a completely different matter, and Fawcett's opinion that the abolition of monopoly and the introduction of lower local rates would lead to a deterioration in the service was firmly held within the Department.

Such a view was not shared by Fawcett's successor in the chair of economics at Cambridge, Alfred Marshall. The ability of the Post Office to prevent the creation of cheap local services imposed, in his view, a net loss of £4½m on the customers of the Department, which was more than the net revenue. Marshall might well have been reflecting on the Department's closure of the Cambridge college mail system when he accused the Post Office of failing to provide services and taking an active role only in order to prevent others from meeting the public's needs. 'Where private enterprise has a fair field the inventions of public departments make no show at all,' argued Marshall, 'and . . . where they make any show at all it is only because the privileges of public departments have enabled them to make it not worthwhile for private enterprise to try expensive experiments.' The conventional wisdom of the Department was to reject Marshall's approach, but in some ways it was closer to Hill's view than to the line followed by his successors. Hill had only justified uniformity of charge by uniformity of cost; he did not favour cross- subsidisation which was incorrectly ascribed to him by Hunter and, during his retirement, he disapproved of the action against the Circular Delivery Company. The name of Rowland Hill was, by the end of the century, used by his successors to justify policies to which he had never subscribed. The history of the Penny Post had been rewritten and distorted.[45]

Rowland Hill was an ardent supporter of competition. He was not prepared to defend the Post Office's letter monopoly, and, at the same time, he was willing to compete with private enterprise in services where the Department did not have a privileged position. The monopoly of the Post Office had never extended to parcels, an area in which road carriers and railway companies provided a variety of services. The London Parcels' Delivery Company, for example, was formed in 1837 and firms such as Pickford's delivered parcels over a wider area.[46] But it was the railways which were to take the greater part of the business, and in Hill's view, it was perfectly justifiable for the Post Office to encroach on their business. Public enterprise, he argued, should be allowed to compete on equal terms with private enterprise. After all, the railways had themselves taken trade away from the stage coaches and 'there is no robbery on either side: those will get the custom who perform the duty most effectively'.[47] How did the Post Office move from its letter monopoly to compete with private enterprise, and with what success?

Book, sample and parcel posts

Rowland Hill had, as early as 1837, urged that the Post Office should provide a parcel post as part of its mail services.[48] Although his suggestion was not then accepted, his proposal of 1847 that books might be sent through the post in open packets, at a preferential rate of sixpence per pound, did receive support. This, argued Hill, merely extended the right to send printed material through the post which already applied to newspapers and Parliamentary proceedings. He anticipated that the service would make a profit without causing inconvenience to the letter service, for it would be possible to send books by the day mail trains which were under less pressure than the night trains. But the main justification of the proposal was the benefit to the education of the country:

> The privilege in question would greatly facilitate the transmission of scientific and literary reports and of other documents tending to the extension and diffusion of knowledge, and would I believe be highly prized by many Literary and Scientific Societies. . . . Private families, also, especially the rural clergy and other residents in remote country places, many of which are not reached by any other system of conveyance, would thus be supplied, at a moderate expense, with much valuable matter, which, under present circumstances, can seldom reach them.

Although Maberly stressed the pragmatic difficulties created by an increase in the weight of the mails, and urged that the post should be restricted to small packets, the book post was introduced in 1848.[49] In 1855, the rate was reduced to one penny for four ounces, two pence for eight ounces, and four pence for a pound, and in 1856 the scope of the book post was widened so that all printed papers could be sent in open covers at the preferential rate. These changes were induced by the abolition in 1855 of the compulsory stamp duty of a penny a sheet on newspapers which had given the right to free transmission through the post. The tax might, until 1870, be paid on a voluntary basis but some means had to be supplied of sending unstamped papers through the post at a comparable rate. The new printed paper rate of 1855 was broadly the same as stamp duty; it made little, if any, profit but the Post Office had been freed of the obligation to carry large numbers of newspapers without any payment.[50]

In the 1850s and early 1860s the Post Office was under pressure from Chambers of Commerce to provide a further mail service: a sample or pattern post which would allow traders to send packets at a cheap rate. These packets would have no intrinsic value but would contain a small quantity of a commodity which might form the basis for an order. The cost of sending a packet of samples weighing a pound by the letter post was 2s 8d, which was felt to be prohibitive, and in 1863 the introduction of a pattern post was under consideration. Frederic Hill took the opportunity to propose the introduction of a parcel post, for he argued that it would be difficult to define a pattern or sample to exclude items of value. A pattern post would, he claimed, inevitably lead to a parcel post and it was better to accept the fact than to attempt impractical limits. The major problem, in his opinion, was the objection of the railway companies to competition with their parcel trade, which might lead them to renegotiate the contracts for the carriage of letters. This danger might, he felt, be avoided by arranging terms with the railway companies which would make the service remunerative to both parties. But Hill's proposal was rejected by the Postmaster General in 1863, who minimised both the problem of defining a pattern or sample and the prospect of opposition from the railway companies. The pattern post was introduced in 1863 at a rate of three pence for each four ounces to a maximum of twenty-four ounces, which was above the rate for books.[51]

Problems soon arose. It did seem anomalous that patterns, which in theory had no intrinsic value, should pay more than books, which did. However, a reduction of the pattern post rate to the printed paper rate would produce a loss, for the cost of the printed paper service was $2\ ^{3}/_{8}d$ per item in comparison with a revenue of $1^{7}/_{8}d$. Nevertheless, the pattern post rate was reduced by a third in 1864, and in 1870 it was brought into line with the printed paper rate.[52] Difficulties also arose, as Frederic Hill had predicted, from the attempt of 'persons, not overscrupulous in this respect, to make the experiment of posting in socalled Sample Packets small quantities of goods sent for sale or in execution of orders, and many private individuals had adopted the practice of sending presents etc at the sample rate'.[53] There were a number of possible responses to this attempt to convert the pattern post into a parcel post. One, which was adopted in 1870, was strictly to limit the pattern post to items of no intrinsic value, and to insist that all other items were sent at the letter rate. This would, of course, entail a considerable and unpopular increase in postage, but it was feared that an extension of the pattern post would produce a loss, increase the workload, and 'provoke the hostility of the railway companies'.[54] The Secretary, John Tilley, conceded in 1871 that the attempt to reassert the regulations was impracticable and he recommended a second response. 'The safest plan', he now thought, 'is to retrace our steps and simply give the public a legal right to send small parcels of all kinds at the pattern post rate.' The pattern post should become an 'open' parcel post for unsealed packets at a rate of one half penny for each two ounces up to a maximum of twelve ounces, alongside the 'closed' letter post for sealed items. However, the Treasury refused to sanction the introduction of this loss-making service and a third solution was implemented in 1871: the pattern post was completely abolished and the rate for letters was substantially reduced to allow the carriage of packets at a reasonable rate. A penny was in future to cover the postage of a full ounce, and the rate for larger items was substantially reduced so that a letter weighing a pound could be sent for 1s 4d rather than 2s 8d. The demise of the pattern post was not regretted by the Department and the restoration of the service in 1887 at the insistence of the Postmaster General, H. C. Raikes, was staunchly opposed by the Secretary.[55] By this stage, however, a separate parcel post had been established.

The adjustment of the letter tariff in 1871 had moderated the punitive rate for heavy items. However, in the opinion of the Hills what was really needed was a separate parcel post operated in co-operation with the railway companies. The Post Office, they argued, already had a system for collection and delivery which the railways could not duplicate except at 'enormous expense', and it was 'more to their interest to avail themselves of our organisation than to attempt to establish one to compete with it'. An equitable division of the proceeds would, claimed the Hills, be profitable to both parties. Frederic calculated that the costs of collection, delivery and management would amount to 75 per cent of the proceeds and the cost of conveyance to 25 per cent. He suggested that the gross revenue might be divided between the Department and the companies in this proportion; alternatively, the net revenue after all expenses had been met might be divided equally.[56] Although this approach was not adopted in 1871, the principle was to be followed when the parcel post was eventually introduced, on terms which were to be considerably more favourable to the companies.

No adequate, cheap parcel service existed in the 1870s. The despatch of a parcel by rail was complicated by the large number of companies and different rates which made it difficult to send a 'through' parcel from one part of the country to another. The Society of Arts had mounted a campaign against these inadequacies, but the companies made only slow progress in devising a tariff for 'through' parcels. A scale was agreed in 1857 which standardised the rate, but the charges were still at a high level, varying by distance as well as weight, and requiring complex procedures to divide the proceeds between the various companies. By 1878, the traffic superintendents of the railway companies had formulated a simpler scheme, which would both establish low rates regardless of distance, and remove the need for complex accounting procedures. But the Railway Clearing House, which handled the financial payments between companies, did not have the power to enforce majority decisions on dissenters and the proposal came to nothing. This failure of the railway companies to develop an efficient parcel service provided the general background for the introduction of the parcel post.[57]

The Post Office by 1877 was considering a further reduction in the postage on heavy letters, for the revised scale of 1871 had proved to be a financial success. Although the increase in the penny rate to cover a full ounce had reduced the revenue by £171,263, this had been more than compensated by the increase in the number of large letters. It was felt that the rate for items above 12 ounces could be reduced, to remove the sudden leap from 4d to 1s 1d (see chart 1). The increased weight of mail might, it is true, create problems and 'interfere with the rapid transmission of letters properly so called', but the most alarming prospect was the attitude of the railway Companies. They might, it was feared, end their present letter mail contracts and demand recompense for the increased weight and the competition with their own parcel trade. It could indeed be argued that the limit of the letter post had been reached, and that any further extension of the service to large items required a change in approach. The parcel traffic should be kept separate from letters to prevent interference with urgent material, and the co-operation of the railway companies should be secured.[58] The possible introduction of a separate parcel post was encouraged by the discussions at the Railway Clearing House and in 1878 Tilley suggested that the railway companies should operate their scheme in conjunction with the Post Office. The gross revenue, he proposed, should be equally divided between the Department and the Clearing House. This followed the general approach recommended by the Hills since the 1850s, but on terms which were much more generous to the companies. 'It is difficult', Tilley admitted, 'to form any decided opinion as to the effect in a financial point of view. The Railway Companies may naturally expect a large share of the profit and in order to secure the ready co-operation of them *all* it is necessary that the Department should deal with them in a very liberal spirit as it must be admitted will be the result of an equal division of receipts. The Post Office will not perhaps make a large profit but I think it will somewhat more than pay its expenses.'[59]

Although the Railway Clearing House had been unable to formulate a parcel scheme because of its inability to force recalcitrant companies to accept majority decisions, the organisation had considerable power in external negotiations and 'could speak for *all* member companies when it came to a question of demanding more generous terms for co-operating in a parcel post scheme'. The Department's bargaining position was further weakened by the urgency arising from an agreement signed at Paris in November 1880 to introduce an international parcel

THE MAN FOR THE POST.

Henry Fawcett was Postmaster General when the introduction of the parcel post was announced. The new service produced a change in the name of letter carriers to postmen, and in 1883 *Punch* published a lament on their behalf:

It wasn't so bad in the days gone by, with letters tied up in a handy pack,
A stick, a satchel, a pair of legs, a sense of duty, a big broad back;
But now it's different quite, look here, when the grave is ready and sexton host,
Let them bury me quiet, and put on the stone, 'His back it was broke by the Parcels Post'.

59

post, which would clearly be impracticable without an inland service. The railway companies could therefore drive a hard bargain; they were assisted by the Post Office's mishandling of negotiations and the lack of agreement with the Treasury which felt 'such a partnership agreement between private companies and a public Department . . . to be of doubtful policy'. The agreement which was finally reached in the Post Office (Parcels) Act of 1882 gave the companies 55 per cent of the postage on rail-borne parcels; it was to run for twenty-one years, and thereafter until terminated by either party. The Postmaster General had the power to alter the tariff without consulting the companies, but in this event they could seek revision of their terms of remuneration by arbitration. The new service was introduced in 1883.[60] Although the Hills had assumed that co-operation would remove the need for a separate railway service, the companies in fact maintained their own parcel service in competition with the Post Office.

'No expectation has been entertained by the Department', admitted the Financial Secretary in 1880, that there would be any large amount of profit.' Although he did not anticipate a loss, others were more sceptical. The Solicitor issued a prophetic warning that the Department would face competition in profitable local services, so that the Post Office 'will have undertaken and be bound by its contract with the railway companies to continue to perform the most expensive and least remunerative portion of the service'. The railway companies indeed retained a scale which was graduated by distance and, in comparison with the flat-rate scale for the parcel post, it was cheaper to use the railway service for local parcels.[61] Neither was it clear that the Department's share of the gross revenue would cover its expenses. It was hoped that the existing establishment would be adequate, but this expectation might be unrealistic. 'The Post Office does not keep more cats than can catch mice, and as its work increases its expenses would increase in nearly the same proportion especially in dealing with articles of so much greater bulk than letters.' There was, in any case, great uncertainty about the level of traffic which would have to be handled. The parcel post system was designed to handle 27 million parcels, with an average weight of four pounds and a postage of sevenpence. In fact, in 1883/4 there were 20.6 million parcels with an average weight of two pounds and a postage of fivepence. There was a serious shortfall of revenue, and the parcel post incurred a deficit in its first year which was variously calculated to be £89,000 and £248,000.[62]

The strategy adopted by the Post Office was to encourage the traffic in larger, more renumerative parcels, since 'the machinery is capable of dealing with a far larger number of parcels without any serious increase

The bustle and excitement of the first day of the parcels post in 1883 was captured by the *Illustrated London News*.

of expense'. The average cost per parcel on the existing traffic was 2.88*d* and an increase of 25 per cent in the traffic could be handled at a cost of

0.58*d* per parcel, which would, it was calculated, convert the overall deficit into a profit. It was therefore decided in 1886 to reduce the postage on parcels above three pounds and to raise the limit from seven to eleven pounds. The companies could, of course, seek arbitration on their terms of payment, but decided not to risk the danger that the decision would be against them.[63] Another possibility which was considered was the introduction of a low rate for local parcels, which would have the additional advantage of increasing the proportion of road-borne parcels on which the Post Office retained the entire postage. Although it had been expected that road-borne parcels would comprise a sixth of the traffic, they had in fact not reached 10 per cent. Local rates were not introduced, and an attempt was instead made to increase the proportion of parcels carried by road. A number of horse-coach services were started from London to nearby towns, [64] and by the First World War a fifth of parcels were carried by road. However, by 1904 the Post Office had the possibility of sweeping aside the original agreement of 1883 rather than attempting to make the best of it, for the 21-year term had expired and the Department had the option of renegotiation.[64]

Parcel mails were transferred to road services in order to reduce payments to the railway companies.

2.7 ROAD-BORNE PARCELS, 1899–1913

| quarter ending | percentage of: | |
31 December	postage	parcels
1899	14.5	14.2
1909	16.3	17.5
1913	19.5	21.2

Source: Post 33/4778, M9339/1935, file 1.

In the 1880s, the Post Office had been convinced that the terms were unduly favourable to the railway companies, and would have positively welcomed arbitration; the companies were just as eager to avoid this.[66] By 1904 the Post Office was less optimistic about the outcome of renegotiation. The revision in the parcel post tariffs in 1886 and 1897 had already reduced the payment to the companies, so that while they received 6.6d for carrying a six-pound parcel in 1883, this had fallen to 5.8d in 1886 and 4.4d in 1897. The attractions of arbitration had also been reduced by the terms of the award made to the Great Western Railway in 1903 for the conveyance of letter mails. This gave the company 67.5 per cent of the railway parcel rate for the carriage of letter bags, whereas the Department paid only 40.03 per cent of the railway parcel rate for the carriage of parcels and their receptacles. Application of the award of 1903 to the parcel traffic would increase the payment to the companies from £0.9m to £1.5m. It was therefore decided that the agreement of 1883 should not be terminated until the Department was placed in a stronger position. It was discovered that over half the gross weight of the parcel post was taken by the heavy wicker baskets in which the parcels were packed, and the substitution of lighter bags by 1912 reduced the receptacles to less than a fifth of the gross weight of the parcel post. This reduction in the weight of the parcel post meant that the payment to the railway companies became the equivalent to 64.6 per cent of the railway parcel rate, which was still not enough for arbitration to offer the prospect of better terms.

In order to strengthen its bargaining position further it was decided to transfer parcels to motor vans, 'for the abandonment of such services would no doubt prove a useful makeweight' in negotiations with the companies. By the First World War, there were eighteen motor services operating from London and another twenty in the provinces, which were viewed less as a long-term solution to the carriage of parcels than as a bargaining weapon to induce the railways to accept lower rates. The Department remained convinced that the payment should be reduced, for it was clear to officials at St Martin's le Grand that the parcel service made a loss. It was difficult to separate the cost of parcels from the total expenditure on mail services, and in 1913 it was calculated that the parcel post was losing £900,000 on one estimate and £1.5m on another. The problem was how to produce a case which would convince the arbitrators.[67] The award of 1903 was not really applicable, for it failed to take revenue into account. A pound of letters might contain twenty or more items each paying a penny, whereas the postage on a one pound parcel was only threepence. The payment of 67.5 per cent of the railway parcel rate for the carriage of letters still left the Post Office with a considerable margin to cover the costs of collection, delivery and management, but this could not be the case with the parcel post. The railway companies certainly received far less than 55 per cent of the gross revenue from letters, perhaps nearer 15 per cent.

The First World War introduced a new set of circumstances. The motor services operated by the Post Office were curtailed and in 1920/1 only 5.4 per cent of parcels were carried by road. The question of restoring these services was under consideration at the end of the war, largely as a bargaining weapon against the railway companies. It was calculated that the payment of 55 per cent of postage to the railways would give them £3.6m if they carried all parcels. This could be reduced to £2.8m if they carried three-quarters of the parcels, and the provision of road transport for the remaining quarter would raise the total cost of carriage to £3.0m. It was therefore financially attractive to transfer a quarter of the parcel traffic to road transport: it would be even more beneficial if the companies would accept 40 per cent of postage in return for the Department's abandoning road services, for this would reduce their payment to £2.6m. Such was the reasoning behind the Post Office (Parcels) Act of 1922. The railway companies agreed to accept 40 per cent of the postage and in return the Department would send no more than 10 per cent of parcels by road, on penalty of an increase in the railways' share of postage. The agreement was short-sighted and inflexible, for it considered road transport only as a bargaining weapon against the railways and did not allow for future changes in the economics of motor services which might reduce costs.[68]

The parcel post was to lose ground in the interwar period with the emergence of new road-carriers. The railway companies were able to respond by offering an express service, by developing motor services which could compete in the local trade, and by negotiating special terms with large users on condition that they gave the whole trade to the railways. The Post Office was much less flexible in the face of competition. A local parcel rate and discounts to large users were both rejected as departures from the principle of flat-rate charges. Although steps were taken to ensure that the road services were increased to 10 per cent of the parcel traffic, restrictions soon had to be imposed for fear of incurring penalties under the Act of 1922. The proportion of parcels carried by road increased from 6 per cent in 1922 to 9.8 per cent in 1936, and motor vans could certainly have been used in the parcel service to a greater extent. The Department had developed a large fleet for other purposes, yet when schemes were formulated for the introduction of motor vehicles no account could be taken of the parcel traffic. 'Apart from possible adverse financial consequences, it would be contrary to the spirit of the agreement with the railway companies to institute official motor services with the main object of transferring parcels from rail to road, or even to provide a larger vehicle than required for ordinary postal needs solely to permit of diverting additional parcels from the railway.' There was only one remaining response to the deteriorating position of the parcel post: to reduce the rates.[69]

There was a great deal of uncertainty in the interwar period about the finances of the parcel post. Although it was estimated in 1927 that the loss was £875,000 a year, in 1929 it was felt that costs had been exaggerated and that the service might even be profitable. However, even on the basis of the most favourable assumptions the reduction in rates in 1935 would produce a loss of £450,000. The railway companies had not been consulted, despite the fact that the lower rates would reduce their revenue by £343,000, and they responded by demanding 50 per cent of the postage. The Department was in a weak position. It could not threaten to transfer parcels to the roads, for the penalty clause of 1922 would be invoked. Arbitration was likely to benefit the companies, for application of the terms of 1903 for the carriage of letter mails would produce an increased payment. The Department considered itself fortunate that the companies were willing to continue to accept 40 per cent of the postage on condition that their payment did not fall below the sum received before the reduction of rates in 1935. The Post Office had certainly mishandled the parcel service in the interwar period. The agreement of 1922 limited its flexibility and any positive response to competition, such as preferential treatment for large customers or local rates, was ruled out. When action was taken to reduce rates, it had disastrous financial consequences which made worse an already unsatisfactory position.[70]

It is hard to escape the conclusion that the parcel post was one of the least successful and most consistently misjudged of the services provided by the Post Office. There can be little doubt that the agreement of 1882 was fundamentally misconceived. The partnership was not a genuine one, for the companies retained their own service which resulted in competitive reduction in rates. It was also difficult to see how the Department's share of the revenue could cover its expenditure. The

65

continuation of the principles of 1882 in the new agreement of 1922, along with the abandonment of the power of extending road services, was in retrospect even more misguided. The Department had surrendered its flexibility by tying itself to the railway companies, and it was also trapped by adherence to uniform rates so that it was unable to develop a positive marketing response to competition. It is certainly possible to sympathise with the view of Maberly in 1848 that the parcel trade was outside the sphere of the Post Office.

Inland postage rates and traffic

Where the State itself conducts an industry there is always a risk that commercial considerations and fiscal considerations will not be sufficiently distinguished. Charges may be fixed at a higher point than is warranted by the cost of the services rendered. The surplus goes to the national revenue. It is a tax, but a concealed tax, and in the case of postal rates it is one of the worst kinds of tax, a tax on communications. On the other hand, charges may be fixed at a lower point than will cover the cost of the service. The deficit is a subsidy, but a concealed subsidy. (H. Samuel, 'Introduction' to A.D. Smith, *The Development of Rates of Postage: an Historical and Analytical Study* (1917), pp. xi-xii.)

The Post Office was a Revenue Department, and the conflict between its tasks of raising income for the Exchequer and providing a service to the public was never resolved. Herbert Samuel, the Postmaster General, noted in 1917 an important consideration in the history of the postal services. Should rates be determined by the cost of the service in order to produce a commercial return; or might they be fixed without regard for costs, whether to produce a large revenue for the State or to subsidise certain forms of traffic? The introduction of the Penny Post in 1840 did not produce a definitive answer.

The basic postage rate for an ordinary inland letter remained one penny from 1840 to 1918, but this did not mean that the tariff was static over the period.[71] There were in fact three significant changes: the weight which could be despatched for one penny increased from half to one ounce in 1871 and to four ounces in 1897; there was a considerable reduction in the rate for heavy letters so that the cost of a packet weighing a pound fell from 2s 8d in 1840 to 4d in 1897; and cheaper services were introduced which allowed postcards and printed papers to be sent for one halfpenny (see charts 1-3).

Did the customer of the Post Office share in the general price deflation which was such a marked feature of the second half of the

Inland Letter Rates, 1840 – 1939

No Limit of Weight

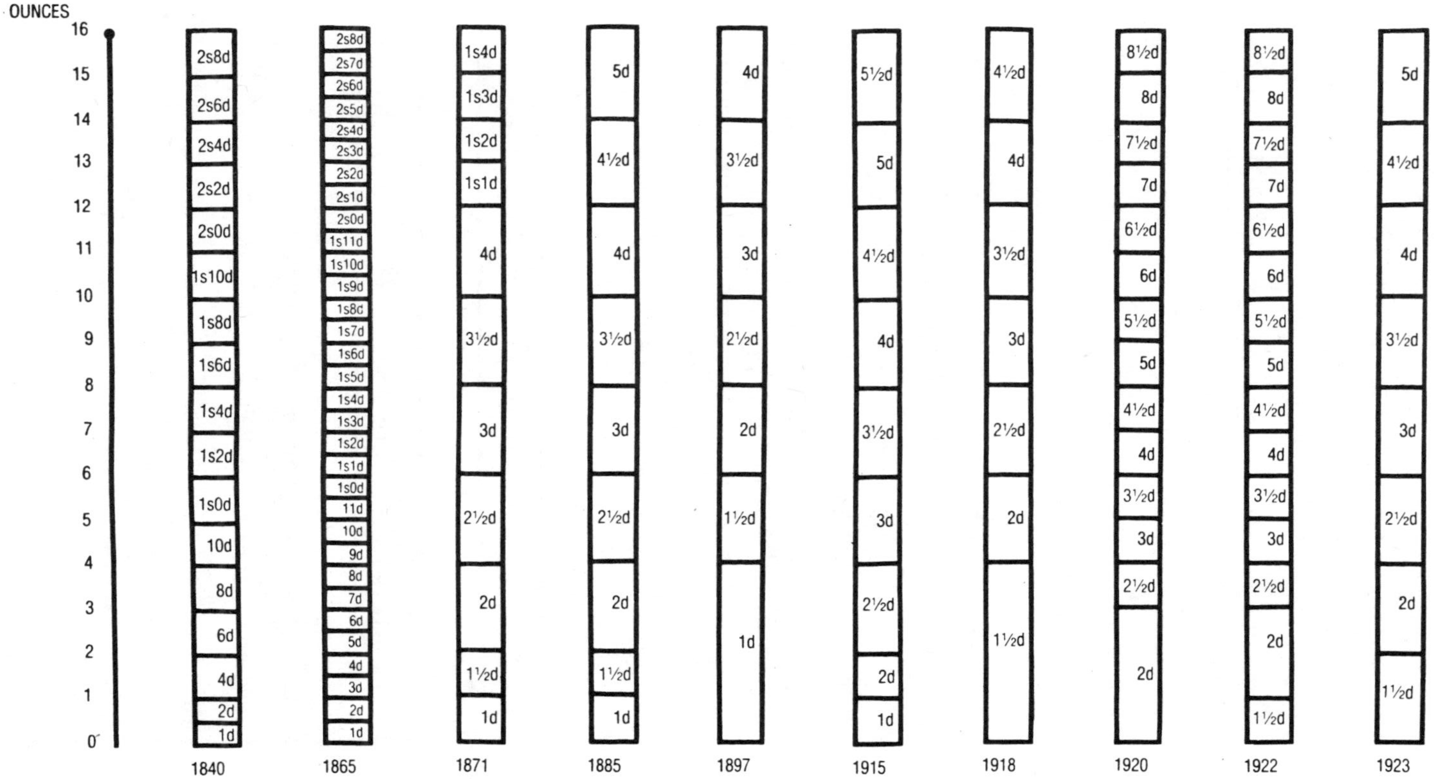

CHART I

Rate steps by year (read from highest weight at top to lowest at bottom):

1840 — 2s8d, 2s6d, 2s4d, 2s2d, 2s0d, 1s10d, 1s8d, 1s6d, 1s4d, 1s2d, 1s0d, 10d, 8d, 6d, 4d, 2d, 1d

1865 — 2s8d, 2s7d, 2s6d, 2s5d, 2s4d, 2s3d, 2s2d, 2s1d, 2s0d, 1s11d, 1s10d, 1s9d, 1s8d, 1s7d, 1s6d, 1s5d, 1s4d, 1s3d, 1s2d, 1s1d, 1s0d, 11d, 10d, 9d, 8d, 7d, 6d, 5d, 4d, 3d, 2d, 1d

1871 — 1s4d, 1s3d, 1s2d, 1s1d, 4d, 3½d, 3d, 2½d, 2d, 1½d, 1d

1885 — 5d, 4½d, 4d, 3½d, 3d, 2½d, 2d, 1½d, 1d

1897 — 4d, 3½d, 3d, 2½d, 2d, 1½d, 1d

1915 — 5½d, 5d, 4½d, 4d, 3½d, 3d, 2½d, 2d, 1d

1918 — 4½d, 4d, 3½d, 3d, 2½d, 2d, 1½d

1920 — 8½d, 8d, 7½d, 7d, 6½d, 6d, 5½d, 5d, 4½d, 4d, 3½d, 3d, 2½d, 2d

1922 — 8½d, 8d, 7½d, 7d, 6½d, 6d, 5½d, 5d, 4½d, 4d, 3½d, 3d, 2½d, 2d, 1½d

1923 — 5d, 4½d, 4d, 3½d, 3d, 2½d, 2d, 1½d

OUNCES scale: 16, 15, 14, 13, 12, 11, 10, 9, 8, 7, 6, 5, 4, 3, 2, 1, 0

Source: The Post Office. Statement showing alterations in inland postage rates and growth of postal traffic 1840-1925
Note: The 1923 scale applied until 1940

CHART II

Printed paper rates, 1848–1939

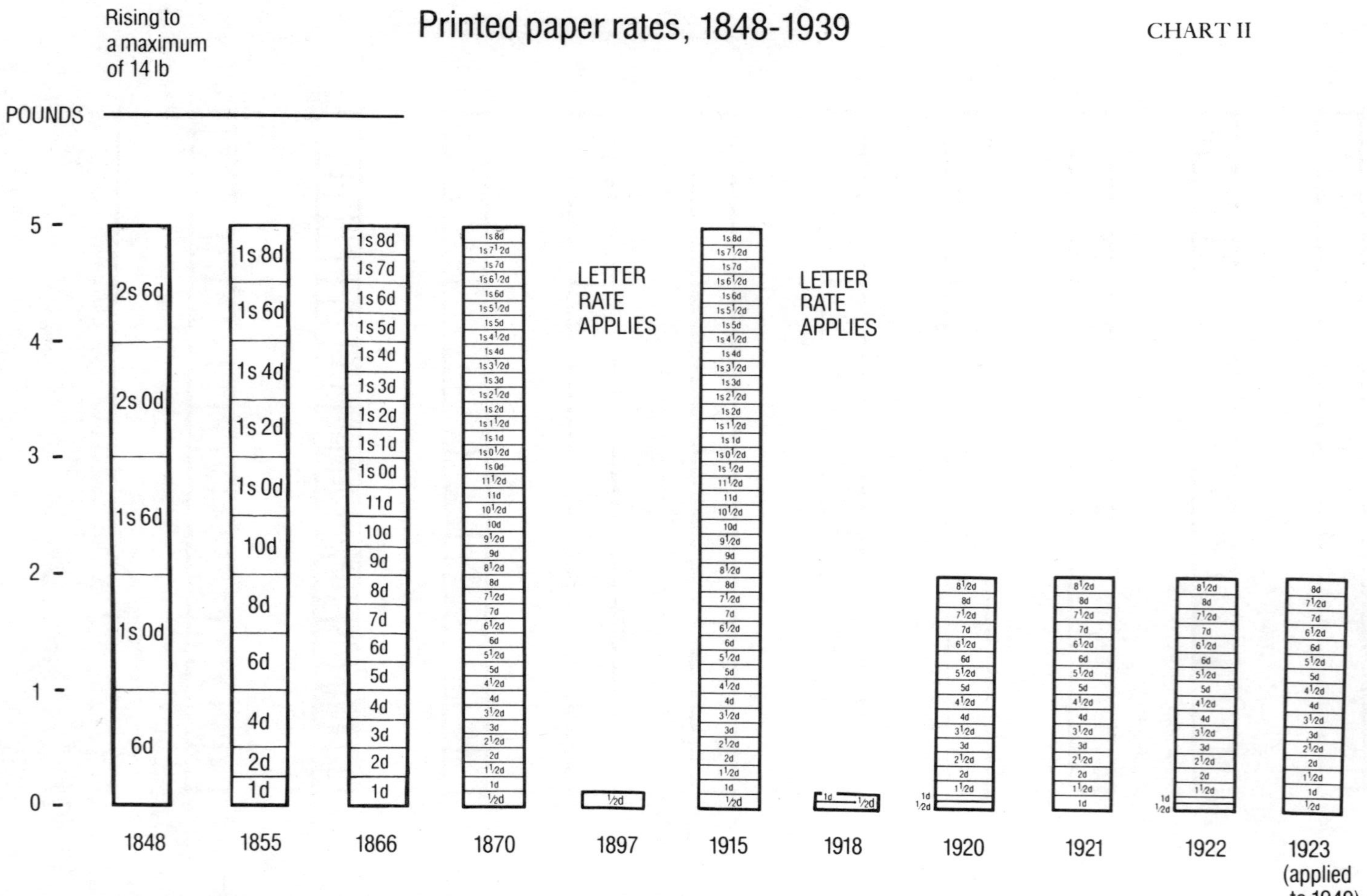

Rising to
a maximum
of 14 lb

POUNDS

5 –

4 –

3 –

2 –

1 –

0 –

1848

2s 6d

2s 0d

1s 6d

1s 0d

6d

1855

1s 8d

1s 6d

1s 4d

1s 2d

1s 0d

10d

8d

6d

4d

2d

1d

1866

1s 8d
1s 7d
1s 6d
1s 5d
1s 4d
1s 3d
1s 2d
1s 1d
1s 0d
11d
10d
9d
8d
7d
6d
5d
4d
3d
2d
1d

1870

1s 8d
1s 7½d
1s 6½d
1s 5½d
1s 4½d
1s 3½d
1s 3d
1s 2d
1s 1½d
1s 1d
1s 0½d
10½d
11d
10½d
10d
9½d
9d
8½d
8d
7½d
7d
6½d
6d
5½d
5d
4½d
4d
3½d
3d
2½d
2d
1½d
1d
½d

1897

LETTER
RATE
APPLIES

½d

1915

1s 8d
1s 7½d
1s 7d
1s 6½d
1s 6d
1s 5½d
1s 5d
1s 4½d
1s 4d
1s 3½d
1s 3d
1s 2½d
1s 2d
1s 1½d
1s 1d
1s 0½d
1s 1½d
11½d
11d
10½d
10d
9½d
9d
8½d
8d
7½d
7d
6½d
6d
5½d
5d
4½d
4d
3½d
3d
2½d
2d
1½d
1d
½d

1918

LETTER
RATE
APPLIES

1d — ½d

1920

8½d
8d
7½d
7d
6½d
6d
5½d
5d
4½d
4d
3½d
3d
2½d
2d
1½d

1d
½d

1921

8½d
8d
7½d
7d
6½d
6d
5½d
5d
4½d
4d
3½d
3d
2½d
2d
1½d
1d

1922

8½d
8d
7½d
7d
6½d
6d
5½d
5d
4½d
4d
3½d
3d
2½d
2d
1½d

1d
½d

1923
(applied
to 1940)

8d
7½d
7d
6½d
6d
5½d
5d
4½d
4d
3½d
3d
2½d
2d
1½d
1d

Source: Post Office Archives, Historical Summary No. 10, 'A history of inland postage rates'.

CHART III

Postcard rates 1870 – 1940

RATE FOR CARD UP TO 5½ x 3½ INCHES 1870 – 1925
5⅞ x 4⅛ INCHES 1925 – 1940

Cards sold with
embossed stamp
at a slight
charge; or private
cards embossed at
inland revenue office

Private cards
with adhesive
stamp

½d	½d	1d	1½d	1d
1870	1894	1918	1921	1922

Source: Post Office Archives, Historical Summary No. 10, *'A history of inland postage rates'*

CHART IV

Parcel post rates, 1883–1939

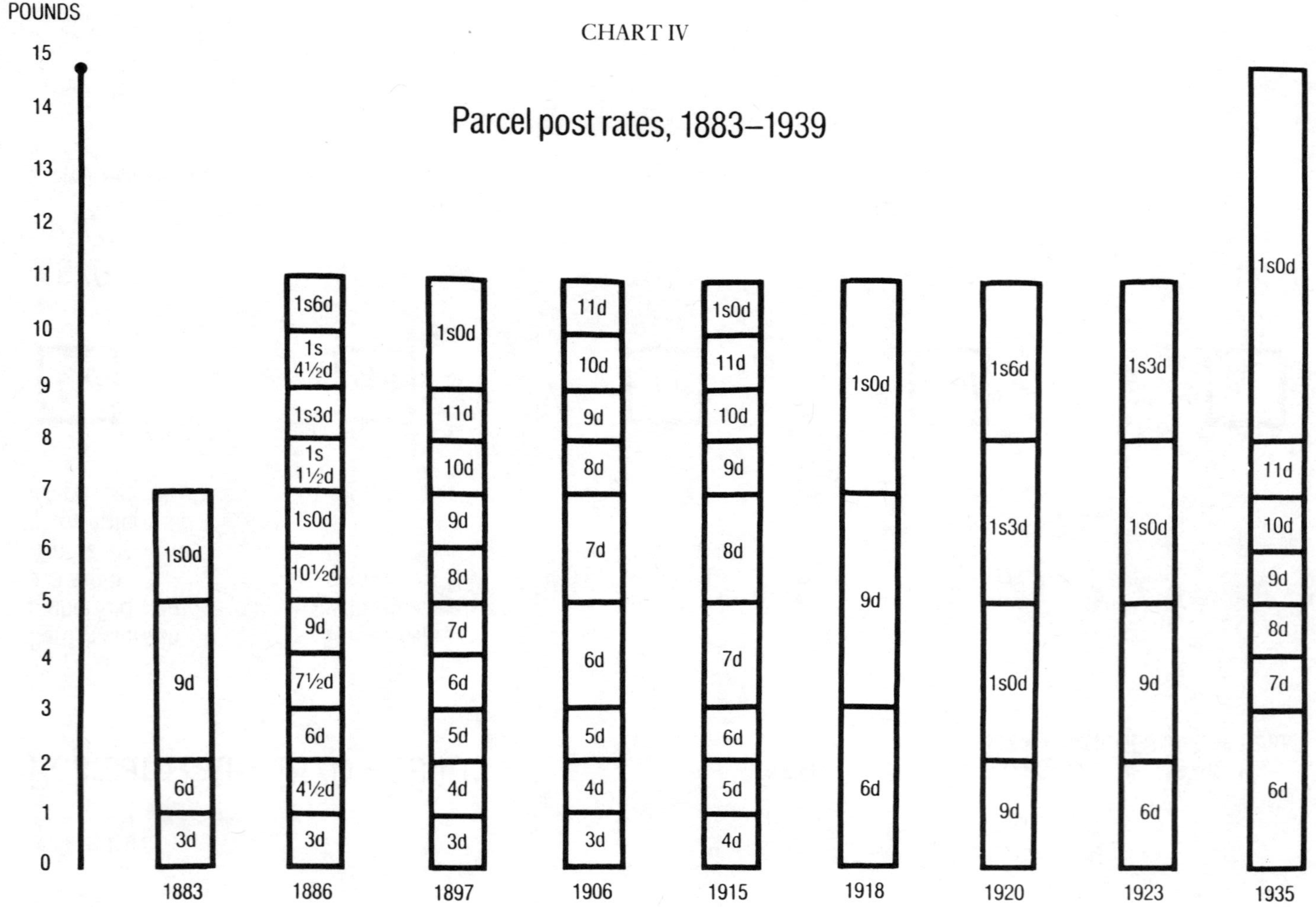

POUNDS

15 · 14 13 12 11 10 9 8 7 6 5 4 3 2 1 0

1883
1s0d | 9d | 6d | 3d

1886
1s6d | 1s 4½d | 1s3d | 1s 1½d | 1s0d | 10½d | 9d | 7½d | 6d | 4½d | 3d

1897
1s0d | 11d | 10d | 9d | 8d | 7d | 6d | 5d | 4d | 3d

1906
11d | 10d | 9d | 8d | 7d | 6d | 5d | 4d | 3d

1915
1s0d | 11d | 10d | 9d | 8d | 7d | 6d | 5d | 4d

1918
1s0d | 9d | 6d

1920
1s6d | 1s3d | 1s0d | 9d

1923
1s3d | 1s0d | 9d | 6d

1935
1s0d | 11d | 10d | 9d | 8d | 7d | 6d

Indices of postage rates and prices, 1840–1940

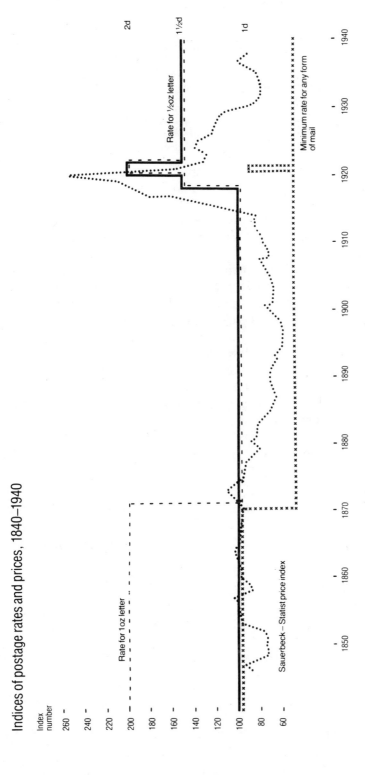

2.8 LETTERS, CARDS AND PRINTED PAPERS IN THE UNITED KINGDOM, 1875 AND 1900/1

	Letters		Postcards		Printed papers	
	no (m)	per cent	no (m)	per cent	no (m)	per cent
1875	1,008.4	80.4	87.1	6.9	158.7	12.7
1900/1	2,323.6	66.9	419.0	12.1	732.4	21.1

Source: *Annual Reports of the Postmaster General on the Post Office.*

nineteenth century? Postcards and printed papers which were carried at a rate of one halfpenny became a significant part of the mail traffic, increasing from 19.6 per cent in 1875 to 33.2 per cent in 1900/1. The reduction in the tariff for heavy letters, and the increase in the weight limit of a penny letter, had less impact. In 1895, only 10 per cent of letters exceeded half an ounce, and only 1 per cent weighed more than four ounces.[72] The penny rate produced over 90 per cent of the revenue on letters and formed the bedrock of postal finances. The halfpenny rate for cards and printed papers at best covered costs and at worst produced a loss. The cost of a postal packet (excluding parcels) was estimated to be 0.536*d* in 1910/1, which meant that postcards and printed papers made a loss of 6.7 per cent while ordinary penny letters produced a profit of 86.6 per cent.[73] Any threat to the highly profitable penny rate would push the Post Office into deficit, and the changes in postage rates were therefore more in the character of minor adjustments designed to protect the penny rate than major reductions. The overwhelming majority of letters did not share in the nineteenth-century fall in prices; most letters in the 1890s, as in 1840, weighed up to half an ounce and paid a penny.

2.9 WEIGHT DISTRIBUTION OF ORDINARY INLAND LETTERS, 1895

	per cent of letters	per cent of revenue
up to 1 oz	95.4	91.3
over 1 oz but not exceeding 2 oz	2.3	3.3
2　　　　4	1.4	2.6
4　　　　6	0.5	1.2
6　　　　8	0.3	0.8
over 8 oz	0.2	0.7

Source: *Postage Rates Committee, 1895* in Post 30/703, E16980/1895.

Prices in general started to rise from the late 1890s, with a period of rapid inflation during and immediately after the First World War. Postage rates rose less rapidly, for the penny rate survived until 1918, and the increases in the minimum rates to 1½d in 1918 and 2d in 1920 were below the general rate of inflation. Prices fell sharply from the early 1920s, but the minimum letter rate remained 1½d between 1922 and the Second World War which was higher in relation to the general price level than at any time since 1840.

What was the rationale behind the tariff? It has been seen that a confused and anomalous pattern had emerged by 1870 with the creation of the book post, its extension to printed papers in general, the acceptance of the demands for a pattern post and the grant of a cheap rate for postcards. These various changes had come in response to a variety of pressures. The book post reflected the desire of Hill to encourage education, but the subsequent reduction in the rate in 1855 was necessitated by the abolition of compulsory stamp duty on newspapers. The introduction of a halfpenny rate in 1870 for printed papers and postcards came as the result of a vote of the Commons against the wishes of the government. The pattern post, the various changes in its regulations and the adjustment in the rate for heavy letters reflected the pressure on the Post Office to introduce a parcel service. There was in consequence no coherent pricing policy, but rather a pragmatic response to particular pressures and problems. There was no good economic reason why rates in 1869 should range from 2s 8d for a letter weighing one pound to 2d for a pattern and 4d for a book. Indeed, in 1870 Frank Scudamore suggested that the time had arrived for the simplification of rates. He based his analysis upon two basic propositions. The first was that simplicity was essential in a business which involved millions of transactions carried out under pressure. The distinction between letters, samples and books offended against this rule, causing increased labour and expense. The second proposition was that charges should be regulated by the work done rather than by the contents of a packet. A letter, book and sample might have the same weight and cost the same to handle, so that the charge should be the same. Scudamore concluded that the various rates should, as far as possible, be assimilated. This would not be easy for, as Scudamore realised, the Department was not operating from first principles in an ideal world. Although some progress was made in the direction he advised, his propositions were never fully implemented. In any case, a more important consideration was the need to preserve the penny rate which formed the basis of postal profits up to the First World War. It made sense to use part of the surplus to reduce rates on more peripheral services in order to protect the profitable penny rate, even if this did offend against Scudamore's propositions. The fear that a halfpenny rate for letters would be forced on the Department was a real one in the early 1870s and this would, it was fully realised, push the Post Office into

73

deficit. The increase in the weight carried for a penny which was granted in 1871 was a relatively inexpensive way of containing the pressure. At the same time, there was a movement to consolidate rates by abolishing the pattern post and reducing the postage on heavy letters as some compensation. The attempt to create a more coherent pricing structure was limited by political expediency and the need to preserve the penny letter.[74]

When the parcel post was introduced in 1883, postage rates were again thrown into confusion. The parcel rate was cheaper than the letter rate for weights above eight ounces, and cheaper than the printed paper rate above twelve ounces. A transfer of letters and printed papers to the parcel post would obviously reduce the Department's profit, for a large proportion of the postage on parcels was paid to the railway companies. It was therefore in the financial interests of the Post Office to retain articles in the printed paper and letter post, provided that the rapid mail services were not disrupted by heavy items. In 1884 a Committee on the Revision of Inland Rates of Postage was appointed to formulate 'harmonious' rates, without imperilling the initial penny rate. The new rates which were introduced in 1885 reduced the postage on a letter weighing a pound from 1s 4d to 5d, and on a printed paper from 4d to 2½d: a parcel of the same weight cost 3d. This was a response to the unremunerative parcel service, and was designed to check the transfer of mail from the letter post rather than attempting any assessment of the cost of handling letters of different weights.[75]

However, the unremunerative traffic in light parcels continued to grow, and an Inland Postage Committee in 1889–90 again considered means of diverting traffic to the letter post. There was no clear agreement on the best strategy to follow. The committee recommended that the printed paper rate for unsealed packets might be converted into a general 'open' or unsealed post for light articles at a lower rate than the parcel post. This proposal was, however, carried only by the casting vote of the chairman and generated opposition from those who argued that an open post cost as much to handle as a 'closed' post, because of the attendant problems of ensuring that the regulations were observed and that articles did not escape from their covers. The committee also recommended that the letter tariff should be reduced on larger items, but failed to agree on the scale. It was indeed argued by some that the more sensible course of action was to make the parcel post profitable by raising the maximum weight and introducing a cash-on-delivery service.[76] These disagreements and uncertainties meant that no changes were implemented.

Profits in the postal services had fallen in the early 1890s and started to recover in the mid-1890s. Public pressure mounted for a better service and reduction in rates, which the Secretary admitted would be difficult to resist but 'very inconvenient and unwise on financial grounds to concede'. The demand for the introduction of an imperial penny postage and cheaper parcel rates should, he felt, be pre-empted:

> The whole of our large surplus is derived from the penny letter, and the profit from that letter is so large that, after providing the surplus . . . it enables us to wipe out the loss on the Telegraphs, the Newspaper and Open Post, and on the Foreign and Colonial Post. It seems reasonable, therefore, that if any concession is to be made it should be made to that class of the public which provides the whole of the profits of the Department. The writers of inland letters, in other words, seem morally entitled both to consideration and to prior consideration.

2.10 RATES FOR LETTER, PRINTED PAPER AND PATTERN POST IN 1895

	1 oz	2 oz	4 oz
Letter post	1d	1½d	2d
Printed paper post	½d	½d	1d
Pattern post	1d	1d	1d

A Committee was appointed in 1895 to consider the introduction of a letter rate of one penny for four ounces and one halfpenny for each succeeding two ounces, which was the same as the printed paper and pattern rates excepting the initial step of one halfpenny for two ounces. This would attract some parcels into the letter post and establish a simpler, more coherent tariff structure. The cost was estimated to be £200,000, but the committee felt that the new tariff offered 'a minimum of ulterior danger to the revenue'. There was, the Committee noted, 'a temper of restless expectancy, in view of which the Post Office is more than ever held to the duty of suggesting appropriations of its surplus revenue to the public benefit instead of waiting till they are wrung from it'. The new rates which were introduced in 1897 therefore had two motivations. One was internal, arising from the desire to simplify the complex and anomalous rates and to encourage light parcels to transfer to the letter post. Scudamore's propositions of 1870 were implemented to a much greater extent, and the various scales were much less confused. The second motivation was external, directed against politicians and publicists who were advocating changes which had no internal, Departmental justification.[77]

The new rates were announced to mark the Diamond Jubilee of Queen Victoria in 1897 and they marked the limit of the reduction in postage rates. The improvement in the net revenue of the Post Office did lead in 1906 to a consideration of a scale of one penny for the first four ounces and one halfpenny for each succeeding four ounces. This would have reduced the postage on a one pound letter from 4*d* to 2½*d*, and at the same time it was proposed that the rate for light parcels should be increased to encourage their transfer to the letter post. However, this adjustment of the tariff was rejected, largely because of its implications for contracts with the railways for the carriage of mail. The transfer of parcels to the letter post would reduce the revenue of the railway companies by £196,076 and it was feared that they might terminate their contracts and secure better terms. In any case, the transfer of heavy items to the letter post would increase expenses and reduce efficiency. The tariff of 1897 had already increased the average weight of inland letters, for the proportion weighing an ounce or less had fallen from 95.4 per cent in 1895 to 87.1 per cent in 1903. The changes recommended in 1906 were therefore confined to relatively minor improvements such as less stringent rules for the use of the halfpenny post, improved deliveries in rural districts, and a slight readjustment of parcel rates, at a cost of £156,250. The Post Office was willing to surrender part of its surplus, but faced a number of constraints on further reductions in the letter tariff.[78]

The outbreak of the First World War changed the emphasis from the reduction of rates to a need to increase revenue. The Retrenchment Committee in 1915 viewed the Post Office as a source of taxation and proposed a special war tax of one halfpenny on every internal postal communication. Herbert Samuel, the Postmaster General, opposed such a policy, arguing that the Post Office was already producing a large net revenue. He decried the taxation of communications and felt that it would be unfortunate if Britain, the inventor of the Penny Post, was the first to abandon it. The Penny Post survived, although the weight carried for a penny was reduced to one ounce, with one penny for the next ounce and one halfpenny for each succeeding two ounces. This new scale would, it was estimated, increase the revenue by £1,181,000. However, by 1918 the increased cost of transport and the mounting burden of wages reduced the net revenue of the postal services to vanishing point. The penny rate still made a profit in 1918, but it was clear that the revenue could not be increased by an appreciable sum unless it was abandoned. Sentiment, it was argued, should give way to considerations of national finance. The scale of 1897 was reintroduced, with the addition of a war tax of one halfpenny at each stage. The Penny Post was ended. In theory, this was a temporary expedient, but the prospects of a swift restoration were slight. The new scale, it was admitted, would 'not nearly cover the increased cost of Post Office services and may indeed be necessary to maintain the Post Office services on a paying footing when normal conditions are restored'. The generosity of the Commons and taxpayer to the staff of the Post Office, commented Evelyn Murray, 'has one drawback – that someone must pay for it'.[79] The expenditure of the Post Office had risen by £26.35m between 1913/14 and 1920/1, of which 79.9 per cent was the result of higher wages.

2.11 PROFITABILITY OF THE MAIL SERVICES, JANUARY 1920

	average revenue	average cost	profit
Letters	1.56d	1.06d	0.5d
Cards	1d	0.9d	0.1d
Printed papers	0.55d	0.95d	−0.4d
Parcels	7.75d	11.5d	−3.75d

Source: Post 30/4648, E18138/1920

The postal services as a whole were profitable, and the new letter tariff produced a surplus of one halfpenny on each item. But by 1920, a further increase in postage rates was necessary, for the postal surplus would not cover the deficit on the telegraph and telephone services in 1920/1, and wages were about to rise again. The only way in which the necessary £8m could be found was to increase the initial letter rate to twopence, with adjustments to the rates for parcels, printed papers and cards. 'As a matter of principle', the Cabinet had decided, 'the Post Office must pay its way.' The Secretary operated on the assumption 'that it is the policy of the Government to place the Post Office services, taken as a whole, upon a paying footing but not to use them as an instrument of taxation, i.e. that the rates should be so fixed as to cover expenditure with a reasonable working margin, but that no attempt should be made to restore the pre-war surplus of four to five millions per annum.'[80] This working assumption was soon to change.

The financial performance of the Post Office improved as the wage bill fell. The 'war bonus' received by the staff was reduced automatically in line with the cost of living index, and by 1922 finances had improved sufficiently to reduce the tariffs for letters, printed papers and postcards. The results were disappointing. The traffic was expected to increase by 10 per cent for letters, 20 per cent for printed papers and 20 per cent for postcards, but the actual rates of increase between October 1921 and October 1922 were 5.5, 26 and 4.5 per cent. The postal revenue fell short of expectations, and the inelastic demand for postal services was to form a major element in the subsequent debate over the reintroduction of the Penny Post. 'All experience goes to show that the inland letter is not highly responsive to minor reductions or increases of charge. The probability is that the vast bulk of letters have to be sent anyhow, and the cost in itself is so small relatively to the value of the service that it does not greatly affect the volume of traffic actually sent.' The growth in postal traffic responded to the general state of the economy rather than to changes in postage rates, and it was argued that the reintroduction of the Penny Post should wait 'until a considerable revival of trade brings a sufficient accession of business and revenue to meet the heavy cost entailed'. Although rates were reduced in 1922 and 1923, the penny rate was not restored: the cost of this change was placed at £6.44m in 1928.[81]

Postage rates remained unchanged until the Second World War, largely because of the fiscal demands of the government. In 1924, the Postmaster General had argued that the Penny Post should be restored, but he was overruled. He complained that 'I have always contested the doctrine that the profits of a State Trading concern, as disclosed in its commercial accounts . . . can legitimately be maintained at an inflated level in order to relieve taxation. Such action is tantamount to the imposition of a tax upon customers.' The government was unmoved, and restoration was similarly prevented in 1934 by the Chancellor, Neville Chamberlain. The Post Office argued that the surplus could be used to finance the 'striking gesture' of reintroducing the Penny Post. 'It would operate tangibly and immediately across the whole community – indeed it might be argued that there are few, if any tonic expedients available of such widespread application and, apart from spectacular reductions in the income tax, that the restoration of the Penny Post would be the most effective indicator of a return to normality.' Chamberlain was highly sceptical of the benefits, pointing out that there was scarcely normality given the level of unemployment, and insisting that lower postage would hardly provide a stimulus to industry. The introduction of Penny Post was more likely, felt Chamberlain, to be seen as an electioneering device. There were, in any case, more deserving claims upon the government. 'The small income tax payer, who still suffers very greatly from the restriction of his statutory allowances, the people who suffered cuts in 1931 and the other claimants for relief from taxation then imposed, including of course the powerful cinema trade, must for the present', argued Chamberlain, 'be regarded as having an absolute first charge on such modest surplus, if any, as I may be able with good fortune in the future to command.' The surplus of the Post Office was to be treated as part of the revenue of the government which could not be sacrificed.[82]

Rowland Hill in *Post Office Reform* had suggested that uniformity of postage should be introduced so far as costs were uniform. Although the Department was to remain loyal to this principle in charging the same rate for an inland letter regardless of distance, it was ignored in many

6　The Earl of Hardwick, PMG 1852.

8　John Tilley, 'as unimpressionable as an oyster'.

7　Lord Stanley of Alderley, PMG 1860–6.

9　Frank Scudamore, 'a great accountant'.

10   Henry Fawcett, 'the blind Postmaster General'.

11   Stevenson Blackwood, 'Beauty Blackwood'

12   Henry Cecil Raikes of 'autocratic bent'.

13   Sir Evelyn Murray, 'born to command'.

other respects. Lower rates were charged for some services, such as printed papers, despite the fact that they cost the same to handle as letters. This is, however, to misunderstand the rationale of postal tariffs, for there was no attempt to establish the cost for each class of service and to add an element for profit. The basic assumption was that the light ordinary letters made a reasonable surplus; this rate should be protected; and the public could be offered a number of concessions in the less important services which would not jeopardise the revenue.

What, then, was the outcome of these changes in tariffs and services for the traffic carried by the Post Office? The reduction in the letter rate in 1840 clearly had an immediate impact, increasing the number of letters by 122.4 per cent in a year. The rate of growth of the letter traffic was 105.6 per cent in the first decade of the Penny Post, thereafter falling to 62.5 per cent between 1850 and 1860, and 31.2 per cent between 1900/1 and 1910/11. The addition of other services such as halfpenny packets and postcards did increase this rate of growth, but even so the increase between 1900/1 and 1910/11 was still only 41.6 per cent. The First World War imposed a check upon the growth of the mail, and the traffic in 1919/20 was slightly below the level of 1913/14. Growth thereafter was at a much reduced rate, of 11.7 per cent between 1919/20 and 1929/30 and 27.3 per cent between 1929/30 and 1938/9. Although the parcel traffic did grow from 22.9m items in the first full year of operation in 1884/5 to 81.0m in 1900/1, the subsequent rate of growth was considerably lower as a result of competition from private carriers. Changes in the tariff after 1840 were probably not of any great consequence for the growth of the traffic in letters, postcards and halfpenny packets. More important than these relatively minor adjustments was the general growth in population and the economy. The situation did change with the development in the twentieth century of the telephone system which produced an important adjustment in the character of the mail. Before the introduction of the Penny Post, most letters were probably sent for business purposes and there was subsequently an increase in personal correspondence. Since the interwar period, there has been a decrease in personal letters which have to a considerable extent been replaced by the telephone, and an increase in the proportion of business letters.

The improvement and expansion of mail services has been considered from the point of view of the Post Office as a business concern. This neglects the impact upon the rest of society. For example, by 1888 Marshall & Snelgrove employed over a hundred clerks who dealt with a thousand letters a day for mail orders from catalogues[83]. Rowland Hill would doubtless have approved neither of the massive traffic generated

2.12 MAIL TRAFFIC OF THE POST OFFICE, 1839–1938/9 (MILLIONS)

	Letters	Books, newspapers, patterns
1839	75.9[+]	—
1840	168.8	—
1850	347.0	—
1860	564.0	82.8
1870	862.7	130.2

	Letters	Newspapers	Half-penny packets	Postcards	Parcels
1880/1	1,176.4	133.8	248.9	122.9	—
1890/1	1,705.8	161.0	481.2	229.7	46.3
1900/1	2,323.6	167.8	732.4	419.0	81.0
1910/11	3,047.5	196.3	1,044.1	871.4	121.8
1913/14	3,477.8	207.1	1,172.3	926.5	137.1
1919/20			5,730		144.7
1929/30			6,400		160.5
1938/9			8,150		184.8

[+] excluding 6.6 m franks

Source: *Annual Reports of the Postmaster General*

2.13 GROWTH RATES OF MAIL TRAFFIC, 1839–1938/9 (PER CENT)

	Letters	Letters, postcards, newspapers halfpenny packets	Parcels
1840–50	105.6	—	—
1850–60	62.5	—	—
1860–70	53.0	53.5	—
1870–80/1	36.4	69.4	—
1880/1–1890/1	45.0	53.3	—
1890/1–1900/1	36.2	41.3	74.9
1900/1–1910/11	31.2	41.6	50.4
1919/20–1929/30	—	11.7	10.9
1929/30–1938/9	—	27.3	15.1

Source: *Annual Reports of the Postmaster General on the Post Office* and *Statistical Abstract for the United Kingdom.*

by the football pools nor the more ribald postcards despatched from Blackpool. He might, however, have taken some satisfaction in the growth in the number of letters per head. The statistics gathered by the Union Postale Universelle for 1900 showed that only in the United States were there more letters per head than in the United Kingdom. The financial performance was also good in international terms, surpassed only by countries such as Spain and Russia where the Post

Office was still viewed much more as a source of taxation. Rowland Hill was mistaken in his detailed calculations, but the Post Office in Britain had an enviable record in 1900 of combining profit and service. Although he has been criticised on many counts, it would be perverse to deny the benefits of Penny Post:

2.14 MAIL PER CAPITA IN THE UNITED KINGDOM, 1839–1914

	Letters	Postcards	Printed papers
1839	3	—	—
1840	7	—	—
1860	19	—	—
1880–1	34	6.1	6.9
1900–1	57	10.2	17.9
1913–4	75	20.1	25.4

Source: PP 1914–16 XXXIII, *Report of the Postmaster General on the Post Office 1914–15*, pp. 889–93.

2.15 MAIL SERVICES AND PROFITS OF SELECTED COUNTRIES, 1900

	Items of correspondence per head	profit francs (m)	or	loss % of revenue
United Kingdom	88	+99.0		+28.1
United States	95	−25.4		− 4.8
Germany	61	+22.4		+ 4.0
France	52	+68.7		+25.4
Italy	26	+ 1.6		+ 2.7
Spain	12	+15.8		+69.1
Russia	4	+62.3		+30.4

Source: Union Postale Universelle: *Statistique Générale du Service Postal, année 1900* (Berne, 1902), tables I and V.

Its object is not to increase the political power of this or that party, but to benefit all sects in politics and religion; and all classes from the highest to the lowest. To the rich, as to the less wealthy, it will be acceptable, from the increased facilities it will afford for their correspondence. To the middle classes it will bring relief from oppressive and irritating demands which they pay grudgingly. . . . And to the poor it will afford the means of communication with their distant friends and relatives, from which they are at present debarred. It will give increased energy to trade; it will remove innumerable temptations to fraud; and it will be an important step in general education . . . A more popular measure could not be discovered. It would bring immediate, substantial, practical, indisputable relief to all.[84]

81

3 Financial Services: Profit or Welfare?

> . . . the largest Banking Establishment that was ever carried on in the experience of mankind. (Lt-Col. W.L. Maberly, Secretary to the Post Office, in 1847).[1]

The Post Office in the nineteenth century developed a widening range of financial services alongside its responsibility for carrying the mail, starting with money orders and postal orders which allowed the transmission of small sums through the post, and adding the business of savings accounts and insurance policies. This extension of the scope of the Post Office raises a number of important themes. The Department was moving into areas in which, unlike the letter services, it did not have a monopoly. This posed the same problem as the introduction of the parcel post: where should the boundary between private and public enterprise be drawn? The commercial banks provided means for transmitting money across the country; there was a well-developed system of savings banks sponsored by private philanthropists and insurance companies, and friendly societies supplied life assurance. The boundary might be drawn so that the Post Office did not directly compete but concentrated on different segments of the market; equally, there might be overt competition which might result in success by public enterprise in some cases and private business in others.

The nineteenth century is often seen as an age of *laissez-faire* or individualism which has given way in the twentieth century to a period of government intervention and collectivism. This contrast is certainly overdrawn, and J.B. Brebner, in his classic article of 1948, had no difficulty in constructing a long list of examples of government intervention which, in his view, showed the readiness of interest groups to use the State for collectivist ends. *Laissez-faire* was, he claimed, a myth. Brebner included in his catalogue the introduction of Penny Post in 1840 and the nationalisation of the telegraph in 1870, and he might have added the use of mail contracts to encourage steam-ships and the establishment of new services such as the parcel post and the Post Office Savings Bank. It may certainly be agreed that the dichotomy between *laissez-faire* and state intervention is false, for the creation of free competition and the unhindered play of market forces required a particular legal framework and institutional structure which could only be created by the active involvement of the State. Brebner had failed to grasp this point: economists and politicians in the mid-nineteenth century were quite willing to accept certain forms of state intervention as consistent with *laissez-faire*. Laws had to be enforced and disputes settled, monopoly combated and competition encouraged, the weak protected and private profit at the expense of society checked. Jeremy Bentham and his fellow utilitarians accepted that free enterprise was most likely to benefit the consumer but, like any other claim to freedom, it had to be justified on the grounds of utility; if it could not, the State might intervene. Further, a bureaucracy became necessary to make democracy effective and to preserve the positive rights of individuals. Bentham wished to create a State of autonomous individuals based on law and rationality in place of a society based upon aristocratic privilege and interest groups. The central government would become a vital source of cohesion in such an individualistic society and this required a bureaucracy to establish control and order, itself observing the legal and rational standards found in the rest of society. Hence the general movement away from patronage to merit for entry into the civil service, which was to be an important feature of the Post Office in the 1850s and 1860s. Bentham's thought could therefore seem to be individualistic and authoritarian at the same time, and much the same might be said of Rowland Hill, who was part of the Benthamite circle.

The reform of the Post Office in 1840 was designed as part of the attack upon privilege and monopoly, and Rowland Hill would certainly have been surprised to discover that he was, in Brebner's opinion, an agent of collectivism. His aim was, of course, to remove a 'tax' on letters which was not justified by the cost of the service, and his ambition, whether in paying shipowners, railway companies or letter-carriers, was to determine expenditure by the rule of the market. It was particularly important in his view that in a State enterprise there should be no departure from the strict application of economic principles: each service should be self-supporting and cross-subsidy between different branches of the Post Office should be avoided. Wages should be determined by comparison with other occupations in the locality, and shipowners should receive no more than the 'sea postage' on the mail they carried. Hill was willing, and indeed eager, for the government to intervene in order to enforce these principles. The aim was always the same: to create free competition and to leave the determination of prices and wages to the market. 'Economical reform' should sweep away the remaining vestiges of privilege and interest which marked the old order before the Reform Bill. The next generation at St Martin's le Grand was more pragmatic and less dogmatic. Hill's successors accepted that it was not necessary for each branch of the service to be self-supporting, providing that the Post Office as a whole was profitable. Each branch of the foreign mail did not need to break even, for there might be other imperial or commercial interests at stake; regularity of shipping services might be more important than the price; wages should perhaps be determined by criteria beyond an assessment of what the market would bear. There was certainly in the 1860s a movement away from the Hills' vision of the principles upon which the Post Office should operate. How did this come about? Oliver MacDonagh has suggested that pressure for government intervention arose within departments as civil servants grappled with problems, and he argues that this process of organic administrative accretion was of greater significance than the impact of abstract ideas. The debate has rumbled on, but surprisingly little notice has been taken of the Post Office which was, after all, acquiring new functions throughout the century. The financial services of the Post Office provide an interesting case-study of the pattern of government growth and the limits to public enterprise in the nineteenth century.[2]

The retail business of remittances

The Money Order Office and the Post Office have at present almost a monopoly of what I may call the 'Retail business of remittances' – that is of the business of remitting small sums. (Report by Frank Scudamore, 5 March 1861)[3]

Money orders were the first financial service to be supplied by the Post Office, for they had their origins in an officially sanctioned private business carried on within the Department from the 1790s. A person wishing to transmit money could go to a post office and buy an order for any sum up to £5 5s in return for a commision of threepence in the pound for orders passing between provincial offices, or fourpence for orders issued or paid in London. The order specified the name of the purchaser and the recipient, and the office at which payment would be made. The purchaser would send the order to the recipient; a letter of advice was despatched to the post office at which it was to be presented and the details were recorded and transmitted to London. This was a cumbersome and expensive procedure, but it did offer protection against 'the Embezzlement of Letters containing money sent by Post'. The aim of the scheme was to rescue 'the general character of the Office from its present degraded condition, of protecting the poor under circumstances so extremely oppressive to them, of correcting the impaired morals of those belonging to the office who might not so err if they were so strongly tempted'. There were doubts whether the Department had the legal power to run the service, and it was also feared that the venture would make a loss. The solution adopted in 1792 was to run the money order office as a private venture within the Department, under the control of the 'clerks of the road' in London with the postmasters as agents. The proprietors of the money order office bore the risk and took the profit, but used the facilities of the Post Office to carry on the service. Private and public business were intermingled.[4]

The limits of the money order system were set to prevent 'interfering with the trade of banking generally through the country, which can be carried on infinitely better by private individuals than by a government establishment'. The intention was to confine it to areas of the market not covered by the commercial banks, that is, 'the poorer classes, who employ it for the purpose of making remittances of small sums to their friends'. But a money order and postage were expensive, and most remittances continued to be made by enclosing cash in letters. By the late 1830s attention turned towards a cheap system of registration of letters to provide an alternative form of security, and concern was also expressed at the ambiguous status of the Money Order Office. In 1838 it became an official service, charging a commission of 6d for any sum up to £2, and 1s 6d for sums between £2 and £5. The rate was reduced in 1840 to 3d and 6d respectively, and the cost was, of course, also decreased by the introduction of the Penny Post.[5]

3.1 MONEY ORDER COMMISSIONS, 1838–97

Up to	1838	1840	1860	1871	1878	1897
10s				1d	2d	
£1				2d		2d
£2	6d	3d	3d	3d	3d	3d
£3					4d	
£5	1s 6d	6d	6d	6d	rising by	
£7	—	—	9d	9d	1d per £1	
£10	—	—	1s 0d	1s 0d	10d	4d

The business of the Money Order Office increased from 188,921 orders for £313,125 in 1839 to 1,552,845 for £3,127,508 in 1841.

There was clearly a buoyant demand for the service, particularly for small sums: 39.6 per cent of the orders issued in the quarter ending 5 January 1844 were for sums of £1 and less, and 62.9 per cent for sums of £2 and less. There were, however, grave doubts whether the administration of the Money Order Office could withstand the pressure of increased demand. By 1847 the accountant of the Bank of England was concerned 'that the whole system of accounts in the Money Order department is so bad as to require a radical change', and he expressed grave reservations about the management of the department. 'The money order office', he remarked, 'is a great banking establishment yet in its infancy. Modes of giving returns accurately are not ascertained, and cheques [sic] which older offices have for years been obliged to adopt, are either not known or not considered necessary.' Rowland Hill saw the money order system as yet another example of the failure to impose tight control on expenditure, for he found 'that the Money Order Office barely defrays its expenses, and shews, what is still more extraordinary and alarming, that of late years every increase of business has been accompanied by a more than proportionate increase of expense'. In his view, 'the Money Order department should not only maintain itself, but supply its quota of that revenue which the Post Office, as a whole, is expected to yield'. Money orders, on the contrary, made a loss of £10,600 in 1847 and £5,745 in 1848.[6] But Hill's plans to convert the money order system into a profitable venture ran into opposition. His critics in the Department felt that the security offered by stringent controls was more important than the economies which might follow from simpler accounting procedures. Neither did his proposal to increase the maximum value of money orders appeal to the Treasury. The expense of a money order was estimated in 1856 to be 3⅛d so that orders for sums up to £2 made a loss, and Hill accordingly wished to develop the profitable traffic in larger sums. The Treasury, however, felt that this would change the character of the business from the remittance of 'small amounts as a convenience to the public' and create competition with 'an open branch of the trade'.[7]

The proposal was finally accepted in 1860 when the Treasury was convinced that bankers in fact did not enter the business of transmitting sums below £10, so that there would be no encroachment on the private sector. The Treasury at the same time laid down a number of principles which it felt should guide the Post Office in running the money order business. The service should be encouraged in view of 'the moral advantages resulting from facilitating remittances of this description especially among the humbler classes', but the Department should not seek profit 'by entering into competition with Bankers or other private traders'. The Treasury also insisted that 'the money order system ought to be clearly self-supporting, so that one class of the community may not be taxed for a convenience to others'. This was to raise a crucial issue: should each branch of the service be self-supporting, as Hill and the Treasury insisted, or should cross-subsidy between profitable and unprofitable sectors be allowed? The spokesman for cross-subsidy was Frank Scudamore. In his view, the Post Office was not solely a commercial organisation; he stressed the welfare implications of remitting small sums and rejected the rigid insistence of the Hills that each class of business should break even. In 1860, he did dissuade the Treasury from increasing the commission on small money orders, but the retirement of Rowland Hill in 1864 gave him the opportunity to pursue his approach with greater vigour. Although the cost of issuing and paying a money order was estimated in 1866 to be $3\frac{1}{7}d$ and money orders below £2 therefore incurred a loss, the commission on small sums was actually reduced in 1871. Scudamore denied that profitability was the prime consideration. Money orders were designed to provide the poor with means of transmitting small sums and if they could not afford the service, profit should be sacrificed in order to bring it within their reach. Cross-subsidies were, he argued, the basis upon which the Post Office operated. In the mail service, letters to Ireland made a loss while letters in London made a profit, and in the same way large profitable money orders paid for the small. 'Such is and has been Post Office practice', argued Scudamore, 'and it is my belief that there is no man of business great or small in the United Kingdom who does not make his account to lose on some part or parts of his business provided he can see his way to making it pay as a whole.' This approach was anathema to Frederic Hill. It was not enough for money orders *as a whole* to break even, he argued, for each category should make a profit. Any other approach was, he felt, 'an infraction of that important rule . . . that every part of the business of the Post Office shall be self-supporting and shall moreover produce a fair share towards the aggregate profit which the Department is expected to yield'. Scudamore and Hill had already disagreed in the 1860s over the correct terms of the payment of shipping companies, and Hill's rigid insistence upon a strict interpretation of self-supporting finance was rejected both on this issue and in 1871. Scudamore was in the ascendant.[8]

The extension in the maximum value of money orders produced disappointing results, for the proportion of orders above £2 actually fell from 37 per cent in 1844 to 29.6 per cent in 1869/70. The reduction in the commission on small money orders pushed the service back into deficit by 1876, and this deterioration in the financial position strengthened the hand of Frederic Hill who urged that steps should be taken 'to secure a reasonable profit, or the business should be abandoned'.

George Chetwynd, the Receiver and Accountant General, took a more positive approach by suggesting that a cheaper and simpler means of transmitting small sums might be found which would produce a profit. In 1874 he proposed a system of postal notes or orders which could be cashed by the bearer on sight, so removing the need for complicated accounting procedures and letters of advice. Chetwynd expected that the new system would attract 2¼ million money orders and would yield a profit of £10,000 at a tariff of ½ d for a postal order of 2s 6d rising to 2d for an order of £1. This was not the first time that such a proposal had been made, but in the past it had been rejected 'on the ground of its impracticability and the facility which it would afford to dishonest persons to commit forgery'. The collapse of the profitability of the money order system changed the priority, and Chetwynd's role was to give a workable administrative structure to schemes which had been suggested since 1840. Frederic Hill was anxious to ensure that the new service was self-supporting and urged that the minimum rate should be one penny. 'To adopt a lower minimum would be', he argued, 'to revert to the vicious principle . . . of attempting to make one class of remitters of money orders pay for another class, instead of each class paying wholly and only for itself; that is to say, each class paying such a commission as shall defray the cost to the Department of their orders and, in addition, yield a moderate profit, an object which could not be obtained by a half-penny commission.' This was the basis on which postal orders were submitted to the Treasury in 1874.

The Treasury was, however, not prepared to sponsor the necessary legislation and merely instructed the Post Office to cut costs in order to produce a profit. This, it was generally agreed at St Martin's le Grand, was no solution to the major problem of the low rates of commission on small orders. The Post Office, argued Blackwood, the Financial Secretary, 'is not justified in carrying on the business at a loss, or on a system inevitably tending to a loss, nor is it right to charge one portion of the community (that sending large amounts through the post) with the loss sustained by the performance of services for another portion of the community (that sending the lower amounts) at a cheaper rate than that which they actually cost'. He did not, however, go so far as Hill, for he felt that to push this principle to its conclusion would subvert the entire basis of the Post Office. Blackwood did not insist that each transaction should be self-supporting, but only that money orders as a whole should be financially solvent. The minimum commission, it was suggested, should be raised to twopence, which was still below an economic rate but which would allow the service as a whole to break even. Postal orders might then be introduced as a cheap alternative. The scheme was submitted to the Treasury in 1876 which still found it 'difficult to understand why regulations which are cumbrous and costly should be insisted upon in the Money Order which can be safely dispensed with in the Postal Note'. In order to answer this question, a committee representing the Bank of England, Paymaster General, Post Office and the City was appointed in 1876.

The Committee recommended that a simpler and cheaper form of remittance of small sums should be introduced, at a commission of 1d for notes under 10s and 2d for notes between 10s and £1. These notes would, it was hoped, replace the small, unprofitable money orders, on which the commission should be increased. The Committee argued that since a profit was earned on the carriage of letters where the Post Office had a monopoly, 'it would therefore be unreasonable to suppose that for the money order service, which it is optional with the public to use, and which is largely used, it is to derive no profit whatever. There are other modes of making remittances . . . it seems only right, therefore, that the public should pay a remunerative charge for the accommodation of which they voluntarily avail themselves.' The new money order scale was implemented in 1878, and was expected to convert a loss of £10,000 into a profit of £35,000. The introduction of postal orders was to prove more troublesome, for the Bill failed in 1877 as a result of fears that the government would be able to create small notes without the safeguards of the Bank Charter Act. The reduction in the registration fee from 4d to 2d in 1877 in any case provided a cheap alternative means for the remittance of small sums, and enthusiasm waned in the Post Office for the introduction of postal orders. In the end it was the Postmaster General who insisted. 'The question I have to ask myself,' commented Lord John Manners, 'is should I have proposed to raise the commission on the lower money orders had I not also intended and announced my intention of granting as an equivalent the 1d postal note? I must answer the question in the negative, and I consequently hold myself bound to proceed with the scheme.' The Bill was passed in 1880, and postal orders were introduced in 1881.[9]

The increase in the money order commission and the introduction of postal orders did result in a fall in the number of money orders and an increase in their average value. Nevertheless, a considerable number of small money orders continued to be sent at a loss. In 1892/3, 57.3 per cent of money orders were for sums of less than £2, and the overall profit of the service was slight. This suggested to the Post Office that the commission on small orders should be increased to threepence in order to encourage a transfer to the profitable postal order service. The Treasury initially argued for a flat-rate charge of fourpence on the grounds that costs were the same regardless of value, but in 1897 it admitted that small money orders were used by people without bank

89

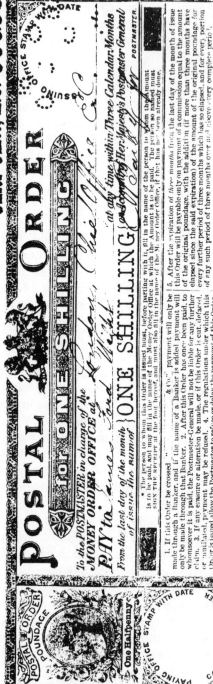

The first postal order was issued in 1881.

90

accounts who needed security, and accepted that the charge should not be increased. Instead, the commission on large orders was substantially reduced which would produce an estimated net revenue of only £565 on the service as a whole. Considerations of profit had been largely rejected in favour of cross-subsidies.[10]

It was generally assumed before the First World War that postal orders were profitable, and little attention was paid to the financial performance of this service. But after the First World War, with the increase in wage rates, the finances of the remittance services were precarious, with a loss of £50,000 on inland money orders and £134,000 on postal orders. Rates were increased in 1920 and 1921, but the remittance service continued to make a loss until the reduction in wages as a result of a fall in the cost of living bonus produced a profit in the late 1920s. By 1930–1, postal orders returned a profit of £270,300 and inland money orders a loss of £7,960. Money orders for small amounts continued to make a loss, while all postal orders above 2s 6d made a profit. The result was that the remittance services as a whole were profitable, and in 1935 the surplus was £529,370.[11]

The scale of the remittance services provided by the Post Office was impressive. Why had the Post Office become such a significant financial intermediary? Commercial banks in the nineteenth century provided services to a restricted clientèle and a large proportion of the economically active population lacked the means of financial intermediation to cater for their needs. Craftsmen and small shopkeepers wishing to transmit funds for a reasonable fee had no obvious institution to which they could turn; and the difficulties of itinerant working men who wished to send money to their families provided a recurrent theme in the literature of social reform. A local agent for financial intermediation simply might not exist, but even where a service was available it was usually not offered to customers outside the high-income segment of the market. The result was that the vast majority of households and small businesses in the early nineteenth century relied upon the transmission of money in coin or bank notes through the post. As the demand for financial intermediation of small sums increased in the course of industrialisation, the Post Office was in a stronger position than a private entrepreneur to supply the service. The Department, with its existing network of offices, could offer a much wider regional coverage than any private business and could attract business by a low cost policy, for it could condone operating losses without the danger of bankruptcy which faced a private business. Above all, the money and postal order service was a natural development from the mail service: money orders had their origins in the problems of security in transmitting money through the post and postal orders were a response to the financial weakness of the money order business. The remittance business therefore emerged from the internal logic of the operations of the Post Office and provided a service with which it was very difficult for private enterprise to compete.[12]

3.2 REMITTANCE SERVICES OF THE POST OFFICE, 1839–1913/14

| | Inland Money Orders Issued in the United Kingdom | | |
	Amount (£)	Number	Mean (£)
1839	313,125	188,921	1.7
1841	3,127,508	1,552,845	2.0
1850	8,494,499	4,439,713	1.9
1860	13,858,404	7,229,146	1.9
1870	19,993,987	na	na
1880–1	24,228,763	16,329,476	1.5
1890–1	23,897,767	8,864,483	2.7
1900–1	34,454,859	11,375,518	3.0
1910–11	41,951,000	10,626,000	3.9
1913–14	47,353,000	11,372,000	4.2

| | Postal orders issued in the United Kingdom | | |
	Amount (£)	Number	Mean (£)
1882–3	3,451,284	7,980,328	0.4
1890–1	19,178,367	48,841,765	0.4
1900–1	30,106,000	85,741,000	0.4
1910–11	50,225,000	132,262,000	0.4
1913–14	57,206,000	159,242,000	0.4

Source: *Annual Reports of the Postmaster General on the Post Office.*

The Post Office Savings Bank

'In every new disciple of the Savings Bank', remarked S. W. Nicoll in 1818, 'I see at least two apostates from the Poor Rate.' He looked forward to the day when 'the inherent and progressive principle of the Savings Bank will have not only stopped the progress but will have entirely routed the influence of its antagonist, the Parish Rate. Next to the road to the Church, I would teach the young the road to the Savings Bank.' But many respectable working men preferred to join a friendly society as an alternative protection against the poor law. These were agencies of thrift emerging from within the working class and establishing a sense of mutuality and co-operation in the pursuit of security, unlike savings banks which were directed by the middle class and assisted by the State. Members of the working class who established organisations which apparently accepted a middle-class ethic of respectability and self-help in fact interpreted these values in a different way. Independence did not mean individualism but freedom from out-side control, a sense of democratic self-government, and collective identity. Friendly societies such as the Manchester Unity of Oddfellows or the Ancient Order of Foresters are examples of this working-class ethic of self-help. Savings banks, in contrast, were run by middle-class trustees *for* the working class, without participation by the investors. The ethic of thrift, respectability and independence might appear to be the same, but the implications were very different, for the savings banks were paternalistic rather than democratic, without a sense of collective identity and purpose. Thomas Attwood did perhaps exaggerate, but he had a point when he denounced the savings banks as 'a sort of screw in the hands of the Government to fix down the working class to its system'.

The Savings Bank Act of 1817 established two general principles: the management of the banks was to be undertaken by local trustees on a voluntary basis; and all funds were to be handed to the State for investment by the National Debt Commissioners which would pay interest to the banks at £4 11s 3d per cent per annum. The system was, therefore, a combination of private philanthropy and state assistance, but by mid-century co-operation had given way to disagreement over three issues. The first was the rate of interest paid to the trustees. Although this had been reduced to £3 16s 0½d per cent in 1828 and £3 5s per cent in 1844, the National Debt Commissioners were still obliged to pay more than they could themselves obtain from investment of savings bank funds in government securities. The Chancellor of the Exchequer therefore aimed to reduce the rate of interest paid to the trustees who were, of course, eager to maintain their favourable position. The second disagreement followed from this conflict over interest rates, for the trustees could argue that the real problem was not the excessive rate of interest paid to them, but that the Chancellor managed the funds of the savings banks for his own ends rather than to secure the best return. The trustees accordingly complained of their lack of control over their funds, while the government for its part felt that the operation of the banks should be supervised by paid officials and inspectors to ensure efficient administration. This assault upon the autonomy of the trustee savings banks formed a third area of dissension. These points were fought in Pariament in the 1850s with the result that deadlock ensued, and the introduction of the Post Office Savings Bank owed its origins to the desire of the Chancellor of the Exchequer, W. E. Gladstone, to break the impasse. 'If the Trustee Savings Banks were determined to oppose him,' H. O. Horne has commented, 'why should he not use the machinery of the Post Office to run a state savings bank which would encourage thrift in places where no savings facilities yet existed, bring more money to the Exchequer and, incidentally, either kill or reinvigorate by competition the old savings banks which had proved such a thorn in the flesh of a succession of Chancellors of the Exchequer?' The political tensions between the Chancellor and the savings banks resulted in the establishment of a State-operated system in place of the existing strained alliance with middle-class philanthropy.[13]

The idea of a state savings bank had been suggested on a number of occasions, including Jeremy Bentham's 'Frugality Banks', but the scheme which came to attention at the critical moment was proposed by C. W. Sikes of the Huddersfield Banking Company. His initial ambition had been to reform the trustee savings banks, whose coverage and hours of operation he felt to be inadequate. He had proposed that Mechanics' Institutes should act as 'feeders' to the nearest savings bank, and he aimed to make the system financially secure by reducing the interest rate on accounts above £100 and creating a central guarantee fund. These early ideas were developed further in 1859. He did not intend that the State should itself become a banker, but only that post offices might remit sums of one pound and over to a chief savings bank in London by means of money orders; the depositors in return would receive 'interest notes' giving the right to be paid interest at 2½ per cent a year.[14] Sikes's plan was drawn to the attention of Rowland Hill in 1859 by Edward Baines, one of the Members of Parliament for Leeds, who felt that 'it is certain that Savings Banks are much less useful than they might be, owing to the short hours they are open, and the distance which many have to travel in order to reach them. If the Post Office could be made available in aid of Savings Banks, it would be an immense advantage, by facilitating the practice of saving among the humbler classes.' Hill agreed that the scheme was practicable, and discussions started both within the Department and with the National Debt Commssion on the assumption that the Post Office should merely *transmit* the money and receive a commission for the use of money orders. The existing facilities of the Post Office would be used according to established principles without an extension into a new area of operation. The central savings bank, it was intended, would be a separate institution unconnected with the Department. The scheme had originated from outside the Post Office, and in its original form had minimal implications for the Department: it merely offered a new customer for the existing means of remittances by money order. But a divergence soon arose within the Post Office between two different conceptions of the role of the Department, which formed part of the wider disagreement between the Hill family and the new generation of officials led by John Tilley and Frank Ives Scudamore.

The tension between self-supporting finance and cross-subsidy emerged here, as so often in the 1860s. Should the money orders issued for savings bank purposes pay the full rate, or should they have preferential treatment? Frederic Hill insisted that 'the great principle of Post Office management is simplicity and uniformity', and he maintained that a lower rate for one class of customer would 'be a great departure from the principle which requires that every part of the Post Office business should yield a share of the surplus revenue required by the State'. Scudamore and Tilley were less concerned that each part of the Post Office should contribute to the surplus, and this conflict over price determination merged with a disagreement over the proper boundary between private and public enterprise. Frederic Hill wished to charge full economic rates so that there would not be any encroachment either on the business of commercial bankers in transmitting money, or on the operations of the existing savings banks. He was alarmed at the prospect of the State taking business from the independent trustee savings banks and throwing a new burden on the Post Office, for 'a duty quite subordinate to the great work of the Post Office – the conveyance of letters – might in many places become the chief occupation of the postmaster to the obstruction of his other duties and render necessary perhaps a larger office and a greater staff of clerks'. Hill had a minimalist view of public enterprise, and suggested regulations which would check the use of the proposed service. The interest rate of 2½ per cent was already lower than the rate paid by many trustee savings banks, and imposition of the full money order commission on any deposit would impose a further severe burden. He also proposed that only multiples of one pound could be transmitted.

Scudamore, by contrast, had an active interventionist approach, eagerly seizing all opportunities to increase the public sector. He explained his philosophy in 1860 when urging the introduction of higher value money orders: 'those parts of the business of the Post Office which are open to public competition are, in my opinion, the very parts which are least liable to sound objection; since the very possibility of such a competition makes it essential that the Post Office should perform those portions of its duty economically and well and to the general satisfaction of the public, otherwise it would soon cease to retain them.' Men such as Scudamore were coming to dominate at St Martin's le Grand in the 1860s, and amongst their number was George Chetwynd, book-keeper of the Money Order Office.

In November 1860, Chetwynd suggested some major modifications to Sikes's plan. The issue of money orders and 'interest notes' was, in his view, unnecessary. A depositer might hand a sum of money to the postmaster who would make an entry in a bank book retained by the investor; instead of purchasing a money order, deposits could be trans-

Charles W. Sikes

ferred to London with cash balances from the money order business; and the depositor could withdraw money by sending a form to the central savings bank which would issue a warrant payable when the bank book was presented at a post office. The change in procedure would allow the deposit of small sums other than multiples of one pound, and the business would be profitable if the Post Office charged one penny per transaction. The proposal was supported and extended by Scudamore. In Chetwynd's scheme, the Post Office was still a 'feeder' to a separate central savings bank. Scudamore felt that this would create the 'expense and inconvenience of a divided authority' and he argued that the whole business should be entrusted to the Post Office which had 'acquired an experience and practical aptitude for the business' through running the money order service. Scudamore grasped the opportunity of expansion into a new area, even at the expense of existing institutions. The cautious, minimalist approach of the Hills was rejected for a policy of expansion of the public sector which culminated in Scudamore's management of the nationalisation of the telegraphs.

Scudamore's view was to prevail, for Gladstone's intention was precisely to weaken the trustee savings banks which resisted reform and imposed a drain on the Exchequer. The establishment of the Post Office Savings Bank also coincided with Rowland Hill's last crisis as Secretary of the Post Office. He complained in May 1861 that 'the Postmaster General has again interfered with my Department. I had placed, or rather left, the management of the new Post Office Savings Banks with Frederic; but the Postmaster General, without consulting me, and against the protest of FH, has transferred the management to Tilley . . . and has himself issued instructions to Scudamore and Chetwynd to prepare plans, etc.' Frederic had attempted to contain Scudamore's enthusiasm by limiting implementation of the plan to three counties where few trustee savings banks existed, and urging that it should earn the 'ordinary rate of profit, which in the case of money orders is about one quarter of the money received as commission and in that of letters about one-third of the postage'. The Hills viewed the Post Office Savings Bank as a distraction from the proper functions of the Post Office and a threat to strict financial standards, but their philosophy was in retreat in the 1860s as economic reform was replaced as the guiding principle of the Department.[15]

Gladstone introduced the Post Office Savings Bank Bill into the Commons in 1861, and the Bank started operations by September 1861, paying interest of 2½ per cent, and accepting deposits up to £30 a year with a maximum of £150 in any account. Deposits were to be transmitted to the National Debt Commission for investment in government securities; unlike the trustee savings bank which received a guaranteed

SEASONABLE ADVICE—"PUT BY FOR A FROSTY DAY."

Mr Punch appears as W.E. Gladstone, Chancellor of the Exchequer at the time of the
introduction of the Post Office Savings Bank. The cartoon clearly indicates the intended
role of the Bank in reforming the working class

interest on its funds from the Commissioners, the Post Office Savings
Bank was to receive the actual interest earned. The proponents of the
trustee savings banks attempted to draw Gladstone on the question of
whether the Post Office Savings Bank was to supplement or to replace
the existing system, but he was careful to avoid a clear statement of
intent. Attention should, he suggested, at first concentrate on areas
neglected by the trustee savings banks, but 'if the old suffered from the
competition of the new, it could only be because the new were better,
and, if so, they ought to have the preference'. The representatives of the
trustee savings banks were in a difficult position for, much as they
might oppose intervention in their affairs, they could hardly deny the
right of the government to supply a service which was agreed to be
socially desirable. Lord Monteagle warned the House of Lords of the
likely outcome. 'He could not see without regret and alarm', he remarked, 'what seemed to him *meant* to produce a breaking up of the

existing Savings Banks and the substitution of the action of a salaried Government Department for what he might call a great public charity, directed by benevolent persons acting gratuituously in their own neighbourhood.'[16] Monteagle had a clear perception of the aim of some officials within the Post Office, and the early years of the Post Office Savings Bank seemed to confirm his fears. The number of trustee savings banks fell from a peak of 645 in 1861, and the Post Office Savings Bank increased from 178,495 accounts at the end of 1862 to overtake the trustee savings banks in 1872. The average account in the trustee savings banks was considerably larger and it was not until 1888 that total deposits in the Post Office Savings Bank exceeded the deposits in the trustee savings banks. Although it seemed in the 1860s that the trustee savings banks would ultimately disappear, by the end of the century it was clear that the result had been the removal of the smaller, less secure, trustee savings banks and the attraction of a new class of small investors to the Post Office system. Public enterprise did not sweep everything before it, and problems were indeed to arise.[17]

3.3 TRUSTEE AND POST OFFICE SAVINGS BANKS, 1861–1939

		Trustee Savings Banks			Post Office Savings Banks		
	Number	Accounts (m)	Deposits (£m)	Mean a/c (£)	Open a/c (m)	Deposits (£m)	Mean a/c (£)
1861	645	1.6	41.7	25.9	—	—	—
1868	513	1.4	37.2	27.1	1.0	11.7	12.1
1872	483	1.4	40.3	28.2	1.4	19.3	13.4
1888	382	1.6	51.5	32.6	4.2	58.6	13.9
1900	230	1.6	57.4	35.3	8.4	135.5	16.1
1913	202	1.9	71.3	37.3	9.2	187.2	20.4
1919	163	2.2	112.2	50.5	12.8	266.3	20.8
1929	113	2.5	162.5	65.2	9.8	285.0	29.0
1939	99	2.5	292.6	117.5	11.6	551.4	47.5

Source: Horne, *Savings Banks*, app. II and III.

The Post Office Savings Bank was an immediate financial success. Scudamore had assumed that there would be 1.75 transactions per account per annum at a cost of 7*d* each, but in 1872 there were in fact 2.55 transactions per account at a cost of 5.1*d*. The surplus of £301,070 in 1872 was an effective answer to Frederic Hill's scepticism, and the issue facing the Department was how to dispose of this sum. One possibility was to raise the interest rate paid to depositors, which was below the maximum of £3 0*s* 10*d* per cent offered by the trustee banks. However, Scudamore felt that the Post Office Savings Bank did not need to compete in the rate offered to depositors, for it had a clear superiority in 'absolute security and unbounded facilities for deposit and withdrawal'. His preference was to raise the limit on deposits to £100 in the first year and £50 in subsequent years, up to a maximum of £300. Chetwynd wished to go even further and remove the time limit on deposits, a suggestion which raised a major issue concerning the proper role of the Post Office Savings Bank. In 1861, Scudamore had been willing to expand the Post Office's sphere of influence at the expense of the trustee savings banks, but raising the upper limit on deposits threatened to encroach upon another interest group, the commercial banks. '[T]hough they did not oppose the original establishment of the Post Office Savings Banks which only proposed to deal with the small savings of the working classes,' remarked the bankers of Leeds, 'it is a very different matter when government proposes to extend that principle in such a way as to attract the middle classes from whose ranks deposi-tors of sums from £100 to £300 are mainly composed, and who are quite able to judge for themselves as to what they will do with their savings or surplus money left with country bankers while awaiting an investment.' The objection to trespassing on the territory of the commercial banks was not so much ideological as pragmatic. There would certainly be 'warm opposition from the banking interest' which would be difficult to overcome in Parliament, but Scudamore was even more troubled by the implications for the Post Office Savings Bank itself. The removal of the time limit might create 'Drawing accounts' used by tradesmen in place of current accounts with country bankers. The result would be a 'great and costly change in the business', for the quieter the accounts the cheaper they would be to manage. The expansion of *deposit* accounts at the expense of the trustee savings banks was welcomed but *drawing* accounts would generate opposition and erode profit. The trustee savings banks imposed a drain on the State and it was hoped to replace them with the profitable and secure Post Office system, but there was a self-denying ordinance against current or 'drawing' accounts. The policy to be pursued by the Post Office Savings Bank was clearly stated by Scudamore: 'as a rule people who accumulate slowly, withdraw slowly, and our object, of course, is to encourage accumulations and discourage withdrawals'. The maximum deposit was only raised in 1893, and the time limit was retained.

Scudamore's policy was the 'gradual extinction' of the trustee savings banks over a period of twelve to fifteen years. This time scale would, he argued, allow the Post Office Savings Bank to build up reserves to write off the deficit on the funds of the trustee banks. The National Debt Commissioners had received less from its investment of the fund than it was obliged to pay to the trustee banks, and this shortfall was met from the capital of the Savings Bank Fund. Scudamore feared that the Post

Office would need to cover the deficit when the trustee banks were taken over. Instead of a sudden demise of the trustee banks, he therefore recommended that 'the gradual and quite natural transfer' of business should be encouraged by 'increasing the facilities and the advantages of the Post Office Banks and thereby slightly accelerating that painless extinction of the old banks'. By the mid-1870s it was clear that the policy was not succeeding. The rate of closure of trustee savings banks had fallen from ninety-four in the five years to 1866, to thirty-one in the five years to 1876, and 'at the present rate of closing', calculated Lewin Hill, 'it would take about 74 years to close them all and thus put an end completely to the loss upon their business'. Deposits in the trustee banks had started to recover, largely as the result of the larger banks exploiting a loop-hole in the Savings Banks Act of 1863. The trustees were required to invest with the National Debt Commission, but they were also permitted to receive money from depositors which was not to be paid to the Commissioners. This power was used in the early 1870s to start 'investment departments' which placed funds in local authority bonds and other securities which were not available to the National Debt Commissioners. Large trustee savings banks in manufacturing towns were able to expand, so that in Bradford the balance due to depositors in the 'ordinary department' was £88,736 and in the 'investment department' £428,068. The result was viewed with alarm, for the business of the Post Office Savings Bank was checked, the investment departments were not regulated, and the solvency of the trustee banks was in doubt.

The Controller of the Post Office Savings Bank in 1878 felt that the time had come for drastic action in place of gradual absorption. He rejected the renewed suggestion that interest rates should be raised, and proposed instead that an Act should be passed closing all trustee savings banks so that the entire business would be 'under complete and efficient control in the Post Office Savings Bank'. Although the Treasury rejected this 'heroic remedy', it was agreed that the pace of absorption should be accelerated. The Post Office fed the Chancellor with information against the trustee savings banks, taking care that the Department 'should not appear as the accuser of the old Savings Banks'. The finances of the trustee savings banks were indeed reformed in the late 1870s. In 1877 it was ruled that any future deficiency of interest should be voted by Parliament rather than paid from the capital of the Savings Bank Fund; half of any surplus should be paid into the Exchequer and half into the fund to provide against depreciation. The fund was thus safeguarded against any further loss, and in 1880 an annuity was created to make good the past deficit. Both the interest paid by the Commission to the trustees and the maximum rate the trustees could allow to depositors were reduced, and by 1888 the trustee savings banks could pay depositors no more than the Post Office. The trustee savings banks were, as a result, less competitive and their finances were placed on a sounder footing. Ironically, it was at this point that the finances of the Post Office Savings Bank came under severe pressure.[18]

3.4 FINANCIAL PERFORMANCE OF THE POST OFFICE SAVINGS BANK, 1876–1912 (IN POUNDS STERLING)

	Interest received from National Debt Commission	Interest paid to depositors	Difference of interest	Expenses of management	Profit or loss
1876	908,441	619,331	289,110	125,912	163,198
1886	1,530,673	1,169,590	361,083	290,555	70,528
1896	2,884,110	2,460,645	423,465	429,627	−6,162
1900	3,644,019	3,145,978	498,041	487,025	11,016
1904	3,921,216	3,495,633	425,583	537,673	−112,090
1906	4,146,784	3,667,729	479,055	598,925	−119,870
1912	4,991,497	4,259,082	732,415	649,207	83,208

Source: *Annual Reports of the Postmaster General.*

The profit of the Post Office Savings Bank fell from 1876 and a deficit appeared in 1896. This was not the result of increased administrative overheads, for the cost per transaction fell from 6.9d in 1876 to 6d in 1896 and 4.5d in 1913. It was rather the result of a fall in the yield of the government securities which were held by the Post Office Savings Bank Fund, from 3.4 per cent in 1877 to 2.9 per cent in 1892 and 2.8 per cent in 1901. The Act of 1861 had provided for the payment to the Post Office Savings Bank of the entire interest on the funds invested by the National Debt Commissioners, and this produced a surplus of £0.9m by 1875 after the claims of depositors had been met. However, the Savings Bank Act of 1877 required that in future 95 per cent of any surplus should be paid to the Exchequer, and it was claimed in 1893 that this had deprived the Post Office Savings Bank of £1.5m, which would have earned a further £0.5m in interest. When the earnings on the Savings Bank money invested by the National Debt Commissioners fell and a deficit appeared, the Bank did not have a reserve upon which to draw. The pressure on the finances of the Bank was intensified because money was attracted by the payment of 2½ per cent interest which in the 1890s became highly competitive, and the net inflow of funds rose from £2.5m in 1892 to £7.7m in 1896. When interest rates in general recovered and the return on deposits in the Bank became less attractive, the net inflow of funds fell to £2.3m in 1900 and became a net outflow of £1.3m in 1904. The Controller of the Bank felt that he lacked effective power over the business. The interest paid to depositors was fixed, he was denied access to any surplus earned on the funds of the Bank, and he had no say in their investment by the National Debt Commissioners. 'An arrangement under which the Department primarily responsible is without any knowledge or authority in respect to the employment of its own funds seems hardly calculated to produce the best possible results.'

There were a number of possible responses to the slide of the Post Office Savings Bank into deficit. One was to vary the interest paid to depositors according to the earnings of the Post Office Savings Bank Fund, but this was thought to be politically unpopular and the 2½ per cent rate survived. Another was to widen the range of investments to include loans to local authorities. However, the Select Committee on Savings Bank Funds advised against this course of action, for the purchase of new securities would have only a marginal impact on the total portfolio and might even be counter-productive by giving them a quasi-governmental guarantee which would increase their price and reduce the yield. The Select Committee in any case argued that any increased income resulting from a change in investment policy 'would properly belong to the taxpayers, and not to those who had deposited their money with them'. This left a third possibility: 'to apply any Savings Bank profits to Savings Bank purposes. . . . The taxpayers', argued the Secretary, 'have no business to make either a profit or a loss out of the bank; and a Reserve Fund would give us something to "come and go" upon.' A surplus reappeared in 1911 after a period of deficit which had been covered by annual votes of Parliament. The Post Office claimed the whole of this surplus to strengthen the Savings Bank Fund, but the Treasury would only surrender half. Indeed, in 1925 the Exchequer's share of the surplus was raised to 80 per cent and in 1934 to 95 per cent. Depositors in the Bank had a certain return of 2½ per cent and the security of the State and beyond that had no concern, so it was argued, with the earnings on the Savings Bank Fund. The scope of the Post Office Savings Bank was severely limited: the task of the Controller was to ensure that an efficient administrative system existed to transfer funds to the National Debt Commission and to credit interest to accounts. It did not, like many of its European counterparts, develop into a giro system but remained strictly an instrument for thrift.[19]

Thrift might have very different meanings to middle-class reformers and members of the working class. Middle-class commentators saw thrift as the acquisition of liquid assets in a savings bank, but to the working class it was more likely to mean the purchase of insurance against unemployment, sickness, or death from a trade union, friendly

103

THE NEW STAMP DUTY.

MR. FAWCETT. "NOW, THEN, ALL OF YOU, 'IN FOR A PENNY IN FOR A POUND.'"

"Mr. FAWCETT's scheme brings saving within everybody's reach."—*Times*.

In 1880 Fawcett attempted to take the Post Office Savings Bank further down the social scale and to children, by introducing a system of affixing postage stamps to cards which could be credited to a savings account.

household could lay aside enough money to provide savings to compensate for loss of income, but the regular payment of small sums to the Oddfellows or Prudential effectively supplied 'a large stock of savings at, and only at, the time when it was especially needed', during sickness or to pay for a funeral. Savings banks were more likely to attract members of the lower middle class who were averse to the mutuality of friendly societies and trade unions, and the most well and regularly paid members of the working class. The impression which emerges from two surveys of depositors in 1879 and 1896 is that women and children dominated the occupational distribution; in 1896 it was calculated that women and children recorded under other headings would bring their share to 60.6 per cent. The deposit of small amounts by children was

3.5 DEPOSITORS IN EIGHTEEN POST OFFICES IN 1879

	per cent	average deposit (£)
Female servants	14.8	14
No occupation	11.4	13
Artisans	11.0	15
Minors over 7	10.5	7
Married women	10.1	21
Tradesmen	7.6	16
Clerks	6.0	11
Labourers	5.1	21
Unmarried women	3.6	16
Minors under 7	3.5	5
Male servants	2.6	22
Public officials	2.0	40
Soldiers and sailors	2.0	18
Professional men	2.0	20
Milliners	1.7	11
Others	6.1	—

Source: Post 75/3, *Annual Reports of Post Office Savings Bank, 1871–94.*

3.6 NEW ACCOUNTS FOR A THREE-MONTH PERIOD IN 1896

		per cent
Professional	1.6	
Official	2.8	9.3
Educational	1.0	
Commercial	3.9	
Agriculture and fishing		1.8
Industrial		18.4
Railway, shipping, transport		3.0
Tradesmen and their assistants		8.1
Domestic service		8.6
Miscellaneous		0.4
Married women, spinsters, widows, children		50.4
		100.0

Source: PP 1897 XXIV, *43rd Annual Report of Postmaster General, 1896–7,* p. 674.

encouraged by the scheme of 1880 by which penny stamps were affixed to cards which could then be credited to an account. Teachers were brought into the system and School Savings Banks were established, which covered 35 per cent of elementary schools in 1902/3. Working men did not dominate the clientèle, and Dr Paul Johnson has concluded that there were 'considerably fewer' members of trustee and Post Office savings banks than belonged to friendly societies. Indeed, 'only those working-class families with an income more than sufficient to buy contingency insurance are likely to direct their surplus funds to the savings banks'. The Post Office was indeed to enter the market in 'contingency insurance' against death and old age, but with a notable lack of success.[20]

The Post Office and provision for old age

The remittance services and the Post Office Savings Bank provided facilities which were popular, in areas of the market not filled by private enterprise. By contrast, the attempt by the Post Office to sell life insurance and annuities proved to be a failure, and the Department was unable to compete either with the aggressive marketing of the commercial companies, or the sociability of the friendly societies. Before the Post Office became involved, the State had undertaken the sale of life insurances up to £100 through the National Debt Commission, with the requirement that an annuity should also be purchased in order to provide 'old age pay'. The cost had prevented the development of the service, and in 1864 Gladstone's Government Insurances and Annuities Act transferred the business to the Post Office, separating life insurance from annuities. It was in future possible to take out life insurance for a minimum of £20 and a maximum of £100, and to purchase annuities for £4 to £50 a year. Gladstone aimed 'without any interference with private establishments, or any attempt to take their proper business, should do all it could to offer facilities for the increase and extension of frugal habits among the industrious classes'. He argued that 'the wide field of the labouring classes is not occupied by sound institutions – nay, that is not finally occupied even by sound and unsound institutions, such is the enormous breadth of the subject'.[21] His expectations were, however, to be disappointed.

The new departure had to some extent been anticipated within the Post Office, for it had since 1854 used funds obtained from undeliverable mail and void money orders to encourage life insurance amongst its staff. In 1858, Scudamore expressed concern that it was postmasters rather than employees earning low weekly wages who took advantage of the assistance which was offered, largely because laying money aside week by week in order to pay an annual premium required

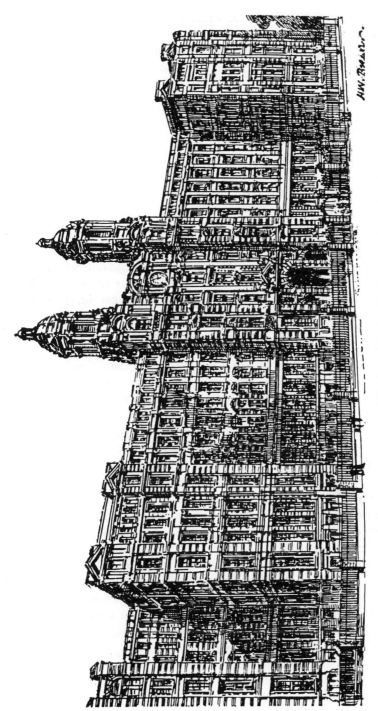

The new headquarters at the Post Office Savings Bank at West Kensington opened in 1903.

'patient, persevering self-denial which very few are likely to display'. Scudamore therefore suggested that the Department should assist by making a deduction from wages each week in order to pay the premium, and the scheme was introduced on a voluntary basis in 1859. This was, argued Scudamore,

> a politic course, because it will gain a stronger hold on their good will, and bind them more firmly to its service – a benevolent course, because it will prevent much misery, and save many helpless and unoffending persons from extreme poverty – and a wise course, because it will create and foster in its officers a habit of prudent and provident economy which they, in turn, will bequeath to their children, a legacy of inestimable value.

Society, in Scudamore's opinion, was dominated by new 'wants and pleasures' which had undermined 'frugality and economy'. Although charity might alleviate distress, it was no cure for the faults which caused hardship and which could only be removed by 'fostering and cherishing a habit of frugality and economy, and I must think that the Government will act wisely if it attempts to promote that habit in this or any other large public department'. Scudamore's vision soon extended from the staff of the Department to the rest of society.[22]

The Post Office had to compete with two existing agencies. The friendly societies were run by their members on a democratic basis of mutual support in order to provide medical assistance, sick pay, and a funeral grant. The payment of sick pay could become a form of disguised old age pension, and Scudamore, in common with many commentators, was concerned that the friendly societies were not financially sound. He accepted the view that the societies should confine themselves to sick pay and that 'some Association of masters or the State should contract to give old age pay and burial money'. This was the context of the Act of 1864 which allowed the State, in the form of the Post Office, to sell annuities providing an income in old age, and to insure lives as a source of money for funerals. Sick pay, argued Scudamore, was the proper responsibility of friendly societies whose members could, more readily than the government, impose a check on malingerers. The Post Office thus saw itself as complementary to the friendly societies, but it was to come into direct competition with a second interest: the commercial or 'industrial' insurance companies such as the Prudential and the Royal Liver which sold life insurance to cover the cost of funerals. Whereas many members of the working class could not afford to join a friendly society, most took out a policy with an industrial insurance company. Indeed, the Act of 1864 had been amended to protect the companies from government competition, by preventing the Post Office from selling life insurances for sums of less than £20. Both the friendly societies and the industrial insurance companies were to prove much more successful than the Post Office in attracting working men in search of such 'contingency insurance'.[23]

3.7 INSURANCE POLICIES ISSUED DURING THE YEAR BY THE POST OFFICE, 1865–1900

	Number	Amount (£)
1865	547	40,649
1870	385	31,254
1875	370	32,022
1880	258	20,378
1885	457	34,768
1890	468	25,466
1895	720	38,358
1900	677	35,511

Source: Post 30/1699–1700, E14099/1909, file III.

3.8 TOTAL NUMBER OF INSURANCE POLICIES IN FORCE ISSUED BY THE POST OFFICE AND COMMERCIAL COMPANIES, 1888 AND 1907

	1888	1907
Commercial: ordinary	905,068	2,397,915
industrial	9,145,844	25,544,045
Post Office	5,859	13,269

Source: Post 30/1699–1700, E14099/1909, file VI.

The friendly societies offered more than the payment of benefits, as was clear in 1865 when Scudamore was negotiating with the railway companies to collect premiums by deductions from their workers' wages. An official of the London and North Western Railway expressed considerable scepticism, for despite the fact that existing friendly societies might be insecure and actuarially weak, there was 'an element of "sociability" in these local clubs which, though not a prudent arrangement, is agreeable to the feelings of a large number of the contributors; and others are gratified by the appointment of their own officers and by a greater or less share in the management and distribution of the funds'. Artisans would not, he accepted, welcome the collection of premiums by their employer, for this would deny their independence and lead to conflict if they assumed that the company was making a profit out of the premiums. This was a more realistic assessment than Scudamore's view of society as essentially conflict-free, with the State as a paternalistic provider of services. Ralph Welby of the Treasury was to remark in 1874

109

that 'Scudamore . . . likes to dry-nurse the British nation, and would like to manage a large Department (with the guarantee of the Consolidated Fund) to feed and manage us all'. Certainly, Scudamore's desire to use the State as a means of inculcating habits of frugality and economy did not take into account the ethic of the 'labour aristocracy'. The friendly societies were exclusively working class both in membership and leadership, and rejected middle-class patronage and State control. The emphasis was upon self-government, independence, respectability and collective self-help rather than individualism or dependence upon the State. Purchase of annuities or insurance from the Post Office simply did not accord with these perceptions.[24]

Neither could the Post Office compete with the commercial companies. This was not the result of unfavourable premiums, which were indeed less in the Post Office for small amounts: it was noted in 1905 that a premium of one penny a week at age 20 gave £8 14s at death in the Prudential and £11 6s 1d in the Post Office. The companies did have the benefit of a higher return on investments, for they were not restricted to parliamentary securities as was the Post Office. However, this was neutralised by their large expenditure on agents and advertising which took nearly half of the contributions.[25] This proved to be a more effective means of attracting custom than low premiums. 'Only a very small number of persons insure with us', remarked the Postmaster General in 1911,

> and the reason is that as a rule the working man will not go to the insurance: he expects it to come to him. It is through a system of active canvassing for new business and through the collection of weekly payments by personal visits that the great business of Industrial Insurance Corporations has been built up. In that field the organisation of the Post Office does not allow us efficiently to compete, and consequently it is for this reason unlikely – unless the whole organisation of the Post Office is altered and we establish a great organisation of canvassers and collectors, that we shall be able to increase to any very large degree the business of industrial assurance which is at present performed by us.[26]

This was precisely what the Post Office could not contemplate.

The attempts to popularise the service fell short of any really effective measures. The minimum sum to be insured was reduced and the maximum raised; premiums might be paid directly from a Savings Bank Account when due or by affixing postage stamps to a book; the staff of the Post Office was offered commissions for attracting business; the premiums were made more attractive. The results were minimal, and it was fully realised that 'success can only be won in one way, and that way

110

is closed'. Expansion, it was generally admitted, required active canvassing but it was as generally accepted it was not possible to contemplate 'an army of Post Office canvassers' with 'ingratiating manners' who would go from house to house seeking custom. 'Such a course would, I fear,' remarked the Secretary, 'be unworthy of the traditions and dignity of the Department.' There was, however, a wider issue at stake than the dignity of the Post Office. Should public enterprise engage in active competition with private companies? The Treasury argued in 1905 that it should not, and suggested that 'where the State engages in business in competition with private enterprise, it should confine itself to making the fact known and should then sit still and wait for people to avail themselves of the facilities offered. I see no sound reason for paying others to induce them to do so.' This was the view taken in 1906 by H. Babington Smith, the Secretary, when he proposed as a general principle that 'it is undesirable for the State to compete with private enterprise in any sphere where a public need is adequately supplied by private enterprise under competitive conditions'. Customers would be better served, and the State was uncompetitive since it was obliged to treat all alike and lacked flexibility, being 'unable to pick and choose and take the remunerative business'. Further, the State paid higher wages than private enterprise and had greater problems in managing its workforce, which provided 'a very strong reason against multiplying to any considerable extent the number of persons in the employment of the State'. The Post Office had entered the insurance business in order to provide security and to fill a gap in the market for small insurances, but these justifications no longer existed in the early twentieth century. Commercial companies had moved into the business and State intervention had developed in a direction unsuspected by Gladstone, with the introduction of old age pensions in 1908 and compulsory national insurance in 1911.[27]

The Post Office was to have a role in the new welfare system as the agent for the payment of pensions and sale of insurance stamps. The postmaster of 1914 was a far cry from his counterpart in 1840, as the post offices in each town and village more and more became the local representative of the State. It was not only that he had a wider range of mail, telegraph and financial services to provide to the public: in 1880 the Post Office had taken over the sale of various licences and fiscal stamps having no relation to postal business. The Post Office did not receive payment for these services, and similarly did not reimburse other departments for work undertaken on its behalf. However, the estimated cost of the various services was included in the accounts after 1897, and in 1922, for example, the agency services supplied by the Post Office were valued at £1.85m, and other departments provided services worth

£1.81m. This was not a significant item in total turnover, but the Post Office had become more than a place to mail a letter: it paid out pensions, issued licences to keep dogs, guns, or male servants, and sold stamps for legal documents.[28]

Giro: the limits of public enterprise

The Post Office had come to provide facilities both for remitting small sums and depositing small savings. A logical progression might suggest a link between the Savings Bank and the means of remitting money in order to provide current accounts and a clearing system on the lines adopted in Austria in 1883, and followed by most continental countries. In the United Kingdom, such a 'giro' service was not provided until 1968, and the failure to develop this service provides some indication of the limit which had been set to public enterprise.

The aim of the Post Office Savings Bank was to encourage deposits and to discourage withdrawals in order to promote thrift: the low level of activity is apparent in 1913 when there was an average of 2.5 deposits and 1.2 withdrawals per account. Money could be deposited by taking the bank book to any post office; withdrawals were more complicated, for a form was sent to London and the warrant which was returned had to be presented to the named post office. The system permitted the deposit and withdrawal of money at offices other than the one at which the account had been opened. These 'cross entries' in 1880 accounted for 24 per cent of deposits and 40 per cent of withdrawals, so that 'the working classes who migrate from town to town in search of work, commercial travellers, travelling actors, singers and showmen, tourists, and generally all who are led by business or pleasure, to move much from place to place in the United Kingdom avail themselves largely of the facilities the Post Office affords them for, as it were, carrying their Bank with them'.[29]

A clerk in the Savings Bank in 1893 suggested that its use as a means of transferring money could be encouraged by introducing 'Savings Bank Postal Orders'. Depositors, it was proposed, would be able to withdraw money from their accounts in the form of postal orders up to a value of £2 which would be payable at sight at any Post Office in favour of the person in whose name it was drawn. This tentative move in the direction of a form of cheque account was firmly opposed by the Secretary as 'altogether contrary to the theory of a *Savings* Bank', and he strongly opposed 'the establishment of a State bank for all the ordinary business of banking'. Neither would he accept a revised proposal that postal orders should be payable only to the depositors and not to a third party. A large inflow of funds in the 1890s and 1900s would threaten the finances of the Post Office Savings Bank, and 'it would be inexpedient, and possibly fatal to the Post Office Savings Bank, if it were to enter into competition with the bona fide Banking Interest'. Above all, it was stressed that the Post Office was responsible for encouraging deposits and not withdrawals. 'The Postmaster General', it was asserted in 1904, 'is not prepared to introduce any such machinery as is suggested for facilitating the withdrawal of deposits from the Post Office Savings Bank. It must be remembered that the Post Office Savings Bank was established to encourage thrift, and the Government has no intention of converting it into a banking institution.' The limits of expansion were clearly drawn, and the Bank was viewed as an agency of social welfare rather than a commercial service. 'It is the object of the Post Office Savings Bank to provide a safe place of deposit with a moderate rate of interest for the savings of the working classes as a provision, not only against old age or death, but also for the other contingencies of life, such as sickness, want of employment, etc.' It followed that the Post Office Savings Bank should not be used either to supply cash on demand or to transfer money. The withdrawal of money by obtaining a warrant from London was considered to be perfectly adequate, 'and seeing that one of the chief objects with which the Post Office Savings Bank was instituted was to provide facilities for *saving* as distinguished from ordinary banking business, it appears both unnecessary and undesirable that any more extended facilities for withdrawals should be afforded than is already furnished'.[30]

The rejection of 'Savings Bank Postal Orders' meant that the continental 'giro' system of cheques and transfers between accounts would not have a favourable reception. Such a development had been rejected on a number of occasions as 'contrary to the spirit of the Savings Bank system', but in 1911 it was seriously considered for the first time, as a result of the wish of the German Post Office to establish a postal cheque service for the transmission of money between the two countries. The Foreign and Colonial Branch of the Post Office was in favour of entering into an agreement with Germany, against which the Home Mails Branch urged caution, fearing that the result would be to stimulate demand for a domestic service. The United Kingdom Postal Clerks' Association was indeed pressing for a domestic postal cheque, to which the official response was that the Post Office Savings Bank existed to accept deposits and that remittance services were the responsibility of the money order and postal order system. There was a rigid divide in the Post Office between the two forms of financial service, which had separate administrative structures and motivations. The savings bank had been created as a medium of thrift, and the money and postal order system had been defined in a similarly narrow sense. Its origins lay in the transfer of money in letters, and it emerged as an adjunct to the mail service with a strict ban on competition with the commercial services of bankers. The Post Office could in any case insist that a 'giro' system was unnecessary in the United Kingdom, for 'in countries in which a Postal cheque system has been adopted by the Government the number of persons having ordinary Bankers' accounts, and drawing cheques thereon, appears to be infinitely smaller than in this country'. It was accordingly decided in 1913 not to enter into an agreement with the German Post Office. 'The position in Germany, where very few people have banking accounts, and where the number of banks is much smaller than in this country, is so different that the system no doubt has advantages there; but it is not seen why the Post Office should embark on a new service of this kind for the benefit of the German public.'[31]

In the interwar period, there was considerable pressure from the unions to develop a postal cheque system. The Trades Union Congress in 1926, for example, passed a resolution in favour of such a service, and the Union of Post Office Workers argued that it would benefit existing depositors and attract new customers. The committee which reported in 1928 was sceptical. The income on a giro system came from two sources, the fees charged on each transaction and the interest earned on balances held in accounts. The Committee argued that when balances were large, there would be considerable income from interest and fees could be fixed at a low level. But when the balances were low, as they would be in the United Kingdom where commercial banks already catered for large accounts, there would be less income from interest and fees would have to be fixed at 'an unduly high level'. The result would 'be a difficulty in making the system pay its way'. This assessment was persuasive, and the introduction of a giro system was delayed until the 1960s.[32]

The pattern of growth in the financial services of the Post Office suggests, as might be expected, a variety of motivations. The introduction of money orders and postal orders provides a good illustration of MacDonagh's view that change came from organic developments within the administrative structure as experience brought new problems to light. The remittance services grew from the insecurity of transmitting money in letters, and the facilities were extended to provide cheaper postal orders when the financial viability of money orders was threatened. However, MacDonagh's interpretation does not answer the major question of where the limit to government intervention should be set. The process of administrative accretion as civil servants grappled with the problems thrown up in their daily work would suggest that there was continuity of change with little ideological conflict, which was not true even of the remittance services. A line was drawn against encroachment into the market supplied by the private banks, and even in the area which it was accepted did fall within the scope of the Post Office there was disagreement over the role of the State. Should each segment of the business earn a profit, or was it permissible for the surplus in one area to cover a loss in another? There was certainly a marked divergence between the views of Hill and Scudamore which would be missed if the emphasis were placed upon a continuous process of administrative accretion. In any case, the administrative structure itself threw up institutional barriers which acted as limits to a gradual process of acquisition of new functions. This was a partial explanation of the failure to develop a giro system, for responsibility for remittance service and the savings bank fell to two separate branches of the Department which made it difficult to make the necessary connection. The rise of government intervention as a process of organic administrative growth may be exaggerated even in the case of the remittance services. Certainly, the movement into the business of savings and insurance did not result from developments within the Department for this was a new departure arising from the desire of Gladstone to provide an alternative to the trustee savings banks and friendly societies which he considered to be financially insecure. This might still suggest, as MacDonagh argues, that the extension of the role of the government arose from the perceived shortcomings of existing institutions rather than the influence of ideas, but this would not provide a complete explanation. Gladstone had a view of the role of government which was obviously different from that of Lloyd George. He wished to provide financially secure institutions which would permit workers to save and insure against the insecurities of life. There was no compulsion: the State was making facilities available for those who wished to help themselves, and those who did not take advantage were left to the care of the poor law. This assessment of the role of the State was to be modified in the early twentieth century by a Liberal government which introduced old age pensions and national insurance. The role of the Post Office must be located in the changing ideology of Liberalism as it moved away from Gladstonian financial orthodoxy to the new nostrums of the welfare reforms of 1906–14. There was more at stake than civil servants wrestling with the daily problems of administration.

Administrative historians have been fascinated by the pattern of government growth, but an economic historian might be tempted to ask what determined the relative prosperity of private and public enterprise. The Post Office did not have a legal monopoly in the provision of remittance services for small sums, but private business nevertheless preferred to ignore this sector of the market. By contrast, when the Post Office faced the industrial insurance companies in the sale of life policies, it could not make any impression on these private concerns. What determined the relative success and failure of public and private enterprise? The demand for a financial intermediary capable of transmitting and receiving deposits of small sums was likely to grow in the course of industrialisation, and the state was at a considerable advantage: it had a national coverage of existing offices and staff; it could provide security; and it might offer low fees without the danger of bankruptcy which would face private firms. Insurance demanded a different approach, of active marketing and the collection of weekly premiums from the household by agents working on a commission basis. This was an area in which the existing administrative structure of the Post Office offered no advantages. There were some areas in which public enterprise had an unquestioned advantage and other sectors in which it was obviously at a severe disadvantage, so that an assessment of the economics of the various services might be of greater value than the political debate of *laissez-faire* versus government intervention which has dominated the historical literature.

PART II
Carrying the Mail

A letter for St David's, posted at Cromer is conveyed – from Cromer to Norwich by Mail Cart (1) – from Norwich to London by Eastern Counties Railway (2) – from London to Bristol by Great Western Railway (3) – from Bristol to Gloucester by Midland Railway (4) – from Gloucester to Grange Court (a short distance beyond Gloucester) by Great Western Railway (5) – from Grange Court to Haverfordwest by South Wales Railway (6) – from Haverfordwest to St David's by Mail Cart.(7)

(UCL, Chadwick Mss, Box 84, Postal and Telegraph Services (1851–80), 'Memorandum on how letters are conveyed between various parts of the country, 1855'.)

Rail and Road:
the Inland Mail

We . . . propose to post an imaginary letter in the metropolis for a village in the far away North, following it from its place of posting till we finally see it deposited in the hands of the person to whom it is addressed. (W. Lewins, *Her Majesty's Mails* (2nd edn, 1865), p. 263)

The letter whose progress was traced by Lewins started on its journey when it was posted at the General Post Office at St Martin's le Grand in the City at shortly before 6 p.m.[1] The ordinary letters were taken from the posting boxes and thrown on to a large table surrounded by a dozen men who 'faced' them by placing the address and stamp uppermost; they were then transferred to the 'stamping' tables where the stamp was obliterated and the date, hour, and place of posting marked on the letter. The next stage was sorting which divided the mail for its outward journey from the office into 'roads' consisting of large towns in the same direction. The letters for each 'road' were then sub-divided until all the mail for one town was gathered together. By 8 p.m. the business of sorting letters at the General Post Office was completed, and all the mail bags were sealed and ready for despatch. Mail vans waited outside the office to transfer the bags to the various railway stations around London where they were loaded on the trains which carried the letters to the provinces. Each train was met at the station by a mail cart which collected the bags from London, and transferred them to the local post office where the process of inward sorting commenced. The mail was divided into the various districts within the town, down to the level of the individual 'walk' of a letter-carrier. When this process was completed, the letter-carriers would sort their pile of mail into the order for delivery from house to house. Of course, these procedures for carrying the mail from London to the provinces were repeated to bring letters to the metropolis.

119

The bustle as mail arrived at the head office in the City and was sorted for the 'roads' leading from London was captured by the *Illustrated London News* in 1875.

The delivery of letters depended upon two vital factors. One was the sorting of letters in a short time under great pressure and the Post Office relied upon an intensive use of labour according to very marked ebbs and flows of traffic during the day. There were, commented the *Quarterly Review* in 1850 with some poetic licence, 'two very violent convulsions, – namely, the morning delivery and evening despatch. . . . Throughout the department, at any period between these paroxysms, there reigns a silence and solitude similar to that which, during the hours of divine service, so creditably distinguishes the streets of Edinburgh on the Sabbath day.'[2] The second was a complex network of rail services. The employment of labour will form the subject of Part III; the concern at present is the transport of the mail around the country by rail and road.

In Lewins's account of the progress of a letter, road transport was used to carry the mail bags from the General Post Office to the London terminus, and from the provincial railway station to the post office of the town. A generation earlier, of course, the long-distance conveyance of letters also depended upon road services provided by the mail coaches. Indeed, the Post Office had in the late eighteenth and early nineteenth centuries taken an active role in improving both the vehicles in which the mail was conveyed and the roads on which they travelled. John Palmer devised a comprehensive network of routes operated by light coaches carrying only a limited load of passengers and luggage, and working to a detailed timetable. This allowed a higher speed and greater regularity, benefiting both the Post Office and the public which was prepared to pay a higher fare for a superior service. The first of these mail coaches was introduced between London and Bristol in 1784, and the network expanded into the early years of the nineteenth century. The Post Office did not itself operate the mail coaches, but fixed the timetable, paid a mileage rate for the carriage of mail, specified a standard vehicle, and provided a guard. The coach was also exempted from the payment of tolls, except in Scotland, and had right of way on the road. The contractor was responsible for providing the horses, coachman, coach and booking of passengers; the role of the Department was to encourage private operators. These operators, however, were facing problems from about 1810 as the stage coach system expanded, and further improved in speed, reliability and comfort. Mail coaches attempted to compete by increasing speeds which resulted in higher costs and lower profits without the compensation of increased payments for the carriage of the mail. The inflexibility of timing for Post Office requirements meant that passenger traffic was lost to the stage coaches, and the mail coaches ceased to be the most favoured form of transport. The mail coach system was encountering problems even before the arrival of railways which were to sound its death-knell.[3]

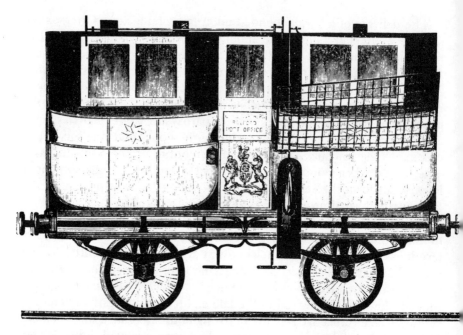

The first Travelling Post Office was introduced on the London and Birmingham Railway in 1838. This coach had a net to collect mail bags while in motion.

The Post Office was remarkably prompt in using the railways for the conveyance of mail. In 1830, Sir Francis Freeling, the Secretary, informed the Postmaster General that the new railway between Manchester and Liverpool must 'demand our serious consideration, whether we ought not to avail ourselves of this mode of communication. . . . The Post Office seems to be bound to keep pace with the wonderful improvements with which the present age abounds.'[4] In November 1830, within two months of its official opening, the Post Office made use of the Liverpool and Manchester railway, and as the rail network was extended in the 1830s and 1840s the circulation of mail became ever more dependent upon this new transport system. The task of 'outward sorting' was eased by the introduction of Travelling Post Offices: the mail could be put on the train serving a 'road' and sorted for individual towns en route, a process which started in 1838 on the London and Birmingham Railway. Mail coaches had stopped at intervals for the sake of the passengers, which provided an opportunity to sort the letters; when longer railway lines came into operation, the only practicable means of preparing letters for towns along the route was to sort them on the train. The Travelling Post Offices became crucial components of the revised circulation system.[5] Their use was linked with another innovation which was introduced in 1839: 'an apparatus for exchanging the letter bags, without the necessity of checking the speed of the train'.[6] The revolution in the circulation of mail was largely complete by 1846 when the last London mail coach ceased operation.

The imaginary letter described by Lewins passed between London and a provincial town, and the correspondence to and from London certainly formed a large part of total traffic. London was also an important point of transit for letters sent between provincial towns. The principle adopted until 1865 was that letters should be circulated through London unless this would cause a delay, but in that year it was decided to revise the circulation system in order to remove pressure on the Travelling Post Offices to and from London. More 'cross posts' were to be introduced directly linking provincial centres, and circulation through London and by Travelling Post Offices was to be avoided as far as was compatible with speed and regularity.[7] This could not, of course, be achieved in all cases and London remained the hub of the mail system.

The trains used by the Post Office fell into two broad categories. The first was the 'ordinary trains' which were run by the companies for their own needs, which the Post Office also found convenient for the carriage of mail. The second category of trains came under the control of the Postmaster General and were further divided into agreement and notice trains. In the case of agreement trains, the timetable, speed and stopping places were fixed by mutual agreement, whereas notice trains were run by the company according to a timetable fixed by the Post Office. A further distinction was that mail might be conveyed either in the charge of railway guards or Post Office staff. The calculation of payment for the service provided by the railways had to take into account four items. Common to all trains was a charge for the weight of mail carried; the second element was a payment for the conveyance of Post Office staff; the third component was the provision of sorting carriages; and the final consideration was the loss of income from other traffic in consequence of the control exercised by the Post Office.[8] Although it was easy to list the relevant factors, it was not easy to determine the exact rates which should be charged. Precedent might be called into play, for the payment to mail coach proprietors had been based upon their operating costs and had ignored expenditure on roads which were used free of charge. Could the State claim a similar right to use the railway's permanent way without charge? It was not even clear whether the Post Office should pay ordinary commercial rates and contribute to the profits of the railway companies, or whether it was entitled to preferential treatment. It did not take the Post Office long to use the railway; it took the rest of the century to reach a definitive statement of the terms for the conveyance of mails.

The Penny Post and the railways

> Detractors ascribed the main success of the measure [Penny Post] to
> the intervention of the railway system. Not so, for the success was
> even greater in the great zone of the two penny post of the metropolis,
> where the railways could have had nothing to do with it. (UCL,
> Chadwick Mss., Box 84, Postal and Telegraph Services (1851–80),
> 'Obstruction to Postal Reform.')

The connection between the development of railways and the carriage of
the mail generated by the introduction of penny postage would, at first
sight, appear to be so obvious as scarcely to merit comment. It was, of
course, in the interest of the railway companies to assert that the work of
the Post Office would collapse without their services, and Robert
Stephenson claimed that if it were not for the railways the costs of the
Penny Post would be so high that a loss would result.[9] At St Martin's le
Grand there was considerable scepticism, and Edward Page, the Inspector General of Mails, argued in 1856 'that the increase which has
taken place in the weight of mails would have presented no difficulty to
their conveyance by mail coaches, and that since the transfer of the
Mails from coaches to railways, the cost of transmission has increased in
a *far greater degree* than it would probably have done had railways never
been constructed'.

Although the number of letters had increased six-fold since the
introduction of Penny Post, their total weight had risen less than
three-fold, and 'the greater part of the Mail coaches would have borne
the increase of weight without any difficulty'. The cost of conveyance of
the mail was £443,000, of which £400,000 was paid to the railways, and
Page remarked that if the expense of mail coaches had doubled the
payment would still only amount to £310,000. He concluded that not
only 'would penny postage without railways have been both practicable
and remunerative, but it would have been even more profitable . . . than
it now is'. The view at St Martin's le Grand was that the railway system
which had developed at the same time as the Penny Post was not an
absolute necessity for the success of the postal service; it was, to use
Hill's phrase, 'an untoward coincidence'. It followed from this line of
reasoning that the rates charged for the carriage of mail were excessive,
produced by the monopoly of a railway company on a route which was
not regulated by legislation. The Post Office had, it was argued, been
protected from high charges for the carriage of mail by coach, for there
was always the prospect of a competitor starting a service. However, 'the
introduction of railways practically destroyed competition, and placed
large monopolies in the hands of a few private companies'.[10]

Rowland Hill could therefore argue that the disappointing financial performance of the Penny Post did not arise from any error in his original calculations, but was the result of the coincidental development of railways. The arrangements between the Post Office and the companies were, in his opinion, inequitable:

> strange as it may seem, that change which to the public at large has so much reduced the charge for the conveyance, whether of persons or of goods, has had precisely the reverse effect as respects the conveyance of mails. No doubt this result is attributable partly to the necessity for running certain mail trains at hours unsuitable for passenger traffic; but even when the Post Office uses the ordinary trains established by the companies for their own purposes, the rate of charge, especially considering the regularity and extent of custom, is almost always higher than that made to the public for like services.

The law, he asserted, was inadequate so that 'the regularity of the mails and the extension of postal accomodation are greatly impeded by the want of better arrangements for enabling the Post Office to obtain the services of railways on equitable terms and for enforcing punctuality in the arrival of the mail trains'. Hill did have some grounds for complaint in that the Post Office's relations with the railway companies had not been placed on a satisfactory basis.[11] It is nevertheless difficult to escape the conclusion that much of his case was based upon special pleading against what he considered to be the monopolistic power of the railways. The market should, in his view, always offer competition; if it did not, it was quite right for the State to intervene. Reality had to be forced into agreement with his view of the world, and this was to lead him and Frederic into difficulties when they failed to adopt a pragmatic attitude. The railways were, after all, providing a much faster service and could justifiably claim a higher payment than the mail coaches. It must be doubted whether a three-fold increase in the weight of mail could have been carried by the existing mail coach services and there would almost certainly have been an increase in expenditure even if railways had not appeared on the scene. The argument in any case had an air of unreality: the railways did exist and the mail coach network was shrinking. It is certainly doubtful whether the introduction of penny postage, which was expected to generate a large volume of new traffic, could have been contemplated if the additional carrying capacity of the railways had not already existed. Hill cannot escape criticism for failing to allow for increased costs of conveyance in his original calculation, although it is possible to sympathise with his feeling that the bargaining procedures were deeply flawed.

The Post Office suggested in 1832 that a clause should be inserted in railway Bills requiring companies to carry mail for a sum not exceeding the fare of one passenger for each guard in whose care the mail was conveyed. The proposal was not pursued at the time in order to prevent delay to Bills already before Parliament, although it was understood that companies would enter into agreements on this basis and would not oppose a future general Bill. The Postmaster General in 1837 accordingly raised the need for 'a legislative enactment compelling rail road companies to carry mail and a guard at a low rate of charge', and the Act of 1838 empowered the Department to despatch a mail guard with bags by any train on the same conditions as applied to any other passenger. This power was soon overtaken by circumstances, for a service based upon a mail guard carrying a bag of letters ceased to be practicable with the growth in traffic after 1840. The Act of 1838 had not specified the terms for the supply of two crucial services: the carriage of mail in a number of compartments or coaches of ordinary trains operated by the companies for passenger traffic; and the operation of special mail trains at times required by the Department. In 1838 the Post Office was, of course, still operating a low-volume, high-price service and these omissions were not so significant as later appeared. The Act merely stated that the companies should have a 'reasonable remuneration' to be determined by two arbitrators representing the Post Office and railway company, who might select an umpire whose decision would be binding. Page had grounds for his complaint in 1856 that 'reasonable' was 'a most indefinite term, and one which has given rise to infinite variety of opinion'. There were no general principles to guide the arbitrators and umpires with the result 'that the most conflicting decisions have been arrived at in cases which, if not identical, have been so nearly alike as to render it impossible to reconcile the strange variation in the rates awarded'. The rate for locomotive power between Chester and Birkenhead, for example, was 2s a mile but between Dublin and Cork 4s 6d a mile. The Post Office could, it was claimed, pay more for the use of part of a train than the entire cost of operation.[12] The payment to the companies was, in the opinion of Hill and his subordinates, excessive both in comparison with the cost of providing the service and with charges to other types of traffic. This was, they argued, a result of the monopoly power of the companies and the inadequacies of the bargaining machinery created by Parliament.

Arbitration seemed at first to offer a satisfactory basis for determining rates for carriage of the mail, for the contract of 1838 between the Post Office and the London and Birmingham Railway was based on general agreement on the criteria to be adopted. The arbitrators – Robert Stephenson for the company and H.D. Harness of the Royal Engineers for the Post Office – reached a settlement without referring to an umpire, by extending to the railways the principle followed in establishing rates for mail coaches. The Post Office had been exempted from most tolls for the use of turnpikes, and therefore made no contribution towards the cost of roads. It followed by analogy – or so it seemed – that the Post Office should not contribute towards the cost of the permanent way of the railways, and should pay enough to give a return of $7\frac{1}{2}$ per cent on the operation of the trains.[13] This consensus between the railway companies and Post Office was to be short lived, and two distinct views were to emerge.

The railway companies, it was claimed by Harness who acted as arbitrator for the Post Office throughout the 1840s, had achieved their monopoly in spite of the legislature and not with its consent. The railway companies were in theory only the proprietors of a line which was open to all, but in practice there were no competing carriers and the Post Office was in consequence unable to put its services out to tender. It was therefore essential, according to Harness, that in calculating the rates for the conveyance of mail he should 'not admit the claim of the railway companies to have the price fixed as if their monopoly was recognised'. He was taking a hypothetical view of the operation of railways which was based upon analogy with the coach services rather than the realities of the railways in the 1840s. He continued to follow 'the same principle upon which the Post Office were paying for their mails on the roads': the Department should allow a 'full commercial profit' to the railway companies as carriers, 'but not pay for the use of the road further than it was clear that the Post Office put the company to an actual expense for it; that is to say, the payment awarded was not to make a return on the capital upon the road'. Harness applied these principles according to a number of formulae. The first was for 'locomotive power'. When the Post Office was using an ordinary train, it should pay in proportion to the weight carried; for special trains, the Department should pay the full cost of 'locomotive power' less any money received by the company for the carriage of passengers and goods. The second component was a payment for the use of carriages, which Harness based upon the rates charged by the companies when exchanging rolling-stock between themselves. This left a third element, the 'toll' for the use of the track. Although the companies should not receive a 'remunerative return', Harness allowed a moderate payment which was calculated on a somewhat curious basis: the rate would give a return of 10 per cent on the capital invested in the line if a mail train ran at half-hourly intervals.[14] The Post Office was considered to be a special case and should not contribute to the profit of the companies. They already had a privileged position, protected by legislation and given large powers of interference with private property. A railway, one arbitrator claimed, was not 'a company of adventurers setting up trade on their own resources only, and subject to the ordinary risk of unlimited competition. It seems to me, therefore, that in a matter of so great national concern as the conveyance of letters, the country has a right to expect a proportionate return of advantage from the railway company.'[15]

On the contrary, argued Mark Huish of the London and North Western Railway and C.A. Saunders of the Great Western Railway, the government had no right to preferential treatment. The operation of special trains at high speeds and at inconvenient times determined by the Post Office disrupted the operation of the railways. The companies should be compensated, and should also receive a contribution towards the permanent way, general management, and interest on capital. The payment for 'locomotive power' and carriages was, they claimed, too low and the companies' receipts on mail trains were irrelevant to the Post Office. The basic point upon which Huish and Saunders insisted was that the Department should have no preference over the public. The Post Office, stressed Huish, 'has neither a legal nor equitable claim to exemption from those fair and reasonable charges which, for a similar service, accompanied by similar constancy, would be made to any member of the public armed with ordinary powers only, and using the highway under the powers granted by Parliament at times suiting the convenience and economy of the company.'[16]

The practical problems which arose in determining the payment to the Great Western Railway illustrated these general points in a particularly clear manner. In the first arbitration of 1843, the umpire was a local MP with no experience of such matters. He made an award which was ambiguously worded and which he subsequently raised when he found he had made a mistake. The Post Office repudiated the whole exercise, only to find that a second arbitration in 1844 produced a still higher award. The Department attempted to reopen the whole affair in 1845. The episode indicated that the arbitration procedure lacked defined criteria for establishing rates, and this shortcoming was intensified by the use of inexperienced, amateur umpires. The award was something of a gamble, and Hill stressed the difficulty of extending services when the financial implications would be uncertain. The companies, for their part, complained that the system was inequitable. The Post Office could obtain a new arbitration at any time by the simple expedient of making a small change in the service required, although the companies could not reopen an award for three years. 'If such is to be the practice', complained the railways, 'there can be no security or fairness in the system of arbitration which certainly implies an even handed, just and final settlement by submission to some impartial and honourable tribunal, by which settlement both parties ought to be equally bound'. Certainly, the experience of the Great Western contract in the 1840s suggested that the arbitration procedure was not operating in a satisfactory manner.[17]

Rowland Hill was indeed eager to jettison the procedure. In his view, arbitration gave the companies favourable treatment, resulting in rates higher than paid by other classes of traffic. Whereas the companies were willing to give low rates to excursion trains or minerals, 'well knowing that it is better to be satisfied with a small profit on such traffic than to lose it altogether', Hill complained that 'the Post Office does not (like the public at large) enjoy the important advantages of increased speed and accommodation at a reduced cost, but . . . purchases them at a greatly enhanced price'. This was a reflection of the nature of the demand for services: high fares might dissuade passengers from travelling whereas the Post Office had no option but to use the railways. In Hill's view, this justified the replacement of the market as the means of establishing the price to be paid, and in 1847 he proposed that the Railway Commissioners – a short-lived experiment between 1846 and 1851 – should issue a general tariff for the conveyance of mails based 'on the principle of repaying the Company the *additional* expense incurred in the service *plus* a fixed percentage (say 5 per cent on such additional expense) for profit'. These charges would vary with the amount of mail and the extent of regulation over the time of the train. The Commissioners should decide all questions between the Post Office and the companies, so that there would be a permanent body to settle points of dispute rather than temporary, amateur umpires. Hill also proposed that each company should be assigned a definite territory in which it would be free of competition, and that the Commissioners should have the power to require the construction of a line in return for a loan at $3\frac{1}{2}$ per cent. The inadequate operation of competition would be replaced by state regulation and this scheme, Hill argued, 'would secure the cheap conveyance of the mails and greatly promote the extension and perfection of the system of Post Office distribution'. It would, in more general terms, 'secure the establishment of moderate fares without resorting to competition, which it is now generally admitted, would, in its permanent results, be as injurious to the public as to the companies'. The railway system of the country would be completed without speculation and waste of capital, relieving the companies from ruinous expenditure designed to defend themselves against the incursion of competitors.[18]

Hill's proposal of 1847 was visionary and impractical; Maberly was content with the existing state of affairs. He felt that the Post Office's powers were sufficient, and that the system of arbitration was 'the most equitable arrangement both for the public and the railway company, as it appears to me that the circumstances under which a train is worked specially for the convenience of the Post Office may vary so much on different lines as to render a fixed rate of payment unjust towards this

129

Department as well as to the railway company'. The only change which Maberly proposed was the appointment of an umpire by the Railway Commissioners in case of delay.[19] The explanation of Maberly's ready acceptance of the existing state of affairs was clear to Hill: he welcomed the increased cost of conveyance which gave 'an excellent handle to the enemies of reform'.[20] Hill, of course, had a vision of a hostile world threatening his plan, and he was inclined to exaggerate. Nevertheless, the system of arbitration did create uncertainties in the operation of the postal services, and there was scope for some modification of procedures, falling short of Hill's heroic remedies.

In 1853, a Select Committee was appointed 'to inquire into the causes of irregularity in the conveyance of mails by railways, and to consider the best mode of securing speed and punctuality, and for remunerating the railway companies for the services which they perform'. The appointment of the Committee arose from concern that the mail service was not sufficiently reliable and that the Post Office was making inadequate use of the railways. Critics of the Department argued that circuitous routes were used, so that mails for the north were centralised at Tamworth rather than despatched by a direct route. Hill defended the practice of concentrating the mail on a few trunk lines on operational grounds, but the dispute was, of course, not simply about organisation.[21] At the bottom there was a matter of finance: the use of any route which might accelerate the mail would impose a greater cost. The question which demanded an answer was whether the Post Office should be guided by considerations of profit, or whether it should seek to provide the best possible service. Hill insisted that his concern was that the letters carried should cover the cost, and argued that this calculation was difficult because of the uncertainty as to the rate to be paid to the railways. The 'convenience of the public' could not, in Hill's view, be considered apart from 'the commercial nature of the transaction', for he insisted that they were identical.[22] This approach did not receive wide support, and the opinion of Sir Charles Grey was more generally accepted:

> it is quite right that the Post Office should be made a source of revenue, so far as that can be done consistently with giving every fair and reasonable accommodation to the public in the transmission of letters; but if we are debarred from making use of any means of sending letters, or of receiving them, except through the Post Office, I think that the first consideration of the Post Office ought to be to give the public every fair and reasonable accommodation with regard to the receipt and despatch of letters.[23]

The question still remained of how to establish the rate paid by the Post Office for the use of the railways. Here the Select Committee foundered, and any positive recommendation was ruled out in view of the wide variety of circumstances 'quite beyond the judgement of anyone looking into the matter for the first time'. Instead, it was recommended that a commission of engineers should be appointed to consider whether a tonnage or mileage rate could be fixed 'which, though not exactly suited to each particular case, might not be generally fair to all parties'. The basic issue had been avoided: should the companies receive a full return on their capital or should the Post Office pay the bare cost of a train? The commission of engineers was to be given no guidance.[24]

Hill became sole Secretary in 1854 and he was eager to settle the matter. He urged that the Department should have the power to require the provision of a special mail train for a multiple of the bare additional cost, excluding the capital expended on the line: the multiple would be fixed by legislation and the cost determined by engineers. In case of ordinary trains, the Department should pay no more than the public paid for parcels; indeed, he noted that newspaper distributors paid only half the parcel rate.[25] Hill claimed that the Department did not require special privileges but only the payment of the same rates as the public.[26] The Treasury decided to follow the advice of the Select Committee and appointed a committee of engineers to arrive at some 'fixed principles'. When the committee reported in 1855 it arrived at different conclusions from Hill. It insisted on taking the capital of the companies into account, and felt that the companies were entitled to an additional sum equal to the 'bare cost' to cover interest on capital and fixed charges. The companies should therefore be paid twice the cost of operation. The report was indeed very favourable to the railways.[27] The engineers recommended, for example, that mail sent by ordinary trains in the care of a company guard should pay twopence per mile for each hundredweight; Hill calculated that the rate should be one halfpenny on the basis of public charges adjusted for the scale and regularity of the trade. The Board of Trade was in broad agreement with Hill, and felt that the rate should be one halfpenny or three farthings.[28] Although the outcome was not satisfactory to the Post Office, it seemed to be essential to secure legislation to place railway rates on a more definite basis and in 1856 a Bill was drafted which incorporated the recommendations of the engineers. A fixed tariff was proposed for ordinary trains 'based upon the principle that the Post Office is to have no pecuniary advantage over the general public'; the rate should be the public charge 'with no other deduction than that which is due for regularity and continuity of service'. Although arbitration would be maintained for special mail trains, this would be on the understanding that the rate should be the actual cost plus 100 per cent, with the deduction of any revenue from passengers. This had gone a long way from Hill's original claim, yet the Department

131

was still not optimistic that the measure would succeed, for 'simple and just as these propositions appear to be, it is probable that they will be vehemently opposed by the railway interest'. The companies in many cases had better terms, and the Bill was abandoned in 1857 in the face of a concerted campaign organised by the railway interest. 'In truth', remarked Hill in his autobiography, 'the railway influence is so strong in Parliament', amounting to ninety-six MPs in 1857.[29]

After this disappointment Hill changed his approach, and suggested that the companies should be offered financial inducements to co-operate. The government should, he proposed, make low-cost loans to the companies in proportion to their postal services. The companies might then replace existing debentures at a saving, and in return mail should be carried at fixed tariffs. An advance of £30m by the government would, Hill calculated, save the companies £300,000 a year in interest changes, and payment for mail services could be reduced from £400,000 to £150,000 and still leave them better off. Hill argued that such a scheme would 'supply the defects of early legislation, by placing the Post Office in a position similar to that in which it would probably have stood, had its interests (and through it those of the public) received due attention from the legislature when railways were first established'.[30] The scheme was obviously impracticable, indicative of Hill's capacity for visionary solutions rather than pragmatic action.

The improvement in the position of the Department in fact came about without any radical change in the method by which rates were established.[31] The Inspector General of Mails noted in 1866 that matters had been transformed in the past ten years from the high charges and strained relations which had characterised the mid-1850s:

4.1 CONVEYANCE OF MAIL BY RAIL, 1854–80/1

	amount (£)	per cent of total costs	per cent of gross revenue from letters, books and packets
1854	462,518	20.0	17.7
1860	490,223	17.4	15.0
1870	587,296	17.1	12.6
1880/1	707,436	17.1	10.9

Source: *Annual Reports of the Postmaster General on the Post Office.*

Within that period the weight of mails generally and of course the weight sent by railway has enormously increased, – the mail trains have in many cases been accelerated and been run at more convenient hours for Post Office purposes and the trains by which mails are forwarded have become far greater in number. . . . But while the value of the service performed by the railway companies has been so much increased the payments of the Post Office have increased to a comparatively moderate extent. . . . The relations of the Department with railway companies are generally of a friendly nature – formal arbitrations having been almost entirely superseded by agreements for settling the rates of payment.[32]

The Great Western Railway provides a good example of the downward drift in the relative cost of conveyance. The Post Office paid the company £74,854 in 1862 and £91,014 in 1882, or an increase of 21.6 per cent; over the same period, the mail carried by the company to and from London rose from 1,149 tons to 4,483 tons or an increase of 290.2 per cent. The payment to the company, if it had increased in proportion, would have been £292,054 in 1882.[33] It is not surprising that the Department had become much less concerned about the cost of railway services.

The Railway Commission and the Great Western award of 1903

The procedure by which rates were established was at last amended in 1873 when the new Railway Commission created that year was authorised to arbitrate between the Post Office and the railway companies, at the discretion of the companies. The Post Office aimed to take this further by inserting a clause in the Railway and Canal Traffic Bill of 1888 which would *require* the use of the Commission for arbitration, but the companies objected and the clause was dropped. The Secretary of the Post Office, S.A. Blackwood, felt that such a measure was urgently required. 'Arbitrations', he complained, 'are unsatisfactory from the want both of continuous experience and of guiding principles on the part of the tribunals; whereas if all cases in which the Department and the Companies were unable to settle the remuneration by mutual agreement were referred to the Commissioners, they would soon acquire a knowledge and a grasp of the subject which could not fail to be advantageous to the public service.' This, of course, was precisely what the companies feared: systematic rate-fixing might reduce the payment received from the Post Office.[34]

The views of the Post Office had changed since the time of Hill's ascendancy. The Railway Commission should certainly be used when arbitration was absolutely essential, but there was less enthusiasm for defined principles for fixing rates which were 'surely a dream'. The Department preferred to rely upon its bargaining skills rather than the introduction of a precise formula, and took the view that 'the advantage of hard and fast rules (if practicable) over friendly bargaining with the companies is very dubious at the best'.[35] The Department did have certain guidelines when negotiating with the companies: it attempted to secure half parcel rates for the carriage of mail bags and in the case of special trains sought to pay the actual cost less the company's income from other traffic, with the addition of a reasonable profit. This basis for establishing payment was not generally accepted by the companies, and only the London and North Western Railway acquiesced in the payment of half parcel rates. By contrast, the arbitrators in 1888 awarded the North British Railway five-sixths of parcel rates.[36] The Treasury, against the inclinations of the Post Office, insisted that the bargaining position would be strengthened by the adoption of 'a more uniform and systematic basis'. Despite the existence of special features in any particular case, the Treasury claimed that there was 'a large and well defined field over which there appears to be no reason why the rates charged by different companies to the government should be more variable and uncertain than the rates charged to the public.'[37] A committee representing the Treasury, Post Office and Board of Trade was accordingly established to recommend the basis for payment.

The committee reported in 1894. It started from the assumption that the Department was entitled to parity with traders and not to special rates.[38] Mail bags should pay half parcel rates in the custody of a railway guard, and 40 per cent when in the care of a Post Office employee. The rate for supplying and hauling sorting carriages should, it was suggested, be $1\frac{1}{2}d$ per mile plus 15 per cent of the cost of construction, and the companies should receive the difference between the traffic receipts of mail trains under the control of the Post Office and normal trains. The Treasury was suitably gratified, and felt that these proposals provided a 'promising basis for building up such a sound and systematic method of assessing the proper remuneration as should be possible where a permanent and regular service is performed for the State under conditions so little onerous to the Companies'.[39] Applications of these formula was a different matter for the proposals did not have legislative force. The Conveyance of Mails Act of 1893 did, it is true, give the Post Office as well as the companies the power to require the use of the Railway Commission as arbitrator, but it was not until the Great Western award of 1903 that there was anything approaching a definitive statement of principle. What was the background to this award?

The contract between the Post Office and the GWR had not been renegotiated since the early 1880s. In 1881, the company decided to renegotiate the contract which had run for over 20 years without fully compensating the Great Western for the increased volume of traffic. 'This is', remarked Blackwood, 'by far the largest question the Department has ever yet had to deal with in the case of any Railway company.' The company suggested a number of possible methods of establishing the payment, which produced figures ranging from a minimum of £115,752 to a maximum of £200,000. The Department's estimate produced a figure of £110,000, with an additional sum to cover the acceleration of services. Settlement was reached in a short time without arbitration, and a new contract was made for five years from December 1883 at a rate of £115,000 to cover both the existing and accelerated services. The Department was well pleased, and assured the Treasury that 'if a settlement is now effected on these terms it will virtually be that of the buyer fixing his own price, which I suppose is as satisfactory a basis for a government bargain as any admits of'.[40] It was not until 1899 that the Great Western Railway decided that a revision of this contract was necessary. The volume of mail had continued to rise at a time of mounting costs, and the company requested an increase in its payment to £182,000. The Post Office was unsympathetic, and the company decided to terminate the contract. 'We have', argued the Great Western, 'too long been parties to an arrangement under which the remuneration has been non-progressive, while the services required of us, and the cost of rendering those services, have increased at a rate and to a proportion which make a readjustment of the terms an urgent necessity.'

The negotiations soon reached an impasse. The company wished to take the contract of 1883 as the basis for any settlement, and to raise its payment in line with the increase in costs and weight of mail. This the Post Office would not accept. The agreement of 1883, it was now argued, was favourable to the company, for why else would it have been allowed to continue so long? In any case, a mere rise in the volume of mail was no reason for an increase in the payment. The company, it was argued, was paid for the inconvenience of running special trains regardless of the weight carried, and an improvement in the passenger receipts from mail trains might even merit a lower payment. The Post Office wished to assess the value of each service rather than to negotiate an inclusive figure, and it was felt that 'the payment now made is more than the present service justifies'. This the Great Western could not accept and the case was accordingly submitted to the Railway Commissioners for arbitration. The company's claim was for £264,821. This was based upon the full parcel rate for mail bags. Letter mails, argued the company, were more valuable and important than parcels; they were carried under strict orders and earned a considerable profit for the Post Office. By right, asserted the company, the rate should be *higher* than for ordinary parcels. This was a view which the Department denied: value and profit were not relevant, and the traffic was regular and easy to handle. One third of the parcel rate was offered. These different

135

assumptions meant that for the carriage of mail bags the company claimed £130,000 plus £10,000 for Christmas traffic, and the Department offered £32,971 plus £1,141. In addition, the company proposed a rate of ninepence a mile for special trains; the Department offered 'to fix the payment at a rate which would not be more than adequate to supply any deficency in the traffic receipts which may be due to the company's having to run these trains at inconvenient hours'. The task of the Railway Commission was to arbitrate between these two claims.[41]

The award was issued in 1903. The Commission decided that for the conveyance of mail bags 'the parcels' scale less 25 per cent will yield the company as good a net revenue as they earn from the parcels which they carry for the public', with an 8 per cent reduction for the regularity and scale of the traffic. The payment for special trains and carriages brought the total sum to £135,536. This was little above the payment of £124,827 in 1901, despite the inclusion of a new service. The Post Office expressed its satisfaction. The principle of appraising the value of each service, rather than making an inclusive payment, had been accepted and clear principles established for future negotiations. Although the rate for the carriage of mail bags might, it was felt, have been lower, the Post Office welcomed two features of the award. The Commission had accepted the right of the Post Office to know how much the company earned from special trains, and had agreed 'that the only payment that the company have a right to expect is a sum which will bring the earnings of each of these controlled trains into line with the average earnings of other similar trains'. The award at first sight meant that mail was carried by the Great Western on terms favourable to the Post Office.[42] There was, however, an attendant danger: the application of the precise formulae could in some cases produce a considerable increase in payments to the railway companies. Free bargaining might still have advantages over the rigidity of the principles laid down in 1903.

A case in point was the London and the North Western Railway's contract. This had been negotiated in 1856, and in 1904 the Department realised that the LNWR would be entitled to an additional £150,000 on the basis of the Great Western award. It was accordingly decided to *'find reason* for making additional payments' to avoid the termination of the contract. However, in 1911 the LNWR decided to seek a revision and the Department calculated that the company might expect £350,000 on the basis of the Great Western award; the actual payment in 1910 was £224,244. The Post Office made an immediate offer of a contract of £295,000, which the company accepted for ten years. Why, it might be wondered, did the London and North Western Railway not take the case to the Railway Commissioners? The failure of the companies to appreciate the worth of the services they fulfilled was not, as F.H. Williamson of the Secretary's Office remarked, as surprising as it might appear. The intricacy of proceedings before the Commission made it difficult for a company to form an idea of the precise application of the principles established in awards, whereas the Post Office had 'close and extensive knowledge'. It was difficult for one company to compare its services with another company, or even to know how much mail was carried without elaborate and complex returns. The Post Office could much more readily judge when it was beneficial to take a case to the Railway Commission, and when to make a settlement without arbitration; the companies were less able to assess when recourse to the Commission would work to their benefit.[43] The apparently rigid principles of 1903 therefore complemented rather than replaced the process of bargaining.

The disruptions of the war and government control over the railways created problems for the Post Office. The services were considerably modified, and the contracts became records of prewar services rather than a statement of the current position. Costs rose during the war and postwar boom, and in 1921 a provisional increase of 75 per cent was agreed; this was reduced to 50 per cent in 1923 as prices started to fall. Permanent settlements took longer to achieve, and were complicated by the regrouping of the companies into larger units in 1922. Generally, the principles of 1903 were retained, with the addition of a variation clause to allow for changes in the volume of mail and in the parcel rate which formed the basis for payment. The Great Western contract of 1926, for example, specified that when the traffic rose or fell by more than 8 per cent, the payment would be adjusted by half the change in volume. This removed the benefit to the Post Office of long, fixed-price contracts which in the past had allowed the unit cost of conveyance to fall as the volume of mail increased. It also meant that the calculation of payments to the railway companies had been reduced to the automatic application of a formula.[44] The disputes of the mid-nineteenth century were a thing of the past.

4.2 CONVEYANCE OF MAIL BY RAIL, 1919/20–1939/40

	Amount (£) ex parcels	per cent of total costs
1919/20	1,567,172	4.8
1929/30	1,979,815	5.6
1939/40	2,182,076	5.0

Source: *Post Office Commercial Accounts.*

Payments to the railway companies had fallen from 20 per cent of costs to 5 per cent since the mid-nineteenth century. Of course, there had been a general fall in freight rates in the nineteenth century and the Post Office benefited in common with other customers. The change in bargaining procedures no doubt assisted. The railway companies were, at the outset, able to gain highly advantageous terms from the Department, made possible by the system of arbitration through the use of temporary and amateur umpires. The development of permanent, professional arbitration by the Railway Commission resulted in a shift in the balance of advantage towards the Post Office. However, the greatest factor in the relative decline in the cost of conveyance by railway was simply the growth in the weight of mail. Until the interwar period, contracts did not contain a variation clause to increase payment with the rise in the weight of mail. An award would therefore be made on the basis of the existing traffic, and would be adjusted only to take account of the addition of new services. The companies would not be aware of the quantity of mail carried except in general terms unless they compiled complicated returns, and they were therefore in a weaker bargaining position than the Post Office. They did not, however, have much cause for complaint. The early contracts had been favourable to the companies, and there was some margin to be squeezed. The companies were in any case not very alarmed, for the revenue from carrying the mail was a relatively insignificant element in their total receipts. There was here a major difference from the development of steamship and air services, where the contract with the Post Office might be crucial for financial success.

Transit services and contractors

When Lewins described the circulation of mail in 1865, road transport was largely used on transit work between the main post offices and the railway stations. In London in particular, at the hub of the distribution system, a considerable fleet of vans was needed to carry mail to and from the major terminuses. This transit work was the responsibility of outside contractors employing horse-drawn vehicles until the First World War, when this started to change as more consideration was given to the introduction of 'official' schemes and the adoption of motor vehicles. The process of change was slow, and it was not completed until after the Second World War. Only in 1949 did the last horse-drawn mail van operated by a contractor cease to run on the streets of London.

In 1920, the Post Office purchased fifty light motor vans to replace contract services in rural districts where the absence of competition had produced high charges. The Treasury gave approval for the expenditure of £12,500 on condition that 'careful cost accounts should be kept of the experiment on a commercial basis, and utilised both for criticising the offers of Contractors and for comparing the relative standard of efficiency in different Post Office districts'. The Department's estimate of the cost of an official service was in effect taken as one tender to be set alongside the submissions of private firms, and it would only be implemented when demonstrably lower. The aim was to force down the price of contracts rather than to make a definite commitment to official schemes. 'Until we are in a position to provide a van service of our own at short notice', remarked one official, 'I do not see how we can bring down the cost of conveyance in places like Leicester or Coventry, where for various reasons there is no effective outside competition for the work.' The formulation of an official scheme 'had a marked effect on Contractors. In the past, high contract prices have had to be paid because the absence of competition in certain districts left the Department no choice in the matter. Now, however, there is a powerful bargaining weapon in the hands of the Post Office which can often be used with considerable effect.'[45]

In 1921 the Treasury authorised the purchase of a further 300 motor vans, and was impressed by the fact that a capital expenditure of £96,000 would produce annual savings of £30,000. The Department, however, was not enthusiastic about extending the use of 'official' motor vans. Although there was an advantage where competition was absent, in general an official service could not be operated at a lower rate per mile than most contract services. The wages paid to contractors' drivers were lower than the wages and benefits received by postmen, and this could be the crucial issue in the relative cost of contract and official services. The Department might opt to employ drivers at 'trade' rates and this strategy was adopted in Birmingham in 1925 when it made the difference between accepting an outside tender and adopting an official scheme. One result was, of course, to create problems with the Union of Post Office Workers which argued that anyone involved with the conveyance of mail should be paid the postman's rate. The issue continued throughout the 1930s, complicating the introduction of official vans on transit work. The irregularity of the demand for vans over the day was a further consideration. Private contractors could use their plant on other business and spread their overheads, unlike the Post Office which was confined to one service. The economic arguments for a move from horse-drawn contract services to motorised official services were not compelling, and the commitment of the Department was unenthusiastic. This scepticism was reflected in the report of the Motor Transport Committee of 1924 which recommended that official schemes should, like outside contracts, be reassessed at intervals or put out to tender. The prevalent attitude was well captured in 1926 when it was decided to invite tenders for the transit services in Manchester. 'We should prepare our scheme with the intention rather of using it as a lever to force down contractors' tenders than of introducing it unless we are forced to do so by the difference between the tender and the official figure.' It was discovered with some surprise that the official scheme was indeed £3,000 cheaper than the lowest tende.[46]

Although official schemes were introduced in a number of provincial cities between the wars, by far the most important contracts were in London. The scale of the work in London was massive and had led in 1909 to the appointment of a committee to consider the conveyance of mail by pneumatic tubes or underground railway. The extent of the London Postal District caused difficulties, for the major office in the City was over three and a half miles from Paddington, and problems of distance were exacerbated by congestion in the streets. The cost of mail van services in London before the First World War was high and rising, amounting to £152,046 in 1900 and £214,733 in 1909. The Committee saw great attractions in the construction of an underground railway which would accelerate the transit of the mail, and it recommended the provision of a small-bore railway from the Eastern District Office to Paddington at a cost of £513,000. The annual expense was taken to be £36,000 which would produce a saving of £14,000 on the existing mail contracts, as well as improving the service. This was, of course, the time at which underground railways were under construction as a solution to passenger transport in London and the scheme had the allure of the fashionable. The proposal was welcomed by the Postmaster General as 'a most attractive scheme, which I trust may be found suitable for adoption in the very near future'. However, in the course of development the anticipated savings were to disappear. This was in part the product of a change in accounting procedures when the Treasury increased the allowance for depreciation. More significant was the under-estimation of the capital cost of the scheme. On most assumptions the scheme would produce a loss and it became clear that the Treasury would not sanction the construction of an underground railway. The Department modified its case to emphasise the social savings which would result from acceleration of mail and the reduction of congestion on the roads. The Cabinet accepted this case despite the warnings of the Treasury. Construction started in 1914, and the railway opened in 1927 after considerable delays during and after the war. The venture did not receive universal acclaim. It was, remarked one Member of Parliament, 'probably about the most ridiculous enterprise that even the Post Office has ever entered into' and the full system linking the major London railway stations was in fact never completed. The decision to construct the underground railway was certainly questionable, although once it was in existence it became an integral feature of the

140

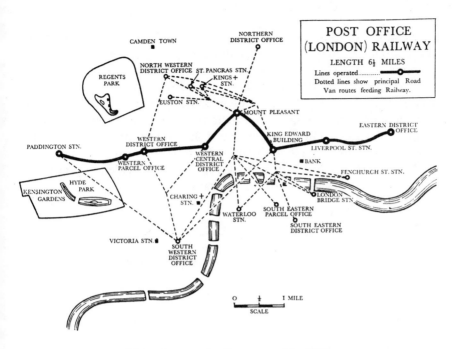

CAMDEN TOWN

NORTHERN
DISTRICT OFFICE

NORTH WESTERN
DISTRICT OFFICE ST. PANCRAS STN.

REGENTS
PARK

KINGS +
STN.

EUSTON STN.

MOUNT PLEASANT

POST OFFICE
(LONDON) RAILWAY

LENGTH 6½ MILES

Lines operated............
Dotted lines show principal Road
Van routes feeding Railway.

EASTERN DISTRICT
OFFICE

KING EDWARD
BUILDING

WESTERN
DISTRICT OFFICE

PADDINGTON STN.

LIVERPOOL ST. STN.

WESTERN
CENTRAL
DISTRICT
OFFICE

WESTERN
PARCEL OFFICE

BANK

FENCHURCH ST. STN.

HYDE
PARK

KENSINGTON
GARDENS

CHARING +
STN.

LONDON
BRIDGE STN.

WATERLOO
STN.

SOUTH EASTERN
PARCEL OFFICE

SOUTH EASTERN
DISTRICT OFFICE

VICTORIA STN.

SOUTH
WESTERN
DISTRICT
OFFICE

0   ½   1 MILE

SCALE

The underground railway opened in 1927.

London distribution system, operating with great frequency and reliability.[47]

The Department could argue, with some justification, that the transit services across London were of such importance to the circulation system of the country that strict financial standards were inappropriate and that a 'liberal attitude towards its cost is justified'. Even so, there was doubt whether the cost at the end of the First World War *could* be justified. There were five contracts in 1919/20 with a payment of £370,451 which rose to £422,993 in 1920/21. The high prices during the postwar boom led to serious consideration of the introduction of official motor schemes, and it was estimated in 1922 that the Department could undertake for £109,933 services for which McNamara was paid £167,848.[48] Robert Bruce of the London Postal Service in 1919 prepared a report on 'the question of dispensing with Contractors in favour of a State-owned service', in which he suggested that the Department should run and maintain its own service. At the same time, horses should be replaced by faster motors which would reduce the workforce and the number of vehicles, and permit greater mobility. The high price of feed had removed the cost advantage which horses usually had in congested areas where the vehicle was often idle.[49] Bruce's opinion was confirmed in 1922 by R.H. Patterson of the London and North Western Railway, who noted that contractors had failed to reduce

141

their charges despite the fall in prices after 1920; it seemed to him that 'the contractors had no fear of competition'. Patterson noted a basic dilemma. Large contracts would be more efficient, for a single firm could reduce the overlap of services and utilise its vans more fully. This would, however, be at the cost of creating a monopoly 'which would soon be autocratic'. Smaller contracts would increase competition but reduce efficiency. 'The only way out of the present position', Patterson concluded, 'is for the Department to become the owners of their own road transport, beginning in a small way.'[50] It was decided to prepare an official scheme to replace the McNamara contract.

4.3 LONDON MAIL TRANSIT CONTRACTS, 1919/20

Contract	Number of vans		Number of horses	Payment 1919/20
	horse	motor		
NcNamara Letter mails between head DOs and stations	309	41	420	£136,994
Allen Parcel mails between Head DOs and stations	257	—	500	£113,170
Birch Brothers Letters and parcels between Head and Sub-District Offices in certain areas	164	—	255	£73,556
Tilling Selected letter and parcel services	—	15	—	£28,916
Leyland Motors Selected parcel services	—	25	—	£17,815
				£370,451

Source: Post 33/1362, M9971/1924, file II.

'The Post Office by the conditions of the transport market since the war, had been forced into a position where throughout the country it had had to face the necessity of becoming its own contractor.'[51] This necessity was short-lived, for the threat of an official service encouraged McNamara to reduce its tender to £127,750 a year, a figure which was only slightly above the estimated cost of £126,000 for a Departmental scheme. McNamara's tender was accepted, and the same process was

14   The issue of uniforms started with the General Post in London in 1793, and was extended to the Twopenny Post in 1837, larger provincial offices in 1856, and finally to the rural letter-carriers in 1872. The original aim was to detect men 'loitering and mis-spending their time in Ale Houses'.

15   This uniform was introduced in 1861: a blue coat with scarlet collar, cuffs and piping; a blue vest similarly piped with scarlet; and blue trousers with a scarlet stripe. It replaced the uniform of 1855 which, with its scarlet frock-coat and tall glazed hat, was 'more fitted for the Fire Brigade than for a peaceful body of men connected with the department of *literae humaniores*'.

16   William Gates, a postman at Hurstpierpoint near Brighton, was photographed in the late 1890s when he had acquired four good conduct stripes as a sign of 'regularity, diligence and fidelity'.

17   A London parcel postman in 1906.

18   Postwomen were employed as a temporary mea[...]
during World War II.

19   Women at work in the Post Office Savings Bank.

20 Derby post office typifies the large offices erected in the later nineteenth century.

21 The sub-post office at Edderton, Ross-shire, was at the other end of the scale.

ABERDEEN
POST OFFICE:
1907
CROWN ST: FRONT:

H·M· OFFICE OF WO
EDINBURGH

22   Aberdeen post office, 1907. 'The State', remarked Herbert Samuel in 1913, 'has the duty of erecting its public buildings in a manner which will contribute to the dignity and the beauty of the towns.'

23   These London postmen in 1908 were undertaking some of the more routine work of sorting.

24   Sorting parcels at Birmingham.

25   Mount Pleasant sorting office in London was the largest in the country. This view of 1929 shows the primary sorting of inland letters.

26   At a later stage of sorting, the letters were divided into individual towns. This is the Birmingham sorting office.

repeated in 1924 when a further Post Office threat induced McNamara to reduce the tender by 20 per cent, which was 'more than sufficient to counterbalance the saving anticipated from the introduction of a Post Office Service'. Although the cost of an official scheme was below Allen's tenders for the parcel service in the 1920s, the Department felt that it was not wise to threaten two major contractors with replacement at the same time. However, when Allen's contract came up for renewal in 1929, the only tender was from McNamara which was accepted. The result was therefore not to replace contractors as both Bruce and Patterson had recommended, but to rely upon a virtual monopoly of one large firm whose price could be controlled by the threat of an official scheme.[52]

The contracts with McNamara were continued throughout the 1930s, until the situation was changed by the outbreak of the Second World War. The contracts were then suspended, and McNamara was paid the actual cost of the service plus prewar profits. This agreement was to run until 1947. Although there was a suspicion that the company was making high profits, and possibly subsidising its commercial operations from the Post Office contract, it was nevertheless accepted that an official scheme would cost more. McNamara had a number of advantages over the Post Office in the provision of transit services: it could pay lower wages; vans could be more fully occupied by switching them between mail and commercial uses; and a smaller reserve fleet was needed. When an official scheme was finally introduced, it was not the result of any change in the economic arguments. It came in consequence of a political decision: the nationalisation of road transport and the commitment of the postwar Labour government to public enterprise. The McNamara contract was phased out between 1947 and 1949 as official motors replaced private contractors in the London transit services.[53]

The 'motorisation' of collections and deliveries

The Post Office not only introduced motor vans in the transit services provided by contractors, for they were also used in a new direction in order to improve labour productivity by 'extending the use of motors to replace pedal cycles for rural deliveries and collections, handcarts for station services and parcel deliveries in towns, and pedal cycles or postmen on foot for letter box collections in towns'. The two uses of official motor vans were, it is true, not always distinct, for it was possible to replace contractors with Departmental vans driven by postmen who could undertake collection and delivery duties as well as the transit work. This readjustment of routines could make comparison between the cost of official and contract services difficult. However, in most cases it is possible to make a distinction between the two motivations and the primary reason for introducing motor vans changed in the 1920s from an attempt to force down contractors' prices to a desire to improve productivity in collection and delivery services. The introduction of vans in place of foot and cycle posts was to have serious consequences for the workforce in the Post Office, and this formed one of the major changes in the Department between the wars. 'There is no motor transport organisation throughout the country', it was claimed by 1933, 'that is in any way comparable with the Post Office fleet.'[54]

The first official experiment in 'motorisation' of postmen was made in 1914 when twenty motor-cycles and side-cars were purchased for rural deliveries and collections. The experiments were resumed after the war, and the number of motor vehicles in use for mail services increased from sixty vans and four motor-cycle combinations in 1920, to 1,002 vans, 176 motor-cycle combinations and forty-eight motor cycles in 1926. Although some of these motors were used to replace contractors' vehicles, they could improve productivity in collections and deliveries, 'because the postman who drives the van can perform work which a contractor's driver could not undertake'. The result was the net loss of about 700 full-time posts and the net creation of about 250 part-time posts, and the major issue which arose from 'motorisation' was precisely this impact on staffing.[55] The first schemes required each van to produce a saving of £120 a year, which was reduced in stages until in 1925 motors could be introduced if they offered a saving of £20, or £5 if there was a desirable improvement in services. These savings came from a reduction in staff costs: between 1920 and 1923, a motor van saved 0.14 of a full-time post; this rose to 0.55 in 1924 as the emphasis changed from replacing contractors to motorising collections and deliveries. In 1928 it was calculated that each vehicle entailed the loss of one full-time post of forty-eight hours a week, and the creation of a part-time duty of nine hours a week. A conflict of interest arose within the Department over the policy. The Establishments Branch faced union pressure to reduce the number of part-time posts, and this was to become a definite commitment; at the same time there was pressure to reduce costs and improve productivity after the war-time collapse of profitability which led the Mails Branch to advocate the use of motors. The issue was put by the union:

> is it right to get rid of two full-time men and to replace them by one full-time man, a motor and a part-time man, where there is no advantage to any one except that the motor and the part-time man together cost less than the full-time man who is displaced? The official answer seems to be in effect that it is sound policy provided that the difference in cost exceeds £20.

It proved difficult to reconcile the aims of the Mails and Establishments

Branches. A disingenuous argument was used to placate the union: vans, it was claimed, were not introduced primarily to reduce the workforce but rather to accelerate the service, which might have the secondary consequence of displacing postmen. This suspect reasoning did nothing to remove the paradox that on the one hand the Establishments Branch was incurring expenditure to replace part-time by full-time posts, while on the other hand the Mails Branch was saving money by the opposite course of action. There was a major inconsistency in the Department's policy, and a lack of agreement whether the aim was to maximise the surplus of the Post Office or to maintain employment. The union pressed during the 1930s for the complete cessation of 'motorisation' and, although this was not accepted by the Department, it is clear that the programme was slowed down and the full benefit of staff economies forgone. It was decided in 1930 that, until there was a general recovery in employment, vans should not be introduced where there was a reduction in the number of full-time posts without an improvement in services. The aims of the Establishments Branch largely prevailed over the ambitions of the Mails Branch.[56]

Although the Post Office had one of the largest motor fleets in the country in the interwar period it had not been created with a great deal of positive enthusiasm. One major use of motors had, indeed, been surrendered: the transfer of parcels from rail to road was abandoned in return for a reduced payment to the railway companies. Official motor schemes for the transit services were intended mainly as a bargaining weapon against contractors, and the Department was relieved when the ploy succeeded. Although the introduction of motors for collection and delivery of the mail promised considerable economies, this was moderated by the desire to maintain employment and to reduce part-time labour. Acceptance of modern technology in inland transport was therefore checked by social considerations; at the same time, the adoption of air transport in overseas services was forced on the Post Office by imperial considerations. This was indeed a major theme in the history of the Post Office: on the one hand the modification of domestic operations by social constraints and on the other the shaping of overseas services by imperial concerns.

Sea and Air:
the Overseas Mail

The decision on Post Office contracts is not a mere Post Office question, but frequently involves considerations of an imperial character affecting our political relations, our colonial empire, the efficiency of our army and navy, and the spread of our commerce. (*First Report from the Select Committee on Packet and Telegraphic Contracts* (PP 1860 XIV), p. 16.)

The inland transport of mail generally rested upon straightforward commercial considerations of securing the best price from the railway companies and road contractors. There was no question of providing a subsidy, and although the procedures for fixing the terms for the use of railways might not have been beyond reproach, they did at least exist. By contrast, the Postmaster General 'has no statutory right to refer disagreements between himself and a Steamship Company to any tribunal'. He could call on a shipowner to carry 'ship letters' at fixed rates, a procedure which was designed for the conveyance of a small pouch of mail and which was 'useless when applied to comprehensive contracts as they give a rate of payment much in excess of that which has hitherto been accepted as reasonable by the Shipping Companies'.[1]

The difference was not only in the legal position of the Department, for the mail contracts with shipping companies could be used in pursuit of a variety of interests unconnected with the Post Office. 'I am certain', remarked Robert Lowe in 1851, 'that it is impossible to exaggerate the weighty political considerations as regards postal matters. It is more important to the colonies than all the constitutions you can give them. . . . If you mean to maintain those colonies, you must either absolutely abandon to them the whole of the government, or else you must shorten the distance; people cannot wait; the larger the communities become, the more impossible it is to wait.'[2] Dr Perry has shown, for example, that the award of contracts to carry mail to Zanzibar was determined as much by a desire to encourage trade, to establish a strategic presence, and to abolish the slave trade, as by postal needs.[3] The carriage of mail overseas by ship and plane clearly raised issues of imperial and foreign policy which did not apply to the use of domestic railways. The mail contract could provide a payment for a better service than was required by strictly commercial considerations. When the Royal Mail Steam Packet Co. lost its mail contract to the West Indies in 1905, the service deteriorated as branch lines were cut and services were altered at will.[4] The mail contract could therefore provide a premium for regularity, frequency, and speed as well as payment for carrying the mail. It might, to go a stage further, also provide an outright subsidy which, particularly in the early stages of development, permitted a service to be established. Mail contracts were never crucial to the survival of railway companies, but they might have been essential, at least in the initial stages, for the viability of steamships and planes.

This raises once again the question of the nature of government involvement in the economy, for a debate was to develop between those who insisted that a strictly commercial relationship based upon adherence to the principle of *laissez-faire* should exist with the companies, and those who were willing to use the Post Office as a means of subsidising British companies. The crucial question was to be: what exactly were mail contracts designed to provide? This was associated with another question: by what criteria should postage rates be fixed? The postage on foreign and colonial letters might be set at uneconomic levels so that the revenue could not cover costs even when the contractors were paid an economic price. A deficit on the overseas mail service might therefore indicate one of two possibilities: the payment of high rates to shipping companies as a form of subsidy; or the use of low postage rates to encourage trade, which might create pressure to economise on the cost of carrying the mail. The desire to foster British commercial and imperial interests might in consequence produce two contradictory impulses, and even when the strict application of financial criteria was rejected there was still scope for disagreement over the best approach. Should companies be paid an uneconomically high rate to encourage shipping and air services, or should the postage be set at an uneconomically low level to foster communications? A consideration of overseas postage rates indicates that there was a trend towards the reduction of charges below the level which was economically viable.

Postage rates: foreign mail

In the case of the inland letters, at the time that my brother made his proposal for the establishment of penny postage, he showed that the cost of conveyance was so small, as not to be appreciable, and therefore

147

he proposed not to take the conveyance into account; but it is very different when you go to distant places, as to India or Australia; then the cost of the conveyance becomes a huge item of account, and that of collection and delivery sinks into comparative insignificance. (Evidence of Frederic Hill to the *Select Committee on Packet and Telegraphic Contracts, 1860*.)[5]

Rowland Hill had argued in *Post Office Reform* for uniformity of charges when justified by uniformity of cost, and he was not in favour of cross-subsidy between profitable and unprofitable service. In the inland post, he had established that the cost of conveyance of a letter was so low that uniformity of charge by distance was justified, but in the overseas post the high cost of transport demanded a variation in the charge according to distance. It was also necessary, in the view of the Hills, for the mail service to each country to cover its costs, and they insisted that the postal revenue must exceed the payment to the shipping company. Postage rates, argued the Hills, could be set at a high level in the foreign service for the volume of traffic was less sensitive to price than in the inland service. Rowland Hill had justified a reduction in the inland rate on the grounds that the traffic would increase to such an extent that the net revenue would be maintained, whereas in the overseas service it was expected that a lower rate would simply produce less revenue. He could point to experience, for he had in 1853 recommended a reduction in colonial postage rates in order to contain the pressure for the introduction of an ocean penny post.

5.1 OVERSEAS POSTAGE RATES, 1840

Colonial: packet. 12 times inland rates, i.e.

up to ½ oz	1*s*
above ½ oz but not exceeding 1 oz	2*s*
above 1 oz but not exceeding 2 oz	4*s*
above 2 oz but not exceeding 3 oz	6*s*

Colonial: private ship. 8 times inland rates, i.e.

up to ½ oz	8*d*
above ½ oz but not exceeding 1 oz	1*s* 4*d*
above 1 oz but not exceeding 2 oz	2*s*8*d*
above 2 oz but not exceeding 3 oz	4*s*

Source: H. Robinson, *The British Post Office. A History* (1948), p.298.

The postage on colonial letters of half an ounce was reduced to sixpence and in his autobiography Hill was to regret his generosity: he had not yet foreseen 'that where long distances are concerned the increase of correspondence bears comparatively little relation to the amount of charge'. The demand for an ocean penny post was, he felt, based on a false analogy between the inland and foreign services: distance did not matter at home so it was assumed to be immaterial abroad; the domestic correspondence increased with lower rates and so, it was believed, would the overseas mail. Rowland was more sceptical, and felt that 'when contractors will undertake to carry letters to India or Australia for the same charge as to Glasgow or Aberdeen – starting at fixed times and proceeding at the highest practicable speed – ocean penny postage will become a practical question. Till then the consideration must, I fear, be postponed.' Cost, argued Frederic Hill, was not an important consideration in writing to the other side of the globe, and he gave greater weight to 'the frequency, regularity, and speed of communication'.[6] These principles for the determination of foreign postage rates were brought into question at the end of the nineteenth century.

A need for international agreement on postage rates had long been apparent, and in the last year of Hill's secretaryship a conference was at last called at the instigation of the Postmaster General of the United States. The exchange of mail between countries at this time involved 'complicated and burdensome' accounting procedures, usually on a bipartite basis, and the Postmaster General of the United States in 1863 suggested that a congress should be held to simplify arrangements. The representatives of fourteen countries, including Britain, met at Paris to consider the introduction of a uniform scale of weights and charges, and to simplify the accounts. The deliberations of the congress resulted in a number of recommendations: the basic unit of weight should be 15 grammes; the charge for the transit of mail across a country should not exceed half that country's inland postage rate; the charge levied by one administration for sea transit of mail for another administration should not exceed the actual payment to the shipping company. Although these recommendations did not have the force of authority, they might be used as the basis of agreements. In 1874 a further congress met in Berne to extend their application. A number of proposals were on the agenda. Each country should, it was suggested, fix its own rates provided that they did not exceed a basic charge for letters of fourpence or forty centimes. Instead of a complicated division of postage between the country of despatch and receipt, it should be retained by the administration in which it was collected. These proposals were not adopted in full, for countries such as Belgium, which provided extensive transit services, argued that they should be recompensed. Rates were therefore laid down for the transit of mail across a country and for the use of shipping services. It was accepted, however, that postage should not be divided and it was also agreed that low, uniform rates should be introduced. The recommended postage rate was 25 centimes for 15 grammes, although it was permitted to go up to a maximum of 32 centimes and to fall to a minimum of 20 centimes, with a surcharge of 50 per cent when a sea voyage of more than 300 nautical miles was involved. These terms were agreed in 1874 and implemented in 1875. At the same time, the Union Générale des Postes was created, which in 1878 became the Union Postale Universelle.[7]

The deliberations of the UPU led to simplification of international postage rates and accounting procedures between administrations. Transit rates were established both for the carriage of mails across a country, and for the use of shipping services provided by other administrations. The postage rate for letters entailing a long sea journey might contain a surcharge in addition to the normal postage, which was in general accord with the principle laid down by the Hills that international rates need not be uniform by distance. However, the situation was to be transformed in the 1880s by the emergence of J. Henniker Heaton, who was elected to the Commons as Conservative member for Canterbury in 1885. Heaton had been born in Kent in 1848, and had emigrated to Australia at the age of sixteen to work on sheep farms and subsequently in journalism. He married the daughter of the proprietor of the newspaper, and in 1884 returned to settle in London. His sole interest in the Commons was the Post Office, and 'nothing happens in the smallest post office of the most remote and obscure township of the whole Empire but Mr Henniker Heaton hears of it, and duly enters the circumstances in his inexorable record'. In 1886 he first moved a resolution in the Commons inviting the government to negotiate the introduction of universal penny postage, and although the motion was defeated his crusade had begun. His policy was: 'Be a Paganini – play on one string' and, as his daughter remarked, 'year after year, he fiddled away on his one string outside the portals of St Martin's le Grand, regardless of all requests to move on'.[8]

A Colonial Conference met in 1887 and considered the virtues of an imperial penny postage. Heaton urged its implementation in the strongest terms. The Post Office, he felt, was 'apt to take narrow and departmental views of postal matters' and 'is undoubtedly hampered by the vicious arrangement whereby it has become the milch cow of successive Chancellors of the Exchequer'. Heaton argued that such an approach was inappropriate and urged that the profit of the Post Office should be fixed at, say, £2.5m; any excess might then be devoted to cheapening and improving services rather than to reducing taxation. High postage charges, he argued, were in themselves a tax which fell on the poor and on 'the initial operations of the most extensive and vital branch of our commerce, that, namely, with our Colonies'. Heaton argued that

The provision of facilities for intercommunication between the various parts of the empire is, like police, defence against foreign invasion, and the raising of supplies, a function of the State. But while it is the duty of the State to provide such facilities even at a loss to itself, the State has no right to turn them into a source of indirect taxation, as it does when it makes a profit out of its postal business.

In Heaton's view, the correct approach was not to make generous contracts with shipping companies in order to encourage the merchant marine; instead he sought to reduce the cost of carrying the mail by fostering competition and removing the subsidies paid to shipping companies. Once costs had been reduced and the services made self-supporting, the postage rate could be lowered. He agreed with the Hills in wishing to fix payment to shipowners at a low level, but he parted with them in his belief that a reduction in postage rates would produce an increase in the correspondence sufficient to maintain the revenue. The service would, in his view, break even at one penny per letter and Heaton claimed that such a charge would allow the Colonial Conference 'by one simple act, to cement the social and political bonds of the empire', providing a 'formidable blow to the foreign competition with which we are threatened in colonial markets', and fostering patriotism. 'It is on behalf of this mighty Empire, this greater Britain across the sea, that we plead for free communication.' Despite this plea, no action was taken, for the existing packet services produced a loss of £292,054 and the reduction of rates to one penny would entail a further loss of £360,000.[9]

The matter of foreign postage rates was raised again in 1897, at both the Washington Congress of the Union Postale Universelle, and at the meeting of colonial premiers in London. At Washington, there was pressure from the German and Austrian Post Offices to reduce land and sea transit rates, as a step towards their abolition. Although their precise proposals were not accepted, the transit rates were reduced for both land and sea services. The Union did not make any change in the international postage rate, but at the Colonial Conference of 1897 Joseph Chamberlain accepted Heaton's case for an imperial penny postage. 'One of the very first things to bind together the sister nations', argued Chamberlain, 'is to have the readiest and the easiest possible communication between their several units, and as far as this country is concerned I believe we should be quite ready to make any sacrifice of revenue that may be required in order to secure a universal penny post throughout the Empire.' A Conference on Postage within the British Empire was summoned to discuss the matter in 1898. The British Post Office suggested a rate of twopence, which was approximately the cost

151

of handling a foreign letter. The Department was loathe to introduce a penny rate which would, it was calculated, reduce revenue by £108,000 in the first year and possibly prepare the way for universal penny postage. It was, however, admitted that imperial considerations might intervene, which was precisely what did happen. At a meeting to clarify the British position at the Conference, the Secretary of the Post Office opposed imperial penny postage. However, Chamberlain felt that 'it was impossible for this country to resist a reduction of postage which large and important colonies were pressing on it': Canada and the Cape had agreed to a penny rate, and it would be difficult for Britain to charge twopence for letters sent to these countries. It was accordingly agreed that the British delegates should propose a rate of two pence, and would give way if Canada and the Cape were strongly in favour of a penny rate. The Chancellor accepted this strategy on condition that steps were taken to reduce payments to shipping companies. The Secretary was alarmed, for 'Imperial Penny Postage would necessarily lead to Universal Penny Postage. We should hardly be able to resist the demand for a $1d$ rate to the States if we were only charging $1d$ for letters conveyed through the States to Canada. Similarly, we should be unable to resist the $1d$ rate to France if we were charging only $1d$ for letters conveyed through France and Italy to India, Australia, and the East.' Despite these doubts, the Department changed its position at the Conference to support an imperial penny rate which was introduced in 1898 for mail to the empire with the exception of Australia, New Zealand and the Cape, who joined over the next few years.[10]

The fears that pressure would develop to extend the penny postage to other countries were soon fulfilled. In 1901 New Zealand introduced a universal penny postage, and the matter was discussed at the Congress of the Union Postale Universelle in 1906. Although the Union did agree to further reductions in transit rates, it did not accept a lower postage rate; instead the weight limit on letters was raised to twenty grammes or an ounce.[11] The British Post Office calculated that a higher weight limit and a penny rate would together produce a reduction in revenue of £640,000, with no prospect that the revenue would recover. The experience of the imperial penny post had not provided a good precedent, for the rate of growth of traffic had not been sufficient to compensate for the loss of revenue. The traffic to India had grown at 3 per cent a year when the postage was $2\frac{1}{2}d$, and during the first year at one penny the growth had been 27 per cent before falling back to 8 per cent. It was indeed fortunate that the increase in traffic was no greater, for each additional letter imposed a loss. The cost of a colonial letter was calculated in 1905 to be $1.3d$, which meant that there was a loss on each item of $0.3d$. The cost of a foreign letter was $1.1d$, so that universal penny postage would push the foreign letter service into deficit with no prospect that the immediate loss of revenue would be restored. However, this damning assessment of the economics of the foreign and colonial mail service did not close the matter.

In 1905, Heaton established a League for Universal Penny Postage, and pressure mounted for a penny rate to the United States and France. In 1908, a penny post was indeed introduced between Britain and the United States when the American Post Office came forward with an offer of a rate of two cents or one penny per half ounce, which was modified at the request of Britain to one penny for one ounce in order to establish uniformity with the empire rate. This, it was calculated, would reduce the revenue by £136,000, and the Post Office was despondent about the prospect of recovering this sum. 'Henniker Heaton and the like', complained the Secretary, 'talk gaily about recouping the loss by the increased correspondence which the reduction would produce; but our estimate is that new matter at 1d an ounce would do no more than pay for the increased cost of handling it.' In 1907, 18 million letters were sent to the United States, and in 1913 24.5 million or an increase of 36 per cent, which was not proportionate to the reduction in postage. The demand for the service was, as Frederic Hill had argued, not responsive to price. The reduction in the rate did, however, have a political attraction. The Postmaster General explained to Asquith:

> The revenue of the Post Office since I have been there shows a very large increase. The public – the Post Office users – have therefore a considerable claim that some portion of the increased revenue that they have contributed should be devoted to postal improvements – and the reduction in the postage to America would be much the most popular and profitable object. . . . I feel confident that the introduction of Penny Postage to the U.S. would be extremely popular, and particularly popular in business circles, as materially very advantageous to trade. From the point of view of the Government, it would, therefore, be well worth doing this year, and give them a fillip in quarters where they most require it.

This was the limit of concession, and Heaton's campaign for a penny post to the rest of the world came to nothing.

It might indeed seem absurd that it cost 1d to send a letter to Fiji and 2½d to Calais, but the conclusion to be drawn from this anomaly was not necessarily that the rate to France should be reduced. Rather, the rate to the empire had been determined without regard to costs, and the principle laid down by the Hills had been rejected.[12] The Hills had also argued that the payments to the shipping companies should exclude any element of subsidy. Competition, they stressed, should be fostered by

153

regular tenders and short contracts, and the payment should not exceed the 'sea postage' on the letters carried. How far were these policies implemented?

Admiralty control and the development of steamships, 1837–60

In the 1830s, mail was carried either as ship letters on any vessel leaving Britain, or by packets operated by the Post Office. The Post Office had been a pioneer of the use of steamships, and between 1821 and 1826 had made the 'bold decision' to establish continuous services throughout the year on the various routes to Ireland. Philip Bagwell has noted 'the superior regularity and punctuality of the sailings of the Royal Mail steamboats' which set the standards of efficiency which private operators sought to match.[13] The Post Office's financial record was less laudable. By 1836, the Department owned and operated twenty-six steamers with a capital cost of £273,018 and ran packet stations at Dover, Weymouth, Milford, Holyhead, Liverpool and Portpatrick. In four years between 1832 and 1836, this considerable enterprise produced a loss of £154,957, and it is not surprising that the Commissioners appointed to enquire into the management of the Post Office complained of 'the total inadequacy of the existing system to ensure efficient service, strict economy, and regularity of accounts'. They concluded that the packets should, as far as possible, be replaced by contracts with private ships, and that the remainder be transferred to the Admiralty.[14] This suggestion was implemented in 1837. In future, the Post Office was to 'point out the services required for the due conveyance of letters from one port to another, and the Admiralty will be charged with the execution of this service'. Whenever possible, contracts were to be used as the best means of securing 'economy and simplicity of arrangement'. The Post Office and Treasury were to agree on the nature of the service to be provided, and would then inform the Admiralty which would 'enter into contracts accordingly and superintend their enforcement and execution'. This was, argued the Treasury, a rational division of responsibility, and such was the administrative system which existed until 1860.[15] The manner in which it operated may be indicated by considering two of the most important contracts, with the Peninsular and Oriental Steam Navigation Co. for the service to India, and with Cunard for the service to North America.

Thomas Waghorn, an ex-naval officer who had joined the Bengal Marine, in the late 1820s proposed the establishment of a steamship service between England and India via the Cape. This was rejected by the Post Office as a 'wild scheme', and in the 1830s attention turned to the shorter 'overland route' through the Mediterranean to Alexandria, across Egypt, and by sea from Suez to India. The eastern leg of the voyage was at first undertaken by vessels of the East India Co. and the western leg by the Admiralty, but by the mid-1840s responsibility for the entire sea-route passed to the P & O. This company had entered the trade with Spain and Portugal after the Napoleonic Wars, and in 1837 secured a contract from the Admiralty to carry mail to Portugal and Malta. In 1840 the Admiralty invited tenders for a steamship service to Alexandria, and the company won this contract; it added a contract for a service from Suez to Calcutta in 1844.[16] The P & O had secured a dominance in the Indian mail service which it was to maintain for the next hundred years, a state of affairs which did not attract universal support. The question arose whether the monopoly of the P & O produced an efficient and cheap service. 'What we dread in India', remarked one merchant, 'is that we should be entirely left at the mercy of one company.'[17]

The SS *William Fawcett* was the first P & O steamship to carry mail.

The contracts could be terminated at the end of 1852, and a Select Committee on Steam Communications with India was appointed in 1851 to consider what policy should be adopted. The company was receiving a considerable sum for the mail services. The contract of 1840 had been worth £38,000 in its first year, falling by £1,000 a year; this was replaced in 1849 by a contract worth £24,000 in its first year, falling by

155

£500 a year. The payment for the service east of Suez came to £115,000 for the route to Calcutta and a further £45,000 to Hong Kong. The critics of the P & O felt that these payments made it a pampered monopolist, immune to the pressures of competition. Merchants and residents of India complained that the P & O had fallen behind the standards attained on the Atlantic, and 'had done little towards introducing into their line those great and important improvements as regards speed, which have of late years taken place in Ocean Steam Navigation'. The vessels, so it was claimed, were crowded, fares high, and freight rates excessive.[18] Shipowners were also aggrieved. The British merchant marine had lost protection against foreign competition, and the General Shipowners' Society argued that the industry's problems should not be aggravated by giving unfair advantages to some owners at the expense of others. Mail contracts had, it was feared, 'become to a considerable degree bounties in favour of contractors, enabling them to defy the competition of less favoured individuals, and partaking in consequence much of the character of a monopoly'. Revenue from the carriage of mail allowed the contractor, so the Society claimed, to undercut competitors in the carriage of passengers and freight.[19] The Select Committee was in general agreement with these critics of the P and O's monopoly, and suggested that there should in future be two distinct services to India, put out to separate tender. The creation of 'wholesome competition' was expected to produce a better service, for

> any arrangement which might tend to promote an exclusive traffic on the Indian lines in the hands of one Company is open to serious objection. . . . [The members of the Committee] wish to lay down the principle, that the only security to the public for the full advantage of these communications, must consist in open and fair competition. . . . It can only be effected by ample notice, and full particulars of the terms and conditions required being given, so as to enable all parties to enter the field who may be desirous of tendering for the service.[20]

But could the strategy succeed?

Competition, claimed Captain J. H. Wilson, late of the Indian Navy, would soon give way to collusion. The cost of establishing a line of steamers to the East was high, and was not analogous with the route to America. 'Competition in Indian steam communication is not a thing which is to be drawn forth by holding your finger up; it is too expensive a matter.'[21] This was fair comment, for operations in the East required not only a large investment in ships but also in coaling stations, dry docks, and engineering works which simply did not exist. P & O employed 60,000 tons of shipping and 3,000 seamen in order to supply coal, at twice the cost of the Atlantic. These high overheads, argued Arthur Anderson of the P & O, meant that long contracts were necessary, for 'if the contract is broken at short intervals, I consider that very few prudent men would embark a large capital in an undertaking attended with so much risk as a steam navigation company, especially if they thought that the principal object for which the vessels were constructed would be taken from them in a short period'.[22] In any case, the benefits of the mail contract were, in Anderson's opinion 'greatly overrated':

> The sum paid for the postal service on that line of communication does not constitute a subsidy or bonus. . . . It was not a premium given to establish Steam Navigation with India, but the consideration for performing a valuable public service. . . . And the disadvantages to which the postal service subjects the company in carrying on its commercial operations, and otherwise, are such, I submit, as in a great degree to neutralize its supposed advantages.

The service could not be reduced in slack seasons, and had to run throughout the year with large, fast vessels; it was also necessary to provide a reserve fleet. Merchandise trade was checked by the need for transhipment on the overland route across the isthmus of Suez, and in general 'the possession of a contract for the postal service is far from being of that overwhelming importance in the Steam Communications with India at which it has been estimated'.[23] This might be dismissed as special pleading, yet it is significant that the Eastern Steam Navigation Co., which had in 1851 offered to take over the service, was not able to compete when tenders were invited.[24] The new contract of 1853 was awarded to P & O, giving the company £199,600 a year for the entire service to India and China.[25]

The Cunard company had meanwhile achieved an equally dominant position on the Atlantic, despite the fact that on this route there was a real prospect of competition. The initial award of the contract to Cunard is, indeed, puzzling. When the Admiralty in 1838 invited tenders for a service to Halifax and New York, offers were submitted by two established companies already operating a transatlantic steamship service: the St George Steam Packet Co., and the Great Western Steamship Co., which both offered to provide a monthly service to Halifax and New York for £65,000. However, neither could meet the Admiralty's terms in full, for the vessels of the St George Steam Packet Co. were underpowered and the Great Western Steamship Co. required eighteen to twenty-four months to provide a full complement of ships. This provided the opportunity which Samuel Cunard eagerly seized. He was a Nova Scotia shipowner who had recently arrived in London, possibly attracted by the government's advertisement. He made contacts with

157

politicians and shipbuilders and in 1839 he offered to supply a service which would start in 1840 and run twice a month to Halifax and Boston. His plan was, as Francis Hyde remarked, 'simple and effective': he ordered enough ships with early delivery dates to implement the mail service in full and he started negotiations from this strong position. Once he had secured the mail contract, he had to raise the necessary capital to build the ships; indeed, he hoped that the security of the mail contract would allow him to secure enough money to build larger ships than specified in his original order. He was taking a gamble by ordering the ships in advance, and he succeeded where his more cautious rivals failed. His initial offer was £55,000 a year, and by 1841 payment had risen to £80,000 to take account of more onerous stipulations and the need to provide an additional ship. Cunard had seized the initiative.[26]

The Great Western Co. in particular was bitterly resentful of the award of the contract to Cunard, and was even more aggrieved in 1846 when it discovered that a fresh contract was to be made without an invitation to tender.[27] Cunard had again taken the initiative. Rather than waiting for the government to seek new tenders, he made a unilateral offer which ensured that there was no point of comparison and no means of securing competition. The contracts, he admitted, 'have all proceeded from offers emanating from myself'.[28] Although a Select Committee was appointed to consider the affair, the contract was signed before it could report. This Committee accepted that the service had been efficiently performed by Cunard, and declined to speculate whether better terms could have been secured by competition. Nevertheless, the Committee did regret that the interests of the Great Western Co. had been injured and 'will be glad if, on any future extension of the Royal Mail Service, it receives the favourable consideration of the Government'.[29] This was little consolation to the Great Western Co., which could claim with justice that it was 'the first to lay down, equip, and send to sea a steam-ship with the object of establishing a line of steam packets between England and the United States, and solving the problem of transatlantic steam navigation, with engines of infinitely larger dimensions than it had previously been thought possible to provide fuel for, or to keep at work the number of days required in a passage across the Atlantic'.[30] Technical dynamism was as nothing besides the superior political skills of Cunard, and the Great Western could only fulminate after the event at 'manifest injustice'.

The continuation of the contract with Cunard came under persistent criticism. One London merchant and shipowner, Robert McCalmont, in 1851 strongly attacked what he saw as a parcelling out of the seas to 'intriguing companies' and 'monstrous and intolerable monopolists'. The award of contracts on the Atlantic, he felt, was 'perfectly preposterous' in view of the number of ships which were available.[31] Rowland Hill had, of course, always argued that mail services should be self-supporting and the deficit on the packets was a standing reproach. In 1853 the Treasury agreed that it was necessary to review the cost and standard of service, for the position had changed since the contracts had first been awarded. Although creation of a 'complete postal system upon the ocean' was 'beyond the reach of merely commercial enterprise', its future operation was a different matter. The cost of packets had, it was felt, grown out of all proportion and rules might be formulated to secure a reduction in payment. A committee was appointed under the chairmanship of Canning, the Postmaster General, to consider the matter.

5.2 COST AND POSTAL REVENUE OF PACKETS, 1852/3

	transmarine postage	contract payment	deficit
North America	£120,863	£188,040	£67,177
East Indies	£127,896	£199,600	£71,704
West Indies & Brazil	£85,410	£270,000	£184,590
All packets	£479,600	£822,390	£342,790

Source: PP 1852–3 XCV, *Return of the amount of postage money actually received by the Post Office for mails conveyed by steamers and other vessels under contract with H.M. government . . .*, p.235

The early contracts were defended by the committee, for 'the heavy expense and serious risk of loss attending the introduction of ocean steamers might probably have prevented the experiments being tried, or at least might have delayed it for a long time, had not aid been granted to its promoters by the State'. The situation was thought to have changed once the lines had been established:

it becomes important to consider whether the lines which have been opened cannot be made self-supporting, that is to say, whether they cannot be so carried on as to produce a postal revenue sufficient to cover the expense involved in their maintenance. Where this cannot be done, the continuance of the line should become a subject of serious consideration, and although there will no doubt be cases in which the political and social interests concerned in it are of such magnitude as to render it a matter of national importance to maintain it even at a pecuniary loss, we think that such cases should be closely examined, and that none but the most convincing reasons should be admitted for the permanent support of any line at a cost exceeding the revenue which it can be made to produce.

159

Where a regular and frequent service was established, 'public competition for the conveyance of the mails can hardly be too frequently, or too openly invited'.[32] Although Hill welcomed the report of the Canning committee as support for his policy,[33] even when he became sole Secretary in 1854 its application remained doubtful because of the division of responsibility between the Post Office, Admiralty and Treasury.

Samuel Cunard, loyal to his policy of seizing the initiative, in 1857 requested an extension of his contract for an additional five years, although it still had four years to run. The Post Office was not impressed, taking the view that the time for liberal subsidies on the Atlantic was over and arguing for short contracts at a rate which merely covered the freight of mail bags. The Admiralty did not agree, and accepted that 'the best course for insuring a satisfactory performance . . . will be by prolonging the contract'; it was 'most important that the superiority of the Royal Packet Line should be maintained'. The concern of the Admiralty was no doubt the competition of the heavily subsidised American Collins Line which had started operations in 1850, in comparison with which the 'pecuniary question of postage is of minor importance'. Cunard's contract was indeed extended in 1858. This did not prevent the award of a further contract in 1859, again against the advice of the Post Office, to the Atlantic Royal Mail Steam Navigation Company. This line commenced operations in 1858, running a service to North America from Galway, and in the same year a mail contract was secured from the government of Newfoundland. The British government came under strong pressure, particularly from Irish MPs, to follow this lead and in 1859 a contract was agreed for a fortnightly service at an annual subsidy of £78,000. The Post Office expressed grave doubts, feeling that any long-term agreement was unnecessary in view of the 'vast mercantile traffic' and the prospect of competition; Cunard was in any case already paid for the service. The 'Galway' contract was indeed to prove a disaster. One vessel was almost immediately lost and the others were quite inadequate for service on the North Atlantic, so that in 1861 the contract was suspended. The whole episode raised grave doubts about the management of the packet contracts by the Treasury and Admiralty. An offer from the well-established Liverpool, New York & Philadelphia Steamship Co. of William Inman to carry mail for the 'sea-postage' had been rejected, and the untried and incompetent novices of the Galway Line had secured a contract. Allegations that the Galway Line had offered large sums to parliamentary lobbyists in order to secure the contract added to the general air of recrimination and confusion. Clearly, the administrative structure which had existed since 1837 needed a thorough reassessment.[34]

The control of packets was indeed returned to the Post Office in

1860. The Select Committee on Packet and Telegraphic Contracts, after considering the events of the late 1850s, concluded 'that it is quite practicable to dispense with large subsidies in cases where ordinary traffic supports several lines of steamers'. Subsidies were, it was felt, no longer required on the North Atlantic in order 'to secure a regular, speedy, and efficient postal service' and, as the Treasury remarked, 'the Packet mail service has become as purely civilian as that of the transmission of mails by railway'.[35] It remained for the Treasury to advise the Post Office on the use of its new powers. 'Abstract principles' were not favoured, although the Treasury did suggest in a minute of 1860 the 'leading considerations' which the Post Office should take into account. Contracts should be made with dependable firms so that an 'apparent saving' did not place commercial and imperial interests at risk as a result of irregularity. Accordingly, the lowest tender should not necessarily be accepted and the Department should be cautious about awarding contracts to inexperienced firms. The Post Office should by preference work with established companies with a proven record, without excluding competition. The Treasury accepted that long contracts might be one-sided, preventing the use of new services and frustrating reductions in payment. Ideally, contracts should be terminable at a year's notice, although this could not be rigidly applied: a long contract might be needed to safeguard a large investment and the Post Office should use its discretion to secure the best results for the public service. Generally, the recommendations of the Canning Report were to be followed: subsidies might be paid to establish a route and a lower rate should be offered to continue a service. The Treasury was alarmed that the deficit had in fact mounted since the Canning Report: in 1853, the packets cost £877,797 and the sea postage amounted to £521,613; in 1859, the cost was £977,000 and the sea postage £393,500. The reduction in postage rates made it all the more imperative to secure economy, and the Treasury urged 'a recurrence to the principles laid down by Lord Canning's Committee'.[36] It was soon to appear that the application of these 'leading considerations' was to cause a major crisis within the Department.

The Post Office and packet contracts in the 1860s

The Post Office is very much averse to loss of any kind on any part of its business; it is a constant object with us to diminish and ultimately to do away with loss. (Frederic Hill, evidence to PP 1866 IX, *Select Committee on East India Communications*, Q 335.)

No item of the public expenditure is so reproductive, and . . . in reference to the so-called 'loss', with equal consistency might the farmer put down the cost of the seed which he sows as a 'loss', without taking into acount the crop produced by it. (Investigator, *Our Ocean Steam Postal Communications: Their Cost and National Advantages* (1867), p. 4.)

The task of applying the recommendations of the Canning Report and the Treasury minute of 1860 fell to Frederic Hill, and he proceeded to pursue economy with such vigour that many, inside the Department as well as outside, considered that the efficiency of the service was threatened. The 'very strong difference of opinion'[37] which resulted was to be one of the major conflicts between the conceptions of the Hills and their successors at St Martin's le Grand. It was in this clash of views over the proper basis for packet contracts that the Hills' ideology of 'economical reform' was to be overturned.

The Treasury, in the period before the Post Office took over responsibility in 1860, did 'not regard it as conclusive' whether a service paid, for there were many political and commercial considerations to set against postage receipts. 'The first charge upon [Post Office] revenue is, to supply reasonably all portions of Her Majesty's dominions with postal communication,' commented George Hamilton of the Treasury, 'I do not regard the Post Office revenue as merely a question of revenue. . . . The primary object is, to have the service very efficiently performed.' In any case, if a service did not pay at once, the traffic would soon increase and so convert a loss into a profit, 'whilst an enormous advantage will arise to the country commercially and socially, in proportion to the facilities which you afford'.[38] Such an approach was anathema to the Hills, and they sought in the 1860s to impose a rigid adherance to the principle that services should be self-supporting. Frederic stressed that the Post Office was 'a great commercial department' in which the aim, as in a private firm, was to secure a profit. The provision of services which did not pay in order to encourage trade and enterprise did not appeal: 'the same arguments appear to me to be applicable to everything else; the conveyance of passengers and the conveyance of cotton, for example. In point of fact, it is protection that is asked for.'[39] In the 1860s he had the opportunity to apply his principles of free competition and financial viability to the packet services. 'Ever since the mail packet contracts were placed under the management of the Post Office', the Treasury was assured in 1865,

it has been the aim of this Department to make the packet service self-supporting; and partly by its success in obtaining contracts on lower terms than formerly, partly by an increase, in certain cases, in the rates of postage, and partly by an augmentation in the number of letters, much progress has been made towards this end; and if the same policy be steadily pursued, I have little doubt that in the course of a few years the large sum which British taxpayers are still called on to contribute towards making good the excess of the packet subsidies beyond the amount of sea postage, will nearly, if not entirely, disappear.[40]

In pursuit of this end, notice was given in 1867 to terminate the contracts with both the Cunard and P & O companies.

Frederic Hill believed that the large number of steamships on the Atlantic made it possible to avoid long-term contracts and to obtain a service in return for the sea-postage. The American Post Office agreed to provide a service to Britain on the same basis, and the intention was that each administration would in future bear the full cost of the outward carriage of mail without any complex reimbursements.[41] Tenders were invited from shipping companies to carry mail from Britain on three days of the week at a rate of one shilling a pound for letters, threepence for newspapers, and five pence for books. Contracts were soon agreed with Inman and North German Lloyd to cover two days, and a third service remained. The problem facing the Post Office was that Cunard had rejected the new approach and instead offered a long, fixed-price contract for both outward and inward services for ten years at an annual payment of £95,000. This would entail the United States reimbursing Britain for the use of the company's ships. The British Post Office stood to lose from the contract if the Americans reduced the rate paid for the carriage of mail or did not use Cunard's ships; the company was, of course, insuring itself against either eventuality. The cherished intentions of Hill had been rejected by Cunard; Frank Scudamore, who took over the negotiations in Hill's absence, was in no doubt that Cunard's offer should be accepted. The company carried 46 per cent of the outward mail, and Scudamore feared disruption of the service and loss of efficiency. Pragmatism demanded acceptance of Cunard's offer which he also justified on financial grounds, for Scudamore calculated that within ten years the fixed payment would fall below the sea postage. Hill was outraged that such a step should have been taken 'without my concurrence or even my knowledge', and he insisted that an adequate service could be maintained without the use of Cunard's fleet. Hill was sceptical that a long contract would produce a profit, for it could not be certain that the American Post Office would continue to use Cunard's ships for the homeward voyage. From the Company's point of view, the attraction of a fixed price for both outward and inward journeys was the security it offered against loss of earnings, and Inman was quick to complain that 'such undue preference in favour of the Cunard company would enable them to compete unfairly with us in the general Atlantic trade'.

Such was the disagreement within the Department, and the Secretary, John Tilley, was to side with Scudamore against Hill. Tilley had treated the foreign and colonial services as a separate department which was not answerable to the Secretary or Postmaster General; in 1867 he only regretted that he had not acted sooner in removing Hill. The opinion of Hill that his approach would create an efficient service was dismissed as conjecture; Scudamore's case – so Tilley believed – was based on the 'plain statement of facts' that Cunard offered a regular, certain service. Tilley was highly critical of Hill's management of the packet contracts:

> It is, it seems to my humble judgement, the paramount duty of the Post Office to make the best arrangements for the carriage of mails which, having a due regard to the revenue, are within our power; and that the merchants and others of this country have a right to demand this at our hands . . . [Hill] having taken up the idea that every separate branch of the Service must be made to pay its own expenses . . . has suffered it to run away with him and has failed to see that it might lead to disaster. From this point of view . . . the advantage of maintaining a service across the Atlantic which has always been mentioned with eulogy whenever it has been spoken of – the pride of the English nation in their ocean mails which hitherto have beaten all competitors are things of nought as compared with a balance on the right side of the ledger.

Lower priority was to be given to a search for economy than to securing 'the best possible service'.[42]

This change in policy entailed both the renegotiation of the postal convention with America, and the termination of the contracts with Inman and North German Lloyd. Meanwhile, Tilley requested Cunard to provide a service for 12 months on the understanding that tenders would subsequently be invited for a longer contract worth £80,000 a year for three voyages a week. At this point problems arose, for when tenders were invited in 1868 Cunard and Inman formed an alliance. They both declined to follow the terms of the official tender, and offered to enter a ten-year contract which would give Cunard £100,000 a year for two voyages a week and Inman £50,000 for one voyage a week. Scudamore was fatalistic, accepting that no other offers were likely to be forthcoming and that 'the only course seems to be to try to obtain better terms by negotiation'. The terms were indeed reduced to £70,000 and £35,000 for a contract of seven years plus one year's notice, in part because North German Lloyd agreed to carry mail from Southampton in return for the sea postage. It is not surprising that when the contract came before the Commons many members were horrified and a Select Committee was appointed to consider the matter. This produced an

164

acrimonious debate between Hill and Scudamore, who both took their stand upon the Treasury minute of 1860. Hill interpreted this as providing firm instructions to the Department to avoid long contracts, to determine payment by the amount of mail carried, and to make services self-supporting. Scudamore with some justification argued that the Treasury had only suggested the 'leading considerations' which should be pursued according to the merits of each case, and that it had not laid down abstract principles to be rigidly enforced. The Select Committee in the event rejected the arguments of Scudamore and agreed with Hill that there was 'no longer any necessity for fixed subsidies for terms of years' on the Atlantic. Despite this endorsement of Hill's views, the contracts with Cunard and Inman were implemented.[43] Although Hill had won the debate he had lost the control of policy at St Martin's le Grand.

The new contracts provided for the carriage of mail in both directions across the Atlantic, which contradicted the postal convention with the United States. By refusing to tender in one direction, Cunard and Inman were passing the risk of a loss of earnings to the British Post Office: they would hand over any payment received from the American Post Office and would be guaranteed a fixed annual sum from Britain. The existing postal convention was terminated, and in 1869 Anthony Trollope was despatched to Washington with 'plenipotentary' powers to negotiate a new agreement which would take into account the change in British policy. The British proposal was that the two administrations should make joint contracts for the carriage of mail; the Americans refused and insisted that there should be unrestricted competition on the basis of annual tenders. The American administration was rightly critical of the British Post Office for stating the payment for the service in advance in its invitation to tender, arguing that if this had been left open Britain would have secured more favourable terms. 'It is not doubted', argued the American Post Office, 'that under the operation of free competition on each side, the cost of the transatlantic service by first-class steamers of approved speed, can be lessened from year to year.' It was eventually agreed that each country was to make its own arrangements for the conveyance of mail, and the postage rate was fixed at sixpence or twelve cents. Trollope was scathing about the convention, for he took the view that the Americans were able to secure cheap services only because the British Post Office agreed to fixed-price, long-term contracts which gave the shipowners security to build suitable steamers. The convention meant, he complained, that 'everything possible should be done, at a heavy expenditure on the part of England, to expedite the mails from England to America, and that nothing should be done by America to expedite the mails from thence to us'.[44]

Although Frederic Hill had fallen into the trap of a dogmatic inter-pretation of the Treasury minute of 1860, and had behaved in a somewhat high-handed manner in his administration of the foreign and colonial business, it is certainly possible to sympathise with his assessment of the state of shipping services on the Atlantic. It is doubtful whether Trollope was right that long-term, fixed-price contracts were necessary by the 1860s for regular, fast services on the American routes. There had been a major change in the economics of steamship operation on the Atlantic since the 1850s. The early steamships had wooden hulls and were driven by paddles, and a change started in 1850 when William Inman introduced iron-hulled steamers driven by screws. Paddle steamers had a much smaller passenger capacity than screw steamers which were able to exploit the expanding market for emigrant passages to America. This gave them a financial edge in competition on the Atlantic, and paddle steamers could only operate so long as they received considerable sums for carrying the mail. Paddle steamers con-tinued to have positive virtues into the 1850s, for they were proven and reliable, and Cunard could therefore offer safety and regularity which were so vital in carrying the mail. This gave some substance to Samuel Cunard's argument in 1860 that 'I do not think that any postal line, a line to be conducted for the service of the Post Office, can exist without a subsidy'. Postal and commercial services were, he argued, different: he employed about thirty screw steamers on the commercial services which were profitable; on the postal contracts he used nine paddle steamers which cost twice as much, carried less cargo and could only operate with a subsidy. The argument had ceased to be valid in the 1860s when screw ships could match paddle steamers in speed and reliability, and could earn a profit without a large subsidy. A separate postal line at this point was no longer needed. The Cunard company was noted for its technical conservatism, leaving the costs and risks of innovations to others, and concentrating upon safety and reliability. The loyalty to the wooden paddle steamer was encouraged by the technical caution of the Admiralty which was slow to accept the virtues of screw propulsion, and it was not until 1862 that permission was given to Cunard to build a screw steamer for the mail service. The company was also slow to move into the emigration business which had formed a main-stay of Inman's trade from the 1850s. Cunard had insisted in 1860 that mail ships should not carry emigrants since it would be impossible to save both post and passengers in the event of an accident. Nevertheless, in the same year he did enter the emigrant trade and it was clearly no longer possible to claim that the mail service required a separate fleet of subsidised steamers operating on long, fixed-price contracts. Inman was quite willing to carry mail on his ordinary commercial ships at freight rates

1840 BRITANNIA 1,135 tons

1862 SCOTIA 3,871 tons

1874 BOTHNIA 4.535 tons

1907 LUSITANIA 31,500 tons

The *Britannia* was one of Cunard's first mail steamers, and the *Scotia* was the last paddle steamer built by the company for the postal service. The switch to screw steamers and the continuing increase in size provided the background to the fall in freight rates and mail contract prices on the Atlantic.

and the special position of Cunard was under threat. Mail contracts might in the days of paddle vessels have provided a crucial element in the development of steam navigation on the Atlantic; by the 1860s they were, if anything, protecting Cunard from more dynamic rivals. It was becoming increasingly difficult for Cunard to maintain its privileged status and at this point collusion with Inman had obvious advantages. The loser was the Post Office.[45]

There was at least a chance that Hill's policy might have succeeded on the Atlantic if a firm line had been taken with Cunard. There was very little likelihood that his approach would flourish in the East where there was no prospect of competition. Frederic Hill, like Rowland, had a tendency to proceed from dogmatic beliefs rather than a pragmatic assessment of the possible limits of action. This was abundantly clear in the handling of P & O's contract for the carriage of mail to India. In the mid-1860s Frederic attempted to increase postage rates in order to make the Indian service self-supporting. This strategy was rejected by the Select Committee on East India Communications, which

> cannot assent to the doctrine, that interests so important from every point of view, whether political, social, or commercial, as those which connect the United Kingdom with the largest and most valuable possessions of the Crown, should be prejudiced by an insufficient postal service, because the establishment of an efficient service might leave an apparent loss of no great magnitude. . . . [A] question of profit or loss, within reasonable bounds, is a consideration entitled to little weight in the case of so important a postal service as that between England and India.[46]

Despite this clear advice, notice was given in 1867 to terminate the P & O contracts. Outrage was expressed by some MPs that the opinion of the Select Committee had been ignored and 'adherence to pedantic theories' upheld. 'It is no secret', claimed one Member, 'indeed, it is evident that the proposal of the Government is based on the peculiar views of Mr Hill. He is a public servant of great experience and ability, but a most dangerous man if you make him your master instead of adviser, and follow out his views with regard to postal communication.'[47]

The existing contract gave P & O a payment of 4s 6d per nautical mile or £230,000, and the company argued that competition from subsidised French ships and the increase in costs entitled it to a larger sum. The attempts of P & O to enter into a private agreement with the Department to continue the service were rebuffed, and Hill insisted that competitive tenders be invited in order to prevent the payment of an 'exorbitant subsidy'. His strategy failed, for only two tenders were received, from the P & O to fulfil the entire service for six years at £500,000 a year, and from the Società Italiana di Navigazione Adriatico Orientale to provide a service between Brindisi and Alexandria. 'The lesson we have now learnt should not readily be forgotten,' remarked Tilley, for

> we shall do well to recognise the fact that the Peninsular and Oriental Co. having established the route to India and China to the practical exclusion of all competitors the question is no longer whether or no we shall employ them for the conveyance of the mails, but simply what sum we are to pay them for their services.
>
> It may be . . . that the Company having come to the same conclusion will be indisposed to make any abatement in their terms; but there is no doubt . . . that they were much alarmed at the possibility of the withdrawal of the Post Office subsidy – as well they might be – and that to be able to calculate upon the subsidy as a somewhat permanent source of income would, to say the least, be very agreeable to the office bearers of the company as well as to the shareholders.

The best strategy might therefore be to suggest a longer contract, and the outcome was to be far removed from the approach advocated by Hill, amounting to a form of partnership between the Department and the company.

The company proposed to open its books in order to show that its tender was justified, and the inspection was undertaken by Scudamore. He felt that the offer of £500,000 was not unrealistic, but he did suggest that a lower price might be accepted if the company's dividend was guaranteed. The P & O agreed to accept £400,000 for twelve years, 'on condition that, when the fund of the company accruing for dividend from all sources rises above the sum required for a dividend of 8 per cent, the Post Office shall have one fourth of the excess, and that, on the other hand, when the like fund, from causes not within their control, falls below the amount required for the payment of a 6 per cent dividend, the subsidy shall be increased by the amount of the deficiency'. This would, felt Scudamore, be advantageous, for the P & O had only once paid a dividend below 7 per cent. The nation wanted 'secure and regular communication', despite the fact that the revenue from passengers and freights fell short of the sum which was required to maintain the service and to pay a modest dividend; the deficiency had therefore to be made up by the government. This should not, argued Scudamore, be viewed as a loss but rather 'as the cost of keeping up communications with the East'. It was not necessary, he argued, to make the service self- supporting, and the correct approach was to ask: what was the proper price to pay for the service which the nation required?

169

Parliament had declared in favour of rapid, regular, and frequent service, and the correct price 'must in every such case be that, which taken together with the revenue from Traffic, will cover the working expenses and give a moderate dividend on capital'. There were two radically different approaches: Hill started from the postal revenue and attempted to reduce payments to this figure; Scudamore started from the cost to the company of supplying the standard of service required by the State. 'It is impossible', argued Scudamore,

> to obtain good service on any other terms. The question cannot be dealt with on commercial principles because the conditions of the Postal service compel the contractors to disregard commercial principles. If they were guided solely by commercial principles the Peninsular and Oriental Company would not sail as many ships – in the dull as in the brisk season – would not sail on fixed days when by sailing a little sooner or a little later they could secure a good freight; would not go at full speed when half speed would serve their turn; and would build no bigger and no better ships than the trade absolutely required. For the sake of keeping up such a communication with the East as the Nation requires they must set commercial principles at defiance, and, cost what it may, the Nation must either pay them what they lose or forego the communication.

A new contract based upon such co-operation between company and Department was signed by the end of 1867.[48]

The defeat of Hill seemed to be complete. Competition and self-supporting finance had been denied on the services to both America and India. In the case of the Atlantic, the explanation was largely the power of the so-called 'Liverpool ring' of shipowners rather than the economics of shipping services. There is a strong suspicion that rates on the Atlantic were unnecessarily high, and the P & O claimed that the application of Cunard's rate to its service would have produced a payment of £744,142.[49] Disagreement on the principles for establishing the payments to shipping companies was to split the Department in the later 1860s, and was to result in the mutual recriminations before the Select Committee on Mail Contracts of 1869 as Frederic Hill and Frank Scudamore roundly condemned each other's policy. Hill certainly did apply too strict an interpretation of the Canning Report and the Treasury minute of 1860 and he ignored the views of the Select Committee on East India Communications. It would, however, be difficult to differ from the opinion of many merchants that the Post Office 'is not firm enough with the Cunard company'.[50] Whatever the assessment of the policy which was pursued, one thing is abundantly clear: the Hills' ethic of economical reform was defeated. 'Mr Scudamore's object', the Postmaster General had commented in 1867, 'is to secure for the merchants the best and most speedy mode of transmission for letters. Mr Hill's object is to secure the Post Office from any loss even should the postal arrangements not be as satisfactory as they would be under another arrangement.'[51] It was Scudamore's opinion which prevailed.

Mail contracts and the merchant marine, 1870–1939

The expenditure of the Post Office on mail packets continued to exceed the 'sea postage'. This did not reflect an indifference to the cost of the service, which was reduced despite the increase in the volume of mail, for the survival of the deficit was rather the result of the downward trend in postage rates, in particular with the introduction of imperial penny postage. The rejection of Frederic Hill's policies in the late 1860s entailed not a disregard for the cost of mail packets so much as the replacement of the dogmatic pursuit of abstract principles by pragmatic assessment of the circumstances of each case. Indeed, it was noted in 1881 that

of recent years, it has been the policy of the Post Office to get rid of fixed annual subsidies, and to pay according to the weight of letters actually carried. Thus, while in 1869 there were twelve companies receiving fixed annual subsidies there are now only seven such companies. In most of these cases it has been found impossible to dispense with subsidies, as, for instance, in the case of mails to the East and West Indies, where, for Imperial purposes, a regular mail service must be kept up and the postage earned would not, of itself, be sufficient to induce ship owners to run their steamers with the necessary regularity, frequency and speed. In other cases, where the rivalry of ship owners is greater, we get the mails carried for a sea rate of so much a pound for letters and newspapers respectively, such rate being generally less than the postage paid by the Public.[52]

The outcome was to be different on the Atlantic and Indian routes.

5.3 COST AND POSTAL REVENUE OF PACKETS, 1860/1 TO 1910/1

	cost of packet services (£)	estimated deficit on sea postage (£)
1860/1	1,041,743	466,200
1870/1	1,047,000	486,111
1880/1	724,621	341,009
1890/1	930,000	270,142
1900/1	771,293	505,604
1910/1	722,249	362,833

Source: C.R. Perry, 'The General Post Office's Zanzibar shipping contracts, 1860–1914', Mariner's Mirror 68 (1982), p. 57.

When the contract with Cunard, Inman and North German Lloyd was terminated at the end of 1876, a system of monthly tenders at 2s 4d per pound of letters was substituted in order to encourage competition and reduce costs. The development of steam navigation on the Atlantic seemed to offer a greater prospect of success, and in the early 1870s the White Star Line of Ismay, Imrie & Co. had indeed mounted a campaign to carry mail. There was no point in diverting mail to the White Star ships so long as the existing contracts remained in force. However, once they were terminated the prospect of rivalry promptly disappeared and Cunard, Inman and White Star formed an alliance. They announced that they would not tender to carry mail after November 1877 unless they had a monopoly at the rate of 4s 8d per pound for letters. The Post Office agreed to pay 4s, and a contract was accepted for twelve months which, argued the Department and the Treasury, 'affords more advantage to the public than could otherwise be obtained'. Although there was criticism in the Commons that the contract was 'wrong in principle and prejudicial to the public service', the Postmaster General could claim with some justice that 'I had not abandoned the previous system. It had abandoned me.' The Department continued to welcome competition and in 1878 obtained offers from the Anchor and Guion lines to carry mail. Although the Post Office was certainly prepared to end the exclusive contract with the allied companies, it met with a firm response from the 'Liverpool ring'. The allied owners refused to abandon their monopoly unless the rate was raised to a level which would give them the same total payment after mail was diverted to other lines. The Postmaster General was alarmed, for in the absence of agreement with these companies, 'no other ships equally efficient will be available, and, consequently, the time occupied in the voyage to New York will, on average, be prolonged'. The stipulation that the Cunard, Inman and White Star lines should carry all the mail to America was accordingly preserved, and the Post Office was confident that it had secured the most efficient steamers which could provide a regular and frequent service at a reasonable rate. The acceptance of a rate of four shillings per pound had increased the payment from £26,000 to £50,000, but even so this was considerably less than the sum of £122,000 which had been paid in 1876.[53]

In the early 1880s there was pressure in the Commons to end the monopoly of the allied companies, and to move to the American Post Office's system of employing any available ship. Although the existing arrangement was defended on the grounds of regularity and efficiency, it was decided to terminate the contract and invite tenders, offering a rate which was expected to be sufficiently attractive to prevent combination and to secure the best ships. Notice was given in 1883, and tenders were invited to carry the mail on a monthly basis at three shillings per pound for letters. The Secretary, S.A. Blackwood, was optimistic that this reversion to the policy of 1876 would succeed. The support of the Anchor and North German Lloyd lines was confidently anticipated, and the rates were 'sufficiently liberal, especially when compared with the rates per ton paid for cargo of the highest quality, to induce the owners of the best Atlantic steamers to place their ships at the disposal of the Post Office, and also such, I hope, as to prevent a combination against the Post Office such as took place in the autumn of 1877'. Although Cunard, Ismay and Inman refused to tender except on the existing terms, there were offers from the Anchor, Guion and North German Lloyd companies. Blackwood urged the Postmaster General to adopt a firm line and to accept the offers of the non-combined owners. 'The Post Office cannot create ships', he argued, 'and the public ought not to blame you for a loyal endeavour to serve them, although, at the outset, your success in obtaining all the swiftest ships is qualified owing to adverse combination against the Department.' He was, however, over-ruled by the Treasury and the existing contract was extended.

In 1886 Blackwood resolved upon a third attempt to introduce monthly contracts, and tenders were again invited from British companies at a rate of three shillings per pound for letters; in order to prevent outcry against the use of foreign lines, North German Lloyd would only be offered the UPU rate of 1s 9½d. It was hoped that the 'coalition' would finally be broken. Although Inman did leave the alliance, the Cunard and White Star companies would only agree to carry the mail on the existing terms for twelve months, with the pre-servation of their monopoly. This would result in a deterioration in the service, for only two, rather than three, voyages a week would be provided. Tenders were also received from Inman, Anchor, Guion and North German Lloyd which could, despite shortcomings, provide a service at a saving of £19,000 a year. But was the risk worth taking? Only Cunard and White Star could offer regular voyages throughout the year, and it was feared that they would be able to dictate terms to the Post Office if their rivals were to fail to maintain an adequate service. The risk was in fact taken: the Treasury was unwilling to accept the offer of Cunard and White Star unless they dropped the demand for a monopoly of mail. At the end of 1886 a three-month contract was agreed with Inman, Guion and North German Lloyd. A 'well-known, long tried and thoroughly regular service' was abandoned, 'but a trail of the system of taking up vessels for short periods would at least show by actual experience whether the plan, which has been so persistently advocated in many quarters, is, on the whole, advantageous or the contrary.' Although it soon became apparent that the new contracts

173

could not offer a regular service, this attempt to break the hold of Cunard and White Star did force them to reduce their terms when the contracts expired in 1887. They offered to provide a twice-weekly service for three shillings a pound of letters on condition that their monopoly was restored; if it were not, the rate would be four shillings a pound. Despite the fact that four other companies tendered at three shillings a pound, the Post Office decided to accept the terms proposed by Cunard and White Star and to restore their monopoly.[54] Blackwood felt that 'the existence of the monopoly is an old public grievance and a notorious one',[55] yet the contract was to survive until 1898 when the prospect of lower postage rates to Canada and the United States created renewed pressure for economy.

The Post Office had expended a great deal of effort in order to substitute payment by weight for fixed contracts; the rationale was that the companies should be paid according to work undertaken rather than a form of subsidy. However, the circumstances were changed by the introduction of imperial penny postage and its extension to the United States. This was expected to produce a substantial increase in the traffic and it seemed that the restoration of a fixed annual payment would have advantages for the Department. The Post Office was faced with the prospect of a heavy loss on the American mail service and argued that the costs to the shipping companies did not increase in proportion to the weight of mail carried. The shipowners, of course, stood to gain from the continuation of payment by weight, and they stressed that their ships had been built specially for the mail service, running at a loss in winter in order to maintain regularity in the face of competition from heavily subsidised foreign vessels. Eventually a compromise was reached and a sliding scale was created by which rates were reduced as the quantity of mail rose. The existing rate of three shillings a pound for letters would apply to the average weight of mail carried between 1888 and 1898, and it would then be reduced to two shillings a pound until earnings reached £120,000; at this point the UPU rate of 1s 9½d would apply. The Post Office felt that it would be impossible to achieve better terms, for it was not politically expedient to use the threat of heavily subsidised foreign competitors.[56] Indeed, in the early twentieth century it became necessary to protect Cunard against its rivals.

In 1902 a combine of American steamship companies, backed by the financier J.P. Morgan, absorbed two British lines, including White Star, and secured the support of the North German Lloyd and Hamburg-American companies. Cunard appeared to be under threat from this combine, the International Mercantile Marine Co. There was concern that the freight rates of British companies would be undercut, and that the absorption of British companies would jeopardise the use of liners for naval purposes in war-time. The government decided upon two courses of action. One was to reach an understanding with International Mercantile Marine so that ships would not be transferred to the American flag without consent, and half the tonnage would accrue to British companies with the Admiralty having the right to use the ships. The second aim was to bolster the independent British lines. Accordingly, in 1903 an agreement was reached with Cunard by which the government would lend the company £2.4m at 2½ per cent for twenty years to build liners. These ships would receive an annual subvention of £150,000, and the mail contract was to continue at not less than the existing rate for twenty years from the first voyage of the second of the new liners.[57] The Post Office was critical of the new contract, complaining that the term was too long and that the payment would continue to mount as the traffic increased. 'The natural policy of the Post Office', argued the Secretary, George Murray, 'would therefore be to attempt to get a fixed annual payment substituted for a payment by weight, so as to secure for ourselves, instead of for the Company, the advantage arising from the growth of the mails.' Agreement was indeed reached to substitute a fixed payment of £68,000, based upon Cunard's average remuneration of the last three years.[58] This method of payment was subsequently extended to the White Star line. The company in 1906 wished to transfer its operations from Liverpool to Southampton, and the Post Office used this as a bargaining weapon to substitute a fixed annual payment of £70,000 in 1908. This produced a considerable saving, for in 1908/9 the company would have received an additional £21,453 if it had been paid on the basis of weight.[59]

When the Cunard contract expired in 1927, the Admiralty had no wish to renew its agreement and the Post Office was left to make terms for the carriage of mail. The existing contract was very favourable to the Post Office, for no account had been taken of war-time inflation. Payment at UPU rates would have entitled Cunard to £118,800 and at the commercial 'fine goods' rate to £144,700, and the company insisted that the contract was hardly worth having. F.H. Williamson was pre-pared to change the basis of the contract, by extending to shipping the method of paying railway companies. The shipping companies should, he suggested, receive two-thirds of the 'fine goods' freight rate, the payment to be based on the volume of mails carried at the time of the agreement with a variation clause providing for adjustment of payment at half the rate of increase or decrease of the weight. It was agreed that the two companies should receive £100,000 each, with a variation clause and a pro rata reduction if a suitable ship was not supplied.[60] This agreement was, however thrown into confusion in 1934 when the two companies merged, reducing the service but still claiming payment in full irrespective of the service. The company argued that the merger had taken place at the behest of the government and that it should not be penalised by a loss of revenue. In 1935 it was agreed that the company would receive £100,000 a year for one fast service a week and £5 per ton for mail carried on any other ship. The Cunard line continued to express its dissatisfaction, for it made a loss on the fast service and its payment was below UPU rates. Nevertheless, when the contract terminated in 1938 the Department adopted a firm line that payment should depend on the amount of mail carried, for 'anything by way of subsidy was contrary to policy and must be ruled out'. In 1939 it was agreed that the rate should be £4 15s a ton, and the balance of advantage had clearly swung towards the Post Office.[61]

On the Atlantic, there had been a long battle between the Post Office and the shipping companies in order to reduce the payment for carriage of the mails. Competition did exist, and the 'Liverpool ring' fought a long campaign to ensure that the Department did not secure the full advantage. On the route to India, by contrast, there was an absence of competition and the hold of the P & O was scarcely troubled. In the 1860s this had gone so far as the emergence of a form of partnership between the Department and the company. However, in 1878 there was a reaction and it was decided that an attempt should be made to secure competition. There was a general feeling at the Post Office, Treasury, and India Office that the P & O contract should be terminated in order to reduce the price and to secure a better service, and tenders were invited for services at both eleven and twelve knots. There were two serious bids, from P & O and Alfred Holt's Blue Funnel line. The P & O's bid was below Holt's for the twelve knots service, but Holt offered a lower price for the eleven knots service and this, it was felt, would 'afford as good a service as can reasonably be demanded by the public'. However, the Post Office's recommendation was overruled by a Cabinet committee which felt that P & O provided a more comprehensive service, and a new eight-year contract was agreed to run from 1880 at an annual payment of £370,000. Holt was deeply aggrieved. He had been given only a month to submit a tender, and would have to build an entire fleet at great expense and risk. 'The whole contract has been an ill-considered one', argued its critics, 'not free from the suspicion that the ability and influence of those having charge of the Peninsular and Oriental Company's interests have gained an advantage over the supineness of those having control of our postal arrangements.' The continued payment of subsidies to P & O, argued Holt, checked the development of other companies so that 'the effect of ceasing to subsidize the P & O would probably be an increase in the number and speed of vessels under the British flag'.[62] On this argument, the P & O did not secure the mail contract because it had a monopoly; it had a monopoly because of the mail contract.

This raises an important point about the role of mail contracts in the development of British shipping. It is common to argue that payments for the carriage of mail were important in encouraging the development of steamship routes in the early nineteenth century, but Holt was claiming that in the later nineteenth century they were, on the contrary, checking the growth of services. Of course, P & O did not accept this analysis and argued that without mail contracts its service on the eastern routes would deteriorate. 'It may be different in the American trade, where the shortness of the voyage, and the gigantic passenger traffic, may render mail receipts less important. But in the Eastern trade, there would not, without a considerable payment for the conveyance of mails, be any mail service at all, properly so called.' Holt could operate cargo ships which cost a third of the price of mail steamers, and it was only possible for the P & O – so the company argued – to operate the fast mail ships on the basis of a guaranteed annual payment. The danger which the P & O stressed was that shipowners such as Holt, who were not burdened with the demands of the Post Office for fast and regular passages, could encroach upon the ordinary cargo business. Mail contracts, so it was claimed, could threaten profitability. The P & O needed, it was remarked in 1896, to earn $£2\frac{1}{4}$m a year in addition to the payment from the Post Office:

> The existence of the Mail Service does not create any special advantages in the way of earning this large general revenue. That has to be accomplished in the way of ordinary every-day competition, to obtain for the company a sufficient share of the Eastern trade. On the other hand, the necessity to construct Mail Steamers which shall be larger and faster than those of former times is an immense restriction on the earning power of the new as compared with the old tonnage. The mail steamer of the present day, which is 3 or 4 knots faster than her predecessor of 10 or 12 years ago, will carry in proportion to register tonnage, something like 50 per cent less cargo.
>
> The task which has therefore devolved upon the Directors up to the present time to improve the Mail Service, and likewise to maintain the revenue which is essential to the existence of that service, has not been an easy one.

On the Atlantic, the Post Office admitted, the shipping companies 'would provide the same services whether they had a mail contract or not', whereas on the Indian and China route it was doubtful whether the P & O would run such a fast and regular service for purely commercial needs. Fuel costs were higher, and 'there is no passenger trade to compare with the colossal traffic between Europe and the American continent'. As a result there were no ships apart from mail steamers running at more than 12 or 12½ knots in the eastern trades. The mail contract was, in the view of both the P & O and the Post Office, not a subsidy which excluded other companies but a payment justified by higher speed, greater regularity and inflated costs.[63] In any case, the relative importance of payments for carrying mail did start to fall in the 1880s and should not be exaggerated. In 1870 the income from the Post Office had been 24.4 per cent of the P & O's total revenue, and was still 24.0 per cent in 1880. This had, however, fallen to 15.1 per cent in 1890 and 8.8 per cent in 1910.[64]

P & O's contract was renewed in 1886, but in 1894 the desire for competition resurfaced when an interdepartmental committee representing the Treasury, Colonial Office, India Office and Post Office recommended that separate tenders should be invited for each section of the service. P & O refused to 'sectionalise' its tender and would only submit terms for the whole service. Only three tenders were received for parts of the route, and there was no practicable solution except a new contract with P & O which ran from 1898.[65] There continued to be doubts about this dependence on a single company, and the Select Committee on Steamship Subsidies of 1902 concluded that free competition was more healthy and beneficial to the Empire than a State-subsidised and controlled system.[66] Accordingly, an interdepartmental committee in 1904 recommended that competitive tenders should be invited either on a sectional basis or for alternating services, and that to give adequate time for competitors to build ships the existing contract should be extended for three years.[67] The policy was even less successful than in the 1890s, for the only tender received apart from P & O came from the inmate of a Mariners' Home. 'The scheme of obtaining competition by inviting separate tenders for numerous sections of the service has', it was admitted, 'signally failed.' A new contract was agreed with P & O to run for seven years from 1907, after which it was to terminate on twenty-four months' notice.[68]

The contract of 1907 was in fact to survive until the Second World War. The payment was £305,000 a year, and the Post Office calculated in 1913 that at UPU rates the company would receive £390,000 for letters alone and £468,900 for letters and parcels. The Post Office, it was agreed, had nothing to gain by terminating the contract for there was little prospect of competition and the company might expect an increased payment. The contract was subsequently reviewed at frequent intervals to establish whether or not it should be continued. It was found that in 1928, for example, the company would have received £399,900 for the letter mails at UPU rates. Nevertheless, P & O was now receiving a higher rate than Cunard, and payment on the same basis of a portion of the fine goods rate would have produced a payment of only £178,000 in 1928 for the carriage of letters and parcels. The two cases were, however, not comparable, for Cunard would run its services regardless of the mail contract while it was doubted whether P & O would continue to operate at high speeds. Although the transfer of mail to the air in the late 1930s did pose a new threat, the contract had still not been terminated at the outbreak of war.[69]

By the 1920s and 1930s the crucial issue which bothered the Post Office had, of course, changed. The concern was less the terms for the use of ships than planes, and many of the debates of the nineteenth century were to be repeated in a new guise. Should mail contracts be used as a means of subsidising air services which were not otherwise commercially viable, or should the Department insist that it was guided by strictly postal considerations?

Air mails: the European 'all-up' service

Sound finance and an economic system are the bed-rock of Imperial commercial aviation. It must be recognised that the British aircraft industry cannot live unsupported. Direct assistance is a necessity. Subsidised competitors are in the field. . . . All that the Aircraft Industry needs is a fair field and no favour. Payment for services rendered to the Post Office, in the form of a guaranteed sum for cargo space, whether used or not, is quite a different affair from a subsidy. (Speech by Sir Frederick Sykes, reported in *The Aeroplane*, 18 February 1920.)

Subsidies, argued Sir Frederick, were 'money for nothing and lead only to laziness', but a guarantee from the Post Office of a full cargo on each trip was a different matter. 'Air mails', he claimed, 'are the real foundation of the whole system.'[70] The Secretary of the Post Office, Sir Evelyn Murray, did not altogether welcome such proposals to turn his Department into the sponsor of civil aviation. 'Our position', he had remarked in 1919, 'is this. As the Post Office, our business is to make our "show" a paying concern. We quite conceive that the Government, for other reasons, may consider that it is desirable to start these routes, even if they do not pay for mails services, but that is outside the province of the Post Office.'[71]

The Department had faced similar pressures in the nineteenth century when mail contracts had provided a means of encouraging the development of steamships. There had, however, been a rejection of such an approach, and an emphasis upon the payment of commercial

179

rates had become firmly entrenched in the mental world of Post Office officials by the interwar period. This assumption was to be threatened by the development of civil aviation. Mail would, after all, utilise a larger proportion of capacity than had ever been the case with steamships: this was the opportunity for the aviation industry and the danger for the Post Office. In the United States, mail contracts were indeed used as an open-ended subsidy to encourage civil aviation, for the Post Office paid the net cost of any flight which remained after revenue from passengers and freight had been deducted.[72] Although there was no suggestion in Britain that the Post Office should guarantee the companies against loss, the prospect of a mail contract which assured a secure income and a definite cargo was still highly attractive. Whatever the inclination of the Post Office, it was to be involved in the intricate business of government encouragement of British civil aviation.

Mail was not to be of great significance in the development of civil aviation in the 1920s. The attraction of air services operating during the day to the near continent was slight, for most letters were posted at the close of business in the late afternoon, and could travel overnight by rail and sea for delivery the next morning. The use of an air service might even entail a delay for the mail would not be despatched until the morning after it was posted, and since the services were unreliable it would be necessary to maintain the existing surface organisation. The expense was also considerably higher, for a kilogram of mail sent to France cost 9d by sea and rail in comparison with 2s 5d by air.[73] Air mail in the 1920s was therefore treated as a special service for which a fee was charged. When the first regular air-mail service was established between London and Paris in 1919, this surcharge was initially fixed at 2s 6d per ounce, which was reduced in 1920 to 2d an ounce.[74] The companies and the Air Ministry did urge that mail should be carried at the ordinary surface rate in order to provide a guaranteed revenue, for 'the establishment of aerial passenger services depends largely upon the question of whether or nor aerial mails may also be carried'.[75] This the Department refused to accept in the early 1920s, insisting that the special air fee should be paid and that the transfer of 'the ordinary continental mail to aerial transport is at present wholly impracticable'.[76] The Post Office should, it was felt, adopt a passive rather than active role in the development of civil aviation which should 'depend on the extent to which it can attract passenger and freight traffic. . . . [T]here is little probability that the conveyance of mails would be more than a 'side-line' giving a regular and useful supplement to earnings from other sources.'[77]

In 1924 the structure of civil aviation in Britain was transformed by the merger of the unprofitable existing companies to form Imperial

Airways as the sole recipient of government aid for ten years. It was to receive a subsidy of £137,000 in the first year falling to £32,000 by the tenth year when the company, it was hoped, would be self-supporting.[78] Income from the carriage of mail was to become a crucial element in the attempt of the company to break even as its subsidy was reduced, and Imperial Airways urged that air conveyance at surface rates should be automatically extended to any mail which would be accelerated. The introduction of this so-called 'all-up' air mail offered 'the fullest possible employment of aeroplanes as mail-carriers' and Imperial Airways urged that it was 'one of the surest methods of enabling civil aviation to become independent of subsidy from the public purse, and even if a small additional expense is entailed to the General Post Office, it will be more than compensated in other ways'.[79] There was some sympathy for this view at St Martin's le Grand. 'The relation of the Post Office to Imperial Airways', it was pointed out, 'is not merely that of an ordinary customer. It is that of a customer who (through the Treasury) is also a creditor, and who therefore has a financial interest in giving the debtor firm as much custom as possible.' Others were more sceptical, arguing that the overseas mails barely broke even and that there was little margin for assisting air transport. The introduction of an all-up service was accordingly rejected in 1927.[80]

The Department in 1927 formulated its views on the future use of air services for the carriage of mail. The usefulness of air services rose with distance since a substantial acceleration of mail would result, but costs also rose in proportion and it was unlikely that surface postage rates would cover the expense of air transport. Air mail should therefore remain a 'superpost' with its own rates. It was, however, conceded that 'in the far future' the superpost principle might be confined to services beyond Europe, and within Europe 'air conveyance would become used indifferently with other means of conveyance for the exchange of ordinary mails'. Imperial Airways was advised not to expect too much from the diversion of ordinary mails to the air, for a greater profit might be expected from a superpost.[81] This was a rational analysis of the economics of air mail, and since the Second World War there has indeed been an all-up service within Europe and a special rate or superpost outside Europe. Sensible as this might appear, air mails were to develop on very different lines between 1927 and 1939: the all-up principle was initially introduced on long-distance imperial routes and not in Europe. The Post Office's predictions of 1927, which proved to be accurate in the longer term, were denied in the 1930s.

Surface mails to Europe had traditionally made a profit and empire mails a loss. Different criteria had applied, and the introduction of imperial penny postage confirmed that communications with the empire

181

had a higher priority than the profitability of the Post Office. Much the same point applies to the development of air mails, for the all-up principle was introduced on imperial services at a loss and surcharges were maintained in Europe until 1938 at a profit. It was calculated in 1930 that air fees to France, Belgium and Holland yielded 3s 4d a pound, whereas the payment to the aviation companies was only 1s a pound. It was agreed in 1930 that the fee should be reduced to a standard rate for all European services, and the combined postage and surcharge were set at fourpence for the first ounce and threepence for each additional ounce. The principle of uniformity was in this way extended to European air services, and the fee was fixed 'irrespective of the actual costs of each particular service' in order to 'cover the cost of the services taken as a whole'. This was as far as the Post Office was prepared to go, for 'no doubt we are a long way off the time when the Continental mails will habitually be sent by air without special charges'.[82] The lower, flat-rate air fee did produce an increase of 52 per cent in the volume of air mail to Europe between July 1929 and July 1930,[83] and it was calculated in 1933 that each European air letter produced a profit of 0.38d.[84]

Pressure started to mount for the introduction of an all-up service to Europe so that letters would be sent by air at the surface rate whenever delivery would be accelerated. In 1935, the letter mail service to Europe yielded a profit of £425,000 and the transfer of letters to the air at a conveyance rate of 7d per pound per 100 miles would leave a profit of only £20,000. The financial viability of all-up services depended on the charges for air carriage, and a conveyance rate of 3½d would produce a profit of £250,000.[85] The decision did not, however, rest entirely upon an assessment of the financial implications, for there was also the important consideration that Imperial Airways had failed to develop its European services. The company had an exclusive right to subsidies for European services between 1929 and 1939, but it had become clear by the mid-1930s that this had created a barrier to enterprise. Imperial Airways had an agreement with Lufthansa not to develop routes in northern Europe, and in return Lufthansa would not compete in the East. The services were scarcely impressive, and the government decided that British civil aviation on the continent could best be encouraged by allowing a new company to operate in northern Europe. British Airways was accordingly formed, without a subsidy, in 1935. It was initially intended that the new company should carry mail to Scandinavia and Berlin, but Imperial Airways eventually secured the German service as the price of acquiescing in the creation of British Airways and breaking its agreement with Lufthansa.[86] The government's decision to encourage civil aviation in Europe was to place pressure upon the Post Office. 'The government', it was remarked in 1935, 'is anxious to foster British civil aviation, which is particularly backward on the European routes, and the question has therefore been studied to see whether the additional payments derivable from the consignment of larger mail loads could be utilised to encourage British air transport in the continental field.'[87]

The Post Office in 1935 laid down two 'cardinal principles' for air mail services to Europe. An all-up service using air conveyance at the existing surface rate of postage might be introduced when it was justified on financial grounds; and this should be used to increase the British share of European air traffic 'by insisting that as far as is reasonably practicable the extension should be provided to the extent of 50 per cent by British aircraft'.[88] The use of the new services provided by British Airways would reduce the profit on the European first-class mail by £88,000, which was considered to be a justifiable surrender of income.[89] The development of the all-up mail to Europe was therefore part of the encouragement of British civil aviation, and the Post Office refused to use air services provided by foreign companies which would accelerate the mails.[90] However, this use of air mail as part of the government's encouragement of British services to Europe was threatened by pressure from other postal administrations to adopt the all-up principle, which made it 'more difficult for us to decline to use foreign services where there is no British service or an inferior British service'.[91] A series of conferences of European postal administrations was held in 1937 and 1938 to consider the matter. The British view was initially one of scepticism, fearing that it was part of a plan by the International Air Transport Association to benefit the aviation companies. At the first conference at The Hague in 1937, the British delegates held to the policy that air services should be used only when there was 'useful acceleration' and half the services were supplied by British aircraft, but it soon became clear that the all-up principle would be generally accepted and that Britain would be surrounded by countries which automatically sent mail by air without a surcharge. The Post Office was forced to abandon its policy of subordinating the development of all-up mail to the interests of British civil aviation, and the rule that half of the services should be provided by British aircraft was abandoned. 'We should be authorised to use any air services in Europe which offer useful acceleration, for the conveyance of our first-class mail, without feeling that we must consult and carry the Air Ministry with us before we do. In other words, that we should decide on the use of air services precisely in the same way as we decide about sea services.' In 1938 an agreement was signed at Brussels accepting the principle of all-up carriage of mail, and providing for the use of foreign services at a rate of 2.5 francs per tonne-kilometre.[92] This was to form the basis for the development of European air mail services after the war.

The Empire Air Mail Scheme

All history proves the close connection between progress, power and communication. . . . [T]he strength of the British Empire depends upon good communications. . . . Air transport careless whether the route be over land or sea, unhampered by foreign frontiers, gives the Empire precisely those essential powers of direct, supple and speedy intercommunication which ship and rail have already shown us to be vital. . . . Steam, cable and wireless have each in turn been evolved to expedite intercommunication, but just as the roads of the Roman Empire failed to keep pace with the requirements of the time, so modern communications are insufficient for an Empire stretching from Great Britain to Australia and the Pacific Ocean. (*Memorandum on the development of civil air communications within the Empire prepared by the Department of Civil Aviation, 1921.*)[93]

Imperial Airways in the early 1930s had to face the prospect of an end to the subsidy granted in 1924 and an increase in earnings from mails seemed to be an urgent necessity. A surcharge air mail service to the East had started to operate as far as India in 1929,[94] which had failed to provide the company with sufficient income and revenue, despite the fact that the fee charged to the public was set at a low level merely covering the additional cost of air conveyance. Although economies and increased passenger earnings had compensated to some extent for the reduction in the subsidy, the future seemed very bleak unless the air mail revenue could be augmented. This led Imperial Airways in 1933 to propose an all-up service for letters to Africa and the East 'as the best means of getting a large and stable volume of traffic on which to base our growth'.[95]

Imperial Airways was in agreement with the view that the Post Office was 'the blackest reactionary in all matters concerned with the air', as Sir Samuel Hoare had put it in 1930.[96] The Post Office, the company protested, was taking no risks for it retained the ordinary postage and imposed a surcharge to cover the additional cost of air transport. Why should the Department not encourage air services by surrendering part of its revenue? After all, it was argued, in the case of other forms of transport unprofitable routes were subsidised by the profitable, 'the financially strong support the weak, all working in together in the interests of the expeditious and economic delivery of the mails'. Service by sea to the Orkneys might make a loss which was covered by the profit on local letters delivered within London. By air, however, all services were obliged to cover their costs and the development of new routes was retarded.[97] Air transport, so the argument ran, was treated less favourably than other forms of conveyance, whereas the special relationship between the government and Imperial Airways should have led to more favourable treatment. 'The Post Office', complained Imperial Airways, in 1934, 'is inclined to look upon us as an ordinary carriage contractor, whereas it is impossible for us to regard ourselves in that position, because the main principles of the air mail and the details, are an essential feature of our agreement with the government, and the air mail revenue . . . represents relatively a far larger item in our Profit and Loss Account than in any other form of transport.'[98] A further complaint of the company was the division between the Air Ministry, which developed new routes, and the Post Office, which denied responsibility despite the fact that its attitude was crucial for financial viability. 'The position which we have today', complained Imperial Airways in 1932, 'of the Air Ministry and Post Office – if I may put it crudely – working at cross purposes, is one which ought not to be tolerated.'[99]

These charges of conservation and obstruction were not totally fair and were, of course, based upon special pleading. There was, in fact, no profit on the imperial letter service, so that the Department could claim with some justice that there was no further scope for cross-subsidisation within the overseas mail service. The basic postage rate was unprofitable, and the air surcharge only covered the additional cost, so that in 1933 each imperial air letter imposed a loss of $0.02d$.[100] 'The Imperial postal service', as F. H. Williamson remarked,

> is run at a substantial loss, and 'ex nihilo nihil fit'. . . . Our relations with Imperial Airways have always been those of an ordinary customer; we pay for the mails actually carried at an agreed poundage rate and on our side we charge the public the lowest possible fee consistent with avoiding a loss in the service. Any reduction of the air fees beyond this point would not be easy to distinguish from an indirect subsidy from Post Office funds.[101]

Those who wished to use air mail should accordingly 'pay for it, as they pay for other exceptional services'. Subsidising civil aviation, it was argued, was properly the responsibility of the Air Ministry and was outside the scope of the Post Office whose role was to follow rather than lead in the use of air services.[102]

Imperial Airways and the Air Ministry resolved to change this attitude, and the Post Office found that the combination of imperial development and the financial needs of the company were too strong to resist. The Department accepted by 1934 that imperial surcharges would have to be reduced and a flat-rate air fee introduced. It therefore concentrated upon reaching an agreement with Imperial Airways 'which would keep the Post Office loss within bounds, and at the same time avoid definite loss to the company'. A reduction in the surcharge was calculated to produce a loss of £49,900 on existing traffic, rising to £136,100 on the additional mail which was expected to result. This could be reduced to £57,200 if Imperial Airways agreed to carry the additional mail at freight rates, and the Department was willing to accept such a sacrifice of revenue as its short-run contribution to the encouragement of civil aviation. 'There would be no question of making the service pay, but only of trying to make such arrangements as would check an increase in the loss which would otherwise follow a substantial increase in traffic.' Agreement was not to be a simple matter. The Post Office concentrated upon the high charge for the carriage of mail in comparison with freight and passengers. 'There appears', remarked one Post Office negotiator, 'to be a delightful insouciance in the manner of arriving at these rates which is altogether charming. On what principle are these charges fixed and why is it that mail charges are generally twice, at least, as heavy as human flesh charges and about four times freight charges?' Imperial Airways started from a different assumption: it should receive the entire revenue of the air fee, which would produce about 20s a pound. The company stressed the risks it would be running in extending services, and that before incurring them it would be necessary 'to feel assured of a considerable increase in mail revenue. Surely', it concluded, 'the great additional postal advantages of such a development are worthy of a substantial guarantee by the Post Office?' The Post Office, however, refused to move from its original offer of 15s a pound. This was accepted by Imperial Airways with some disappointment that the rates offered were so low, bearing in mind the risks involved.[103]

A flat-rate air fee of sixpence per half ounce was introduced on imperial routes in 1934. The initial loss was expected to be £20,000, which would gradually fall as the traffic grew.[104] The Post Office had made a concession to assist Imperial Airways which was finite and narrowly defined. This was, however, soon to be surpassed by the Empire Air Mail Scheme which was finalised in 1934, offering automatic transmission by air of letters to Africa and the East. Surcharges were to be abandoned, and all letters would be sent by air at a rate of 1½d per half ounce in place of the previous surface rate of 1½d for a full ounce. The scheme was to run for fifteen years from 1 January 1938, during which the Post Office was to pay a fixed annual sum of £900,000 to Imperial Airways regardless of the amount of mail. The Air Ministry was, in addition, to pay a subsidy of £750,000 a year during the first three years, falling to £450,000 a year during the last three years.[105] The Post Office would initially incur a loss of £162,000, although it was expected that the growth of traffic would produce a profit of £8,000 by 1952. Imperial Airways was attracted by the prospect of a large sum at the start of the service, and the Post Office 'gambled on the possibility of obtaining such a growth of traffic during 15 years' as to cover the initial loss.[106] The agreement seemed to have benefits for both parties, but it soon became clear that Imperial Airways had made a major miscalculation which jeopardised the scheme.

The increased volume of mail which the Post Office saw as the main attraction of the Empire Air Mail Scheme would threaten the company with insolvency. Imperial Airways made the crucial assumption that there would not be a considerable increase in the weight of mail. The reduction of the initial weight limit from a full to half ounce was expected to secure a reduction of 15 to 30 per cent at the outset, and the quantity of mail would, it was believed, remain within 14m ton-miles a year throughout the term of the scheme. The total capacity of the empire services was 24.65m ton-miles a year, and it was necessary to earn £900,700 from passengers and freight to break even. On the assumption that mails took 14m ton-miles, this would require an average passenger load of 73.64 per cent. Any increase in the volume of mail would encroach upon the passenger capacity and threaten the financial viability of the company, particularly in view of the reduction in the Air Ministry subsidy. An increase of 5 per cent in the volume of mail would require an average passenger load of 80.29 per cent in order to break even, which was felt to be unattainable. The company insisted that there was no financial margin for the carriage of more than 14m ton-miles of mail. 'In fact, the greater the success of the Empire Air Mail Scheme, the quicker the ruin of the company.'[107]

Imperial Airways had without doubt entered into an agreement to carry an unlimited amount of mail, but it was clear to the Post Office that it was impossible to insist upon the payment of a fixed sum.[108] The company at first claimed five shillings per ton-mile for any excess above 14m ton-miles; this was equivalent to £1,750 for a ton of mail to India, or five times the net postal receipts and two and a half times the cost. It was finally agreed that the Department should pay £350 a ton for any mail in excess of 1,250 tons in the first seven years of the agreement, or in excess of 1,500 tons in the last eight years.[109] The Post Office could feel justifiably aggrieved. There had always been doubt about the automatic use of air transport which 'compulsorily imposes an increase in postage on all letters except the lightest'; it would have been preferable to allow letters to be sent by sea and to charge an optional higher rate for air mail. Nevertheless, in order to assist the Air Ministry, the Post Office had agreed to 'mortgage the future' by accepting a present loss in the hope of distant profit. When it became apparent that this would spell economic ruin for the company, the Department was forced to accept modifications which would not have been accepted at the outset.[110]

Although the Post Office might feel that the additional cost should fall on the Air Ministry, there was no escape from the increased payment. 'The fiction that [the Empire] service is not subsidised out of Post Office funds is', commented Sir Thomas Gardiner, the Director General of the Post Office, 'so transparent.'[111]

The outbreak of war in fact put an end to the Empire Air Mail Scheme long before its full term of fifteen years, and it was soon realised that it had been based upon a serious misunderstanding of the economics of air transport. In the case of railway and shipping companies, mail was not a high proportion of total capacity and it was unusual for an increase in volume to encroach on the revenue earned from passengers and freight. Mail was, however, a high proportion of the total capacity of planes, and an increase in volume would seriously erode revenue. The Post Office tended to work on the same assumptions with Imperial Airways as with P & O, expecting to benefit from an increased weight of mails in return for a fixed payment and, as the company remarked in 1945, was 'astonished when we started to talk about the weight of individual bags'. Imperial Airways could, for its part, be accused of remarkable naivety in assuming that the total weight of mails would not rise. It is not surprising that when the war terminated the agreement discussions almost immediately started to place postwar services on a different basis. The company was to be paid according to the weight carried, and a distinction was drawn between light air letters and heavier items which could be sent by sea. 'I can find', the Air Ministry reported in 1943, 'no friend for a renewal of the pre-war all-up Empire air mail scheme.' It had proved to be a short-lived and expensive misconception of the proper role of air mail on long-distance routes.[112]

Railways and motor vehicles, steamships and airplanes have transformed domestic and international communications since 1840, and the Post Office was involved in each of these major innovations. The Department was in some cases reacting to changes in which it played no active role, such as in the use of the Liverpool & Manchester Railway. Certainly, the payment for carriage of the mail was not crucial to the early development of the British railway system. Similarly, the Post Office acquired a large fleet of motor vehicles which cannot be claimed as a significant component of total demand for the British motor industry. The domestic carriage of mail was kept on a strictly commercial footing, and the revenue of the inland mail was always adequate to cover transport costs. There was a very different story overseas, for mail provided a sizeable proportion of the earnings of the steamship and aviation companies in their early days, and the contracts with Cunard, P & O, and Imperial Airways had an active role in encouraging the provision of a regular service. This support was important on the Atlantic up to the 1850s during the era of the paddle steamer when the earnings from freight and passengers were relatively low, until the emergence of screw steamers meant that mail contracts ceased to provide the basis for continued improvement in services. On the contrary, the most dynamic firms on the Atlantic did not receive assistance, and moved instead into the emigrant trade and experiments with new shipping designs. Mail contracts did remain significant in encouraging services to the East for a longer time, given the absence of a large passenger traffic and the additional costs of providing fuel and facilities, although even there the relative importance of earnings from the Post Office fell in the late nineteenth century. Attention at this point turned towards the reduction of postage rates within the empire and to the United States, and the revenue from international services could not cover costs. The application of strict financial criteria to the international postal service, which had been urged by the Hills, had little success against wider political and commercial interests, and this was very apparent in the negotiation of the Empire Air Mail Scheme in the 1930s. Of course, British governments in the 1930s had accepted a policy of protection and active intervention in the structure of industry, and the support given to Imperial Airways was part and parcel of the policies which were pursued during the depression. The support given to Cunard and P & O in the 1830s and 1840s fits less easily into the vision of nineteenth-century British governments pursuing principles of *laissez-faire* and non-intervention. Reality was more complicated than the usual description of the mid-nineteenth century as an era of free enterprise might suggest.

5.4 CARRIAGE OF MAIL AND LABOUR AS A PERCENTAGE OF TOTAL COSTS (POSTAL SERVICES)

	inland transport	overseas transport	total transport	labour
1854	27.6	34.4	62.0	na
1870–1	20.4	32.0	52.4	35.4
1900–1	15.0	7.6	22.6	62.5
1913–4	12.7	5.0	17.7	67.6

Source: PP 1864 XXX, *10th Report of the Postmaster General on the Post Office*, p. 607; PP 1902 LV, *Return of revenue and expenditure of the Post Office for each year from 1869–70 . . .*, pp. 334–5; PP 1916 XIV, *Report of the Postmaster General on the Post Office, 1915–16*, pp. 686–7.

There was a remarkable change in the structure of costs in the Post Office from about 1870. Payment for the conveyance of mail had dominated expenditure on postal services in 1854, and still came to more than half of costs in 1870–1 when labour accounted for only a third of expenditure. By the early twentieth century, payment for carriage of mail had fallen to less than a quarter of costs, and labour had risen to two thirds. The management of the workforce came to form an increasingly dominant concern of the administrators at St Martin's le Grand, and the next two chapters turn to a consideration of the recruitment, control and payment of the huge staff of postmen, sorters and counter clerks employed by the Post Office. The payment of railway and shipping companies had been reduced to order by the early years of the twentieth century, whilst the emergence of trade unions and the insistent pressure for higher wages posed a new set of problems.

PART III

Working for the
Post Office

Talk of armies! Why, the number of officers . . . of whom I may say I am for the time being the Commander-in-Chief, are more numerous than any regular forces which the Secretary of State for War can show within the compass of Her Majesty's dominions. (H.C. Raikes, Post-master General, quoted in H. St J. Raikes, *The Life and Letters of Henry Cecil Raikes, late Her Majesty's Postmaster General* (1898), p. 328.)

———————————————

Workers and Wages

Friends and acquaintances who came to the Post Office used often to say to Laura: 'How dull it must be for you here.' But although she sometimes agreed mildly for the sake of not appearing peculiar, Laura did not find life in the Post Office at all dull. (Flora Thompson, *Lark Rise to Candleford* (1945), p. 489.)

'Until a few years ago', remarked Sir Evelyn Murray in 1927, 'the Postmaster General was the largest employer of labour in the country', for it was only with the combination of the railways into large groups in 1922 that the Post Office 'lapsed into second place'.[1] At the peak of 1913/14, the Postmaster General was, to use the terminology of Raikes, the commander of an army of 249,696 men and women, and the control of this vast workforce became an ever greater burden for the administrators at St Martin's le Grand. One of the major differences between the Secretaryships of Rowland Hill and Evelyn Murray was certainly the amount of attention paid to labour relations. Hill in 1860 had a workforce of 25,191 as yet untouched by trade unions, while Murray had come to face not only the problems of management of a workforce of almost a quarter of a million but also had to negotiate with powerful trade unions claiming a voice in the management of the Department. Labour costs had come to dominate the finances of the Department, rising from 35.4 per cent of total costs in the postal services in 1870/1 to 67 per cent by the First World War. There could be no escape from the increasing domination of policy by labour relations and personnel management; the development of techniques to control and order its vast workforce was one of the most remarkable features of the history of the Post Office in the nineteenth century. The creation of these new methods of labour management was in many ways more significant and impressive than the invention of the postage stamp.

193

The workforce: size and structure

The statistics of employment in the Post Office are a mass of inconsistencies which make a coherent analysis of the main changes a difficult exercise. The figures in the early annual reports of the Postmaster General included only the full-time staff, and the basis of these statistics was changed first by the acquisition of the telegraph companies in 1870, and then by the inclusion of part-time workers. The statistics did not capture one group at all: subpostmasters might employ assistants to work at the counter in their offices who would not appear as employees of the Department. The workforce, however it is measured, was growing more rapidly after 1870 than before, and continued to expand to 249,696 in 1913/14 after the nationalisation of the private telephone companies in 1912. After the First World War, the staff fell below the level of 1913/14 which was only regained in 1936.[2] The staff of the Post Office had been rising at a moderate rate until 1870, when a period of considerable growth ensued until the First World War which marked the onset of relative stability.

6.1 THE WORKFORCE OF THE POST OFFICE, 1860–1930/1

		number	percentage increase
Full-time postal workforce	1860	25,192	—
	1870	28,359	12.6
Full-time postal and telegraph workforce	1880	46,956	65.6
Full- and part-time postal and telegraph workforce	1890	113,541	—
	1900	167,075	47.1
	1910	212,310	27.1
	1920/1	234,008	10.2
	1930/1*	231,877	−0.9

* excluding Eire

Source: *Annual Reports of the Postmaster General* and *Statistical Abstract for the United Kingdom.*

A close analysis of a single year will clarify the main characteristics of the structure of the workforce. A number of features emerge from the employment pattern in 1910. One important division was between the established and unestablished staff, between those with and without the security of regular employment, pensions and benefits. The unestablished staff consisted both of full-time employees such as boys engaged to deliver telegrams, and a considerable number of part-timers who provided a cheap and convenient means of adjusting the staff to the irregular flow of traffic. The majority of the women fell into this category of unestablished workers although there was also a sizeable number in the 'indoor' force of counter staff and telegraphists, in the ranks of postmasters and subpostmasters, and in the clerical grades. The Department was, indeed, a pioneer in the employment of female clerks, although they were in 1910 still confined to routine tasks and excluded from promotion to 'male' posts. The proportion of women in the workforce fluctuated within narrow limits between the late nineteenth century and the Second World War, standing at 25.0 per cent in 1885, 20.3 per cent in 1900, and 22.8 per cent in 1935.

6.2 THE WORKFORCE OF THE POST OFFICE, 1910

	men		women		total	
	number	per cent	number	per cent	number	per cent
Superior officers	537	0.3	4	—	541	0.3
Subpostmasters and postmasters	15,534	7.3	8,064	3.8	23,598	11.1
Clerks and superintendents	7,582	3.6	3,439	1.6	11,021	5.2
'Indoor'	25,483	12.0	10,750	5.1	36,233	17.1
'Outdoor'	47,780	22.5	10	—	47,790	22.5
Unestablished	69,131	32.6	23,996	11.3	93,127	43.9
Total	166,047	78.2	46,263	21.8	212,310	100.0

Source: PP 1910 XLV, *Annual Report of the Postmaster General on the Post Office for 1910*, pp. 221–2.

Postmasters in 1910 accounted for only 11.1 per cent of the staff, and they had experienced a considerable relative decline since the mid-nineteenth century. In 1855, they had formed the largest category, with 46.6. per cent of the permanent workforce, and had fallen to 29.7 per cent by 1875. The national network of offices had been largely completed and growth was rather in the workforce which collected and delivered mail throughout the country. In 1910 the 'outdoor' staff made up 22.5 per cent of the workforce, most of which comprised postmen. The 'indoor' workforce was responsible for sorting letters, operating telegraphs, running the counter and providing clerical support at local offices. The clerical grades were largely engaged on routine work in the central administration, such as calculating interest on Savings Banks accounts. The superior officers who were involved in the general administration of the Department were remarkably few. The Secretary's office at St Martin's le Grand was responsible for the formulation of policy and in 1910 consisted of nine secretaries and assistant secretaries and forty-four first-class clerks. There were also the Solicitor's office, the Accountant General's Department and the superior officers responsible for the efficient functioning of the various services, such as the Controllers of the Savings Bank and Money Order Department. In addition to the central administration there were officials responsible for a particular area. The Secretaries in Edinburgh and Dublin had general responsibility for the service in Scotland and Ireland and in London there was a Controller of the Postal Service, a general manager of the Telephone Service and a Controller of the Central Telegraph Office. The remainder of the country was divided among Surveyors who acted as the local agents of the central administration. Although the number of superior officers would appear to be small, even this figure is inflated by the inclusion of about 200 clerks who assisted the Surveyors, and their exclusion would give an even clearer notion of the marked concentration of power in the structure of the Post Office.

The wage differentials between the highest and lowest paid members of an organisation might reflect social expectations rather than the operation of economic principles. Income distribution is usually explained in terms of the supply of and demand for particular types of labour and the value of the goods or services produced. However, such considerations would not necessarily apply within an organisation such as the Post Office where wage scales were set by administrative decision rather than the free play of market forces. The important factor might be the mental image held by the administrators of the proper distribution of income, and wage scales in large bureaucracies were frequently determined by these assumptions.[3] The scale of incomes in 1910 indicates a wide differential. The highest-paid officials were the Secretary, Sir Matthew Nathan, and the solicitor, Sir Robert Hunter, who both received £2,000 a year. The officials in the next rank earned between £1,000 and £1,400, so that A.F. King, the Second Secretary, had an annual salary of £1,400 and H. Davies, the Controller of the Savings Bank, £1,150. The third-class clerks at the bottom of the clerical grade were on a scale rising from £80 to £200 by annual increments of £7.50, so that the highest-paid official earned twenty-five times the salary of the lowest-paid clerk. The great majority of the staff in the 'indoor' and 'outdoor' grades were on lower scales than the clerical grades. In London, counter clerks started at a wage of £46.80 at age 18 rising to £161.20 at age 36, and postmen started at £49.40 at age 18, rising to £96.20 at age 46 in outer London or £106.60 in inner London. Provincial postmen earned between £39 and £46.80 at age 18, and could rise by age 46 to £93.60 in large towns and £70.20 in the country. The differential between the lowest-paid full-time postman and the Secretary was therefore more than fifty-fold. Women's earnings were consistently lower, the best paid posts being the superintendents of the female staff in the Savings Bank and Money Order Office, who received £600 and £390 respectively. Differentials between men and women in clerical grades were wide, for male principal clerks in the Savings Bank earned three times the salary of women. Indoor posts had a narrower differential, male counter clerks in London at the top of their scales receiving only one and a half times the salary of women. These differentials between grades, and between men and women, must be explained by the internal organisational history of the Post Office rather than the simple operation of the market.

6.3 WAGE DISTRIBUTION, 1910

Male

Secretary		£2,000
Controller of Savings Bank		£1,150
Principal Clerk, Savings Bank	min.	£450
	max.	£600
Third-class clerk	min.	£80
	max.	£200
Counter clerk and telegraphist, London	min.	£46.80
	max.	£161.20
Sorting clerk and telegraphist, provinces	min.	£36.40
	max.	£145.60
Postman, London	min.	£49.40
	max.	£106.60
Postman, provinces	min.	£39.00
	max.	£93.60

Female

Superintendent of female staff, Savings Bank		£600
Principal clerk, Savings Bank	min.	£150
	max.	£200
Second-class clerk	min.	£65
	max.	£110
Counter clerk and telegraphist, London	min.	£41.60
	max.	£104
Sorting clerk and telegraphist, provinces	min.	£31.20
	max.	£93.60

Source: *List of Officers . . .* (1910).

It is not possible to discuss each of these grades in detail, but the main segments into which the workforce was divided may be considered. One of the most significant was the distinction between the established staff and the large fringe of workers, whether part-timers such as the auxiliary postmen or full-time workers such as the boy messengers, who did not share in the benefits of establishment. The treatment of these 'outsiders' and their claims upon the Department for admission to the privileged world of the establishment provide a major theme in the history of the Post Office. The separate spheres of men and women form a second significant division within the Post Office. Of course, many women fell into the category of unestablished staff, but when they were taken on to the establishment they were treated very differently from their male colleagues. Sexual divisions cross-cut the distinction between established and unestablished workers, a point which may be illustrated by a consideration of women clerks. Another important distinction was between the 'outdoor' staff, dominated by postmen, and the 'indoor' staff of counter clerks, sorters and telegraphists. The Post Office's workforce had a bewildering array of grades and classes, and it is hoped that a consideration of these three lines of division will provide a sense of the complexity which bedevils the analysis of labour relations in the Department.

Unestablished workers: auxiliaries and boy messengers

The duties of the auxiliary postmen do not differ in any material way from those undertaken by Established Postmen. They are a most useful body of men and their services are used to fill up temporary gaps in the permanent force, or to supplement the permanent force at certain times of the day – as, for instance, at the General Post and Evening duties – when additional help is much needed. . . . The employment of auxiliary labour is indispensable. It is certainly economical and valuable. (Post 30/938, E4060/1901, file V, *Report by Controller of the London Postal Service*, 11 December 1890.)

It appears as if the Post Office is one of the least promising occupations into which a boy can enter. The better boys go into it and it is very depressing to see . . . how few of the very large number discharged at 16 or 17 get into as good employment as their good social standing and general standard of education should have guaranteed for them. (PP 1901 XLIV, *Royal Commission on the Poor Laws and Relief of Distress. Volume XX, Report by Mr Cyril Jackson on Boy Labour . .* , p. 940.)

The work of the Post Office 'varies sharply in volume at different periods of the day, instead of flowing evenly in such a manner as would permit of its allotment to full-time staff only', and the Department faced a greater spread of its 'peaks' than other services. In London transport, for example, the peaks came at 7.30 to 9.30 a.m. and 4.30 to 7 p.m. which meant that the covering period of duties was at most twelve hours. In the Post Office, the peaks were spread from 6 to 8.30 a.m. until 6 to 10 p.m., and the covering period was sixteen hours. It was possible to cover both peaks by requiring men to work 'split' duties with two periods of attendance. These were unpopular and a larger workforce would be required than was needed for the remainder of the day. Auxiliary labour eased the problem, allowing a flexible adjustment of the labour force to the irregular flow of the traffic in order to cover the first morning delivery and also, in London, to assist with the last evening delivery.[4] The part-time staff held a wide range of occupations outside the Post Office, and in London in 1887 included 345 shoemakers, 106 gardeners, 55 porters and 51 tailors; their weekly earnings were in most cases between 10s and 15s 6d. It was reported in 1891 that 23.3 per cent of auxiliaries in London were engaged for between five and six hours a day, 32.0 per cent for between four and five hours and 22.3 per cent for between three and four hours a day. The income they derived from the Post Office was a welcome supplement to their main source of earnings, and they provided a workforce which was more economical than the employment of full-time men 'who are more highly paid and entitled to pensions and holidays'. John Tilley explained the case for the use of auxiliaries in 1872 when the postmaster of Liverpool planned to increase the full-time staff:

> The employment of auxiliary force is decidedly cheaper. . . . For 11s a week we get 5 hours a day whilst with established men for 8 hours work a day, we should pay . . . 21s a week. . . . To the 21s must be added the estimated cost of a pension, equivalent say to 2s 6d a week, and the cost of substitutes for men absent on holiday. The total mean weekly cost of an established man on this computation may be stated at 25s a week, whereas 8 hours of work by auxiliaries if paid for at the present rates would cost only 17s 6d a week.[5]

The Post Office adopted a strict policy that the part-time staff could not share in the benefits of the established officers. The auxiliaries were 'exempted from all the rules and regulations for admission to the Civil Service, and it is only by this exemption that their partial employment by the Post Office at all is rendered possible. . . . [I]t must be clearly understood that when persons accept partial employment as auxiliaries they cannot have the advantages, the wages, or the position of the Established Service which they have never entered.'[6] Auxiliaries might, however, provide a useful source of experienced and trusted recruits when vacancies appeared in the ranks of the established postmen. It was decided in 1849 that promotion of auxiliaries to the establishment could not be laid down as a general rule, 'because auxiliary and permanent letter carriers may advantageously be selected from different classes'. Although the prescriptive right of auxiliaries to advancement was denied, they were in fact considered for a vacancy if they were felt to be deserving and competent, and a large number of posts were in fact filled from their ranks. Indeed, the Controller of the London Postal Service noted in 1890 that 'during the past three years as many as 420 auxiliaries, or about 28 per cent of the entire Force, have been nominated to fill vacancies on the Established classes'. Although men signed a form on appointment as auxiliaries which specifically excluded any right to filling a permanent established post, this practice of filling vacancies from the part-time staff provided an incentive to recruitment and a reward for efficient service.[7] It was, however, to be threatened at the end of the century, for in 1897 it was decided that half the vacancies for established postmen should be reserved for ex-servicemen, which had serious repercussions for auxiliaries who could no longer expect advancement.

A major change in the system of part-time labour was recommended by an interdepartmental committee in 1897 which wished 'to discourage the employment of this class of labour, and to express the opinion that where practicable all work should be performed by officers on the established staff'. It was accepted that operational necessity made it impossible to dispense completely with part-time staff, and the committee concentrated upon a reform in its structure. The auxiliaries were divided into two categories. The first were to be called assistant postmen, consisting of men waiting to be placed on the establishment who would be employed for about six hours a day and who were to receive many of the benefits of establishment. The second class was made up of genuine part-timers with no claim to established appointments. They were to work no more than three hours a day, and were to receive none of the benefits of the establishment. The scheme meant that part-timers were excluded from advancement and had to face a future limited entirely to auxiliary labour. There was some concern that the posts would cease to be attractive but until 1914 there were enough men with other occupations which made them able and willing to accept part-time appointments.[8] The closure of their avenue of advancement did mean that care had to be taken to ensure that auxiliaries were not over-dependent on their Post Office earnings, or were not working excessively long hours in two part-time jobs. The general aim was to remove any suggestion that the Post Office was exploiting a source of underpaid labour which had been denied all prospects of advancement.[9]

After the First World War, changes in the structure of the labour market made it difficult to deny the claims of the auxiliaries to consideration, for a collapse in part-time employment outside the Post Office left many auxiliaries dependent entirely upon their earnings from the Department. In the 1920s the Union of Post Office Workers mounted a persistent campaign for the automatic establishment of auxiliaries after a number of years' service. It was claimed that men had given up their outside work during the war to take temporary full-time appointments, and had subsequently reverted to auxiliary posts with no other means of support. Auxiliaries who had returned from the war were in a similar predicament and were often dependent upon Departmental earnings which were inadequate to support a family. The Union demanded not only a 'direct line of advancement to the establishment' but also the abolition of part-time employment. 'It is now generally recognised', argued the Union, 'that unemployment or underemployment is an evil. . . . [T]he claim of the auxiliaries must be examined from the standpoint that it is the duty of the Post Office to provide full-time employment for these men.' The relationship of the Post Office to its staff was not merely 'the market one of the buyer of labour power. As an industry owned by the Nation it has a moral responsibility to lead the way in attacking the problem of under-employment.'[10]

The Post Office response was unsympathetic. The scale of the problem seemed to defy solution, for in 1920 there were 13,368 auxiliaries and any attempt to advance them to the establishment would absorb a large proportion of vacancies. The Post Office throughout the 1920s maintained that part-time labour was operationally necessary, and that it could not be treated as a back-door to the establishment. 'Post Office conditions demand the employment of large numbers of part-time men and . . . the ideal person for such posts is the village cobbler whose sedentary occupation necessitates a daily walk and who therefore welcomes a walking duty for the small payment which it warrants. He should not desire, certainly not expect, establishment.'[11] Although the operational arguments might be against change the Post Office was open to serious criticism on social grounds, and in 1930 steps were taken to reduce the use of part-timers. In the provinces, a gradual process of abolition started, limited to individual cases where substitution of a full-time post would cost no more than £45, provide a daily attendance of at least 7½ hours in towns and 6 hours in the country, and impose no undue hardship on the displaced part-timers. In London, promotion of auxiliaries to the establishment after a number of years' service was preferred, and 150 permanent posts a year were made available to auxiliaries. The impact of this policy was certainly limited. The Treasury gave its reluctant consent but 'cannot pretend to be favourably impressed with the scheme. . . . We have to recognise the fact that the

201

incidence of postal work makes the employment of a part-time force inevitable. We cannot abolish this force, and a reduction of about 400 of their numbers on a total of some 20,000 is not likely to give satisfaction.' Indeed, the problem was at the same time exacerbated by the extension of motor services which had the opposite effect of replacing full-time by part-time posts. In 1926, part-timers comprised 27.8 per cent of the total force of postmen and they were still 27.4 per cent in 1933. The policy adopted in 1930 had little measurable impact, and significant change was delayed until 1935 when the union agreed to an extension of the 'covering period' of duties in London to sixteen hours. This permitted a modification in the structure of shifts which would permit the abolition of part-time work in London within three years; at the same time the process of abolition was accelerated in the provinces. The number of part-time duties began a steady fall from 21,306 in 1933 to 14,180 in 1938. Although the demise of auxiliaries was still some way in the future, it was Post Office policy from 1935 to abandon this central feature of its operations. Instead of the adjustment of staff to handle the irregular flow of traffic, the emphasis moved to the adjustment of the traffic to a staff of full-time workers.[12]

The boy messengers who delivered telegrams posed some of the same problems as the auxiliaries. What claim did they have upon the estab-lished grades of employment? At the turn of the century, there was considerable concern about the problems of 'boy labour'. A distinction was drawn by contemporary commentators between learners or apprentices on the one hand, who were employed to acquire a skill which would maintain the supply of adult labour, and boy labourers on the other hand, who were employed for their immediate commercial utility without regard to their future. The work of the boy labourers did not provide a skill qualifying them for future employment, and more were employed than could be absorbed into adult grades. These boys were, it was argued, expelled from such 'blind alley' occupations on reaching manhood, and entered the casual labour market which so troubled Edwardian social reformers. The employment of boy labourers was considered to be 'parasitical', entailing the waste of human capital and the imposition of social costs on society. 'The mass of un-employment', it was argued, 'is continually being recruited by a stream of young men from industries which rely upon unskilled boy labour, and turn it adrift at manhood without any general or special industrial qualification.' The issue which had to be faced by the Post Office was whether telegraph messengers were to be treated as apprentices learning a skill which would secure a permanent adult engagement on the establishment, or as boy labourers employed for their immediate com-mercial utility.[13]

Boy messengers spent their leisure awaiting telegrams to deliver in rest rooms, such as this one in London in 1882. It was feared that they lacked discipline and supervision and might fall into bad habits.

The private telegraph companies had promoted the messenger boys to the adult grade of telegraph clerk, and when the companies were acquired by the Post Office the boys had the choice either of entering the competitive examination for sorters and telegraphists, or seeking nomination as postmen. This new source of recruitment alarmed the Controller of the London Postal Service who in 1881 looked back with nostalgia to the days when postmen had been recruited as young men direct from the country, 'with a fine physical constitution, somewhat blunt in manners, though sound in morals'. It was feared that 'contaminated sources' had been substituted, and there was indeed a scandal in the late 1870s arising from male prostitution among the telegraph messengers in London. A 'bad source of supply for Telegraph messengers' resulted from the low starting pay of five shillings a week and the failure 'to ascertain the antecedents of the boys before admitting them to the Service'; the problem was only made worse by the lack of supervision, frequent idleness and 'the naturally demoralising influence of a street life on juvenile character'. Action was urgently required in 1877 when it was discovered that the boys had 'a willingness to prostitute themselves even for very small sums. They had no particular liking for the vice, as a vice', remarked a baffled official, 'but whatever dislike they had for it, was entirely and easily overborne by the money which was tendered to them by their seducers.'[14] It was hoped to attract a better class of entrant by raising the starting pay, and greater attention was paid to the character of recruits and their supervision. Clearly, these reforms were not enough, for in 1889 it was discovered that messenger boys were *habitués* of a homosexual brothel in Cleveland Street patronised by members of the aristocracy.[15] It was perhaps as a result of this renewed concern that an earlier suggestion which had not been implemented in 1877 was revived: boys should be examined at the age of 16, and all those who were unsuitable for permanent appointment on the grounds of 'physical defect, educational deficiency, questionable character' should be dismissed. The boys who were retained would be offered permanent appointments when they reached the age of 18, while those who left at 16 would still be young enough to learn a trade. This system of 'weeding' at the age of 16 was introduced in 1891 in London and 1892 in the provinces. The result would, it was hoped, be a better class of recruits for the adult grades, without imposing hardship on the boys who were forced back on to the labour market.[16]

The Postmaster General, Arnold Morley, inspected the telegraph messengers at the Tower of London in November 1894 as they marched past carrying their carbines.

The training of boys had become a matter of renewed concern in the early 1890s, when more radical schemes came under consideration. One proposal in 1891 was that messengers from London should be appointed to postman vacancies in the country where their character would improve, and men transferred from the country to raise the standards of the force in London. But H. C. Raikes, the Postmaster General, suggested an alternative: the army was 'the best possible school for promoting habits of obedience and smartness of appearance' so that messengers should enlist at the age of 18 with the promise of employment as postmen after five years' service. This so-called 'enlistment scheme' was introduced in 1891 in a slightly diluted form. A fifth of the messengers might pass straight to the adult grades, but all others were obliged to join the army as a condition of permanent employment. Officials at St Martin's le Grand were, at best, sceptical, for service in the Army was unpopular among respectable working-class families, and the result was a fall in the social status of recruits. The scheme was abandoned in 1893 because 'parents take alarm at the very name of enlistment and refuse to let their sons enter the Post Office'.[17] Although the attempt to enlist boys in the army did not succeed, military training could still be introduced into the Post Office. 'It should be impressed upon the boys', it was argued in 1892, 'that, wearing as they do the uniform of the Queen, they are under an obligation to conduct themselves in a manner which shall never bring that uniform into disrepute.' The messengers were to be drilled when they came on duty, and were to learn how to march and salute. Carbines were borrowed from the War Office, corporals were appointed and prizes awarded to the best offices. The Inspector of the Board of Education was impressed by the smartness and precision of the drills. 'There can be no doubt that this kind of work is most valuable,' he remarked in 1912, 'helping as it does to promote habits of strict obedience, attention and neatness among the boys, besides fostering a sense of self-respect and esprit de corps.' This military training survived until 1921 when it was abolished as an economy measure, to the relief of the Union of Post Office Workers which opposed drill 'as alien to the general administration of the Post Office and as savouring of militarism'.[18]

Until 1897, auxiliaries and 'weeded' messengers had a good prospect of securing appointment as an established postman but the decision to reserve half the vacancies for ex-servicemen led to severe pressure on these unestablished grades. This so-called 'alternate scheme' threatened to upset the relationship between juvenile and adult posts:

the employment of an Ex-Soldier involves the displacement of a Boy Messenger, and conversely, the retention of a Boy Messenger leaves a

Soldier on the labour market. The Soldier *v* Messenger problem
resolves itself, therefore, into the question whether a soldier on
quitting the Army is, on account of his greater age, at a greater
disadvantage as regards his future than a discharged Messenger of 16
years of age, and whether the obligation of the State to find him
employment is consequently greater also.

The decision in favour of the ex-servicemen created difficulties for the
Post Office in its treatment of telegraph messengers, and the only
solution was to remove a higher proportion of boys at 16, many of whom
were satisfactory for permanent retention in adult grades. It was feared
with some justice that such extreme selectivity 'will in all probability
seriously lower the class of boys applying for employment'.[19] Although
the Boer War provided a breathing space by reducing the supply of ex-
servicemen, the return of troops after the war meant that 'it is no longer
possible to provide for the large number of boys retained'. In 1909/10,
5,527 boy messengers reached the age of 16, and 'weeding' resulted in
the discharge of 4,471 and the retention of 1,056, although it was
admitted that twice as many were satisfactory for permanent
appointment. The Post Office was concerned about the scale of this
'purgation', and attempts were made to find employment for redundant
messengers. The Department approached employers in 1905, and instituted a system of employment registers in 1907, with little positive
result. The problem of discharged messengers even induced a recon-
sideration of the 'enlistment scheme' which was introduced in a
voluntary form in 1910, so that boys who had been dismissed would be
accepted back if they agreed to join the army.[20] It was, however, becoming clear that the dismissal of boys was no longer acceptable and the
Department feared that its policy would be criticised by the Royal
Commission on the Poor Laws and the Relief of Distress which was,
amongst its other concerns, considering the employment of boys.

The fear proved justified, for the Commission was scathing in its
denunciation of Post Office practice. The 'telegraph messengers who
are discharged', it was claimed, 'exemplify in a very striking way the evils
of a parasitic trade which lives by cheap boy labour partially supported
by parents' wages.' The Post Office contended that dismissal at the age
of 16 did not harm the boys, for they were still young enough to learn a
trade, but the Report came to a different conclusion. 'A large number of
boys are leaving the Service year by year badly equipped for the necessity of making their way through life, and too large a proportion of these
lads are finding employment in casual labour and unskilled work.' The
employment of boys should be 'on the lines of a kind of apprenticeship.
An adjustment of numbers could surely be made so that all the boys in

the towns (except a small proportion definitely unsatisfactory) could be absorbed in the adult service.'[21] The Postmaster General was in broad agreement. 'It is wrong', he wrote, 'that the State should use up two of the most important years of a boy's life and then let him drift away, unprepared for any occupation offering permanence of employment.' One approach was to provide boys with further training to enable them to obtain outside employment. Boy Messenger Institutes had been encouraged since 1877, and in 1911 compulsory attendance at continuation classes for four hours a week over two years was introduced. More significantly, a Standing Committee on Boy Labour in the Post Office was appointed in 1910 to arrange for the 'complete absorption' of boy messengers into the adult grades. This was done by reducing the total number of messengers for whom vacancies had to be found: the age of advancement to adult grades was raised from 18 to 19, and a smaller number of boys was employed continuously between the ages of 14 and 19 rather than a large number up to the age of 16 and a small number after that age. The force of boy messengers fell from 15,788 in 1910 to 13,171 in 1914; at the same time the range of classes which the boys might enter was widened. The boys were required to pass a qualifying examination at the age of 16 to indicate that they had reached a minimum standard. Some did fail and others opted to leave the Post Office for alternative employment, but by 1914 any boy who wished to remain and who had met the minimum standard would be offered a permanent post. In 1908/9, 4,322 boys had been dismissed without prospects, which had fallen to 1,227 in 1911 and none in 1914; the number gaining permanent positions increased from 1,697 in 1908/9 to 2,578 in 1914. By the First World War, telegraph messengers had ceased to be a class of boy labour employed for immediate commercial utility and had become instead a class of apprentices.[22]

The Standing Committee on Boy Labour had no sooner congratulated itself on the absorption of all boys fit and willing to remain in permanent employment, than the war upset the calculations. Recruitment of boys ceased during the war, their numbers falling to 4,679 in 1919. After the war, girls who had been employed in their place were gradually phased out, and the number of boys reached 8,209 by 1921. The age distribution was consequently distorted, which resulted in a cycle of peaks and troughs in the number of boys requiring permanent posts. The trough allowed the Post Office to utilise vacancies to meet other demands, and the peaks resulted in a higher age of promotion to adult grades which was unpopular both with the union and with officials who argued that messengers were of a higher standard than other recruits. However, these were largely matters of minor adjustment and the major problem of boy labour had been solved. The contentious issue in the interwar period was rather the treatment of the auxiliary workforce.[23]

The Post Office in its treatment of these unestablished workers was responding to the changing definition of social problems in society at large, rather than to its own operational requirements. The ability to select the best amongst the boy messengers was an advantage until the government's concern for the deterioration of boy labour, with its impact on 'national efficiency' and the creation of unemployment, forced a modification in policy. A major department of state could not set a bad example. The treatment of boy labour by the Post Office was defined as a social problem around 1910, whereas in the 1890s the government had willingly sacrificed the messengers in order to solve another problem which was considered to be more imperative: the treatment of ex-servicemen. Similarly, the auxiliaries lost their opportunity of advancement to the establishment, despite the fact that from the Post Office's point of view they were a better source of recruits than ex-servicemen with no experience of work in the Department. In the interwar period, this treatment of the auxiliaries became a matter of concern and the Post Office was to abandon its traditional practice of employing part-time labour to adjust the workforce to the peaks and troughs of the daily traffic. The recruitment of labour was shaped by external social concerns as much as by internal operational needs

Indoor and outdoor: postmen and sorters

The outdoor staff undertook collections and deliveries; the indoor staff sorted the mail, worked on the counter, and operated the telegraph. Although this appears at first sight to be a clear and simple division of functions, it was in fact the product of administrative decisions allocating particular jobs to certain grades. There was, after all, nothing self-evident about the division of responsibilities: it could equally be argued that the postman's grade should be responsible for sorting the mail as that it should be left to a separate category of workers; it was by no means obvious that sorting clerks should be in the same grade as telegraphists and counter staff whose work differed in many respects. The allocation of duties was, in other words, a matter of bureaucratic decision rather than technical necessity. The result was a particular social structure of the workforce based on the allocation of tasks to grades according to certain assumptions.

The division between postmen and sorters did not arise from an obvious division of function, for both were involved with handling mail. It was rather the result of a social difference in the patterns of recruitment. This was clear in the use of the postmen's grade as a means of employing ex-servicemen, at the expense of auxiliaries and messengers with the benefit of experience in the work of the Department, who often had a better education and higher social status than recruits to the army. The attractions of the Post Office as an outlet for ex-servicemen may be easily understood. The volunteer army of the nineteenth century faced an endemic problem of a lack of recruits; the response was to reduce the term of service in order to attract men who feared a lengthy commitment to army life; the result was that the army had to find more recruits each year in order to maintain its establishment; the corollary was that a large number of men were discharged in their mid-twenties with few marketable skills. The War Office was fully aware that the worst possible advertisement for army life was the unemployed ex-soldier, and an obvious solution seemed to be an obligation for other government departments to employ ex-servicemen. 'Employment in different Government Departments may, to a certain extent, be looked on as employment in different capacities under one master. . . . No one can . . . complain that the sailor or the soldier getting this amount of consideration with regard to civil employment under the Crown.' The State, it was argued, had a 'moral obligation' to men who, by enlisting, had lost the chance of learning a trade. How better to redeem this pledge than by offering employment in the Post Office?[24]

In the early 1890s, the Post Office had viewed ex-servicemen with some favour. The memorials from postmen demanding improved pay, the formation of trade unions and the strike in London in 1890, all suggested a collapse of discipline, and the army appeared to offer an antidote to 'rising discontent and insubordination'. The army's Inspector-General of Recruiting remarked in 1890 that the Post Office 'would have at command a practically inexhaustible supply of well-disciplined and responsible young men, who would not be likely to quarrel with their Bread and Butter. . . . The Army on the other hand would benefit by the steady flow into its ranks of respectable and fairly educated young men, whose employment on quitting the ranks would be assured.' The result was the introduction in 1891 of the 'soldier scheme' of preferential employment of ex-servicemen.[25] This was a limited scheme, for ex-servicemen only had priority over applicants who were not already in the employ of the Post Office. The enthusiasm for soldiers in any case soon waned, the number who were offered employment falling from 1,230 in 1892 to 589 in 1895. 'While recognising to the full the claim which Soldiers have upon the country', the Postmaster General responded to the complaints of the War Office in 1896, '[he] holds that his first duty is to his own Department and that he is constrained therefore to provide first for persons in the Post Office service who have done well and established a claim upon the Department.' There were 1,056 appointments as postmen in the provinces in 1896, of which 537 went to boys, 391 to auxiliaries, 127 to ex-servicemen and one to an outsider. The Post Office feared that a

The introduction of ex-servicemen into the Post Office possibly delighted domestic servants, but less impressed postmasters who felt that they lacked the necessary training and attitude.

definite obligation to employ ex-servicemen would upset the balance between numbers in the juvenile grades and adult vacancies. However, when the issue went to Cabinet in 1897, priority was given to the interests of the War Office. The 'alternate scheme' was produced and, in future, half of all vacancies in the minor grades of the Post Office were reserved for ex-servicemen. This had, it has been seen, serious implications for both the auxiliaries and boy messengers: the auxiliary staff lost its prospect of promotion to the establishment, and the 'weeding' of boy messengers became more selective.[26]

The Post Office in 1913 was responsible for 77.5 per cent of ex-servicemen in government employment. The needs of the War Office

210

had been met, with the result that the Post Office experienced a deterioration in the quality of its labour force. 'We find the old soldier has become a sort of machine,' reported the Controller of the London Postal Service, 'Put him on a Porter's duty and say "Carry that bag from there to there", he can do it: but send him out with a bundle of letters for delivery, when he has to exercise some discrimination, then he is not so intelligent as the ordinary man. He does not think for himself, that is really what it is. He has had all the thinking done for him while he has been in the Army. He has been forbidden to think there.' The actual quality of the men was lower, quite apart from the results of army training. 'The Soldier . . . is often picked up at the street corners at periods of unemployment and has not always a respectable past.' Once in the army, 'the young soldier is brought into frequent contact with undesirable comrades to a greater extent than his civilian brother, and this is often reflected in his character in later life, making him, perhaps, crafty or idle'. The conclusion was clear: a consideration of Post Office interests alone demanded the recruitment of established officers from boy messengers who were 'subjected to and become accustomed to the kind of discipline which is specially suitable for the Post Office, but which differs considerably from that of the Navy and Army. They look forward to spending their lives in the Post Office, and do not get unsettled, as so many ex-soldiers do, by going abroad and doing nothing when not actually on duty.' The problem was, of course, that it was impossible to curtail the employment of ex-servicemen 'if national interests are to prevail, and on broad grounds there is much to be said for this point of view'. There was, indeed, some pressure before the First World War to go further and replace boy messengers by ex-servicemen. The proposal was, fortunately for the efficiency of the Department, not implemented.[27]

The immediate issue which arose after the First World War was a different one, involving a decision on the preference to be given to different categories of ex-servicemen, that is, professionals who had enlisted before the war, 'hostilities only' men, and postwar recruits. The War Office was concerned about future recruitment, and was anxious to find occupations for professional soldiers. The Post Office agreed, with the proviso that disabled 'hostilities' men should have preference over able-bodied professionals. By the mid-1920s professionals who had enlisted after the war were also claiming jobs and the Post Office was alarmed that these peace-time professionals might obtain preference over men who had fought in the war. 'It appears to me', wrote the Secretary in 1924, 'that to give a preference to a man who enlisted after the war and is probably therefore quite young over men who possibly threw up or lost their civilian occupation in order to enlist during the

211

war, would be repugnant to public sentiment.' Although the Secretary of State for War disagreed on the grounds that professional soldiers had a higher claim, the order of preference which was laid down in 1927 ran from professionals with war service to 'hostilities only' men, and only then postwar professionals.[28]

The curtailment of the recruitment of boys during the war had freed a large number of vacancies on adult grades, and this did permit the minimum requirements of the 'alternate scheme' to be exceeded by a comfortable margin: ex-servicemen had 78.8 per cent of vacancies in 1920, 91.1 per cent in 1921, and 81.4 per cent in 1922. The position of ex-servicemen was less secure by the late 1920s. The standard of the soldiers appointed was often unsatisfactory, and 'it is felt that the Department should be recruiting better material at a time when the Post Office service is unusually attractive'. The number of adult vacancies was falling because of the introduction of motor services, and claims on the available appointments had risen because boys engaged after the war were demanding adult appointments, and because the Department had a new obligation to advance part-timers to permanent posts. The share of vacancies taken by ex-servicemen accordingly fell to 49.3 per cent in 1929 and 39.2 per cent in 1930, and complaints were soon received from the War Office. Although the right of ex-servicemen to half the vacancies was reaffirmed, the War Office abandoned its claim to priority in filling any vacancies not required for boy messengers. The Post Office could instead use these vacancies to meet the needs of auxiliaries for permanent posts.[29] Until the Second World War, the Post Office had a continuing problem in recruitment to the ranks of postmen: despite the great attractions offered by regular and secure employment, it was obliged to recruit a large part of its 'outdoor' workforce from the ranks of ex-servicemen who were less suitable than the alternative sources of labour. Although postmen were part of the 'uniformed working class', this did not imply that military training was necessarily a welcome preparation. Discipline in the Post Office was in fact not militaristic, resting instead upon the bureaucratic rationality of career progression and benefits.

The postmen were in this way marked off from the indoor staff by a particular pattern of recruitment. The fragmentation of the workforce went further than a simple division between indoor and outdoor grades, for the postmen were themselves further subdivided into a complex and confusing variety. The terms and conditions of rural postmen were very different from their colleagues in London and the provincial towns. 'Of all the numerous classes into which the Post Office servants are divided', it was remarked in 1884, 'there is none that has been so lost to sight, – I had almost said neglected, – as the rural letter-carriers.' They continued to be appointed by patronage until 1892, long after this had ceased for other postmen, and they were also paid a fixed wage when others received an incremental scale. In 1883, for example, rural postmen had a flat rate of 16s a week, for which they normally walked 16 miles a day with a load of 30 or 35 pounds. In 1884, the rural postmen were brought into line with other grades when they were awarded an incremental scale, although it was specific to them.[30] Another peculiarity of the employment of rural postmen was that many possessed a horse and cart to undertake the work. The Department did not provide the capital, and the postman was expected to supply the horse and cart himself in return for a weekly allowance. 'Individual postmen', the Secretary pointed out, 'have often experienced great difficulty in obtaining the necessary money for the capital outlay. Usually, an old-established postman is helped, in meal or in malt, by the local gentry. But of course this is not always the case.'[31] The work of the rural postman was to be eased in the twentieth century, at first by the bicycle and then by the motor van which speeded the collection and delivery of mail. Bicycles were introduced around 1900, and the duty of a cycle post was fixed in 1903 at 26 miles, or 28 miles where roads were good, with a load of 50 pounds.[32] Motor vans in the 1920s and 1930s further speeded the work of rural mail services and allowed a reduction in the workforce.

The rural postmen clearly had a different pattern of work from their urban counterparts, for they had longer distances to cover and less frequent collections and deliveries. This is not, however, to say that urban postmen were undifferentiated. Until the 1870s, wages scales had been determined on a local basis and there was not a national standard scale: a postman in Liverpool would receive a different wage from a postman in Plymouth. The result, it was pointed out in 1881, was a 'great variety of scales which appear to have been adopted on no very clearly defined principle, and to have resulted in difference of pay at places where the circumstances would seem to call for uniformity'.[33] In the last decade of the nineteenth century the variety of rates was reduced to order, not by creating a single national scale but by formulating a coherent hierarchy which could be applied to different towns. This was initially based upon the staff or workload of an office, and was modified by the recommendation of the Select Committee on Post Office Servants in 1907 that the classification 'should be based upon the volume of work . . ., plus the cost of living, in each locality as a whole, as ascertained by the Board of Trade'. By 1907, wage rates in provincial towns were divided into seven classes, ranging from class I offices where the scale ran from 19s at age 19 to 36s at age 51, down to class VII offices where the range was 15s to 24s. The whole structure of scales could now be revised in a single exercise which could be applied to the whole country; it did also mean that the postmen were segmented according to the class of office at which they were employed.[34] This complication of rates and fragmentation of the grade of postmen was very obvious in London, which had its own specific scales. At the time of the wage revision of 1891, there were nine scales for 4,105 postmen, comprising three classes of town postmen in the central areas, first- and second-class postmen in each of three suburban divisions, and an outer London grade. The scales varied from 24s to 32s for a first-class town postman to 18s to 22s in the outer district. The elaboration of the London salary scales was reduced, yet in 1907 there were still four divisions in the capital in addition to seven in provincial towns and the rural grade.[35] The apparent similarity of work was complicated by the elaborate system of classification.

A clear line was drawn between the duties of the postmen and the indoor staff, between the uniformed outdoor workforce and the higher status white-collar indoor occupations. This was not technically necessary, and in some offices postmen did indeed undertake at least part of the simpler sorting at the 'primary' stage. It was perfectly feasible for the Post Office to argue that the specialist sorters were overpaid for these less onerous tasks, which could be undertaken more economically by postmen on a lower pay scale. The matter was considered at length in the decade before the First World War, when an impasse was reached. The postmen were eager to achieve a complete 'unification' of indoor and outdoor postal work as a means of increasing their pay scales on the grounds that they were undertaking higher grade duties, and of creating better promotion prospects. The sorting clerks for their part saw a threat to their status. In other words, the social divisions between indoor and outdoor grades, and the union structure which had emerged as a result, acted to frustrate what might appear to be the most efficient and economical organisation of work. The Post Office retreated and the line between the two groups was reinforced.[36] However, even if 'unification' of indoor and outdoor work was rejected, it was not clear how the indoor duties should be allocated. Should the tasks be separated or amalgamated, should the workforce be composed of specialists or generalists?

When the telegraph companies were transferred to the Post Office in 1870, the postal and telegraph staffs were initially kept distinct. A process of amalgamation started in the smaller provincial offices in 1876 which was extended to the larger offices in 1882. The motivation for 'dual training' in postal and telegraph work was in part to permit a more flexible adjustment of the indoor staff to variations in traffic, although the more immediate justification was to reduce the threat of disruption from any strike of telegraphists. A class of provincial 'clerk and telegraph learner' was created, and entrants would be trained in both branches before passing to a unified class of 'sorting clerk and telegraphist'. The postmasters of the largest offices were soon to cast doubt on the scheme, which produced 'great waste of time and of instruction' in acquiring a smattering of knowledge which was soon forgotten when a newcomer settled to work in one branch or the other. Specialisation might well be more economic than flexibility, and dual training might *extend* the likelihood of strikes for 'the tendency of the successful amalgamation must be to bind up the whole service in a common interest and in the event of discontent to expose it, therefore, to a common danger.' It was accordingly decided in 1883 that specialisation was preferable in large offices. 'A large contractor', it was pointed out, 'might as well mix his carpenters and his bricklayers as the Department mix its telegraphists and sorting clerks.' Provincial offices were in future organised in one of two ways. The larger offices were 'divided' and the sorting clerks and telegraphists specialised in one branch or the other; the smaller offices were 'amalgamated' for the work was insufficient to justify two separate staffs. The desire to create a united grade in fact as well as in name did not entirely disappear, for it was hoped that 'the exclusive spirit and narrow traditions' of the old telegraph companies might be replaced and flexibility increased by breaking down the barrier between postal and telegraph work. Specialisation was, however, to triumph in the large provincial offices.[37]

In London, the indoor work was organised in a different way. The three tasks of sorting, telegraphy and counter-work were in the provinces contained within a single grade of sorting clerk and telegraphist, but in London there were two distinct grades. Sorting the mail was the responsibility of a separate class of sorters, and the remaining tasks were covered by the counter clerks and telegraphists. The sorters had lower status and pay, and in some ways they were closer to the postmen than the more strictly clerical tasks of the counter clerks and telegraphists. The result was that in London the line between indoor and outdoor occupations could be blurred, and between 1879 and 1885 there was a trend towards the recruitment of postmen and sorters in London from a common pool using a single examination. The experiment did not succeed, for 'the duties of a sorter require more intelligence than those of a postman', and in 1887 there was a return to separate examinations for the two classes. Nevertheless, a proportion of vacancies as sorter was set aside for postmen and the chances of promotion from outdoor work to this lowest grade of indoor work was greater in London than the provinces where the different structure created a wider gulf. The remainder of the indoor work in London was undertaken by the counter clerks and telegraphists, and the same question of training arose as in the provinces. Counter staff was recruited entirely from the postal workforce until 1889 when it was decided that recruits should in future be trained in telegraphy and the title of the job was changed to counterman and telegraphist. However, the requirement for dual training was dropped in 1908, and the exact nature of the relationship between telegraph and other branches of indoor work remained a question of doubt and uncertainty.[38]

The indoor grades were considered to have a higher status than the outdoor grades, and they were in part recruited from an open competition for 'learners' or trainees in telegraphy. This examination was taken by adolescents, and 'most of the successful candidates come from Cramming Establishments which make a speciality of preparing boys and girls for Learner Competitions'. This had the disadvantage that many of the recruits were not local, and many indeed came from Ireland, although it did mean that the learners had the advantage of a more extended schooling. A proportion of vacancies was also reserved for a competition limited to boy messengers and postmen. Their share was raised in the early twentieth century until by the First World War recruitment to the postal side of 'divided' offices was entirely through the limited competition. Between the wars, concern was expressed that the standard of the indoor workforce in the divided offices had been reduced by this emphasis upon internal recruitment and the Secretary pointed out in 1933 that 'practically none of the candidates has received more than an Elementary school education; and experience has shewn that the material recruited does not throw up a sufficiently large number of men capable of performing the higher class writing duties . . . or of adequately filling the higher supervising positions'. It was accordingly decided that in future a sixth of the indoor staff at the divided offices should be recruited from local candidates aged between 16 and 18 who had the benefit of a secondary education. The Secretary was perhaps unduly pessimistic, for the attractions of a secure job in the Post Office did attract capable boys into the ranks of the messengers, and at least one current director started his career in this way. Despite the fact that a clear line was drawn between the indoor and outdoor grades, they were to a large extent recruited from the same class of boy messengers by a process of selection based upon written examinations; only recruits to the offices where telegraphy was a necessary skill continued to be recruited from outsiders. There were, then, two 'gates' into the indoor workforce, which were to some extent also differentiated on the grounds of sex. The entrants through the limited competitions for boy messengers and postmen were obviously entirely male, and many of the candidates in the open competition were female.[39]

216

Sexual divisions: women's employment

It is especially desirable that we should extend the employment of women. Permanently established civil servants invariably expect their renumeration to increase with their years of service, and they look for this increased remuneration. Women, however, will solve these difficulties for the department by retiring for the purpose of getting married as soon as they get a chance. . . . If we place an equal number of females and males on the same ascending scale of pay, the aggregate pay to the females will always be less than the aggregate pay to the males; that, within a certain range of duty, the work will be better done by the females than the males, because the females will be drawn from a somewhat superior class; and further there will always be fewer females than males on the pension list. (Evidence of F. Scudamore, *Report on the Re-organisation of the Telegraph System 1871*, quoted in P. Hollis (ed.), *Women in Public: The Women's Movement, 1850–1900* (1979), p. 104.)

'The Post Office has throughout', it was claimed in 1929, 'been the pioneer Department in the employment of women.'[40] A sense of proportion must, however, be kept about the record of the Post Office. The percentage of women in the workforce fell from the late nineteenth century, from 25.0 per cent in 1885 to 22.8 per cent in 1935. This may in part be explained by union opposition to women's employment, which is readily understandable when it is remembered that a male principal clerk in the Savings Bank earned between £450 and £600 a year and his female counterpart only £150 to £200. The employment of women was explicitly justified by the Department as a way of reducing the wage bill. The claim of the Post Office to be a pioneer in employing women in the civil service must certainly be treated with scepticism in the interwar period when it had in some respects become a laggard. The Post Office continued to insist that jobs should be labelled as male or female, which meant in effect that the more responsible positions were denied to women and their prospects of promotion blocked. These points may be illustrated by considering two grades in particular. The first grade consists of women clerks who became an important element in the functioning of the Savings Bank and Money Order Department, in which there was a great deal of routine clerical work, calculating interest on savings accounts and entering money orders in ledgers. The second grade comprises the counter clerks and telegraphists who worked on the counters in post offices in London. Both of these grades were established and so shared in the security and benefits of working for the Post Office. It should, however, be noted that a disproportionate number of women were unestablished workers: in 1910

51.9 per cent of women were on unestablished grades in comparison with 41.6 per cent of men.

Women clerks were first employed in the Savings Bank in 1874, a year after the Treasury first permitted their engagement in the Returned Letter Office. The justification for the employment of women was quite clearly one of economy, for additional staff was urgently needed 'and of the several kinds of force adapted to the purpose, the least expensive, although not perhaps the least efficient, would be a corps of Female Clerks'. These women were not only considered to be economical; it was also felt to be essential that their social status should be beyond reproach. The Controller of the Savings Bank had some doubts about the virtues of the scheme, and he insisted that 'the class of young ladies who are employed in the higher grades of schools and private families would be more likely to furnish candidates both able and willing to undertake the duties'. Social exclusiveness and economy were dual requirements, and would be secured by a process of selection using literary examinations set at a higher standard than could be reached by pupils from state schools. This point emerged clearly in 1896 when a new class of girl clerks was created, with the prospect of promotion to woman clerk after three years of service. 'In the scheme for the employment of women clerks as originally introduced, it was desired', remarked the Controller, 'that successful candidates would be drawn from classes of good social position . . . but if the new class of Girl Clerks is . . . to be filled by girls passing an inferior examination, it will mean practically that . . . [those] educated at the Board schools will . . . be the successful candidates, to the exclusion of girls better educated and of a higher social position.' It was therefore decided to add a foreign language to the examination for girl and women clerks in order to 'render it easier for the better educated girls and women to secure places than is the case at present'. Knowledge of Latin or German was, of course, superfluous for women who spent their days calculating 2½ per cent interest on savings bank accounts, yet it fulfilled its role of pre-serving the social position of women clerks.[41]

This emphasis upon social exclusiveness was causing problems by the early twentieth century. The principal of Clark's College in 1906 com-plained to the Post Office that the 'inadequate scale of remuneration' and the 'very high standard of qualifications' was reducing the field of recruitment. The market for women clerks had changed since the 1870s, for it was possible to earn as much 'with a little general knowledge of the ordinary subjects and a certain proficiency in Shorthand and Typing'. The number of candidates for women clerkships indeed fell sharply, and Miss C.L. de Renzi, superintendent of the female staff, accepted that 'the more intelligent and highly

218

educated girls from good schools are no longer attracted by appointment in the General Post Office, and that the only reason for this change is that they can now obtain better salaries elsewhere as Teachers, Inspectors, Chemists, Doctors, etc with better prospects as regards the future and often longer holidays. . . . Some years ago things were different, a woman without private means had practically no alternative but to become a teacher or a clerk in the Post Office.' The solution adopted was to maintain the social selectivity of the examination for women clerks, while raising their salary and transferring some of their more routine tasks to a new and cheaper grade of female assistant clerks or writing assistants.[42]

Women were also employed from the 1870s as counter clerks and telegraphists. In London, 33.0 per cent of telegraphists and 55.5 per cent of counter clerks in 1897 were female; in the provinces, 25.6 per cent of sorting clerks and telegraphists were female. These figures are not directly comparable, for sorting, which was entirely undertaken by men, appeared in a separate grade in London and was combined in a single category in the provinces. Although there was a definite agreement that two thirds of the staff of the Central Telegraph Office in London should be male and one third female, there was no such agreement for the counter staff and this offered temptations. 'There appears to be a very serious determination on the part of the Postal authorities', complained the Postal Telegraph Clerks' Association in 1909, 'to substitute the labour of women for that of men. . . . The action can only be regarded as having been induced by a desire for cheapness.' The Department admitted the charge, for the Treasury would not have sanctioned the policy of substituting crown for sub-post offices in London if expensive male staff were employed. The Department was caught between two conflicting pressures. On the one side was the union, complaining that 'the desire of the Department is to employ the cheaper rate of labour wherever possible', and on the other side there was the Treasury insisting that there was no justification for the greater cost of a male staff. It was admitted in 1913 that 'the expansion of the male staff, apart from that resulting from growth of work, must be taken to have practically reached its limit'. Women were certainly being used, as the Postal Clerks Association argued, 'to undersell the men'.[43]

The female staff of the Post Office had to accept two main conditions of employment: they were to resign on marriage; and they were placed on separate grades which were allocated work considered to be suitable for women. The requirement that women should resign on marriage was considered in the mid-1870s when opinions were by no means uniform. It was argued by some that 'in steadiness and attention to duties the service rather gains than otherwise by the presence of married women'.

219

Others felt that married women would be under the influence of their husbands, indifferent to their work, and irregular in their attendance. 'Directly they get married', it was claimed, 'other and high duties devolve upon them, and it is not . . . for their own good nor for the good of their husbands, children or society, that they should be encouraged to neglect those duties.' The Secretary agreed with these sentiments, and in 1876 it was decided that married women should not be appointed and single women should resign on marriage. This policy was reconsidered in 1891 when the Postmaster General expressed doubts on its wisdom. 'I do not think', remarked Sir James Fergusson, 'that it is for a Government Department to settle for married people whether it is desirable for the married women to seek employment away from home. It is certain that countless numbers do so. I should be surprised to learn that private employers would discharge efficient servants on their marriage.' The departmental committee which reported in 1892 did not accept his arguments, and the ruling of 1876 was maintained. This decision was welcomed by many of the women themselves, who feared that 'a fatal blow would be dealt at the employment of women by any act which would materially reduce their efficiency'. There was much concern that permitting married women to work would encourage early and improvident marriages, lead to the immorality of birth control, and force women to neglect their duties in the home. There was also a more immediate economic argument, for the committee feared that the attendance of married women would be irregular, which would 'counterbalance the comparative cheapness of women's labour. . . . [A] deadly blow will be struck at the very system which it is desired to promote.' The regulation was indeed extended in 1913 to apply to subpostmistresses, and it was only in 1946 that married women were allowed to work for the civil service and Post Office.[44]

The Post Office was a pioneer in the employment of women in the civil service, but this involved the formulation of regulations which were to be much less flexible than in departments which came later. '[In] the early days, in the seventies', it was pointed out in 1929, 'when women were first employed in the Post Office, it was considered a daring experiment; and it was quite natural that the experiment should take the form of segregating the women for particular work.' The Post Office held to the principle of 'segregation' of women into separate grades and distinct avenues for promotion longer than other Departments which accepted the principle of 'aggregation' and placed men and women on the same grades with a common seniority list for promotion. The Association of Post Office Women Clerks complained in 1922 that women were pushed into 'watertight compartments' and prevented from gaining experience in more than a few branches. The Department admitted the charge but was unsympathetic. The Post Office did not, as was the case in other branches of the civil service, have 'neuter' posts which could be filled by either men or women drawn from a common seniority list. Since all jobs in the Post Office were rigidly allocated to either men or women, this meant in effect that women were 'confined for the most part to comparatively routine work in the large accounting Departments, and that they have not been employed to an appreciable extent in the Branches of those Departments where the most difficult and complicated work is done'. In any case, so long as women were obliged to retire on marriage '(*a*) it is less worth while to train them for the better work and (*b*) they are more tolerant of routine'. The Post Office's case was in fact based upon a tautological argument: women's work was defined as routine and therefore they were not suitable for anything better. So long as posts were 'sexed' on this principle, it was impossible for women to gain the wider experience which would qualify them for superior posts. This position caused concern to the Civil Service Commission which recruited both men and women to the executive and administrative class for the civil service as a whole. The Commission could 'not see how any Department employing the class in large numbers can claim that its own members of the class must belong to one sex'. The explanation of the conservatism of the Post Office was in part the hostility of the Civil Service Clerical Association, which feared that common seniority lists and aggregation would reduce the prospects of men. The counter claim of the Association of Post Office Women Clerks that the Department differentiated between men's and women's work to the detriment of women, and that segregation did not allow a true comparison, received little attention. In the 1920s a number of the more responsible jobs were transferred to women's grades, 'without departing from the system of segregation and allowing men and women to compete for the higher posts, a course which would involve the possibility of placing women in control of bodies of men. It is an open question whether public opinion is ripe for such a change, which would certainly be opposed by the male staff.' So far as Sir Evelyn Murray was concerned segregation was simply more efficient and productive, even if it did confine women to inferior jobs with poor promotion prospects. 'There is no doubt', he asserted, 'that in the past, and at present, the system of separate lists has worked and continues to work extremely well.'[45]

These were, then, the major divisions of the workforce into established and unestablished, indoor and outdoor, male and female. The result was a complex hierarchy of pay scales which reflected the social expectations of the administrators as much as the economic worth of the work performed. However, it is necessary to consider not only the structure of pay at a point in time, for another major issue was the adjustment of rewards over time. On what basis should increased wages be offered or refused?

The determination of wages

The method of determining wages in the public sector has remained a topic of controversy which has haunted British governments. It has been a particularly important issue in the 'mixed' economy which has developed since the Second World War, and many of the arguments had already been rehearsed by the Post Office in the nineteenth century. Should wages in the public sector be determined by the market imperatives of supply and demand for labour, should they be regulated by rates in comparable occupations in the private sector, or should they be settled by a concern for social equity apart from ecomomic considerations?

'The working classes', Rowland Hill had argued in 1832, 'must be made familiar with the circumstances which regulate the price of their labour.' When he moved to the Post Office, Hill sought to apply his belief that the free play of market forces was the only reliable means of establishing wage rates, and in 1855 the Department and Treasury were able to agree on 'the principle of fixing the scale of salaries to be paid according to the nature and locality of each place'. Wages, it was decided, should not be determined by the size of the office, for this might mean 'that the high salary and wages, which a thriving manu- facturing town commands, would be paid also at an agricultural town where a lower rate of pay would be sufficient'. The result was a series of local scales determined by the supply of labour and the prevalent wage in any area, so that wages would be adjusted on a piecemeal basis as problems arose in recruiting and retaining labour. This general principle of determining wages by the state of the local labour market could be interpreted in a more or less strict manner, as appeared in 1860–1 in the conflict between Rowland Hill and the committee considering the wages and conditions of the London workforce. The dispute over the propriety of the appointment of this committee has already been discussed, and this was linked to a disagreement over the determination of wage rates. This episode illuminates the assumptions upon which the Post Office operated.[46]

There was general acceptance of the principle laid down by John Tilley that 'to pay every person according to the real market value of the work which he performs can be the only right principle; to go beyond this is profligate and mischievous'. This left open the question of how the 'real market value' should be established, and it was over this, rather than the general principle, that Hill and Tilley parted company.

Although Tilley felt that wages were adequate, he considered that a committee should be appointed to consider wage rates in order to curtail discontent. Hill disagreed, arguing that this was a partial acceptance of the men's case and that Tilley's task was to suppress unrest. This divergence over the necessary administrative action extended to the assessment of the 'market value of the work'. The committee concluded that wages were inadequate, basing this conclusion upon 'the un-popularity of the service, the difficulty of inducing efficient men to enter it, the still greater difficulty of inducing them to remain in it'. Hill, by contrast, argued that the supply of labour exceeded the requirements of the Department; he stressed that the turnover of labour was less than 1 per cent a year and that wages in the Post Office were so superior to similar occupations as 'to render further comparison unnecessary'. The committee could counter that the shortage was one of *efficient* men, that the turnover was high among *young* men, and that comparison should be made with *responsible* and highly paid occupations. Although the simple theoretical proposition that wages were determined by the market commanded general assent, it had become problematical in application.

The determination of wages was indeed to move imperceptibly away from the discipline of the market, towards the position adopted by the Postmaster General in 1861 that recourse to a free market was not enough 'without even considering whether that course would be calculated to secure really efficient and trustworthy services'. Although it might be possible to find workers at lower wages, 'such persons when once admitted would soon become discontented, and clamourous for an improvement in their condition'. The existence of dissatisfaction might itself be taken as a measure of the inadequacy of wages which should, he felt, be fixed so as to 'give an adequate pay for the work to be performed, and to hold out sufficient inducements to the Public Servants to perform their duties with fidelity by enabling them to look forward to securing a fair reward for good conduct and length of service'. This was to give far greater emphasis than Hill to the expectations of the workers. He had insisted upon the unreality of seeking wages higher than dictated by the laws of the market, and feared that the workers might conclude

that their treatment and remuneration must not be governed by those of servants under private masters, but that some other standard, as yet undiscovered, is to be applied in their favour. It is the undisputed right of every individual in the State to employ his fellow subjects on terms of mutual agreement, subject only to the general law of the land; the practical consequence from which proposition is that labour bought by the private employer is purchased at the market price. But it is now implied, if not openly laid down, that when the individuals, of

223

which the State is composed, form an aggregate body, and as such employ labour, the aggregate body loses the right to pay only the market price and becomes subject to some undefined, and, indeed, utterly incomprehensible duty to pay some higher price, or, what is tantamount to increase of price, to pay similar wages for a less amount of labour.

Hill was pointing to a significant theme in the history of the Post Office: should wages be determined by the Department according to its own assessment of a fair rate, or should the process be left to the operation of the market? In 1861, the Treasury was in general agreement with Hill and refused to sanction a general increase in wage rates. It remained to be seen how long this position could be held.[47] Essentially, the principle that wages should be determined by the prevalent local rate and state of the labour market was enforced during the 1870s, and was to be rejected in the early 1880s.

Wages in general increased rapidly in the early 1870s, and the staff of the Post Office wished to share in the gains. 'There is', it was admitted, 'no doubt that in manufacturing towns, in the north of England, there is growing difficulty in procuring youths of 16 years of age, as their services are required in warehouses, and mills, owing to the extraordinary prosperity existing in every branch of trade.' Wages, it was argued, were higher in comparable jobs and 'it would be very inexpedient to refuse the men who make a well-grounded application in a legitimate way an advance which is justified by all the circumstances'. It was therefore proposed to increase the pay in Liverpool, Manchester and Birmingham. The application was, however, rejected by the Treasury which felt 'that the forfeiture of Pensions may be relied on to prevent a strike'. Stoppages did occur at Warrington and Huddersfield; the prospect of serious disruption and resignations worried the Post Office and a renewed application was made to the Treasury. In 1874, the Treasury conceded an allowance of two shillings a week for two years, which was not to be incorporated in the wage scale or to count towards superannuation. The relation of the Post Office to its workforce, the Treasury claimed, was not the same as other employers who could take advantage of a deterioration in the labour market in order to reduce wages, for in the public sector 'a rise in wages once conceded . . . is in effect permanent'. Wages should therefore be established by the price at which labour was forthcoming, and in 1874 vacancies in north London were thrown open by public advertisement in order to ascertain whether wages were 'sufficient to attract suitable candidates'. The answer seemed to be obvious, for 1,200 candidates appeared for 22 vacancies. 'If the Government is to fare simply like other employers in good times', argued the Treasury, it ought to be equally free in bad times to reduce any excess which may have been forced upon it in particular places where labour happens for the time to be in exceptionally great demand. But, seeing that the balance never gets in this way redressed, where Government is concerned, there ought to be a corresponding resistance against committing it to wages which are those only of prosperous times in particular places.

Despite these assertions, the Treasury was obliged to renew the allowance it had reluctantly granted in 1874, and in 1880 it was forced to bow to the incorporation of the 'temporary' increase into the pay scale. Reality could not always be forced to accord with theory.[48]

The assessment of wages by the test 'whether such scale is or is not sufficient to attract and retain the services of suitable persons' did create a resistance to increases in payment. Labour costs in the 1870s nevertheless increased at a faster rate than revenue, and in 1876 the Treasury proposed another criterion based upon the financial performance of the Post Office rather than the state of the labour market at large. Costs, it was argued, should not increase at a faster rate than revenue and the Treasury formulated the principle that pay increases 'will not be entertained unless it can be shown at the same time that the revenue derived from the place or branch of the service concerned has increased in a proportionate rate'. The suggestion alarmed the Post Office, for it was scarcely possible to pay lower wages in the Money Order Office which 'barely pays it way' than in the Savings Bank which was 'highly flourishing'. The Treasury's principle that wages should be determined by revenue implied more generally that 'instead of the social and commercial interests of the country being considered as of paramount importance . . . the Department is to be a mere machine for raising revenue, and is to be conducted as an ordinary mercantile establishment'. The Departmental view, expressed by S.A. Blackwood, was that since policy was not determined by the need of any particular service to raise the maximum revenue, it was not possible to set wages by the financial results. The Post Office was, so it was argued, different from a private concern:

Any attempt to pay a lower scale of remuneration than the labour market enabled persons to demand would only result in a deadlock, a state of things which might be endurable and even justifiable in private enterprises, but which it is needless to say, would not be tolerated for 24 hours in a Service carried on by the State, of which it is given a monopoly for the public benefit, and which is known to bring in a very handsome profit to the Exchequer.

The Treasury's attempt to impose the new criterion of revenue was rejected, and reliance on the state of the external labour market was reasserted.[49]

225

This position was seriously challenged in the early 1880s from another direction. The letter-carriers in 1881 submitted memorials for increased pay which the Secretary considered was 'very difficult to justify . . . on the ground of absolute necessity'. Blackwood, who became Secretary in 1880, had opposed the Treasury's criterion of financial performance but he was strongly convinced of the necessity to determine wages by the state of the labour market. There was no difficulty in obtaining 'good and suitable men', and although concessions might, he agreed, create 'a spirit of contented and willing service', he had other priorities. 'Those who believe that the remuneration of those employed in the Public Services should be regulated in accordance with the stern laws of supply and demand will be slow to admit that an addition to the pay of Letter Carriers is called for at the present time.' He held that the principles of political economy were part of God's law for the welfare of the human race and that their abandonment would place men 'at the mercy of the wildest vagaries'. The rules of the economist might lead to hardships for some, but would be

> less than those which must certainly be the result of attempts to regulate traffic upon principles of man's devising. The Scriptural principle governing all transactions of the nature of commerce, is that of paying a *fair* price. And to the question, How is that *fair* price to be ascertained? I reply, The operation of the laws of supply and demand must settle that price.

High principle therefore demanded the rejection of the letter-carriers' claim, although Blackwood admitted that this would result in 'a very dangerous agitation' and that expediency suggested some concessions. Blackwood was reflecting the Post Office view of the 1860s and 1870s that the local labour market determined wages, with some flexibility in order to contain discontent.[50] However, in 1881 such an approach was rejected by the Postmaster General and wages were freed from the constraints of the market.

Henry Fawcett, the husband of the suffragette, is himself remembered as the 'blind Postmaster General'. He had been blinded in a shooting accident in 1858 when he was 25 but neither this mishap nor his ignorance of the subject prevented his election to the chair of political economy at Cambridge in 1863. His biographer admitted that he made no contribution to the development of economic theory, and sceptics argued that in his term as Postmaster General he broke the laws of political economy. Rather than setting wages at the lowest rate which would attract labour, Fawcett argued that the Department should 'secure really efficient service by obviating discontent'. It was wrong, in his opinion, to grant improvements only as a result of pressure and he felt that the Post Office should be prepared to take the lead by diverting part of the surplus to the staff rather than handing it to the Exchequer. This approach did not receive enthusiastic support within the Department, for, as one sceptic argued, 'paying people more than is sufficient to secure permanent good service does not make them contented, or prevent them from demanding still higher wages. . . . When once the principle of paying according to the market value of labour is departed from generally, on what principle could a further addition of pay be refused?' The Treasury continued to assert that letter-carriers' pay should be determined by the state of the local labour market, and refused to 'admit the pretensions of Civil Servants that, once appointed and to a certain extent relived from the competition to which all other classes are subjected of the open market, they are to dictate, irrespectively of the terms on which they were glad to take service, those on which they are to continue to serve'. The Postmaster General nevertheless had his way and the 'Fawcett revisions' of 1881–2 departed from the principles which had dominated in the 1860s and 1870s. On the contrary, 'financial considerations have been left almost out of sight, the well- being of the Servants of the Department, the inducements to them to render zealous service, and the consequent advantage to the Department and to the public being the main objects sought to be obtained'.[51]

Pressure for improved pay and conditions was to reappear in the late 1880s at a time of widespread unrest and unionisation. The Post Office, as will be shown in the next chapter, was resolutely opposed to unions and mounted a vigorous campaign to contain 'insubordination'. This did not, however, necessarily entail a return to the stricter principles of wage determination of the 1860s and 1870s. This is apparent from the report of 1891 of the committee appointed to examine the pay and conditions of postmen. Although the Board of Trade provided evidence on wages in other occupations the committee doubted the value of the exercise, for 'as between postmen on the one hand and other bodies of men on the other, – such, for instance, as the police or persons engaged in various kinds of labour, skilled or unskilled, – the conditions of employment or mode of remuneration are so different that no useful comparison can be made. There is, in short, no common measure.' The committee was reduced 'to the necessity of examining the case of the postmen by itself, and with little reference to extraneous conditions'; the change in policy announced by Fawcett was confirmed.[52]

The criteria used to establish wages had altered although in other respects little had changed. The Post Office responded to pressure from the staff or to problems of recruitment, and suggested concessions to the Treasury. Negotiations took place between civil servants at St Martin's le Grand and Whitehall rather than with the staff, which was simply informed of the result. In the 1890s there were two changes in this procedure. The first was that consideration of wages was transferred to committees of outsiders appointed for the purpose, starting with the Inter-departmental Committee on Post Office Establishments of 1895 (the Tweedmouth Committee) which represented the Post Office, Treasury and Board of Trade. Its successors had no Departmental membership: the Bradford Committee of 1903 was composed of businessmen; the Hobhouse and Holt Committees of 1906 and 1912 were Select Committees of the House of Commons. The second change was in the role of the staff. There was, it is true, still no direct negotiation between the Department and the workers but representatives of each grade could present evidence to these Committees. This process had started in 1891 with the internal committee appointed by the Department to consider postmen's pay, and it was continued by the committees drawn from outside the Department. The scale of the exercise could be formidable, for the evidence presented to the Tweedmouth Committee came to 1,009 pages, and to the Holt Committee to 1,774 pages. These changes in procedure might at first sight seem to pose a threat to the Department, removing its ability to determine wages and increasing the influence of the staff. However, the new procedure in fact offered certain advantages. Pressure from the staff was directed towards securing the appointment of a committee, which was not lightly granted, and the scale of the enquiries imposed further delay. The result was that the adjustment of pay scales tended to become more inflexible.

The Committees adopted criteria for determining wages which were stricter than those formulated by Fawcett. The Tweedmouth Committee was instructed by the Postmaster General that 'in conducting this inquiry, I can have no doubt you will recollect that the Post Office is a great Revenue Department, and that, in the words of the Select Committee on Revenue Departments Estimates in 1888, it "is more likely to continue to be conducted satisfactorily, if it should also continue to be conducted with a view to profit, as one of the Revenue Yielding Departments of the State".' The Bradford Committee was instructed to base its enquiries upon comparisons with wages in other occupations. However, the Committee failed to follow its terms of reference and accepted three other criteria, namely the number and character of recruits, their capacity when employed, and their contentment. Although it was admitted that the supply and efficiency of labour were indeed adequate, the existence of discontent was felt to justify higher wages. The Committee was, in other words, following the Fawcett view by rejecting a strictly economic assessment and arguing instead 'that postal employees are justified in resting their claims to remuneration on the responsible and exacting character of the duties performed and on the social position they fill as servants of the State'. On this occasion the Postmaster General set aside the Committee's conclusions and the Fawcett approach was not followed. This changed emphasis was also apparent in the case of the Holt Committee. While the staff's claim was based upon a belief 'that "the ideal of family life" ought to be within the reach of everybody', the Committee was instructed to compare the Post Office staff 'as far as may be, to the standard rate of wages and the position of other classes of worker'. The Holt Committee found it difficult to make comparisons, but was confident that 'no evidence was adduced to support the proposition that Post Office servants suffer any disadvantage in the matter of wages as compared with persons engaged in other occupations'. The criteria adopted had clearly been narrowed since the Fawcett revision.[53]

The determination of wages by appeal to external committees was replaced after the First World War by direct collective bargaining between the Department and the staff. The situation had become unacceptable by 1914 as massive and detailed volumes arrived from the Select Committees for discussion by the House of Commons. 'One may expect a certain amount of confusion and verbiage in State documents,' remarked one Member in the debate on the Holt Committee, 'but certainly no big commercial enterprise would ever regard a Select Committee of the House of Commons as a suitable tribunal on duties and wages.' Continuity of negotiations, it was felt by many MPs, was preferable to sporadic committees, and the Commons recommended the creation of permanent machinery to bring the Department and representatives of the workforce into direct contact:

> The system of allowing abuses to accumulate for years and then
> appointing a party tribunal to make a revision is . . . entirely wrong.
> What happens? You have an accumulation of abuses; you appoint a
> tribunal; you clear things up. No sooner is that done than new abuses
> begin to accumulate, like a new debt on a church, and you have to
> appoint another Committee to go over the matter again, and so it goes
> on at short intervals. It is quite impossible for this House to deal
> satisfactorily with the details of the present dispute or of any other
> similar dispute. There ought to be some sort of permanent committee
> or board of arbitration.

The appointment of a committee representing the unions, Post Office and Treasury under the chairmanship of the Board of Trade was approved, although action was prevented by the outbreak of war.[54] After the First World War, direct negotiation between the Department and union officials replaced the cumbersome procedure of presentation of

229

evidence to a third party. The new procedure was inaugurated with the wage claim of 1919 which brought the representatives of the Department to the negotiating table with union officials for the first time.

It soon became clear that there was a lack of agreement between the two sides on the criteria to be used in determining wages. The first postwar settlement of 1920 was based upon comparison with wages in the Post Office in 1914 rather than with earnings in other trades, and the Committee on the Pay of State Servants in 1923 claimed that wages had in consequence been set too high. The Post Office was defined by the Committee as a 'sheltered' occupation which did not face foreign competition and which could, as a result, pay higher wages than 'open' trades. The Committee expected 'that in due course the rates in sheltered occupations will be brought into closer harmony with the level of wages in the open trades on which they depend, and we think the Post Office should consider whether such high maximum rates as are now paid are necessary'. Although the Department doubted whether it would be possible to reduce real wages below the level of 1914, it did accept that rates should not go any higher and insisted upon comparisons with 'outside industries' in negotiations, even if it was difficult to find close analogies.[55] The Postmaster General stressed that 'the wages of the Post Office staff are, at present, in general, commensurate with the duties which they are required to perform', and the award of higher wages would, it was felt, 'become the most conspicuous example of the disparity between the wage level in a sheltered industry and that prevailing in competitive undertakings'. The wages of the Post Office staff could not, remarked the Postmaster General, be set 'as though he and they were the only employer and employee in the country'. The line pursued by the Department was therefore based upon comparison with other occupations.

The staff denied the relevance of such an approach and followed the line of the Bradford Committee 'that postal employees are justified in resting their claims to remuneration on the responsible and exacting character of the duties performed and on the social position they fill as servants of the State'. A public servant, it was argued, 'must maintain a certain social status and standard of life. . . . It is contended that while the State demands and obtains a high standard of service and status from its servants, it does not offer in return that remuneration by which such a standard can be adequately maintained.' The claim for higher wages could also rest upon economic arguments. Productivity, it was maintained, had increased as a result of intensification of work, mechanisation, and rationalisation of methods. 'The staff did not object to changes in methods but they claimed that they should share in the gains which arose. The whole of the benefits however had gone to the

230

Post Office and the Exchequer.... [T]he workers had a fair claim to a better share of the results of a good service which everyone endeavoured to provide by a high quality of service.' However, as Clement Attlee remarked, 'the Post Office was a branch of government and could not act independently of the Government or the Treasury'. Economy and a balanced budget were the order of the day, and the Post Office was expected to contribute a larger sum to the Exchequer. It was admitted that the surplus contained an element of taxation, and 'it would be fallacious to regard the produce of this tax as a ground for increasing wages, just as it would be fallacious to propose a reduction in wages in the event of the Chancellor of the Exchequer finding it practicable to remit the tax and so to reduce the charge to the public and the Post Office profits'.

The Department was able to maintain its position in both pay claims in the interwar period, in 1924 and 1931. The result was that the settlement of 1920, which had been based upon the rates of 1914, remained in force until the Second World War.[56] This was not the end of the matter, for there were also, in addition to the basic pay scale, cost of living bonuses which had been granted as a result of the severe inflation during the First World War. These bonuses were regulated after the war by a formula which was introduced in 1920: the bonus was to be raised or lowered by 5/130ths for every five points by which the cost of living index rose above or fell below 130. The adjustment was made twice a year, on 1 March and 1 September. The peak was reached on 1 March 1921 and for the remainder of the 1920s there was a steady fall, with an additonal emergency reduction in 1931. The system was modified in 1932 when rates were stabilised for two years provided that the cost of living remained within a band of 25 points, and the ultimate aim was to incorporate the cost of lving bonus into the basic pay scale which would only change in the light of comparison with outside occupations. This consolidated scale was introduced in 1934, at which point the cost of living index started to rise. Wages had therefore fallen automatically during the period of price deflation, and did not rise automatically during the period of recovery.[57]

The procedure for the determination of wages in the Post Office had passed through three stages. In the first phase, the Department responded to problems of recruitment and discontent; there were no negotiations with the staff and the Department decided unilaterally on the appropriate concessions which were submitted to the Treasury for approval. Although the criteria did change, this procedure survived until the early 1890s when a second technique was introduced. This was wage determination by committee, which took the process outside the Post Office. The cases of the Department and staff were presented to a

231

committee of outsiders which then made recommendations. There was no direct negotiation between the Department and the staff, and instead there was a reliance upon a cumbersome indirect procedure of appeal to an outside body. This phase lasted until the First World War, when a process of direct negotiation was introduced. The mechanics of wage determination changed over time, and so did the criteria which were applied. The strict reliance upon market indicators at the beginning of the period was gradually undermined by a greater emphasis on non-economic considerations. This trend reached a peak in the early 1880s during Henry Fawcett's term as Postmaster General. During the second phase from the mid-1890s to the First World War this trend was halted, and in the interwar period the principle of wage determination by comparison with outside occupations was asserted. The application of these procedures and criteria for wage determination had practical implications both for the standard of living of Post Office workers, and for the share of labour in costs.

Wages, labour costs and productivity

The changing procedures and criteria for the determination of wages resulted in significant divergences between trends in the standard of living in the Post Office and in the rest of society. The general British pattern was for real wages to rise rapidly between the early 1870s and mid-1890s as a result of a sharp reduction in prices and relative stability of money wages: the index of real wages rose from 128 in 1873 to 174 in 1895. This was followed by a period of stagnation of real wages as prices rose at a faster rate than money wages, and in 1914 the index of real wages still stood at 174. The First World War resulted in severe inflation and an initial erosion of real wages, but in the latter part of the war and during the postwar boom money wages outstripped prices and real wages rose above the prewar level. When the postwar boom broke in 1921, employers initially attempted to reduce money wages in line with falling prices, a strategy which was abandoned in the mid-1920s when the real wages of those in employment started to rise. The index of real wages in Britain, calculated on a base of 100 in 1924, fell from 102 in 1920 to 97 in 1923, and subsequently rose to 118 in 1938. Wages in the Post Office differed from this general trend in a number of respect.[58]

Money wages in the Post Office during the period of falling prices in the last quarter of the nineteenth century rose almost five times as rapidly as the national average. The outcome was a remarkable increase in real wages by 71.9 per cent between 1875 and 1897. Clearly, the more lenient application of the laws of supply and demand had allowed the standard of living of Post Office workers to increase at a rapid rate.

6.4 TREND IN WAGE RATES, 1875–1938 (PERCENTAGE CHANGE)

Postmen and sorters	money wages	real wages
1875–97	+32.4	+71.9
1897–1914	+12.7	−4.2
1923–38	−3.0	+8.3
National average		
1875–97	+7.8	+33.3
1897–1914	+19.0	−2.0
1923–38	+7.1	+19.2

Source: G. Routh, 'Civil Service pay, 1875–1950', *Economica*, ns 21 (1954) and B.R. Mitchell and P. Deane, *Abstract of British Historial Statistics* (1962).

The period between 1897 and 1914 stands in marked contrast, for the cumbersome procedure of investigation by committee and the renewed emphasis upon economic criteria meant that money wages in the Post Office were less buoyant than in society at large. Real wages fell by 4.2 per cent between 1897 and the First World War. Neither did Post Office employees receive the same increase in real wages in the interwar period as other workers, for the cost of living bonus fell and there was no increase in the basic pay scale. The result was that money wages were reduced by 3 per cent between 1923 and 1938, and real wages rose at less than half the national rate. The changing process of wage determination clearly had an immediate effect on the relative position of Post Office workers.[59]

The course of money wages also affected the profitability of the Post Office in an immediate manner, for most services provided by the Department were labour intensive, whether it be the handling of letters or the calculation of interest on Savings Bank accounts. An increase in money wages would have serious financial implications, unless it could be offset by an improvement in productivity. The introduction of Penny Post did produce a marked rise in productivity, although it has been seen that it was not to the extent anticipated by Hill. The workforce in England and Wales rose by 80.5 per cent and the cost by 94.2 per cent between 1839 and 1849, which may be compared with an increase of 309.1 per cent in the postal traffic of the United Kingdom. The fall in the cost of handling a letter continued until about 1880. For the 1860s labour costs are unfortunately not available, and it can only be noted that the postal traffic increased by 53.5 per cent between 1860 and 1870, and the workforce by 12.6 per cent. Labour costs are available for the 1870s when there was a clear improvement in the financial performance: between 1870/1 and 1880/1 traffic rose by 69.4 per cent and labour costs by 50.2 per cent. Productivity rose and unit labour costs fell during the first forty years of Penny Post, a trend which was reversed in the 1880s: between 1880/1 and 1890/1 the traffic increased by 56 per cent and the cost of labour in the postal services by 77.8 per cent. Labour costs continued to rise faster than traffic until the First World War, and although the discrepancy was reduced – traffic rose by 41.8 per cent between 1900/1 and 1910/1 and labour costs by 48.3 per cent – the trend was not reversed. The outcome was a marked increase in unit labour costs in the postal services between the 1880s and the First World War.[60]

Unfortunately, it is not possible to measure productivity in the postal services after the acquisition of the telegraph system in 1870, for although labour *costs* were allocated between the services, no attempt was made to apportion the *staff* between posts and telegraphs. Certainly the generous wage settlements of the late nineteenth century would not appear to have been offset by gains in productivity. The Department was concerned that the cost of providing services rose with the size of an office, and there appeared to be serious diseconomies of scale as the traffic increased. The relationship between traffic and staff was measured by 'Treasury units' or the 'table of normal costs'. Each type of work was expressed in terms of letters, so that a money order transaction was equivalent to thirteen letters, a postal order transaction to three letters, and so on. The total volume of work was reduced to units of 1,000 letters a week; the average cost of dealing with a unit was calculated at a number of offices; and a table of normal costs derived which showed the expenditure involved in handling any level of traffic. The table indicated a serious problem for the Post Office, for as the size of office increased, the average cost per unit rose. In 1895, the cost of a unit of work in a small office which handled up to ten units was £5 11s 7d, whereas the cost in a large office handling over a thousand units was £16 13s 3d. 'As work increases and the division of labour becomes possible economies of organisation are to be expected. But as different categories are entered upon new sources of expense are encountered which have, in the past, more than neutralised the saving thus effected in the postal work.' The economies of scale in the sorting and delivery of letters were offset by various diseconomies such as the substitution of permanent for part-time staff, the separation of telegraph and counter work, increased costs of supervision, the creation of first-class duties at higher wages, and the division of staff for branch offices. Specialisation led in many cases to a 'fractional waste' of the men engaged on each separate duty, for

> the more grandiose organisation of a very large office results in a
> disinclination of men to lend a hand to inferior duties in their intervals
> of leisure. At the smallest Offices a Sorting Clerk will help to unload a

mail cart or to stamp letters. At the largest Offices, a Money Order clerk, though he may be unoccupied cannot sell a postage stamp. There is a grave reason to fear that many duties performed by first class men are really second class duties with a minimum spice of first class work to afford a *prima facie* justification for first class pay.

The increase in the unit cost with the size of office meant that the growth in traffic in the late nineteenth century contributed to the deteriorating financial performance of the Post Office.[61]

Few attempts were made before the First World War to raise the productivity of the indoor workforce. The chief engineer did visit America in 1909 and he returned with great enthusiasm for the techology he had inspected. He urged its application 'with the same general objects in view, namely, reduction of labour, increase in the speed of passage through the various processes and increase in general convenience by the reduction of obstruction and bustle in the gangways and by extending the capacity for dealing with the work at times of great pressure'. He was 'convinced that very great advantages may be obtained by the use of mechanical appliances on a large scale'. In 1910, the Treasury authorised the expenditure of £150 on experiments, and in 1911 it was decided to proceed with a prototype installation at Liverpool. Stamp-cancelling machines were in general use and some offices had conveyor belts, and the intention was to link them so that letters were passed automatically from the facing tables through the stamping machines to the sorters. Trials and modifications continued until 1916 when a committee reported unfavourably on the use of machinery which was 'costly in construction, restricted in its utility, and liable to break down'. The 'present cheap, adaptable and reliable fittings' were preferred.[62]

In the interwar period, the relationship between the growth of traffic and labour costs was reversed, for postal traffic rose by 16.1 per cent between 1920/1 and 1930/1, and labour costs fell by 18.8 per cent. This was in part the result of the changed procedures of wage determination which have been described, and in part the outcome of improved productivity. There was desultory discussion of improvements in sorting in the 1920s, and the need for mechanisation was seriously considered in the 1930s. Experiments began in 1934 to develop automatic letter-facing equipment, and in 1935 a Dutch 'Transorma' sorting machine was installed in Brighton. By 1938, the Post Office was able to agree on the specifications for a sorting machine, and the Department was ready to press ahead with development. At the outbreak of the Second World War, there was unprecedented interest in the mechanisation of sorting offices although it was not to have a practical impact until the late

1950s.[63] The greater contribution to productivity in the 1920s and 1930s came less from mechanisation of sorting than from the 'motorisation' of collections and deliveries which has been discussed in an earlier chapter. There were, it is true, a number of constraints on the adoption of motor vans, but the trend towards a less labour-intensive service had commenced. After the Second World War, the emergence of full employment was, for the first time, to cast doubt upon the ability of the Post Office to recruit labour and the possibilities offered by investment in mechanised sorting became ever more seductive.

On the Establishment

Independently of the money value of these places, there is the great advantage which employment in the Public Service possesses over private employment. However industrious a man in private employment may be, he is liable at any time to be the victim of adverse circumstances such as loss of health, the caprice or want of success of his Employer, or an overstocked labour market. In the Public Service, a man of good conduct is assured regular wages, or a Pension ... from the day he enters it to the day of his death. (Post 60/89, *Memorandum on the wages of the minor establishment in the Post Office, Feb. 1874.*)

Employment in the Post Office granted a security which few other workmen possessed in the nineteenth century, for 'Every established Post Office servant has practical certainty of continuity of employment independent of fluctuations of business'.[1] The Post Office also offered a wide range of benefits which were not generally available to the majority of the population until the Liberal social reforms of 1906–14 and the creation of the welfare state after the Second World War. When entry had been gained to the Post Office, the newcomer joined a bureaucratic organisation which could operate according to its own distinctive principles and policies. There was an internal labour market within the Post Office which connected with the external labour market of society at large only at certain clearly defined points of entry. Once inside, its members were shielded from the impact of competition for jobs. Positions within this internal labour market were filled by the promotion and transfer of those who had already gained access. Wage differentials between grades and by age were determined by the needs and expectations of the organisation rather than by simple economic considerations of supply and demand. In internal labour markets, personal relationships with opportunities for favouritism or capricious discipline were replaced by formal rules and regulations, and such organisations offered 'jobs with relatively high wages, good working conditions, chances of advancement, equity and due process in the administration of work rules, and above all employment stability'. The Post Office was a pioneer of this bureaucratic system of labour organisation in Britain and its acceptance was a slow process with many conflicts and ambiguities.[2]

From patronage to merit

There had arisen in England a system of patronage, under which it had become gradually necessary for politicians to use their influence for the purchase of political support. . . . In this there was nothing pleasant to the distributor of patronage. Do away with the system altogether, and he would have as much chance of support as another. He bartered his patronage only because another did so also. The beggings, the refusings, the jealousies, the correspondence, were simply troublesome. Gentlemen in office were not therefore indisposed to rid themselves of the care of patronage. I have no doubt their hands are the cleaner and their hearts are the lighter; but I do doubt whether the offices are on the whole better manned. (A. Trollope, *An Autobiography* (1883; 1946 edn), p. 51)

Rowland Hill in his pamphlet of 1837 defined reform of the Post Office in a precise manner, as a change in the method of collecting postage and a reduction in rates. By the 1840s and 1850s, the debate on civil service reform had produced a new emphasis: patronage and favour were under attack and entry to the civil service was to depend upon the impersonal assessment of competence rather than the favour of an influential figure. The practice of patronage had often been associated with the appropriation of income from the office in addition to the salary, and a second strand in the reform of the civil service was the assertion of a strict line between private profit and public position. In the mid-nineteenth century, patronage and profit were in retreat as the foundations of a modern bureaucracy were laid.[3]

The use of public office as a source of private gain can be seen in the Post Office. The Money Letter Office, it has been noted, was initially run as a private venture within the Department. In 1838, the Commissioners appointed to enquire into the Post Office recommended the 'abolition of private trading under official privileges', and the service was taken over by the Department. The right of the 'proprietors' to compensation for the appropriation of their business was nevertheless admitted.[4] A similar trend from the coincidence to the separation of

27 Horse-drawn vans such as this one in 1908 were used for transit work in towns.

28 Contractors provided short-distance road services, such as this mail-cart which ran between Redruth and Land's End in the early 1890s.

29　The maximum distance for bicycle posts was set in 1903 at 28 miles.

30　Postwomen delivered letters in Barnet during World War I.

31　Letters were sorted on Travelling Post Offices. This is the Irish T.P.O.

32 A fleet of Morris commercial vans in the yard of the head office in the City of London, 1931.

33 Collecting mail in 1937. Motor vans were first introduced for mail collection in the 1920s.

34   Motor-cycles were introduced in 1932 for the delivery of telegrams. They were ridden by messengers aged 17 and above.

35   A streamlined air-mail van is shown delivering the mail at Croydon aerodrome in 1935.

36 Mail being loaded on the underground railway at Mount Pleasant in 1956.

37 Letters are separated from packets in the segregator, a rotating drum with slots in the sides.

38 The coding-desk operator types the post code which is printed on the envelope in phosphor dots.

39   Coded mail is fed into sorting machines, a scanner reads the phosphor dots, and the letter is directed to 150 selection boxes at a rate of 9,000 letters per hour.

40   A postman clears letters from a pre-sorter which gives priority to mail with the furthest to travel. The whole business of sorting mail has become more capital intensive.

private profit and public office was apparent in the case of letter-carriers in London. In the early nineteenth century they had a proprietary interest in their 'walks', from which they could earn substantial sums in addition to their wages. Businesses were willing to pay the letter-carriers for an early delivery before the regular service, and fees were also charged for 'bell ringing' which announced the collection of letters. The income could be substantial. Letter-carriers in 1845 had an average wage of £46 16s which was augmented by £44 17s 4d from early deliveries, £13 5s 4d from bell ringing and £10 in Christmas gratuities. The Department had attempted to control the system in 1807 by determining the 'profits' of each walk and regulating the official wage to produce a greater equity of income. In theory, any surplus produced by the walks would be used to provide a pension fund; in practice the letter-carriers retained a considerable sum. Total payment for early deliveries in 1845 was £4,152 and the letter-carriers retained £3,389 after the deductions for the pension fund; a further £2,038 was received for bell ringing and £2,770 at Christmas. The wages paid by the Department amounted to £13,354, so that the private income amounted to 61.4 per cent of the official payment. The letter-carriers referred to this practice as 'working the walks', a phrase which indicates a sense of private trading. Although early deliveries and bell ringing were abolished in 1846, the claim of the letter-carriers to a property right in the walk was nevertheless accepted at the same time as the source of private profit was removed. Compensation was granted for the loss of income, which was to recognise that workers did have a vested interest in their jobs. By 1857, John Tilley was prepared to go a stage further, arguing that no individual could have a property right in a public office, and that it was therefore 'very objectionable' to compensate for the loss of something which should not exist in the first place.[5] Tilley concluded that fixed salaries should be the sole reward for public service. This was a relatively recent position, marking the adoption of the bureaucratic principle of a complete separation between the personal property of the official and the property belonging to the organisation.[6]

This trend was associated with the gradual acceptance in the third quarter of the nineteenth century of another distinctive feature of bureaucratic organisation: personal recommendation gave way to objective examination of ability. The process started in the mid-1850s and was not completed for forty years. Letter-carriers in the provinces, for example, had been appointed by the Postmaster General under a system of patronage, the nominee of the local Member of Parliament usually being selected. This patronage was abandoned in provincial towns in 1855 and the local postmaster was entrusted with the selection, a practice which was extended to the country districts in 1892. The

The bellman, until their abolition in 1846, walked the streets of London attracting the attention of anyone wishing to catch the last post, a service for which they were paid a fee.

postmasters usually selected the postmen from the ranks of either the part-time staff or the boys employed to deliver telegrams, and their recommendations were generally accepted by the Secretary.[7] Similarly, the method of appointment of postmasters was modified as patronage was removed in stages between 1854 and 1895.[8] The demise of patronage might, as Trollope remarked, lead to cleaner hands and lighter hearts; more practically, alternative procedures were needed for the filling of vacancies in the civil service in general and the Post Office in particular.

Selection was not a great problem for private employers who could draw upon the labour market at will and dismiss workers with ease; the Post Office, which offered a permanent career rather than a short-term job, had to take greater care. 'Resignations are of rare occurence', it was remarked in 1874, 'nor are dismissals in the Post Office numerous.'[9] The vital point was how entry was to be gained to this privileged and protected world. The *Report upon the Post Office* of 1854 had no doubt:

> the Postmaster General should lay down strict rules for the examination of all Candidates for admission, either into the class of Clerks, or into that of Sorters and Letter Carriers, in order to test their capacity, and should take care also to satisfy himself as to their characters, before making any appointment.[10]

This was, of course, an extension to the Post Office of the principles formulated by Stafford Northcote and C. E. Trevelyan for the civil service in general. Reform of the civil service required, in their view, the abandonment of patronage and the substitution of entry by examination, preferably through a competition open to anyone who wished to be a candidate. Although this far-reaching proposal was not immediately accepted, in 1855 the Civil Service Commission was established to introduce a limited form of examination. Patronage and nomination were not immediately abolished, but candidates for clerical and administrative posts who were put forward by influential persons had to pass the examination set by the Commission in order to ensure that they met certain standards. The implementation of open competitive examinations was delayed until 1870, when two categories of written tests for administrative posts were introduced, under Regulation I for university graduates seeking senior posts, and Regulation II for lower-grade recruits. The morality of merit had triumphed over the power of patronage.[11]

Anthony Trollope was sceptical about this 'damnable system of so-called merit' and his fiction often associated ability to pass examinations with untrustworthiness, and patronage with a sense of a person's real worth. This is most apparent in *The Three Clerks*, which took the introduction of the Northcote-Trevelyan reforms as its theme. Gregory

Hardlines, the fictional counterpart of Stafford Northcote, was appointed to create the Board of Civil Service Examiners, and his old post as head of Weights and Measures was obtained by Alaric Tudor through his ability in an examination. Alaric was also a Commissioner of the Board of Civil Service Examiners, and was in all respects the representative of the system of merit. But he fell into bad company, accepted bribes and indulged in speculation with trust money so that his career ended in ruins and prison. Charley Tudor, who represented Trollope, led an idle and dissipated existence in the Internal Navigation Office where he had secured his post by the old methods of favour and patronage. Charley's appointment was, indeed, a thinly disguised account of Trollope's own entry to the Post Office.

Trollope secured a nomination to a clerkship because his mother knew the daughter-in-law of the Secretary of the Post Office, Francis Freeling. When he arrived at the Post Office in 1834, his competence was tested by Freeling's sons in a somewhat casual manner:

> I was asked to copy some lines from the *Times* newspaper with an old quill pen, and at once made a series of blots and false spellings. 'That won't do, you know', said Henry Freeling to his brother Clayton. Clayton, who was my friend, urged that I was nervous, and asked that I might be allowed to do a bit of writing at home and bring it as a sample on the next day. I was then asked whether I was a proficient in arithmetic. What could I say: I had never learned the multiplication table, and had no more idea of the rule of three than of conic sections. 'I know a little of it', I said humbly, whereupon I was sternly assured that on the morrow, should I succeed in showing that my handwriting was all that it ought to be, I should be examined as to that little of arithmetic. . . . I went to work, and under the surveillance of my elder brother made a beautiful transcript of four or five pages of Gibbon. With a faltering heart I took these on the next day to the office. With my caligraphy I was contented, but was certain that I should come to the ground among the figures. But . . . I was seated at a desk without any further reference to my competency. No one condescended even to look at my beautiful penmanship.

Trollope was hardly a more efficient civil servant than Charley, and he found himself in debt and trouble. But author and character were both to be transformed, for when Charley was transferred to Weights and Measures he ceased to be an idle and impudent 'Navvy' and became a well-conducted and zealous 'Weights', an experience similar to Trollope's metamorphosis when he was posted to Ireland. The Civil Service Commission and examinations had, Trollope feared, done more harm than good. The successful candidate had merely been 'crammed' by a tutor to answer a string of questions which were unconnected with education. The examinee was not prepared for his future work and, on the contrary, 'his very success fills him with false ideas of his own educational standing, and so far unfits him'. Patronage gave, in Trollope's view, a sense of responsibility, whereas under a system of examinations 'no one is in truth responsible either for the conduct, the manners, or even for the character of the youth'.[12]

The views of Trollope had some support from other officials of the Post Office. The Northcote-Trevelyan reforms were designed to recruit high-ranking administrators to such departments as the Home Office or the Treasury, and it was not clear that the procedures had much applicability to the Post Office. The staff which dealt with matters of policy was located in the Secretary's office, and was firmly distinguished from the great majority of the clerical staff which dealt with routine business of a mundane description. Rowland Hill argued in 1854 that an examination could not test such necessary qualities as 'good principles, good habits, sound judgement, general intelligence, energy', and he remarked in his autobiography that competitive examinations excluded many useful men and admitted others of little value. Hill himself would, of course, have been excluded under an examination system based on a classical university education. His successor, John Tilley, similarly lacked the necessary preparation to succeed in the Northcote-Trevelyan system, and he feared that this new method of recruitment might deter 'men of strong native talent, energy, and zeal who, though possessing in a high degree qualifications really required, may be deficient in ordinary knowledge'. Such doubts about the virtue of literary examinations led the Post Office in 1855 to adopt a narrowly based examination for clerical posts on the grounds that it was

> disadvantageous to require candidates to show a knowledge beyond that needed for the performance of the duties which they will have to discharge upon their appointment; these, as respects the large majority of post-office clerks, are of a simple, routine character; and to demand of such persons high educational attainments would be to ensure discontent.

When open competitive examinations were introduced after 1870, the Post Office was obliged to appoint clerks in the Secretary's office from the successful candidates in the Regulation I examinations. It was not clear that this system produced the type of recruit needed by the Department. The Secretary, S. A. Blackwood, in 1888 complained that the Regulation I entrants were 'above their work' and bored with their duties, 'which must be for some years, to a certain extent, of a mechanical and routine character'. He would have preferred to recruit

243

boys straight from public school at the age of 18 who would be 'more amenable, more susceptible of official training'. They might not be so clever but Blackwood felt they would still be excellent public servants for, after all, 'the Civil Service does not want brilliant men'. Candidates who entered Regulation I examinations were not, for their part, eager to accept exile from Whitehall to the strange world of St Martin's le Grand, and Leonard Woolf preferred a post in Ceylon to the prospect of joining the Department. The Post Office had less prestige than other departments, and did not attract those who were most successful in the open examination.[13]

The elite of the Secretariat was recruited through Regulation I examinations which were common to the civil service as a whole, but the great majority of vacancies were filled by specific examinations for grades unique to the Post Office. The Secretary's office, it was remarked in 1888, was a 'close borough' for 'a better type of man', and in other parts of the Department, the leading officials were recruited by promotion from the lower grades. 'Each of them', it was claimed, 'may carry a field marshal's baton in his knapsack, and be fit ultimately to be Controller of his own office.' The relevance of literary examinations of any form to postmen, sorters and counter clerks was highly doubtful. John Tilley argued that the introduction of open competitions for postmen would be 'very unfortunate' since success would provide no indication of ability in delivering letters, despite the claims of advocates of examinations that they would 'stimulate mental culture, increase self-respect, and probably guarantee good conduct'. The Civil Service Commission and Treasury claimed that the introduction of open competitions for postmen would establish the market value of the job but this principle was implemented only briefly in the mid-1870s when vacancies in London were thrown open to indicate the abundant supply of labour at existing rates. The normal procedure, however, was to secure a nomination to a vacancy and to pass a qualifying or test examination in reading, writing and arithmetic which simply excluded those falling below a minimum standard. These tests were introduced in London and some provincial towns in 1855, and were extended to all offices in 1859. The Civil Service Commission pressed for a higher standard of examinations, but care had to be taken not to exclude a large number of candidates by a test which was too 'literary'. When postmen were required to pass the same test as sorters in the mid-1880s, half failed. 'The duties of a Sorter', it was pointed out, 'require more intelligence than those of a postman.'[14] Entry for the qualifying examination was increasingly confined to specified groups of auxiliaries, boy messengers and ex-servicemen and the examination was not in itself the means of recruitment into the Department and its internal labour market.

244

Qualifying examinations after nomination were used for the appointment of postmen and open competitive examinations for clerks; sorting clerks formed an intermediate category where it was not clear which pattern should be followed. The initial response was to adopt open competition, which was to be supplemented by a limited competition confined to postmen and boy messengers, so providing an avenue of promotion within the Department. The proportion of vacancies assigned to the limited competition was gradually increased until in 1910 the open competition was abandoned. The result was that one point of entry to the establishment was closed, for it was not possible to secure a position as a male sorter or counter clerk except through prior service as a boy messenger or postman. Boy messengers in the limited competition attained the same standard as outsiders in the open competition, so their recruitment did not entail a fall in the educational standard of the workforce. The postmen were, however, less satisfactory for 'they are considered to be inferior in education, less intelligent and less efficient when trained; and their standard of work and rate of working is lower. Whilst many will be able to perform their sorting duties in a satisfactory manner only a small percentage will ever make first-class Counter Clerks and Writing Clerks; and concern is felt as regards obtaining suitable officers for supervising posts in the future.' A balance had to be struck between the benefits gained by providing postmen with the incentive of promotion, and a possible decline in standards by reliance upon limited competition.[15]

In 1840 the only means of securing an appointment in the Post Office, whether as a letter-carrier or leading official, was by nomination. Although the last vestiges of patronage had ceased to exist by the 1890s, this did not mean that open competitive examinations on the lines recommended by the Northcote-Trevelyan report had entirely taken its place. Indeed, this method of entry was largely confined to members of the Secretary's office who were appointed from the open competition for the elite of civil servants. This was a literary examination which assumed attendance at a public school and university with a predominantly classical curriculum, and 'practical' men like John Tilley or Frank Scudamore could not have reached their positions under the new dispensation. In most other posts, the examination was either a 'closed' competition confined to those who had already gained access in other grades, or a qualifying test to impose certain minimum standards. Entry through an open competition was indeed curtailed in the case of sorters and counter clerks, and greater emphasis was given to internal recruitment through limited competitions. The point of entry for the majority of staff was through an initial unestablished post as auxiliary or boy messenger, or after service in the armed forces. It was necessary to pass a qualifying test in order to satisfy the Civil Service Commission that a permanent established position could be offered, and it might be possible to move up the hierarchy through success in limited competitions. These various gates which gave access to the privileged world of the Post Office were strictly defined and jealously guarded, whether it be the administrative elite recruited from the public schools and universities through a literary examination, or ex-soldiers with a claim upon the state. The connections between the internal labour market of the Post Office and the wider labour market outside were highly specific, and once entry had been gained the established employee was in a privileged world of benefits, job security and advancement. The Post Office was indeed to be one of the pioneers of the development of techniques of bureaucratic organisation of internal labour markets which have come to dominate large business corporations in the twentieth century.

The benefits of establishment[16]

A definite point of retirement was unusual until the twentieth century and old age, with its promise of a drift towards less remunerative and irregular employment, was faced with trepidation. Occupational pensions were confined to a few trades such as the railways, and better-paid workers joined friendly societies which paid a kind of disguised pension in the form of sick benefits. But for the majority of workers, old age meant dependence on children or the poor law. 'We cannot escape the conclusion', wrote Charles Booth, 'that poverty is essentially a trouble of old age.' Retirement was not a concept which most working men would have understood, for there was no precise age of departure from the labour market; the aim was to remain at work of some sort for as long as possible. The introduction of state pensions in 1908 at the age of 70 marked the beginning of change, and in the twentieth century retirement at a fixed age has become an inescapable fact for most people.[17] The change from drawing a wage to receiving a pension has set a clear limit to participation in the labour market, whereas in the nineteenth century the boundary was vague and blurred. One of the few exceptions was the Post Office.

The terms and conditions of pensions in the government service were specified by the Superannuation Act of 1859. Pensions were paid after the completion of at least ten years' service, at the rate of one-sixtieth of the retiring pay, up to a maxiumum of forty-sixtieths. The usual retiring age was 60, but when retirement resulted from ill-health before the completion of ten years' service, a gratuity of one month's pay for each year of service was paid. These terms of superannuation were modified in 1909, when the pension was reduced and two other benefits introduced. A year's service was in future to give only one-eightieth of the retiring pay to a maximum of forty-eightieths, with the addition of a lump sum of one-thirtieth of the retiring salary for each year's service up to a maximum of eighteen months' income. Further, when an officer who had served at least five years died in post, his dependants would be awarded a year's salary.[18]

Old age was one major cause of insecurity and poverty in Victorian Britain; another was ill-health. Protection could be secured by joining a friendly society which provided both sick pay and medical attention from a doctor under contract to the organisation. The first State scheme was introduced in 1911 which provided sick pay and medical treatment for manual workers and all others earning less than £160 a year. This extended to the private sector what the State had long provided for at least some of its own employees.[19] The Post Office provided free medical attendance to all established officers whose pay did not exceed £150 in the provinces and £160 in London, who were employed at an office to which a medical officer was attached. The doctor would make home visits if the employee lived within three miles of the office. These terms were modified shortly before the First World War, to extend the benefits of medical treatment to all members of the 'manipulative' grades without a limit of income and regardless of the presence of a departmental medical officer. The Post Office did not only provide medical treatment, for sick leave with pay was permitted for any absence which arose from ill-health on condition that a certificate was obtained from the departmental medical officer and there was a reasonable chance of future 'ability to render regular and efficient service'. Full pay was allowed for six months in any twelve and half pay for a further six months, on condition that sick pay ceased when the total absence amounted to twelve months in any period of four years.

The Post Office therefore freed the worker from the worst insecurities of existence: irregular employment at low wages, old age and ill-health. The benefits extended beyond protection against hardship, for the staff also received annual holidays with full pay. The Post Office was one of the few employers of manual workers which provided paid leave before the First World War. Staff on outdoor duties received fourteen days a year, whilst those engaged on indoor duties started with fourteen days and rose to twenty-one days after five years' service.[20] Employment in the Post Office offered conditions of service superior to the great majority of occupations in Victorian Britain. Although the Liberal welfare reforms of 1906 to 1914 started to reduce the differential, the balance of advantage remained in favour of the Post Office until the Second World War, and it was only full employment and the welfare state which eroded the attractions of employment in the civil service. However, these benefits were not awarded to the entire staff, for a firm line was drawn between those who were part of the privileged and protected core 'on the establishment' and the part-time or temporary staff who were denied the benefits and security. Moreover, the established workers were located in a hierarchy which offered advancement and promotion; the Post Office offered not only a job but also the prospect of a career.

Rising in the service

> The theory of promotion by merit, – that theory by which promotion is to be given, not to the senior man who is fit, but to the man who is fittest, be he senior or junior, – is thoroughly Utopian in its essence; but it has in it, as I think, this of special evil, which is not inherent in most Utopian theories, that it is susceptible of experimental action, and that the wider the action grows the greater is the evil done. (Anthony Trollope to Rowland Hill, 24 May 1863.)[21]

Promotion by merit was the twin of competitive entry to the civil service in the Northcote-Trevelyan reforms. 'In order to obtain men of the proper degree of education and of trustworthiness at low wages', the *Report on the Post Office* concluded in 1854, 'it is necessary to hold out prospects of advancement to those who conduct themselves well, and who manifest the qualifications which are required for superior posts. By a proper system of encouragement to merit, economy and efficiency may be combined, and the Office may be worked at a moderate cost.' The *Report* recommended a change in the structure of the Post Office in London to create a single clear hierarchy with 'promotion from class to class to be according to qualification and merit in all cases'.[22] These changes were welcomed in the first annual report of the Postmaster General. 'The habit of trusting to external influences, and of engaging the solicitation of private friends, or members of parliament, for their promotion', the report noted, 'has been very prevalent amongst the officers of this Department.' The 'dispensation of promotion' should, it was agreed, not be influenced by such considerations but should be decided only on the basis of 'meritorious conduct'.[23] But could this 'Utopian theory' be applied to the Post Office?

Promotion by merit did not necessarily lead to economy and efficiency for it could produce grievances and discontent. A memorial of 1860 from clerks in the Money Order Office, Circulation Department and Receiver and Accountant General's Office remarked that

> the principle of promotion by merit, without due reference to length of service, was intended to advance the efficiency of the public service,

and to stimulate its officers in the zealous discharge of their duties; but that in consequence of the difficulty of discriminating nice differences of merit, a few individuals only have been benefited, while the energies of the general body have been weakened and depressed by the small proportion of reward held out for the many, and its uncertain administration. . . . [A] system which excites the passions of envy and jealousy amongst the clerks of a department who have seen their juniors in service preferred, when no demerit could be urged against themselves, tends to depress their exertions and thus becomes detrimental to the public service, as the advantage gained by promoting a meritorious junior officer before his turn is more than counterbalanced by its injurious effects upon those who have been superseded.

The system of merit, the clerks argued, had produced unprecedented dissatisfaction and 'a widely spread feeling of dismay', and they urged the substitution of promotion by seniority.[24] Many of the leading officials in the early 1860s were in agreement.

Anthony Trollope was perhaps the most vigorous in his denunciation of the system of merit as impracticable, unjust and injurious. Merit, he felt, could not be accurately measured for while it might be possible to say that a man was fit it was impossible to say who was *most* fit. Measures did not exist to weigh merit in the balance, for 'zeal recommends itself to one man, intelligence to a second, alacrity to a third, punctuality to a fourth, and superficial pretence to a fifth. There can be no standard by which the excellence of men can be judged, as is the weight of gold.' No position required, in Trollope's view, more than actual competence so that if a man had worked well for twenty years and was fit for higher duties there was no reason to give preference to a more recent recruit. 'If a man be in all respects fit to do the work he has engaged to perform, no better man can be had.' The system of 'odious comparisons' led, in Trollope's opinion, to serious disadvantages. The disappointed men who had been passed over 'cannot but be broken-hearted, and from a broken hearted man no good work can be obtained'. The successful man was, for his part, 'deteriorated by the act of selection' for 'he is taught to imagine himself to be too great and too good for the very ordinary work which, in spite of the glory of his selection, he is generally called upon to perform'.[25] Trollope, of course, was thoroughly opposed to the ethic of bureaucratic rationality, but his position was supported even by officers who were not hostile to the general trend away from patronage and personal favour.

The full application of the principle of merit could be criticised precisely on the standards of bureaucratic rationality. This is clear from

249

Frank Scudamore's report of 1863 which recommended that seniority should apply to all except the most demanding positions. The case was made on pragmatic grounds. The system of merit, he argued, was not uniformly applied in the civil service, for clerks in other departments might rise within a class by length of service to £300 a year without promotion, whereas in the Post Office a third-class clerk could rise only to £150 unless he secured promotion to a second-class clerkship with a maximum salary of £240 or to a first-class clerkship with a maximum salary of £350. He also felt that the connection made by the Northcote-Trevelyan report between open competitive entry and free competition within the service was based upon a false premise. Candidates for entry were 'on one and the same relation to the judges' for 'one kind of merit, and always the same kind of merit, is required from, and equal opportunities for the display of that merit are given, to all the candidates. The judges in this competition have the means of ascertaining readily and with certainty whether the candidates possess the required merit, and which of them possesses it in the greatest perfection.' But competition within the service was not so simple. There could be no single, constant measure of merit, and equal opportunities could not be given to all candidates to show their worth. The relation between judge and candidate was no longer anonymous, for the superior officer might have no knowledge of some of the candidates, work closely with others, dislike one man and be friendly with another. In a large office, it was simply not possible to give equal opportunities to all members of the staff to bring their merits to notice and the result, argued Scudamore, was precisely the feeling of jealousy and discontent which the Northcote-Trevelyan report attributed to the system of patronage. Scudamore therefore supported competitive entry into the service and selection of superior officials by merit, but he argued that for minor positions seniority was a fairer and more efficient system:

> Men can bring themselves to witness with composure and even cheerfulness the good fortune of a rival; but when that rival is declared to have owed nothing to fortune, and everything to superior merit, and when there is a general belief that the process, by which that superior merit is supposed to have been discovered, is more likely to ensure the success of the most fortunate than that of the most meritorious man, no such ready acquiescence in the decision can be expected.

Promotion by merit did not only offend against Trollope's strongly held views of the proper basis of society; it was, in the view of Scudamore, simply inefficient and unworkable.[26]

The committee which considered the operation of the system of merit in the Post Office in 1860 readily accepted that in classes such as sorters 'the work is not of a nature to display in a sufficiently marked degree the relative merits of the men', and could lead only to suspicions of favouritism. There was greater opposition to abandoning merit in the clerical posts, and the Treasury and Rowland Hill were hostile to a change 'so opposed to the spirit of the age'. Nevertheless, the principle of seniority was introduced into the minor classes in 1861 and extended to the lower grades of clerks in 1863. The result was generally welcomed, for the demise of promotion by merit in the lower grades had 'removed one of the greatest causes of dissatisfaction, discontent, envy, and disorder that ever existed in the public service'.[27] However, the extent to which merit had been rejected and seniority substituted should not be exaggerated. What was at issue was promotion within a grade from a third- to a second-class clerk or from a second- to a first-class postman, and there was little reason why these categories could not be contained in a single scale without any need for promotion, since the duties were similar or even identical. Seniority should, it was felt, apply to progress within a job which was essentially the same, and selection by merit should apply to movement into fundamentally different posts such as entry into a supervisory grade or advancement from a manipulative to a clerical grade. It had taken some time for this distinction to emerge and the full application of merit had certainly been impractical.[28] The workforce wished to extend the principle of seniority still further. 'A belief apparently exists amongst the staff', complained the Select Committee on Post Office Servants in 1906, 'that every officer who has once obtained a Civil Servant Certificate is entitled thereafter to proceed upward merely by virtue of his seniority in each succeeding class.' This proposition the Committee could not accept, for 'promotion from the ranks should depend upon the distinct exhibition of qualities superior both to those of the ordinary officer, and to those required for the performance of the duties of the class from which promotion is sought'.[29]

The avenues for promotion from one grade to another were three-fold. 'Direct' promotion entailed selection for a supervisory post without entering an examination. A sorter or postman in London, for example, might be chosen as an overseer and might subsequently rise to higher supervisory posts as an assistant or chief superintendent. In theory, this direct line of promotion ran as high as the Controller of the London Postal Service; in practice, it was a limited avenue for a sorter did not usually secure promotion to overseer until the age of 45 and further advancement to superintendent was unusual. James Graham, for example, was born in 1859 and entered the London Postal Service in 1877 as a sorter on a pay scale of 20s to 25s a week; he was promoted overseer in 1910 and retired in 1913 on an annual salary of £210. W.C. Dix was more successful; he entered the London Postal Service in 1875, and advanced to overseer in 1897 and assistant superintendent in 1909. The 'direct' method usually gave a single step up the hierarchy, and the most successful careers relied upon 'indirect' promotion which involved leaving the ranks of postmen or sorters for the clerical class through success in a competitive examination. A proportion of vacancies might be reserved for candidates from the lower grades, although there was a strict age limit. In the case of sorters entering examinations for clerical posts, for example, the maximum age was set in 1898 at 26 years. W. Howson was one of the most successful to rise by this 'indirect' method. He entered the service in 1872 as a sorter, and secured appointment as a clerk in 1884. He rose to principal clerk in 1899, and in 1905 he moved into a supervisory position as chief superintendent. In 1909 he was appointed assistant controller of the London Postal Service at a salary of £700. This was a common means of recruiting the clerks who managed the day-to-day operation of the postal services: the clerical staff of the Controller's office in 1910 comprised 156 men, of whom 100 had started their careers in non-clerical grades. Only one had entered as a postman: G. T. Evans, who had started his career in 1890 as a postman and had been promoted sorter in 1893 and clerk in 1897. It was indeed exceptional to cross two barriers in this way, and Albert Joyce was more typical of a postman who received a measure of 'indirect' promotion: he was born in 1872 and entered as a postman in 1891 on a wage scale of 18s to 32s a week; in 1910 he was appointed sorter on a scale of 20s to 62s a week. The third avenue of promotion was to secure appointment as a subpostmaster or postmaster. These positions were open to all members of the service, and a large proportion were filled by men who had started their careers in the non-clerical grades, for 444 of 489 postmasters and subpostmasters appointed between 1908 and 1911 had started in manipulative jobs. E. Willcocks, for example, had entered the service in 1872 as a sorting clerk at Hull; he obtained a clerical post in 1885, rising to assistant superintendent in 1891 and chief superin-tendent in 1895; in 1909 he became postmaster of Doncaster at a salary of £460, where he remained until his retirement in 1913. 'The ladder of promotion is necessarily a narrow one,' commented Evelyn Murray in 1927, 'but it is there for those who are able to climb it.'[30]

The majority of the staff in fact did not mount the narrow ladder of success, and an accurate picture of the Post Office should not emphasise Howson or Dix or Evans at the expense of employees such as Daniel Desmond or Arthur Byron. Both retired from the Post Office in 1913 on grounds of ill-health after serving as postmen at Hereford and Leeds for twenty-six years and thirty-one years respectively. They had the benefit of regular employment over a long period, and the security of a pension on retirement. They had also retired at a considerably higher wage than they entered. Byron had received 18*s* a week in 1883, and by 1913 he was earning a wage of 32*s* 1*d* a week and other benefits valued at 8*s* 5*d* a week.[31] He had, in other words, risen from the income level of an unskilled labourer to a skilled craftsman whilst remaining a postman. Increments provided an alternative means of rising in the service, for the bureaucratic organisation of the internal labour market gave considerable freedom to determine wage scales independently of the value of the work performed. 'The Government', the Committee on Postmen's Pay reported in 1891, 'adopts one method of payment and the private employer another. With the private employer there is not, as there is with the Government, security of tenure; and of course the labourer receives from the first the full value of his hire. The Government, on the contrary, holds part of the hire in reserve, which does not become payable until after several years.'[32] Coal miners, for example, might expect to be paid the same piece-rate regardless of their age, although their earnings would vary according to their individual capacity to produce coal. Income would reach a peak in early manhood, and would decline with the onset of middle age as strength and health failed. This was the normal pattern in working-class occupations, but the experience of Post Office workers was different. A postman aged 25 might have the same duties and responsibilities as a colleague aged 45 but the payment in this case rose with the length of service. The precise nature of this incremental scale depended upon the administrative decisions of the Post Office and not upon the operation of economics, for rising wages were not a return for increased productivity or efficiency so much as an incentive for continued service. The Department required loyalty and trust, and the promise of an improved standard of living in the future with a pension in retirement was an effective means to this end.

The award of increments was in practice automatic, and this led to some concern that the positive incentive to loyal and efficient service was slight. Promotion out of one class into a superior grade might well provide a reward to capable and meritorious workers, but this was scarcely applicable to the 'manipulative' workers who were likely to remain within the ranks of postmen for their entire career. In the early 1870s it was argued that these workers required an incentive which was neither automatic, such as an increment, nor dependent upon promotion out of the class. The 'utopian' application of merit which had led to such scepticism in the early 1860s was to be revived in a new form and applied to postmen in London. The Treasury was informed in 1872 that 'the practical officers of the Department have long been of opinion that it would tend to excite a spirit of emulation among the Letter Carriers in

London, and improve the discipline of the Force, if to those who have distinguished themselves by a long course of good conduct, a distinctive Badge were given, such as is worn in the Army, to carry with it distinctive wages'.[33] It was a common phenomenon in the nineteenth century for members of the working class who came into contact with the public to wear distinctive uniforms as visible signs of their function and official position, and the line between uniformed and non-uniformed was carefully drawn to distinguish between occupations which could be designated as working-class and middle-class. On the railways, a ticket inspector was uniformed but not a clerk in the booking office; in the Post Office, postmen had distinctive clothing but not sorters and counter clerks. The uniform separated the postmen from other grades in the Department, and a distinctive and appropriate reward was required to provide a recognition of merit.

'Good conduct stripes' were introduced in 1872, and were at the outset confined to London and strictly limited in number. The award of a stripe carried both a visible sign of 'regularity, diligence and fidelity' in the performance of duty, and a monetary reward of six pence a week. At least ten years' service was required for the first stripe, fifteen for the second and twenty for the third, and they were awarded only to the men who had 'most distinguished themselves' in the service of the Department. The privilege would be surrendered by any postmen who defaulted or who joined a society whose rules were 'opposed to discipline'. The good conduct stripes offered a form of advancement to men who passed their career within the uniformed grade, and provided a financial reward which was not an automatic increment. The system was modified in 1874 when the length of service for each stripe was reduced to five, ten and fifteen years, and the money value raised to one shilling a week. The Controller of the London Postal Service applauded the benefits which resulted. 'The good men', he remarked, 'pride themselves on the decoration, and value the stripes as highly as soldiers and sailors do their good conduct chevrons.'[34] But the scheme created as well as solved problems of discipline and control.

The department wished to award stripes as a reward for exceptional conduct while the postmen were more inclined to treat them as increments to which they should be entitled after a specified period. The number and value of stripes had indeed been increased in London in 1874 as an alternative to a wage increase, and it is not surprising that the men argued that, since good conduct was expected of all, the stripes should either be awarded on completion of a certain period of service or be abolished and a better pay scale substituted. A spirit of emulation was closely allied to a sense of jealousy and injustice: a man who felt his

The issue of new uniforms to London postmen in 1861 was captured by the *Illustrated London News*. The uniform issue was carefully specified: in 1885, London postmen received a coat every six months, a waistcoat every twelve months, a pair of trousers every six months, a cap every twelve months, an overcoat and waterproof cape every two years, and a pair of leggings every three years. Postmen were part of the uniformed working class which was a growing sector in Victorian Britain.

conduct had been irreproachable yet who did not receive a reward because no stripes were available, was likely to feel aggrieved rather than inspired to good conduct. The stripe had become a 'mere lottery' rather than a mark of merit, less a sign of bureaucratic rationality than of inequity.[35] Scudamore's warnings of 1863 on promotion by merit had renewed relevance. Doubts mounted about the benefits of the stripes system. The stripes 'practically ceased to be regarded as badges of distinction of which the letter carriers should be proud', and the staff had become interested in their 'mere money value'. There was perhaps more to be said for an incremental system which gave the certainty of reward for long service.

In 1880, the number of stripes in London was increased and the role of competition reduced so that selection would, in future, apply only to the award of the first stripe to those postmen with five years' service who had most distinguished themselves by regularity, accuracy, usefulness and civility. The second and third stripes would then be awarded according to seniority. In 1882 it was proposed to remove the element of selection in its entirety, and to extend to the rest of the country the award of good conduct stripes based upon the principle of certainty. The limit on the number of stripes would be removed and they would cease to be badges of exceptional merit, instead becoming increments which would be automatically granted after five, ten and fifteen years to mark long and satisfactory service. However, the Treasury refused to accept this changed definition, and insisted that 'the system of good-conduct stripes was introduced expressly to break up the dead level of seniority, and to reward *superior* activity, intelligence and devotion to duty'. The principle of merit accordingly survived when the award of stripes was extended to the whole country, and the problems which had been apparent in the 1870s persisted into the 1890s.[36]

The Committee on Postmen's Pay in 1891 complained, not surprisingly, that the 'men either cannot or will not understand' that the stripes were marks of distinction. 'They seem possessed with the idea', the Committee remarked:

> that after the prescribed periods of service, the condition of good conduct being fulfilled, one man is no less entitled to a good conduct badge than another. That they should have to wait for vacancies is to them unintelligible. There is, as they point out, no waiting in the Army, where, as in the Post Office, a system of good conduct stripes prevails. Yet the postmen are required to wait, and this difference they are at a loss to understand.

The Committee suggested that stripes should be awarded automatically on the completion of five years' service, up to a maximum of six after thirty years. These proposals were implemented in full in 1897 when the confusion between good conduct stripes and increments appeared to be complete. The Secretary did nevertheless attempt the impossible task of maintaining a distinction between the ordinary incremental wage scale and the stripe allowance as 'a *reward* conferred for five years of good conduct'. The ordinary wage provided, he argued in 1900, adequate remuneration without the stripe allowance so that 'anything which a man earns by stripes is therefore in the nature of a bounty for good conduct not of payment for services rendered; and if it is to be an incentive to good conduct it is very necessary that this distinction should be maintained'. It was, however, scarcely possible to convince the postmen of the validity of this distinction when the allowance was paid as a matter of course. The Secretary was 'inclined to regret' the introduction of the stripes system which 'suggests by implication that a man in the service of the state may legitimately require and receive some special inducement, over and above his wages, to conduct himself properly'.[37] It is not surprising that the Select Committee on Post Office Servants of 1912–13 recommended the abandonment of the spurious distinction between wages as a payment for work performed and the stripe allowance as a bounty for good conduct. The Committee accepted that the allowance was 'to all intents an integral part of wages', and in 1914 the allowances were incorporated in the pay scale.

Good conduct stripes came to an end, and it must be doubted whether they had ever achieved the aim of improving discipline and exciting emulation. Rather, the sense that it was 'very much of an accident whether a Letter Carrier does, or does not, obtain the reward' fostered a feeling of grievance and injustice. Stripes became a source of conflict between the Post Office and its staff rather than a device to encourage loyalty, and the certainty of a pension and regular increments over a long service proved to have a greater effectiveness in securing the efficient performance of duties.[38]

Increments could not be justified by any increase in efficiency over time. 'The work performed by the different individuals, whether of long or short service, is so similar', concluded the Inter-Departmental Committee on Post Office Establishments in 1896, 'and that proficiency is so quickly reached, that no great prolongation of the nunber of years over which their scale of pay ranges is necessary.'[39] This was to misunderstand the issue, for increments were not intended as payment for increased skill or efficiency. The Post Office in the last third of the nineteenth century lengthened wage scales, particularly when good conduct stripes are taken into account. Letter-carriers in London in 1862 could rise from 20*s* to 25*s* a week in the second class, and from 26*s* to 30*s* in the first class, by annual increments of one shilling.[40] The

257

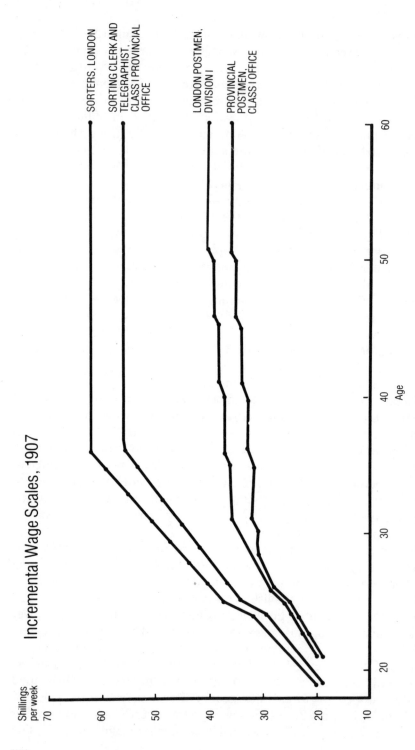

Incremental Wage Scales, 1907

Shillings per week

70
60
50
40
30
20
10

SORTERS, LONDON

SORTING CLERK AND TELEGRAPHIST, CLASS I PROVINCIAL OFFICE

LONDON POSTMEN, DIVISION I

PROVINCIAL POSTMEN, CLASS I OFFICE

Age

20   30   40   50   60

Source: P.P. 1914 LXXI. Return showing the changes in the wages and conditions of service of Post Office servants, pp. 732–72.

258

majority of London postmen in 1891 were on a scale which rose by annual increments of one shilling from 18s to 32s a week, before the payment of good conduct allowances for men with five, ten and fifteen years' service.[41] The award of a maximum of six stripes for thirty years' service further lengthened the scale, so that a postman in London who entered at the age of 21 would not reach the maximum of the scale until he was 51. The lengthening of scales was even more remarkable in the provinces. The postmen in provincial towns were, until 1882, on short scales with only three or four annual increments which entailed 'an utter absence of reward for long and faithful service'.[42] The pattern for indoor staff was somewhat different, for the scale rose at a faster rate to an earlier peak in the mid-30s. A sorter in London in 1907 could rise from 20s a week at 19 to 62s a week at 36, and a provincial sorting clerk and telegraphist in a large office from 19s at 19 to 56s at 37.[43] There could, as a result of these incremental wage scales, be a notion of a long-term career in the Post Office and a sense of advancement even in the absence of promotion. The sense of rising in the service during a life-time of regular employment was a crucial characteristic of bureaucratic forms of organisation.

Unions: from rejection to recognition

Members of the Civil Service must remember that the public interest requires that their official action must be regulated by authority just as much as that of Her Majesty's soldiers and sailors, and the formation of any association intended to coerce those responsible for the administration of the Post Office to make concessions which in their judgement are not justified by the public interest must be regarded as a most serious breach of discipline. (Post 65/3, H. C. Raikes to S. A. Blackwood, 25 January 1890.)

The benefits of establishment implied loyalty to an employer who had removed the worst insecurities of life, and the bureaucratic structures of the Post Office provided rational and equitable rules for the treatment of the workforce. The workforce was expected, in return, to accept the necessity for hierarchy and obedience, and unions were viewed in the nineteenth century as unacceptable intrusions into the Post Office. The attitude of the Department closely paralleled the approach of the railway companies, which had a similar internal labour market and an equally intense opposition to union organisation. This policy of the private railway companies was threatened in the early twentieth century by a Liberal government which was pledged to redress the legal grievances of unions, and this placed the Post Office in a difficult position. The government could not on the one hand give unions a privileged legal status and on the other hand deny them a role within its own workforce. The result was a realignment of labour relations in the Post Office in the early twentieth century: rejection of unions gave way to recognition.[44]

The Post Office in the mid-nineteenth century adopted an uncompromising stance against any organisation of its workforce. When a group of letter-carriers called a meeting in London in 1866 to consider their conditions of service, the response was swift. The organisers were dismissed or disciplined, and it was laid down that no further meetings were to be held to discuss official matters beyond the walls of the Post Office. Applications for improved conditions should be made to superior officers, and 'attempts to obtain by irregular means what reason and mature deliberation with-hold will be summarily repressed'. When the author of a public appeal on behalf of the Post Office Employees Agitation Committee was expelled from the service in 1868, the Treasury stated 'that for any officer in the public service to become secretary to such a committee . . . or to join in any organised agitation for obtaining an increase of pay, is contrary to proper discipline and subordination and renders such person justly liable to dismissal'. The Treasury was indeed inclined to adopt a stricter line than the Post Office. In 1872, the London letter- carriers were forced to disband a committee formed to call for higher wages and were banned from holding public meetings, yet the Department did sanction a meeting at the Post Office. The Treasury felt that this concession should not have been granted:

> It was obvious that the position whether of the Departmental authorities or of the Treasury was inconsistent with meetings of public Servants to organise petitions to Parliament in their own name relative to their own pay and promotion. . . . [The Treasury] regarded those who took part in them as renouncing by their conduct all title to have their claims considered in the ordinary course of administration.

The Department feared that a complete ban on meetings would be denounced as 'tyrannical and un-English', and preferred to permit gatherings at the Post Office where 'the men were to a certain extent under control and . . . strangers who were very likely to incite the men to insubordination were necessarily excluded'. The limits of protest were tightly drawn: the staff could gather at the Post Office building to discuss grievances under official sanction; they could not form an organisation, invite outsiders to attend, or meet at any other location.

This position was somewhat modified by Henry Fawcett, who in 1880–1 adopted a policy of compromise when faced with pressure from telegraphists for better conditions. He rejected the outright hostility to organisation which was urged by the Secretary, S.A. Blackwood. Fawcett's approach was, in the opinion of Blackwood, an abdication of responsibility which would create turmoil and render control impossible. When the Postmen's Union and the aptly named Fawcett Association of sorters were formed in London in the late 1880s, Blackwood was eager to reimpose authority. 'When persons of this class collected in bodies', he urged, 'they could not be humoured or indulged with impunity; any disposition not to press rules against them being pretty sure to be regarded by them as weakness; and if one concession were granted they only presumed upon it to ask another.' His chance to reassert control came in 1890.[45] Blackwood did, it is true, give some ground. Public meetings had been held in defiance of the regulation of 1866, and it was decided that in future they should be sanctioned on three conditions: notice should be given to the authorities of the place and time of any meeting; attendance should be confined to Post Office employees and those directly interested in the matters to be discussed; and an official shorthand reporter was to attend if required by the authorities. The effect of these conditions was that the union secretary could represent only his own grade, and a permanent union officer was out of the question. The union responded by demanding both the right to call meetings as it pleased, and recognition of its secretary as the channel for negotiations. The conflict had moved from matters of pay to questions of organisation and recognition. The union set a deadline for a reply to its demands, and called a strike when no answer was received. This strike failed in the face of limited support from the staff and the firm response of the Department. Blackwood had prepared for the stoppage by engaging a relief force, and retribution was visited upon 457 men, who were dismissed. The Departmental view was that 'the postmen were being duped and led on to ruin by a few ringleaders', and that the resolute action of Blackwood had removed 'the machinations of dangerous people from outside'. The workforce would, it was believed, be loyal and content when it was freed from external influence and there should certainly be no recognition of any trade union. The Postmaster General, H.C. Raikes, was adamant that he

> could not admit that servants of the State stood on precisely the
> same footing as the servants of a private employer with regard to
> combination and without expressing an opinion as to the ordinary
> rights of Trade Unions in regard to ordinary questions between the
> employer and the employed it was impossible in his opinion for the
> government to recognise the interference of such bodies in the
> relation between the State and its servants. Whilst the men were free
> to form or join any Associations; to act together for their mutual

261

The threatened strike of London postmen in 1890 led to demonstrations outside St Martin's le Grand as pickets attempted to call out working postmen. Deliveries were made with police protection, and strikers were dismissed.

benefit and mutual consideration of matters affecting their status, to discuss matters on any subject of interest to them; and to meet when they like and where they like, he never would concede to them any right to form an association the object of which was to supersede the authority of Parliament and the Government in fixing the conditions of labour in the public service. All applications to him must be sent to him by officers immediately concerned and not be sent through a third party or an association.

The Post Office held tenaciously to Raikes's definition of labour relations in the 1890s. It was no longer a breach of discipline to join an association, and the right to hold public meetings was admitted on condition that outsiders were excluded, but unions were not recognised and had no role in negotiation of wages and conditions of service.

The Postmen's Union collapsed in 1890 and in 1891 the Postmen's Federation was formed in London. A strategy was developed by the Federation and the Fawcett Association to overcome the exclusion of unions from discussions with the Post Office: appeals were made to Members of Parliament and parliamentary candidates to vote for the appointment of a Select Committee to enquire into the position of labour in the Post Office. This strategy was in breach of Post Office regulations, for although civil servants secured the vote in 1868 and were permitted to campaign for candidates in 1874, a rule of 1885 laid down that 'it was expected of [Post Office servants] that they should maintain a certain reserve in political matters'. In 1892, the staff was warned not to extract pledges from parliamentary candidates, and the chairman and secretary of the Fawcett Association were dismissed from the service. This meant that the leading officials of the Association were barred from any public meeting called to discuss conditions of employment in the Post Office, a position which Blackwood defended. In his view, a fundamentally loyal though easily misled staff had been subverted by 'outside and professional agitators', and it was necessary to protect the men in their own interests. A failure to do this would 'be most detrimental, I would almost say cruel, to the men themselves. It would be placing them under the influence, and therefore at the mercy of those who having . . . generally their own ends to gain by the fostering of agitation, care little or nothing for their unhappy dupes, or for the ruin which they bring upon the unoffending families of those who are led into acts of misconduct by their efforts.' Blackwood's patriarchal concern for his subordinates made it essential to exclude outsiders from public meetings held with the permission of the Postmaster General, for to admit them would, he felt, 'seem to me like the action of Theodosius, when he invited the Goths into the Roman Empire and made Alaric Master General of Illyricum. We know the result.'

The Cabinet was clearly less alarmed than Blackwood, for it decided in 1893 to rescind the restrictions on public meetings. Permission was no longer to be required from the Postmaster General, and outsiders could attend. This made organisation less difficult, although there was of course no suggestion that the unions should be recognised or that outsiders could take part in representations on wages or conditions of service. The Department continued to insist that grievances should be presented 'by persons in the Service alone and in the channels pre-scribed'. The limitation on political activity was also maintained on the ground that it was wrong to offer votes to a parliamentary candidate in return for a pledge to support improved conditions of work. 'We have done away with personal and individual bribery', it was remarked in 1898, 'but there is a still worse form of bribery, and that is when a man asks a candidate to buy his vote out of the public purse.'

The Post Office was by the turn of the century less convinced of the need to exclude unions from involvement in labour relations, and the policy gradually changed to incorporate them into a formal system. In the early twentieth century unions ceased to be defined as antagonistic to discipline and authority, and were brought within a new structure of control. This trend may be dated from the request of the Postmen's

263

Federation in 1899 that the Postmaster General should receive a deputation representing all classes of postmen throughout Britain. 'It has not hitherto been the practice to recognise any such bodies or to deal with them directly,' remarked the Secretary in 1900, 'but I am inclined to think that it will be difficult to maintain this position permanently, nor does there appear to be any important object to be gained in doing so.' A deputation was received, and this was the first time that unions had been accorded any official sanction in the Department. The limits of the deputation were, however, strictly drawn. Outsiders were excluded, which meant that full-time union officials could not attend, and the scope of discussion was narrowly defined. Issues which concerned particular individuals or classes were excluded, and representations were 'confined to matters which directly concern the whole body on whose behalf they are made. . . . In other words the Postmaster General cannot entertain any representation made by one person on behalf of another unless the interests of both are substantially identical.' The deputation could therefore discuss only matters which affected the service in general, and could not raise pressing issues, such as the employment of auxiliaries, which affected a particular class. Neither could the auxiliaries be represented by the union secretary, even if he was employed by the Post Office, unless he was himself an auxiliary. It was this very limited scope of representation which the unions challenged in 1901 through the Joint Committee of Postal and Telegraph Associations which had been formed in 1899. The members of a union had, claimed the Joint Committee, delegated the right to represent their interests to the union executive 'although they might not be directly affected by the special grievance they are deputed to explain'. The right of a man from one grade to represent others was indeed crucial to acceptance of unions in the Post Office, for the 'fundamental principle of combination lies in the power of representation'. The Post Office might accept membership of unions but, argued the Joint Committee,

> in the absence of the power of one person to act on behalf of another we are denied the necessary corollary of trades unionism, or combination, and that is the power of representation. . . . Our argument is, primarily, that in the absence of the right of representation we have not freedom of combination. . . . The position today from the point of view of the associations is that combination in the Post Office is tolerated, and not recognised. Full recognition means full acceptance of the representatives of the associations; toleration simply means as it obtains today, that you, representing the Post Office, will not accept our representatives unless they are

personally affected by the questions raised. That strikes at the root of the principles of trades unionism.

Acceptance of the full representation of the staff by union officers would, from the point of view of the Post Office, strike at the hierarchical structure of power in the Department. 'We have taken up the position', remarked the Secretary in 1901, 'that the Postmaster General is always ready to listen to any man, or body of men, who have (or think they have) a grievance; but it must be their *own grievance*; and not the grievance of somebody else. If we depart from this rule, a man might equally well claim to be heard by his counsel or solicitor; and there would be an end to all personal relations between the Head of the Department and the Staff.'[46]

Recognition of the representative power of associations was granted in 1906 with the election of a Liberal government pledged to meet the demands of unions for a privileged legal position. The Trades Disputes Act was passed in 1906, and in the same year the Postmaster General, Sydney Buxton, announced that

> he is prepared frankly to recognise any duly constituted Association or Federation of Postal Servants. He is willing to receive representations from members or representatives of the Association if they be in the Service, or through its Secretary (whether he be a member of the Service or not), on matters relating to the Service as a whole, or on matters affecting the class or classes of servants of which the Association is representative.[47]

Blackwood would certainly have felt that the Goths had been invited into the Roman Empire. The policy adopted by Buxton was to tame and order the invaders by formulating precise rules for the submission of grievances. Labour relations were systematised upon the basis of recognised unions and specified channels of communication. Initially, this meant that unions were able to participate directly in the submission of memorials and the despatch of deputations to the Postmaster General, for there was as yet no permanent machinery for bargaining between the Department and the unions. The full incorporation of the trades unions into permanent, formal institutions came as a result of changes during the First World War.

The crucial document in the post-war realignment of labour relations was the report of the committee chaired by J. H. Whitley on the relations between employers and employed. The main recommendation was that Joint Industrial Councils should be established for each industry which would bring together the representatives of employers and workers, not only to discuss wages and conditions of work within a framework of conflict, but also to consider the management of the industry in a spirit of co-operation and participation. It did not have universal assent. Many employers were unsympathetic to the abdication of power which was implied and unions might interpret the report, with its implication of an identity of interest between capital and labour, as a stratagem to circumvent collective bargaining. However, the War Cabinet decided in 1918 that Whitleyism should be implemented in government departments where conditions were 'sufficiently analogous' to those in private industry, a definition which was considered to include the Post Office.[48] The response of the Department was guarded but not overtly hostile. The Whitley report, it was felt, could be accepted subject to safeguards which would ensure that the Post Office was administered for the benefit of the public rather than the staff. The role of the Whitley machinery should also be consultative, excluding matters of management and policy. This limitation was a matter of some importance, for the Secretary, Evelyn Murray, feared that 'the Staff Associations, whose ultimate object is avowedly the 'control of the Post Office' will naturally aim at extending the scope as widely as possible'. Murray's concern was well-grounded, for the Union of Post Office Workers adopted a syndicalist policy of workers' control which would entail 'joint management of the Post Office in conjunction with the State'. The Whitley report was, as a result, enthusiastically welcomed by the postal unions as a means towards full participation in administration and the formulation of policy. 'Here at last appears the immediate prospect of that system of joint control for which we have striven for years, and which but for the war, seemed almost as unobtainable as the Garden of the Hesperides.'[49]

A hierarchy of institutions was created to implement the recommendations of the Whitley report. A National Council was responsible for the civil service as a whole, with a Departmental Council to cover the Post Office and local committees for each office. Representation on the Departmental Council was granted to all unions which were currently recognised, and membership of the local committees was confined to these organisations. The Post Office was obliged to consult the Whitley committees prior to any revision of staff or alteration of duties, and in a labour-intensive service this inevitably had wide implications which threatened to bring the postal unions into the framework of administration. The unions were aware that attitudes and prodedures would need to change in order to grasp their opportunity. Petitions and deputations belonged to the past, and 'the local and national committees would become training grounds for the new type of trade union leaders, who would largely cease to be critical and denunciatory, and would have to be constructive, patient, quietly insistent, and exceedingly

266

capable. . . . To visualise these changes is to see a new trades unionism, bringing with it serious possibilities and wide opportunities.'[50] But Whitleyism was not without its problems.

The Union of Post Office Workers had been formed in 1920 from a number of postal unions, but in 1921 there was a secession by some discontented members who formed the National Federation of Postal and Telegraph Clerks. This was partly the result of resentment by grades whose interests had been submerged, and partly a response to the UPW's acceptance of strikes and political involvement which the National Federation considered to be incompatible with a public service. The question of representation on the Whitley council soon arose, a problem which was particularly serious in London where the Guild of Postal Sorters had organised half the grade. This was blocked by the existing members of the staff side, although the Post Office had granted recognition to certain bodies affiliated to the National Federation. In the early 1920s, Evelyn Murray was not prepared to press the point, for an attempt to admit the Federation would 'lead to the breaking up of the Whitley machinery. This would be unfortunate.' The withdrawal of the UPW, it was felt at this stage, was to be avoided, for it 'would lead to the disenfranchisement of a much larger body of the staff than the Sorters at present excluded and would in effect wreck Whitleyism in the Post Office.' The conflict between the UPW and the secessionists placed considerable strain upon the Whitley machinery, particularly in London, and in 1923 the Post Office decided to withdraw from the London committee on the grounds that it was unrepresentative. Participation in the departmental council continued, and the 'considerable value' of the council was still noted in 1925. The changed circumstances after the General Strike did, however, suggest that it was no longer worth conciliating the UPW. Civil service unions were in 1927 forbidden from having any political involvement, and the secessionists had supported precisely such non-political trades unionism. 'It seems a great hardship', complained one Conservative Member of Parliament, 'that these people whose special quality is their loyalty to the Civil Service and their opposition to politics being introduced into the administration of Government Departments, should be deprived of what is their legitimate right.' When the Staff side in 1926 refused to admit the secessionists, the official side announced that it would need to consider whether the Council was sufficiently representative to continue. This statement produced a decision in 1928 by the staff side as a whole to widen the membership, but the UPW and the Civil Service Clerical Association withdrew. Although the secessionists had gained representation, the absence of the two largest unions resulted in the suspension of Whitleyism in the Post Office until 1932.[51]

The temporary demise of the Whitley council did not in fact make a great deal of difference. 'I should expect', remarked Evelyn Murray, 'that the UPW will be ready to co-operate in discussion through the medium of informal committees which will be just as effective as the formal machinery which the Whitley machinery provides.'[52] This was indeed the case, and in the 1920s and 1930s administrators at St Martin's le Grand were obliged to take almost as much note of the union officers at Clapham as of the Treasury chambers in Whitehall. There had been a remarkable change since the turn of the century. The dominant attitude of the nineteenth-century administrators of the Post Office was that membership of an association was both unnecessary and a subversion of discipline. The established workforce had been incorporated into the organisation through the wide range of benefits, and they had been offered the possibility of career progression from grade to grade, or at least the prospect of rising on the wage scale from increment to increment. Rational bureaucratic standards of discipline and reward had been created to remove the dangers of victimisation and favouritism. The development of unions threatened two aspects of the system of labour relations which had emerged in the Post Office. There was, in the first place, an almost patriarchal attitude to the workforce on the part of the administrators, a sense that they needed to be protected against misguided agitators. The second feature, which was perhaps more important, was the fear that the unions might threaten the bureaucratic system of control which had been erected, relying upon the individual loyalty of members of the workforce to the Post Office and a competitive desire to rise within its internal labour market. Unionisation might weaken loyalty to the department by creating another point of reference, and might also produce solidarity rather than competition. A policy of outright opposition to unions did succeed until the end of the nineteenth century but in the present century considerable adjustments have had to be made; the changed political environment gave unions an accepted role and opposition to membership would be counterproductive. The aim of the Post Office, as of most British employers, was to make unions a source of stability rather than conflict. The staff might no longer have complete loyalty to the Department and they might be willing to join unions which subjected the decisions of the administration to criticism; the solution was to bring the unions within the system of administration, most obviously in the Whitley councils. It might be argued that this process was taken too far, particularly after the Second World War, but the change in the system of labour relations from the exclusion to the incorporation of unions was remarkably successfuly in maintaining industrial peace.

PART IV

Officials
and
Politicians

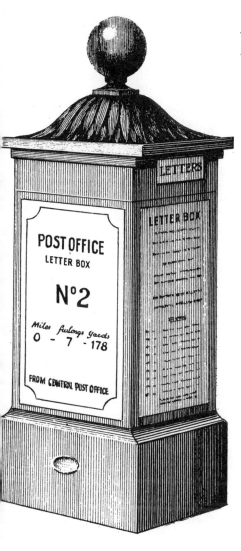

Instead of experts in administration are found amateurs in business, instead of complete cohesion are found a large measure of confusion, instead of harmony there was discord, instead of a succession of Political chiefs there had been a series of Parliamentary figureheads. Instead of a Department that could make its voice felt in Cabinet, there was an appendage of the Treasury. (Viscount Wolmer, *Post Office Reform: Its Importance and Practicability* (1932), p. 14.)

———————————

Centre and Region

The Establishment of the Post Office necessarily extends over the kingdom. . . . Its Headquarters are in London; there are Metropolitan Offices in Edinburgh and Dublin; and there are District Offices in every town, and almost every village, throughout the country. (PP 1854 XXXVII, *Report upon the Post Office*, p. 399.)

The Post Office was one of the few agencies in the nineteenth century with branches providing a nationwide coverage. Most public services were provided by local authorities with a considerable degree of autonomy from central government, and in the private sector only the railway companies had a geographic range which came close to the scope of the Post Office; the Army and the Navy were amongst the few organisations which surpassed the reach of the Post Office. It is not surprising therefore that there was a continuing debate in the Post Office on the most efficient means of controlling an institution which entered into the life of every town and village in the kingdom. Did efficiency demand the creation of uniformity by strict centralisation, or could it be achieved by the encouragement of flexibility through devolution of powers to the localities?

Centralisation: the power of St Martin's le Grand

Unlike almost all other Departments, the Post Office is primarily a trading or commercial undertaking. As a State monopoly the Post Office cannot determine wholly by reference to considerations of profit or loss the extent and character of the services which it provides; but this does not alter its essential character.

It follows that the type of organisation and the methods of control appropriate to a Department charged with administrative or regulative

271

The General Post Office at St Martin's le Grand was completed in 1829 to designs by Robert Smirke; it was demolished in 1912–13.

functions are not necessarily those appropriate to the Post Office. In the former, a high degree of centralisation is inevitable, and the organisation must be framed accordingly. In the latter, the nature of the undertaking suggests *prima facie* that a considerable degree of devolution of authority is possible. (PP 1930–1 X, *Report of the Royal Commission on the Civil Service*, pp. 587–8.)

The Royal Commission on the Civil Service had located a tension between the functions of the Post Office as a business which demanded decentralisation, and its status as a department of the state which forced it to adopt an inappropriate model of central control.[1] Lord Wolmer, after his term as Assistant Postmaster General, complained that 'the Post Office is a great business which is organised not as a business but as a Government Department'.[2] The status of the Department did indeed create a strong impetus towards central control, and the Post Office in the nineteenth and early twentieth centuries was ruled by the autocratic power of St Martin's le Grand. Why should this be?

In the early and mid-nineteenth century it was unwise to devolve many powers upon the postmasters throughout the country, for they were appointed by the Patronage Secretary of the Treasury, a system which produced officers with 'insufficient qualifications'. Although the most important postmasterships were appointed by the Postmaster General after 1854, there was still the problem that promotion within the service at a time of rapid expansion entailed the advancement of men with little experience and poor education. 'It was no doubt necessary that Postmasters selected in this manner should carry on their work under close supervision, and it was found inexpedient to entrust to them the decision of matters of importance.' The role of the Surveyor was therefore largely to inspect and check the work of the local postmasters, rather than to take decisions on the application of policy in the locality.[3] The force of this argument for centralisation had been reduced by the end of the nineteenth century, when postmasters were 'appointed from officers of the major establishment who have spent their whole lives in the Post Office service, and who have, presumably, been selected for their positions because of their special fitness, and in consequence of their efficiency, good character and length of service'.[4] However, another consideration had arisen in the late nineteenth century: the growth of trade unions. It was remarked in 1909 that

> The main difficulty which attends decentralisation of authority is the maintenance of uniformity in the application of rules and policy, and any deviation from uniformity at once gives ground for criticism. Thus one result of the growth and activity of associations of Post Office servants has been rather to encourage centralisation as a means of securing uniformity.[5]

The prospect of local variation in the terms and conditions of service was not welcomed by officials who were adjusting to the minute inspection of their actions by recently recognised trade unions.

The Post Office was a government department answerable to the Treasury with a political head under the close scrutiny of Parliament; the outcome was strong pressure for central control. The Decentralisation Committee of 1909 remarked that

> the Postmaster General is liable to be challenged by Members of Parliament, and to receive inquiries from them, on all points of administration, whether large or small. . . . In the second place, the control of the Treasury over expenditure has been . . . very close and minute. When the sanction of the Treasury had to be obtained for practically all new items of expenditure, delegation of authority in such matters was impossible.[6]

The constant need to seek Treasury approval for even minor expenditure, and to answer Parliamentary questions on the performance of the Post Office in every town and village, created a strong case for the retention of power in the centre. Austen Chamberlain, the Postmaster General, complained in 1902 that 'it is deplorable, absolutely deplorable' that he and the Secretary spent so much time with matters of very small detail, because these matters of detail are asked by honourable Members, and because we do not feel an honourable Member will accept an answer from anyone but the highest authority. I think a third of the time – I am putting it at a low estimate – of the highest officials in the Post Office is occupied in answering questions raised by Members of this House, and in providing me with information in order that I may be in a position to answer the inquiries addressed to me concerning matters which, in any private business, would be dealt with by the officer on the spot.[7]

Centralisation was the result, which it was feared led to inefficiency and inflexibility. Matters as petty as the temporary hire of a bicycle or the employment of a part-time cleaner were submitted by postmasters to the Surveyor, who then sought authority from the Secretary in London. These procedures might not really be necessary for administrative uniformity, for the central Secretariat could, after all, formulate policy and leave its execution to local officers. However, a distinction between the formulation of policy and executive control was not accepted until well into the twentieth century with the result that the Secretariat formed a bottle-neck in the operation of the Post Office, its 'autocratic position' leading to inflexibility and delay. 'One of the fundamental principles of organisation', it was suggested in 1931, had been contradicted:

> viz:- the distinction between policy and practice, between the administrative and the executive functions. . . . The Secretariat of the Post Office, as at present constituted, is concerned not only with the framing and formulation of policy and with the supervision of its execution, but also with the conduct of the daily business of the Post Office services, for which it is unsuited, both by training and experience.[8]

The officials at the centre were, it was argued, submerged in a mass of detailed executive work which resulted in 'waste of power and loss of efficiency'.[9] The duplication or triplication of work as it was referred up the hierarchy to London was, critics claimed, 'costly, cumbrous, in a large measure useless, and without compensating advantages'.[10] The growth in the volume and complexity of work threatened to overwhelm the highly centralised system which had developed at a time when its tasks were relatively simple. By 1909, it was suggested,

> The business of the Post Office has so increased in quantity, complexity and variety, that the pressure of detailed work on the higher officers of the Service has become excessive, with the result that it is difficult for them to devote an adequate amount of their time and energies to the systematic consideration of the more important

274

questions of policy which should properly occupy them. At the same time, a large amount of unnecessary work is created by the reference to higher authority of unimportant and routine matters.[11]

Another weakness of the centralised system was the neglect of financial and engineering considerations in the formulation of policy. The Engineer-in-Chief and the Comptroller and Accountant General were not members of the Secretariat, and could only contribute to debates on policy when their opinion was specifically sought. This division between administration, finance and engineering ran through the hierarchy of the Post Office, with particularly serious consequences for the telegraph and telephone service. The Surveyors who had general responsibility for a district reported to the Secretary, and the Superintending Engineers in the regions reported to the Engineer-in-Chief who was answerable to the Secretary. The result was that connections ran upwards through the hierarchy rather than laterally within the district, and the result was a lack of co-ordination except at the top.[12] It was not only the specialists in finance and engineering who were excluded from the Secretariat, for the same may be said of the heads of major services, such as the Controllers of the Money Order Department or the Savings Bank, and the head of important districts such as the Controller of the London Postal Service. There was a gulf between the Secretariat and the practical officers who ran the service. This was, in the opinion of some critics, a harmful division which entailed both the neglect of the talents of provincial officers and a misapplication of the abilities of officials at St Martin's le Grand.

The divide between the Secretariat and other branches had been less marked in the mid-nineteenth century. John Tilley had risen from the ranks of Surveyor to become Secretary, and Frank Scuadmore had served in the office of Receiver and Accountant General. The introduction of open competition for administrative posts created a rigid barrier between the Secretariat drawn from university graduates successful in 'literary' examinations and other branches of the service, so that the practical experience of officers in charge of operations was excluded from the elite which considered policy. 'The limited power of decision allowed to Postmasters and other provincial officers', it was complained in 1909, 'tends to diminish their sense of responsibility and to create, especially among the more active and intelligent of them, a feeling of undue and unnecessary restraint.' Sceptics doubted the value of success in a literary examination for candidates who might 'spend the remainder of their official career, not merely in administering, but to a considerable extent in controlling, the execution of services of which they may have considerable theoretical, but little practical, knowledge'.[13]

275

Postmasters and surveyors

The officials at St Martin's le Grand faced the task of controlling a national network of offices which had expanded from 4,028 in 1840 to 24,354 in 1913.[14] The system in 1840 was simple and straightforward. The postmaster of a town was appointed by the Patronage Secretary of the Treasury on the advice of a local MP, and he provided the necessary office and clerks in return for allowances from the Department. There were in addition receiving houses where letters might be handed in, which were usually small shops providing the service in return for a commission. This simple pattern was to change from the middle of the nineteenth century as the power of political patronage declined, the cost of providing an office mounted, and the range of services widened.

8.1 POST OFFICES IN THE UNITED KINGDOM, 1854–1913

	1854	*1880*	*1900*	*1913*
Head Office	935	912	906	789
Branch Office	—	—	255	309
Town sub-office			4,964	6,620
Country sub-office	9,038	13,300	15,815	16,636
Total	9,973	14,212	21,940	24,354

Source: *Annual Reports of the Postmaster General on the Post Office.*

In 1854, the power of appointment to postmasterships worth more than £175 a year was transferred to the Postmaster General, which was subsequently extended to cover posts worth more than £120 a year in England and £100 in Ireland and Scotland. The Patronage Secretary still had a large number of positions in his gift, for in 1895 there were 17,874 postmasterships and subpostmasterships below these limits. This vestige of patronage was not greatly valued. Sir William Hart Dyke, the Patronage Secretary, remarked in 1878 that the usual response of Members of Parliament 'was that they had great difficulty in finding a fit person to fill the post, and in many cases they had to apply to the clergyman of the parish to recommend a candidate'. Dyke viewed his task as 'a rare burden and distress' rather than a source of influence. Politics could nevertheless play a part in the selection of a postmaster, as was evident when a vacancy was filled at Winslow in 1877. The Patronage Secretary asked a local Conservative Member to select a candidate; the assistant postmaster was a Liberal, who immediately offered to vote Conservative in the future in return for the nomination. His political apostasy did not succeed, for another candidate was preferred who had proved his dependability by voting Conservative in the past. Such patronage was abandoned in Ireland in 1887, simply because the dearth of Conservative Members in the South was creating problems in filling posts, and in 1895 it was dropped in England, Wales and Scotland.[15] The disappearance of patronage had taken forty years to accomplish.

The method of appointment of postmasters changed, and so did the way in which their buildings were provided. The head post office in a provincial town, William Lewins remarked in 1862, 'is metamorphosed into quite a grand establishment' which might be mistaken for a first-class bank.[16] When a larger building was required, the Surveyor would enquire if it was possible for the postmaster to supply the premises in return for an addition to his allowance, a solution which became increasingly unusual in bigger towns where the cost was likely to exceed the resources of one man. The alternative was to provide a Crown Office owned by the Department. At first, Crown Offices were erected by the Department which employed a local arthitect or builder, excepting the main offices in London, Edinburgh and Dublin which were entrusted to the government's own building department, the Office of Works. However, when the Treasury was asked in 1858 to approve the appointment of a travelling surveyor to supervise building work, it was ruled that all building should in future be the responsibility of the Office of Works. There was a further possibility which was stressed at the end of the century: the Department might rent or lease a building on the open market, for 'in this way the ingenuity and resources of local builders and house-owners may afford the most economical means of furnishing the necessary accommodation'. This policy did not prove practicable in the largest offices where it was difficult to find suitable premises or to induce a developer to make a large investment in a special building, but in the case of smaller offices it was possible to rent buildings provided by 'outside capitalists'. There was therefore a distinction between 'Crown Offices Class I' built and maintained by the Office of Works and 'Crown Offices Class II' which were the responsibility of the Department. The result was an artificial and uneconomic division of powers.

Indeed, the Select Committee on Post Office Servants recommended in 1907 that the Department should take over responsibility for buildings from the Office of Works. This proposal was not accepted by the government, and the division of responsibility and dual control became an increasing problem when the premises of the National Telephone Company were acquired in 1912. A Treasury committee was appointed to consider the whole question. Essentially, the Office of Works was responsible for freehold offices and the Post Office for offices held on lease; the Department proposed to the Committee that it

277

should instead have responsibility for all small offices, with the power to build on its own account, leaving the Office of Works to provide all large buildings. The Committee disagreed, arguing that all government building work should be placed in the hands of the Office of Works, to secure 'economy, efficiency and uniformity'. Acceptance of the Post Office's proposal would, it was feared, 'very soon result in the establishment of a large new and independent Office of Works within the Post Office' which, unlike the Office of Works, could not be employed upon any other projects. 'The Postmaster General', it was argued, 'should be in the position of a building owner employing the Office of Works as his architect.' The Post Office was horrified: why, it was lamented, should Surveyors and postmasters who conducted 'with much ability the largest business in the country' not deal with repairs and maintenance in their buildings? The arrangement with the Office of Works had been made when the Department had a very different character: it was argued that its work was now hampered by the difficulty of getting a sufficient sum voted for building works, and by the delays arising from the need to deal with the Office of Works. And, as Herbert Samuel complained, the architectural style was mean. 'The State has the duty of erecting its public buildings in a manner which will contribute to the dignity and the beauty of the towns in which they are situated, and particularly is this the case when those buildings are for the purpose of conducting a vast and very profitable business, and are daily entered by great numbers of people.' The Treasury was unmoved by the economic and aesthetic case of the Department, and the matter was left unresolved at the outbreak of the war. Building did not revive until the late 1920s when there was, by contrast, a general atmosphere of co-operation between the Office of Works and the Post Office. The divison between Class I and Class II offices survived, but fewer leasehold premises were taken because of the more complex requirements for telephone exchanges and the development of uniform standards for working conditions. Emphasis was instead placed upon the efficiency which resulted from centralisation in the hands of the Ministry of Works, as the Office had become. Delays, it was admitted, were more likely to arise from the difficulties of the Post Office in deciding upon its requirements. The relationship between the Ministry of Works and the Post Office was much more one of architect and client, and this was confirmed in 1938 when the Ministry created a self-contained Post Office Section of its architects' division.[17]

Post offices must be categorised in two ways, by the type of building and also by administrative status. The head post office of a town provided a full range of services and the postmaster had general responsibility for the efficient handling of the town's mail. In larger

8.2 PAYMENT TO SUBPOSTMASTERS, 1879

(a) *A small fixed salary for work connected with the receipt and disposal of letters, newspapers etc.*

	Per year
Primary salary	£3
for each 200 letters posted weekly	£1
for each bag beyond one made up daily	£1
for each bag received daily but not made up	10s
for one or more bags made up daily for branch messenger	£1
for each disturbance between 10 p.m. and 6 a.m.	£1
for each quarter of an hour daily in delivery, etc	£1

(b) *Commission on the issue and payment of money orders*

first 500 issued in year	£2 15s
second 500	£2 5s
each 1,000 after first 1,000	£4
first 500 paid	£2 5s
second 500	£1 15s
each 1,000 after first 1,000	£3

(c) *Commission on Savings Bank deposits and withdrawals per 1,000 transactions*

£5

(d) *Commission in respect of annuity and insurance business per 1,000 transactions*

£5

(e) *Commission on telegraph business*

1d per message but fixed payments of 2s to 7s 6d a week if this does not produce a minimum sum.

(f, g, h) *Poundage on sale of stamps*

postage	1 per cent
telegraph	1 per cent
receipt	2 per cent

(i) *Commission on issue of inland revenue business*

1d per licence

Source: Post 30/408, E8935/1881, file III.

towns there would be branch offices treated as 'detached counters' of the head office. The postmaster and his staff were established members of the Post Office, with all the rights which that entailed; the head office might be owned by the postmaster, but was more likely to be a Crown Office Class I or II. Far more numerous were the sub-post offices, which comprised 23,256 out of 24,354 offices in 1913. The subpostmasters were, until the late nineteenth century, all treated in the same way, receiving a commission for the transaction of various services and providing the necessary staff and accommodation. They were not established members of the workforce, and were often small shopkeepers who welcomed this side-line. By 1906, there were 21,601 of these so-called scale-payment or commission subpostmasters, whose income ranged from as little as £8 to about £1,000 a year at a total cost of over £900,000. These subpostmasters, it was admitted, 'form a very important link in the Post Office system, and there can be no doubt that in no other way could their service be supplied with such little expense to the public purse'. Recruits were attracted not as much by the generosity of the payments as by the 'ulterior considerations' of attracting customers, for a sub-post office produced extra private profit in addition to the official pay. The Department in the early twentieth century questioned the morality of exploiting this calculation in order to offer low rates, particularly in the larger town offices where the post office business was complex, the initial outlay large, and the scale of official business such that other trade was precluded. It was indeed not always possible to find suitably qualified shopkeepers to run the largest sub-offices, so the subpostmasters in these cases were often recruited within the Department from men who had few alternative sources of income. These considerations meant that from the late nineteenth century the large sub-offices were converted from scale-payment to salaried status, which might be run either by an unestablished officer who carried on his own business, or an established officer who devoted his whole time to the Post Office. The wages and office costs of the salaried sub-offices were paid by the Department. In 1906, there were 320 established and 181 unestablished salaried subpostmasters, who were paid sums ranging from £55 to £314 a year. The trend towards the substitution of salaries for commission was accelerated in 1907 when it was decided that any office with an income above £250 in the provinces or £500 in London should change its status. The distinction between branch offices and salaried sub-offices was becoming somewhat anomalous and came in for criticism between the wars. However, this system survives. In 1936 it was decided that branch offices should predominate in an inner circle around head offices, with salaried sub-offices at a greater distance and in the less important locations.[18] More recently, the number of salaried sub-offices has increased as head offices have been reduced in number and regraded. The result, therefore, was the emergence of a complex pattern of post offices which varied according to the type of building and the status of the postmaster.

Clearly, the officials at St Martin's le Grand could not deal directly with such a large number of postmasters spread across the country, and

8.3 TYPES OF POST OFFICE C. 1900

1 Head post office	a. The building might be owned by the Post-master,
	b. but was most likely a Crown Office Class I built and maintained by the Office of Works, or
	c. might be a Crown Office Class II leased by the Post Office.
2 Branch office	Essentially a 'detached counter' of a Head Office; usually a Crown Office Class II leased by the Post Office.
3 Salaried sub-office	Usually a Crown Office Class II,
	a. Where the subpostmaster was established no private business was carried on,
	b. but if he was unestablished there might be some other trade.
4 Scale-payment sub-office	Premises and staff supplied by the subpostmaster who was usually a shopkeeper.

an intermediate category of officers was essential to inspect and supervise local services. The system differed between London and the provinces. London generated a massive postal traffic and also formed the hub of the distribution system for the country: a letter posted in Southampton for delivery in Edinburgh would arrive at Waterloo station, be transferred to a mail van and delivered to King's Cross Station for conveyance onwards to Scotland. The officer who had charge of London was responsible both for the efficient performance of the local services within London, and for the smooth operation of these complex and sensitive connections in the national mail system. Whereas the provinces came under surveyors, London was the responsibility of a controller.[19]

The supervision of services in London and the control of the circulation system had, at the beginning of the period, been divided between the Inland Office which was responsible for mail to and from London, and the District Office which handled the traffic within London. The *Report upon the Post Office* of 1854 recommended the amalgamation of these offices under a single Controller, and a new, unified Circulation Department was created.[20] The organisation of the Post Office in London differed in a number of respects from other areas of the country, for the provincial organisation was based upon geography and the metropolitan organisation on function. When the Department acquired the telegraphs, the surveyors in the provinces were given responsibility for the new service whereas in London the scale of the traffic resulted in a functional division between the Controller of the London Postal Service and the Controller of the Central Telegraph Office.[21] The grading system and pay scales also differed between London and the provinces, but perhaps the most remarkable feature which distinguished the Controller of the London Postal Service from a provincial surveyor was the scale of his task. In 1911/12, the outdoor workforce in the London Postal Service was 15,078 or 29.8 per cent of the national total.[22] The Controller of the London Postal Service was the most important local officer in the Post Office and, despite his proximity to the Secretary's office, the most independent. His background had more in common with the members of the Secretariat than with the surveyors. The Controller in 1910, for example, was Robert Bruce who had entered the Secretary's office in 1876 by means of success in the open competition for civil service posts, and he served there until 1896 when he was appointed vice-controller of the London Postal Service.[23]

The remainder of the country was divided between surveyors who were responsible for inspecting the various offices, checking that services were efficient, and ensuring that the postmasters obeyed the regulations issued from St Martin's le Grand. 'The importance of these officers', it was remarked in 1854, 'can hardly be over-estimated. They are sometimes called the eyes of the department; and the well-working of the complicated and extensive machinery of the Post Office undoubtedly depends in great measure upon their intelligence and vigilance.'[24] Their scope for independent action was slight, limited to the flexible interpretation of rules, for they were essentially a channel of information from the locality and of instructions from the centre. A postmaster might, for example, wish to increase the workforce at his office, and he reported his case to the Surveyor who passed it on to the Secretary. There were some exceptions to this three-tier system of administration, and a fourth tier was inserted in the case of Scotland and Ireland where the Secretaries in Edinburgh and Dublin passed the reports of surveyors to the Secretary in London.[25] By contrast, in some large towns there were only two tiers, for the postmaster was given the power to act as surveyor for his own office and, in some cases from the late nineteenth century, a number of head offices in neighbouring towns. In 1907 there were seven postmaster-surveyors and four 'independent postmasters' who had the right to report directly to the Secretary in London, of whom four had the right to survey other head offices. The postmaster-surveyor of Birmingham, for example, inspected fourteen other head offices.[26] The chain of command thus varied over the country. The postmaster of, say, Dundee reported to the surveyor who informed the Secretary in Edinburgh who sought a decision from the Secretary in London; the postmaster of Norwich would report to the Surveyor of the Eastern counties who would pass the case to the Secretary; the postmaster-surveyor of Birmingham could go direct to St Martin's le Grand. But in all cases the same general point applied: the scope for local initiative was minimal.

The surveyors were not recruited in the same way as the officials of the Secretary's office, for they worked up the hierarchy of the Post Office from lower-grade clerical posts and were not appointed from the open competition for administrative posts in the civil service. The senior Surveyor in 1910 was W. S. Rushton, who had entered the Post Office in 1866 as a temporary clerk in the Savings Bank; in 1873 he was appointed clerk to a Surveyor, and promoted to the rank of assistant Surveyor in 1885 and surveyor in 1890. Experience was in some cases gained as a postmaster. H. S. Wooster, for example, entered the service as a clerk in Bath in 1876, and he was promoted to chief clerk in 1884 and postmaster of Worcester in 1891. He was subsequently appointed assistant Surveyor in 1898 and surveyor in 1906. Appointment rested upon long service: none of the seventeen surveyors in 1910 had served for less than 23 years and one had been in the Post Office for 33 years.[27] A firm line was drawn between the surveyors who inspected at the local level on the basis of many years of experience and the staff of the Secretary's office who were involved with wider questions of policy. The surveyors were, indeed, a conservative force in the Department.

The surveyors' districts had been fixed in 1787, when there were thirteen surveyors in the United Kingdom. By the 1850s, the boundaries of these districts had long ceased to accord with either the distribution of population or the circulation of mail by railway. In 1856, the surveyors' districts in England were increased from seven to nine, and their boundaries redrawn on the basis of population and the night mail circulation from London. These changes also meant that four districts instead of two radiated from London, which made it possible to hold more frequent consultations at headquarters. Indeed, the offices of the surveyors for the districts adjacent to London were to be relocated at St Martin's le Grand, and Rowland Hill went so far as to claim that 'the leading principle in the proposed revision of Districts was to make London the Head Quarters of several of the English Surveyors'. There was a centralising tendency at work, but the experiment did not succeed. The surveyors argued that they should work from home because of their irregular hours and the need to be in the area under their inspection. The force of this point was accepted, and the scheme was soon abandoned.[28] Although the strategy of incorporating surveyors into the

283

organisation at headquarters was again pursued in the early 1870s, it had no greater success. In 1873, the work of three districts was transferred to the Secretary's office, and it was planned to extend this further. John Tilley, who had risen to the Secretaryship from the ranks of the surveyors, was a strong advocate of centralisation. 'It is very desirable that so much of the Surveyors' work as is not necessarily done away from Head Quarters should be done in the Secretary's Office', and he argued that direct management would allow greater speed 'in executing the work in the country'.[29] The scheme collapsed by the end of 1874 in the face of opposition from the surveyors who stressed the virtues of flexibility and local knowledge which arose from residence in the locality, and minimised the benefits of direct communication with the Secretary. By 1876 the surveyors had all been removed from headquarters and returned to their districts.[30]

8.4 COST OF SURVEYORS, 1855–85

	1855		1885	
	No	Cost	No	Cost
Surveyors	12	£6,060	16	£11,598
Travelling clerks	24	£5,464	72	£19,965
Stationary clerks	7	£420	36	£1,080
Expenses, rent	—	£14,025	—	£30,960
Total	43	£25,969	124	£63,603

Source: Post 30/507, E9038/1887, File VI.

The cost of surveyors rose by 145 per cent between 1855 and 1885, at a time when the gross revenue increased by 278 per cent. The surveyors were being overwhelmed with detail as a result of the increase in the number of offices and the introduction of new services, and it was feared that 'the amount and variety of duty now performed by that staff are such as to leave no sufficient margin for the effective attainment of the primary function of a Surveyor, viz, the methodical and complete, as compared with the hurried and inadequate, or the partially intermitted, inspection and supervision of his district'.[31] By 1885 each surveyor was responsible for, on average, 60 head and 900 subordinate offices, and the system was under pressure. Nevertheless, the report of the Committee on the Relief of Surveying Staff of 1886 left the basic structure untouched, and change was confined to minor adjustments. Certain duties were transferred from the surveyors to 'selected' postmasters in 1887, despite some misgivings about their competence. The number of subordinate clerks was also increased and their status raised, in order to release surveyors for their primary function of methodical inspection.

These marginal changes did not offer a satisfactory solution, and in the early 1890s attention turned to the possibility of reducing the number of surveyors 'to the smallest number consistent with the effective discharge' of their duties. This had the advantage of reducing the work of the Secretariat in consulting and controlling the surveyors, but greater emphasis was placed on the disadvantages of weakening their personal knowledge of their district, their subordinates, and the postal arrangements. Such concerns acted as a check on the size of districts, for 'there can be doubt that the more a Surveyor is driven to manage his district on paper, the more dependent he is on others for what he ought to know himself, and the less efficient he becomes as an Inspecting Officer'. Although there was continued discussion of the surveying system in the 1880s and 1890s, practical action did not move beyond marginal adjustments.[32]

It was becoming clear in the late 1890s that more fundamental change was necessary, and it was also apparent that surveyors could be granted a measure of independence only when the Secretary was freed from the need to refer cases to the Postmaster General. The Secretary in 1897 noted that 'it is surely unnecessary that the Head of the Department should personally perform so many of the minor acts of Administration as now fall to his share, and that so large a portion of his time should thus be occupied while the claims of important business become more and more pressing'. A number of minor classes of business were no longer to be submitted to the Postmaster General, including promotions up to a salary of £300, the award of good conduct stripes, and discipline cases which did not involve dismissal or loss of pay. The delegation of powers from the Secretary to the surveyors was similarly minimal, including the right to grant permission to postmasters to sleep off the premises. The devolution of powers in the late 1890s was checked by the fear that a lack of consistency might be exploited by unions, exposing the Postmaster General to criticism in the Commons on cases which he had never considered. The limits of change had been drawn very tightly, but in the early twentieth century the debate over centralisation was to become ever more insistent.[33]

Decentralisation: the frustration of reform

The issue of substantial reform could be avoided no longer in the early twentieth century in the face of the imminent nationalisation of the telephone companies whose administration would have to be incorporated into the structure of the Post Office. This structure had in any case been strongly criticised by the Select Committee on Postal Servants in 1907 which provided an external assessment of administrative procedures in place of the introverted debates of the past twenty years. The Select Committee recommended 'considerable decentralisation of authority' to surveyors and postmasters, with the control of policy remaining in London.[34] This coincided with pressure from provincial postmasters to have greater freedom of action in place of the existing 'obsolete and superfluous system of check' on 'every little detail of duty'.[35] In response to these various pressures a committee was appointed in 1908 to consider decentralisation, under the chairmanship of the Secretary, H. Babington-Smith.

There were a number of possible approaches. One official, P.V. Turnor, proposed the creation of a new tier of authority between the surveyors and the Secretary, on the lines of the system in Scotland and Ireland. These divisional surveyors or secretaries would deal with all papers which did not involve a change in practice or principle, and the Secretary in London would in consequence have fewer provincial officials to consult.[36] The postmasters, on the contrary, suggested that the surveying districts should be broken up and the work redistributed amongst the more experienced of their number. This would, in effect, increase the number of surveyors and impose a greater burden on the Secretary.[37] The addition of a new responsibility – the telephone service – created further difficulties. It could be argued that the Post Office had an efficient administration, and that the managerial structure of the National Telephone Company should be adjusted to fit. Even if this contention was accepted, there were various ways of proceeding: it might be sensible to create two parallel regional systems, with one surveyor for posts and another for telephones; alternatively, a new higher grade of provincial controller could be created to whom the postal surveyors and telephone superintendents would report.[38] The Babington-Smith Committee had not only to settle the unresolved problems of how the existing services should be controlled, but had also to create an administrative structure for a major new departure.

The existing administrative structure (chart 1) had an upper echelon of thirty-two provincial officers above the rank of postmaster. The Committee proposed (chart 2) to reduce the number of surveyors in England from eleven to six, who would be renamed surveyors-general; Ireland and Scotland would each become a single surveyor's district under a secretary; the number of postmaster-surveyors would be reduced to four; and the independent postmasters would be subject to the control of the surveyors-general. The result would be to reduce the number of local officials reporting to the Secretary in London to thirteen, who could meet in conference four times a year. Additional powers should, it was suggested, devolve upon the more senior postmasters who received more than £350 a year, which in turn required a greater delegation of authority from the Treasury to the Post Office. The question which remained was how to deal with the National Telephone Company. It would be possible either to bring the company entirely within the Post Office organisation under the surveyors, or to leave its organisation intact by transferring the existing Post Office telephone service to the company's system. Both of these options were rejected. The first solution would disrupt an existing administrative structure designed for the telephone service and replace it with a structure intended for different purposes, while the second approach would, it was argued, remove telephones from the aegis of postmasters who were the recognised public face of the Department and involve duplication of staff. The outcome was a compromise which, 'while retaining, as far as practicable, the existing organisation of the Company, should combine that organisation with the existing organisation of the Post Office wherever that can be done without loss of efficiency'. The regional superintendents of the National Telephone Company would act as chief advisers to the surveyors-general and to the secretaries in Ireland and Scotland, and the engineering staff would be transferred to the control of the Post Office superintending engineers. This would create an unfortunate division of authority, for the engineering organisation of the Department formed a separate structure alongside the surveying establishment, unlike in the National Telephone Company where the engineers were answerable to the district managers in the locality. It was accepted that the functional division of the Post Office system might create problems of communication between engineers and managers, but the Committee felt 'that there should be no serious difficulty in making the necessary detailed arrangements to secure this result, even although the engineering staff is under separate control.'[39]

These proposals were initially accepted as Departmental policy, and were forwarded to the Treasury with the support of the Postmaster General:

> The proposals . . . will affect a revolution in Post Office organisation. Excellent and efficient as I have found the existing organisation to be, I have been impressed . . . by the unnecessary reduplication of work, and by the excessive centralisation, entailed under the present system. . . . The proposed decentralisation should promote not only economy, by lessening waste in labour; but also efficiency, by raising the standard of the work of the Postmaster and Surveyor, whilst it would not run counter to that general uniformity of administration which is important in the Post Office.[40]

This was to be overturned in 1910 when Sir Matthew Nathan succeeded Babington-Smith as Secretary, for he suggested a number of mod-

CHART 1
ADMINISTRATIVE STRUCTURE OF THE POST OFFICE, 1907

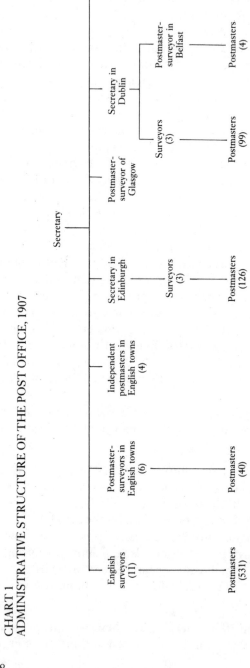

Source: Report of Decentralisation Committee and Post 30/1918, E26128/1910, file III a.

CHART 2
DECENTRALISATION COMMITTEE'S PROPOSAL, 1907

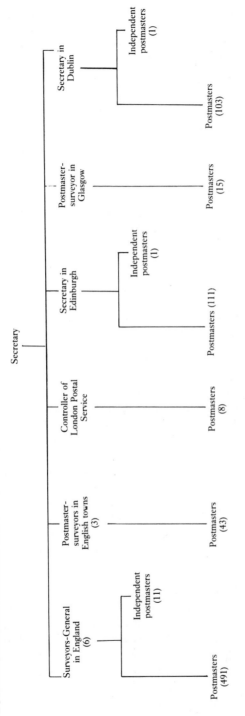

Source: Report of Decentralisation Committee and post 30/1918, E26128/1910 file III a.

CHART 3
SIR MATTHEW NATHAN'S PROPOSAL, 1910

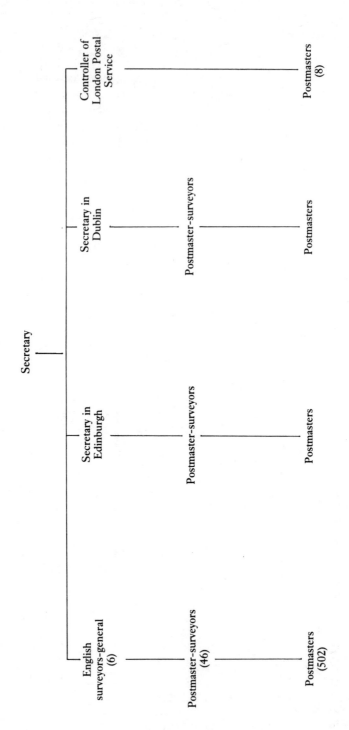

Secretary

English surveyors-general (6) — Postmaster-surveyors (46) — Postmasters (502)

Secretary in Edinburgh — Postmaster-surveyors — Postmasters

Secretary in Dublin — Postmaster-surveyors — Postmasters

Controller of London Postal Service — Postmasters (8)

Source: Post 30/1918, E26128/1910, File IIIa

ifications (chart 3). He felt that the Committee's scheme would not avoid excessive centralisation in the Secretary's office, and he proposed that the surveyors-general should take a larger responsibility. The Secretariat should deal only with nine officials of the rank of surveyor-general or its equivalent; the postmaster-surveyors would form a subordinate grade and postmasters provide a third layer. Nathan had reduced the number of officials in the highest level of provincial administration, but had created an intermediary grade which extended the chain of command.[41]

The officials of the Post Office were split between the two schemes, and the Postmaster General, Herbert Samuel, was alarmed that repeated changes might ensue. 'One does not want to be always tinkering with the organisation of the Post Office, there should be some finality about the changes that are made.' He expressed doubts about the virtues of undertaking work in the provinces rather than at Headquarters, for 'it does not make very much difference whether you bring the work up to eight men sitting at eight great centres or whether you forward the same work to a central office'. Specialist knowledge would be lost, for the provincial officers would be generalists, unlike officials at Headquarters who could handle a particular class of business. He was also sceptical of the virtues of inserting another step in the hierarchy. Samuel proposed instead to transfer work from both Headquarters and the surveyors to the larger postmasters, and to devolve part of the control of smaller postmasters from Headquarters to the surveyors. The creation of surveyors-general was rejected: Samuel doubted whether it would be possible to secure uniformity, particularly on labour questions, for 'unless you have rather close control from the Head Office you may get into greater difficulties with the Associations'. He was also sceptical of the argument that it was necessary to have fewer provincial officers in the highest grade in order to hold conferences, for it was possible to invite selected surveyors to Headquarters for consultation. Surveyors-general would in any case control too large an area to have much personal knowledge. The solution favoured by Samuel was to leave the basic structure as it was, with some minor readjustments of powers:

> This proposal to create a staff of Surveyors General is a very fundamental one. I confess that I am a bit afraid of it, since the case in its favour is by no means clear, and I am wondering whether it may be more wise in the first place to delegate to the larger postmasters such powers as every one is agreed that they ought to have, and also to the Surveyors, and see how that works for a year or two.

Nathan summed up the outcome, with some contempt. 'The general idea is delegation but not reorganisation.'[42]

291

Samuel was not without his supporters. C.A. King, the Accountant General, feared the consequences of the creation of a tier of post-master-surveyors, for 'it interposes an additional barrier between the Postmaster who has to report, and the Secretary who has to consider, the facts. Indeed, the scheme would extend to England and Wales the circuitous method now operative in Ireland and Scotland.' The duplication of work would also be excessive, for 'the distribution of the clerical work done in the (present) Surveyors' Offices amongst sixty Postmaster-Surveyors' offices must be uneconomical as each of these latter offices will tend to reproduce, in miniature, the present organisation of a Surveyor's stationary staff'.[43] The result, it was pointed out by the opponents of Nathan's scheme, would be the 'localisation of the Surveying Staff' which would 'practically "scrap" the present highly-trained, thoroughly experienced, Surveying staff, and to place their duties, and in addition largely increased responsibilities, upon a body of untrained men'.[44] There can be little doubt that Nathan's scheme was misguided, the work of a newcomer who had little understanding of the needs of the Department. Unfortunately, his intervention meant that the arguments of conservatism and minimalist approaches to administrative change triumphed, despite the problems which existed in running the present services and the prospect of acquiring a major new function.

The outcome of the debate was that the structure of the surveying force was unchanged, with the delegation of relatively minor powers to postmasters and surveyors. In future, postmasters could, for example, appoint charwomen and arrange for the repair of bicycles; surveyors could on their own authority appoint subpostmasters paid up to £50 a year, and repair huts provided as shelters for rural postmen up to a limit of £5.[45] Sir Matthew complained that 'For the present at any rate there is to be no reorganisation of the Post Office – only delegation of greater powers to surveyors and postmasters. We shall now have to consider the fitting in of the National Telephone Company's organisation with ours as it at present exists.'[46]

The avoidance of the serious problems which had been clearly perceived does indicate an even more deep-seated source of anxiety about the administration of the Post Office: there was an ingrained caution and inflexibility which arose from the scale and complexity of the organisation. When major changes were proposed, they could be frustrated by barriers to effective action which arose from the divided opinion of Secretary and Postmaster General. There had been a rapid turnover of Secretaries which led to discontinuity of policy, and Samuel had not involved himself with the details of administration. The result was to be an inability to make fundamental changes in structure. Sir George Murray of the Treasury, who had himself been Secretary between 1899 and 1903, had welcomed the Report of 1909, remarking that if only half the proposals were implemented, it would 'constitute the most drastic revolution in Post Office methods which has ever been made at one time'. Even so, he felt that the trend towards de-centralisation would need to go further in the future, for 'the highly centralised system under which Post Office administration has hitherto been carried on has been slowly breaking down for some years; and things cannot go on as they are much longer'.[47] Nevertheless, the recommendations of the Report were not implemented, and the main features of the Post Office's administrative structure were to survive.

There was some change in the aftermath of the war which affected the administrative structure at St Martin's le Grand rather than the regional organisation. In 1919, all government departments were in-structed to reorganise their Higher Division staff on a common basis of assistant principal, principal and assistant secretary. The new grades were introduced into the Post Office in 1921, and this soon produced discontent amongst the small 'corps d'élite'. There were seven assistant secretaries, each in charge of a Branch dealing with Staff, Estab-lishments, Buildings and Supplies, Home Mails, Foreign Mails, Tele-graphs, and Telephones. They received between £1,000 and £1,200 a year, and in 1921 they complained that the differential between their salaries and the Second Secretary who received £2,200 and Secretary who received £3,000 was too great. The Secretariat of the Post Office had been regraded at a lower level than other parts of the civil service where a category of principal assistant secretaries had been inserted. The Department also had a less favourable ratio of assistant principals to principals, for while the Post Office had thirty-one assistant principals to twenty principals, the Ministry of Labour had twenty-five in each grade. The result was discontent amongst the members of the Secretariat whose chances of promotion were slight. Accordingly, in 1921 the assistant secretaries proposed that two new posts should be created by merging the Home and Foreign Mails branches under a Director of Postal Services, and the Telegraph and Telephone branches under a Director of Telegraphs and Telephones. This suggestion was implemented in 1922 when the new posts were created on a scale of £1,200 to £1,500. This regrading did not only mollify the assistant secretaries, for it also checked the demand that the telegraph and telephone services should be separated from the Post Office, a change which had been recommended by the Select Committee on Telephones in 1922. Instead of creating two distinct organisations the new Directors would be responsible for the mail and telecommunications services, answerable to the Secretary; the remaining branches provided common services under the Second Secretary; and the Engineer-in-Chief and

293

294

CHART 4
ADMINISTRATIVE STRUCTURE: 1922

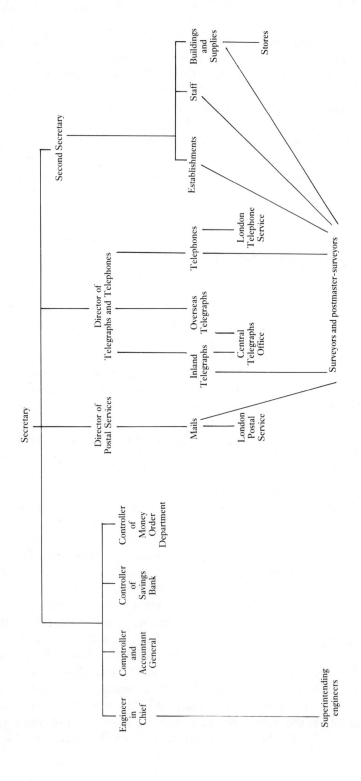

Source: Wolmer, *Post Office Reform*, p. 233.

Comptroller and Accountant General reported to the Secretary. The system was still hierarchical, based upon vertical chains of command rather than lateral consultation and the only co-ordination between functions came at the top in the Secretary's office which formed a bottle-neck in the administration (see chart 4). A more radical reform of the administration of the Post Office, both at the centre and in the regions, was to wait another decade.[48]

Regionalisation

By the early 1930s, there was renewed concern about the centralisation of administration, the control of the Treasury, and the political involvement of the Postmaster General and Parliament. Clement Attlee in 1931 reflected upon his experience as Postmaster General, and he urged both a definite limitation to the Post Office's contribution to the Exchequer, and the abolition of Treasury control which 'is wholly incompatible with the flexibility necessary in the conduct of a business concern'. He felt that the use of civil service structures might be appropriate for the mail services, but was less applicable to 'other services . . . which required for their successful operation not the mere passive provision of facilities, but an active campaign of salesmanship in a competitive field'. He was also sceptical of the virtues of parliamentary control:

> I think it tends to timidity and centralisation and has militated against the adoption of a public relations technique in the service. Its effect on the organisation of the department is bad. The Minister and his principal officials, who ought to be concerned with major problems, are constantly diverted to deal with matters which owe their importance only to the status of those who bring them forward.
>
> As regards policy, parliamentary control is very perfunctory and there is little informed criticism. The principal objection to the present system is, however, the constant change of the head of the Post Office for political reasons.[49]

Attlee's views were confirmed by Viscount Wolmer, Assistant Postmaster General from 1924 to 1929, who was certain in his diagnosis. Control by the Commons, he argued, entailed over-centralisation and timidity; the power of the Treasury meant 'pettifogging interference' without securing economy; civil service conditions of employment resulted in low salaries which were inadequate in important posts with an 'absence of financial stimulus to the lower ranks'; reliance on examinations 'results in a preponderance of theoretical over practical

295

ability'. 'The combined result of all these factors', stressed Wolmer, 'is to produce a Service which is extravagantly and inefficiently administered, whose charges to the public are consequently excessive, and which is therefore prevented from expanding as it should.'[50] These views commanded wide agreement, and 320 MPs submitted a memorial requesting an enquiry into the Post Office. This was established under the chairmanship of Lord Bridgeman, and the report appeared in 1932, dealing with the external relations of the Department with Parliament and Treasury, as well as with internal organisation.

The provincial organisation of the Post Office had scarcely changed since the debates before the First World War (chart 5). The Controller of the London Postal Service, nine postmaster-surveyors, thirteen surveyors and the Secretary in Edinburgh were answerable to the central Secretariat. In addition, there was the telephone organisation run by district managers answerable to the surveyor, and an entirely separate engineering organisation answerable to local superintending engineers and the Engineer-in-Chief. The Bridgeman Report recommended radical changes in this structure, based on five general principles: the Headquarters should determine policy; the district organisation should execute this policy; the administrative, technical and financial services should be co-ordinated and not left to operate as parallel systems; the district organisation should be able to implement policy without hindrance and should be judged on performance; and financial measurements should be decentralised in order to compare and assess local performance. In order to implement these general propositions, the Report proposed the replacement of surveyors with regional directors who would have an overall responsibility for posts, telephones and telegraphs, engineering, finance and personnel. This would, it was suggested, 'ensure that all the interests involved were co-ordinated and brought into focus'. It was also proposed that the existing barrier between the Secretariat and provinces should be breached, by ensuring that the career structure of officials gave experience both at Headquarters and in the regions. Recruitment would still be through the common civil service examinations for the administrative class but entrants should no longer remain in London so that the Secretariat would have a greater understanding of practical problems and provincial staff would appreciate the issues of general policy.[51] The problem which remained for the Post Office was how to implement these recommendations.

The conservative response was to reject the proposals and to argue for the status quo. Such was the view of Sir Evelyn Murray, the Secretary of the Post Office since 1914. The problem of liaison with the engineering staff could, he argued, be solved by less revolutionary means than a

CHART 5
ADMINISTRATIVE STRUCTURE OF THE POST OFFICE, 1932

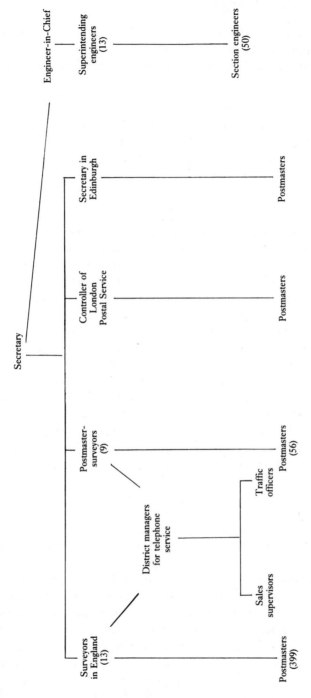

Secretary

Engineer-in-Chief

Superintending engineers (13)

Section engineers (50)

Secretary in Edinburgh

Postmasters

Controller of London Postal Service

Postmasters

Postmaster-surveyors (9)

Postmasters (56)

District managers for telephone service

Traffic officers

Sales supervisors

Surveyors in England (13)

Postmasters (399)

Source: Post 73, *First Report of the Committee on Metropolitan and Regional Organisation.*

complete change in the structure which would involve upheaval of personnel, additional cost, and the creation of a superfluous 'fifth wheel' in the administration. Murray was dismissive of the recommendations of the Report:

> in attempting to weld the postal and the engineering services we are attempting an impossibility and . . . the Bridgeman recommendations are based on incomplete knowledge and a misconception of the position, e.g. they assume that wide delegation would become practicable, whereas there is little left to delegate. Do Railway Companies, the nearest analogy, attempt to fuse their Engineering and Traffic District arrangements?

The existing organisation had, claimed Murray, proved itself, and 'it would be safer to mend it rather than to scrap it'.[52] The official who was charged with devising means of implementing the Bridgeman recommendations had arrived at similar conclusions, for E. R. Raven made a detailed assessment of various schemes and came to a jaundiced view. 'I should not like it to be inferred that . . . I am in favour of such a reorganisation as that proposed. The more I look into it, the more I am impressed by the amount of disturbance involved; and I am not at present convinced that the anticipated advantages are such as to justify what must in any case be a hazardous experiment.' He preferred 'grafting on to the existing organisation some machinery calculated to secure that increased measure of co-ordination and local initiative which is the main object of the Bridgeman recommendations'. In this he had the support of Murray, for 'we do not want to create a number of Secretariats in miniature in the Provinces'. Although the Bridgeman proposals would allow greater co-ordination, there was opposition to the excessive cost of creating 'minor Secretariats' covering areas which were too large for effective personal control.[53]

The arguments against change were as strong in the 1930s as in 1910, but political control now demanded the abandonment of caution. Murray admitted that 'my own inclination by temperament is to the conservative side', but he accepted that others might have a bias in favour of the scheme 'simply because it is conceived on grandiose and revolutionary lines and furnishes an opportunity for 'constructive' thought'. Certainly, it would be difficult for the Postmaster General to ignore the Parliamentary pressure and the recommendations of the Bridgeman Committee, and Murray admitted that regional directors would have to come for purely political reasons. 'Though it is a cumbrous means to achieve a relatively small end,' he remarked, 'we cannot say that it is entirely impracticable.'[54] There were a variety of means of implementation. The first or 'small region' approach would simply regrade the existing surveyors and postmaster-surveyors as regional directors with control over engineers, and this had few advocates apart from the Association of Surveyors and Assistant Surveyors. The devolution of further powers would be difficult, both because of the problems of consistency between the large number of regions, and because 'the present control units are too small to warrant their being provided with a full range of functional officials'. It would also be unwise to place engineers under the control of the existing surveyors, for they were inclined to neglect functions outside their narrow postal training. Certainly, this would have been anathema to the engineers who were inclined to favour a separate regional organisation for themselves, possibly controlled by a separate regional director. A second approach was to leave the existing surveying organisation unchanged, but to insert a new regional organisation between it and the Secretariat. This had even fewer advocates, for 'we should', remarked Murray, 'simply be introducing a large, expensive and useless cog into the machinery'. The faults of the old Scottish system would be extended to England, and it was felt that 'this system was intolerable. The local Secretary's office simply led to delay and irritation and inefficiency; and it was a dull inert mass, which impeded the progress of the work.' This left the third or 'large region' option which would sweep away the existing surveying system and create a new regional structure of bigger units.[55] The Departmental Committee on Metropolitan and Regional Organisation chaired by Thomas Gardiner came down firmly on the side of large regions in its first report in 1934:

> if further devolution of powers to the extent envisaged by the Bridgeman Committee is to be achieved, it is essential to enlarge the Regional unit within which those powers are to be exercised to the greatest possible degree that is consistent with efficiency. Moreover, we do not consider that it would be possible to justify the provision of a full range of functional officials to assist the Regional Directors in their task, unless the unit to be administered by them is very appreciably larger than a Surveyor's or Superintending Engineer's District.

The scheme which emerged from the Gardiner Committee (chart 6) was based upon organisation under the regional director, with technical and financial guidance from the Engineer-in-Chief and the Comptroller and Accountant General,[56] except in London where there would be separate telecommunications and postal regions.[57] The introduction of this new regional organisation would 'be accompanied by the widest possible measure of devolution from the respective Headquarters Departments'[58] and in 1935 the Devolution Committee was instructed to

CHART 6
GARDINER COMMITTEE: PROPOSED ORGANISATION

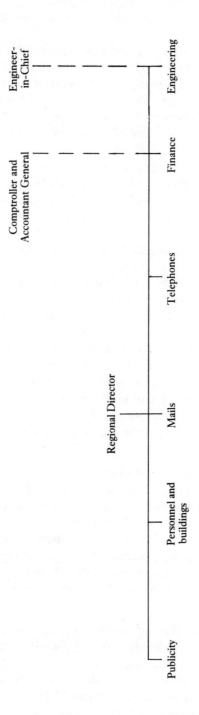

Source: Post 73, *First Report of the Committee on Metropolitan and Regional Organisation.*

implement this policy, 'the main principle to be kept in view being that Headquarters should, as far as possible, be relieved of all functions other than those of framing policy and securing the necessary measure of uniformity in its application and of watching performance'.[59] It was also essential to create financial and statistical measures of regional performance.[60] The implementation of these complex changes began on an experimental basis in 1936 in Scotland and the north-east of England, and in 1938 it was decided that the new system should be extended to cover the whole country. It was agreed that 'the new financial machinery constitutes a valuable contribution to the financial management of the Post Office as a whole, in the sense that it is already possible to obtain a much better picture of the problems for consideration in the Regions than is possible in the rest of the country'. The gross staff costs of regionalisation were put at £487,000, with savings at Headquarters of £85,000. There was a substantial net cost, but the new system did have a greater capacity for expansion and a number of compensating advantages:

> Firstly its services to the public had undoubtedly been improved if only for the reason that living as it does in closer touch with the public that it serves it is more directly responsive to public needs. Secondly, the regional organisation within the limits of its delegated authorities, now of course greatly increased, has proved itself to be a machine capable of striking efficiency and speed of action. This characteristic is due to the concentration at Regional Headquarters of functional authorities possessed of the necessary technical knowledge and experience who are adequate for the work but not so numerous as to be unwieldy, the result being that decisions can be taken with the maximum of speed and at the same time with full knowledge both of the general policy of the Department and the local facts applying to the particular case under consideration.

The regional organisation was completed by 1940, and marked the most significant change in the administrative structure of the Post Office since the report of 1854.[61]

The changed relationship between centre and locality was associated with a restructuring of the Secretariat. The Bridgeman Report in 1932 recommended the abolition of the autocratic position of Secretary, and the creation instead of a functional Board with the Director-General as 'primus inter pares'. The new structure was to follow the pattern of a large company in the private sector. The Postmaster General was in the role of Chairman, the Director-General was the chief executive, and the Board members were in effect directors. The Board members were to

CHART 7
HEADQUARTER'S ORGANISATION IN 1934

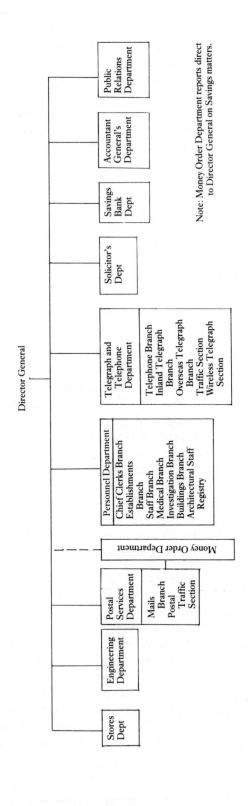

Director General

Stores Dept

Engineering Department

Postal Services Department
Mails Branch
Postal Traffic Section

Money Order Department

Personnel Department
Chief Clerks Branch
Establishments Branch
Staff Branch
Medical Branch
Investigation Branch
Buildings Branch
Architectural Staff
Registry

Telegraph and Telephone Department
Telephone Branch
Inland Telegraph Branch
Overseas Telegraph Branch
Traffic Section
Wireless Telegraph Section

Solicitor's Dept

Savings Bank Dept

Accountant General's Department

Public Relations Department

Note: Money Order Department reports direct to Director General on Savings matters.

Source: Post 33/4314, M6019/1934.

have general responsibility for particular aspects of the work of the Post Office, and were not to be so overburdened with executive tasks as to prevent the consideration of general principles.[62] There would be three general administrative departments dealing with Postal Services, Telegraphs and Telephones, and Personnel; six other departments would deal with stores, engineering, finance, public relations, legal matters, and the Savings Bank (see chart 7).[63] These changes would remove the dominant power of the Secretary, replacing the rigidly hierarchical system by a greater degree of lateral consultation between those responsible for various functions, including finance and engineering. The recommendations were implemented in 1934 when Sir Evelyn Murray was replaced as the last Secretary of the Post Office by Sir Donald Banks, the first Director General.

The large businesses which emerged in Britain and America in the late nineteenth and early twentieth centuries faced a common administrative problem. How should a wide range of activities spread over a considerable area be controlled within a single firm rather than by the independent concerns which had previously existed? The solution which emerged in the early twentieth century in both countries was to create a strongly centralised organisation with functional departments. This strategy of centralisation was adopted by the large British firms which developed in the 1920s, but problems soon arose as a result of pressure placed upon the centre which was unable to view the organisation as a whole. The next stage was to devolve responsibility to the individual units, and this new administrative structure developed in America in the 1920s, and was pursued by British firms such as ICI in the 1930s. The debate between central and devolved control was, therefore, not peculiar to the Post Office, and it formed an important feature in the emergence of a corporate economy in the interwar period. The Post Office faced the same problems as firms such as ICI at an earlier date, and perhaps it would be wrong to criticise the performance of the Department in creating an administrative structure to cope with its massive scale, diverse functions, and wide geographical coverage. Business historians have shown that in the private sector it took a considerable time for firms to develop a coherent centralised structure from which it was then practicable to devolve powers. It would not, indeed, be too much of an exaggeration to claim that the British Post Office anticipated and pioneered many of the procedures required to manage large-scale business corporations.[64]

Autonomy and Control

[The Post Office] is under a financial control by the Treasury so strict as to leave very little chance for independent action. (A.L.Lowell, *The Government of England*, volume I (1908), p. 112.)

A succession of short-term Postmasters General leads either to discontinuity of policy or to the passing of real control into the hands of permanent officials. (C. Attlee, 'Post Office reform', *New Statesman*, 7 November 1931, pp. 565–6.)

The Post Office was a government department with some attributes of a buisness concern, and this dual identity created a continuing source of tension. A business enterprise has a clear objective – to produce a profit – and the performance of the managers may be judged by their ability to maintain profitability in changing circumstances. There might be some room for disagreement over the extent to which profit in the short run should be sacrificed for growth in the long term, but the basic framework within which success should be measured is clear and un-equivocal. The Post Office did not have that single objective and it was not necessarily accepted that the role of the Post Office was to maximise its surplus; the Department might as easily be guided by considerations of social benefit or political expediency as by a requirement to make the largest possible contribution to the Exchequer. The debate over the rates paid to shipping companies in the 1860s, the introduction of imperial penny postage, and the formulation of the Empire Air Mail Scheme, have already indicated the tension between a narrow assessment of postal profit and wider concerns about imperial com-munications. The formulation of policy could not be left to the permanent officials at St Martin's le Grand, but was modified in the light of the needs of the Admiralty, War Office, Foreign Office and Air

Ministry. At the same time, any neglect of financial considerations or sacrifice of revenue which could not be justified by wider political considerations, would be opposed by the Treasury. The Secretary might therefore be pushed in two directions at the same time: he might be encouraged to provide non-economic mail services to the empire which were not justified by the revenue; and his wish to increase the number of deliveries in a provincial town or to pay higher wages might be checked by the Treasury. The Post Office was part of a wider political structure, and the Secretary had to be acutely sensitive to the varied interests which shaped policies. He was, of course, subordinate to the political head of the Department, the Postmaster General, and this might produce another tension in the determination of policy. The decisions of the permanent officials might be accepted by a Postmaster General with minimal interest in the details of the Department, but might be fundamentally altered by a politician with a desire to impose his views upon civil servants. This amounts to asking a simple but crucial question: what was the extent of autonomy of the officials of the Post Office? Did the controls imposed by the Treasury and politicians lead to major changes in policy or did they produce only minor adjustments?

Treasury control and political leadership

Let us first remember that the Post Office is in all things completely under the thumb of the Treasury. (Viscount Wolmer, *Post Office Reform* (1932), p. 216.)

. . . in general the control of the Treasury is neither excessive nor embarrassing and the theory that the two Departments are engaged in a continual guerrilla warfare is pure fiction. (E. Murray, *The Post Office* (1927), p. 38.)

The Post Office was, in the view of some commentators, firmly under the control of the Treasury with a limited scope for independent action, whereas other observers have concluded that the Department had considerable freedom under purely nominal guidance. R.W. Welby of the Treasury was inclined to minimise the power he exercised. 'My view of the control or check entrusted to the Treasury', he argued in 1887, 'is that it is purely a financial check, instituted for purely financial purposes, and that from the moment it interferes in any shape or kind with policy it is departing from its proper sphere.'[1] This distinction between financial control and concern for policy was certainly disingenuous, for the policies pursued by the Post Office might entail the rejection of financial performance as the guiding principle. Welby was assuming that the use

305

of financial criteria to assess the performance of the Post Office was agreed, which was far from being the case. The reliability of packet services, for example, might be given higher priority than the cost, and the maintenance of a contented workforce might be more important than a rigid insistence on low wages. The financial controls imposed by the Treasury could not be divorced from policy as readily as Welby claimed. Whether or not they were effective is, of course, another matter.

The controls imposed by the Treasury were negative and haphazard, for they usually came into play when a department requested an *increase* in expenditure, and there was little possibility that the Treasury could intervene to require the efficient allocation of *existing* resources. 'The Treasury', remarked Welby, 'is of course responsible mainly for economy, and the head of the department is responsible for efficiency; but the Treasury would not, I think, start an enquiry on the subject of efficiency.'[2] The result was that the Treasury could seek economies only when under pressure to increase expenditure which, in the opinion of Dr Roseveare, produced 'head-on collisons'. This was particularly the case in the nineteenth century when it was felt that the administrative reforms of mid-century were not complete and that expenditure could still be reduced. The Treasury in consequence insisted on compensatory economies before sanctioning any increase in departmental estimates, and the 'characteristic effect was to produce a curious departmental shuffle, two steps forward, one back'. Dr Roseveare argues that this 'central dilemma' of the Treasury in securing economies only as a response to demands for increased expenditure 'goes some way towards acquitting the Treasury of the glib and commonplace charges of pettifogging obstruction'.[3]

The outcome of the 'departmental shuffle' depended upon a number of factors. The Treasury found it difficult to control expenditure which was required by political policy, and there was a lack of expertise to assess the validity of technical or professional expenditure. The position of a department in the hierarchy of the civil service; the status and seniority of its Minister; and the network of personal relationships available to a Minister and his permanent secretary, could all determine the effectiveness of Treasury control. The Post Office was in a weak position in certain respects, for it was not one of the major Departments of State and was usually headed by a Minister who was a novice or a worthy nonentity. Although it was possible in some cases to claim a technical expertise which was not available to the Treasury, and some issues did have political repercussions, the majority of cases which were forwarded to the Treasury were straightforward and susceptible to control. Even so, the power of the Treasury to impose its wishes upon the Department should not be exaggerated. The relationship between the Treasury and the other government departments took the form of 'a very formal and elaborate game'. A proposal would be submitted to the Treasury and encounter an inflexible rejection; this might be followed by a re-submission with minor adjustments and a more elaborate justification; the Treasury would then usually accept the proposal with a show of reluctance and the imposition of certain conditions.[4] There might be no fundamental change in the policy as a result of these time-consuming procedures, and the impact of Treasury control might rather be felt through the deterrent effects of playing the game too often. Specific policies might not be modified, but the inflexibilities and pro-crastinations which were an integral part of the system might reduce the responsiveness of the Post Office, increase administrative costs, and produce rigid centralisation. Treasury control might have serious in-direct consequences for the administration of the Department rather than an immediate and direct influence on policy.

The formal and elaborate game which was played between the Post Office and the Treasury was mirrored within the Department. The Secretary, when he had decided on a particular course of action, drafted a minute which was submitted to the Postmaster General. In many cases, this was simply initialled and forwarded, without amendment, to the Treasury as a letter from the Postmaster General. But the Post-master General had the option of rejecting or amending the advice of his permanent officials by making a detailed response to the minute. The Postmaster General was in these cases reacting to policies formulated by his permanent officials, and it was also possible for him to initiate policy which the permanent officials would be required to execute. The signature of the Postmaster General on letters submitted to the Tre-asury might, in other words, range from a mere matter of form via responsive adjustments and emendations to the authorship of the pro-posal. The autonomy of the Secretary in determining policy might be constrained by the political head of the Department as well as by the Treasury.

A Postmaster General who wished to impose effective control on the Department should, it was suggested in 1829, view his appointment 'as an executive office, requiring scrupulous disinterestedness, a zealous regard for the public service, considerable skill and laborious attention in the discharge of the duties'. It was perhaps not surprising that the Commissioners of Revenue Inquiry found his ideal to be far from reality, for the Postmaster General was generally absent and consider-able discretion was left to the Secretary who acted on his own judgement.[5] It was indeed suggested that the political office of Post-master General should be abolished, and a Board of Commissioners substituted which could impose more effective executive control.[6] This suggestion was not implemented, and the Commissioners appointed to enquiry into the management of the Post Office arrived at a similiar conclusion in 1835:

> it is the strong tendency of the present system to place all the duties and powers, both of control and execution, in the hands of a single subordinate officer. . . . When we consider how ineffectual any control over such a department must be, without an intimate knowledge of its details, we feel satisfied that as long as it is vested solely in a high officer of state, liable to be removed with every change of administration, it is not likely that it will be much more than nominal.

A Board of Commissioners would, it was suggested, 'be peculiarly calculated to conduct the management of such a department as the Post Office, which requires daily attendance, constant supervision, and a general control of the various branches connected with it'.[7] The only reason for retaining the post, it was cynically remarked in 1866, was 'to pay a compliment to some person of high rank, and give him a salary for doing nothing'.[8] Despite these attacks on the office, the only significant reforms were in 1866 when the Postmaster General was allowed to sit in the Commons, and the introduction in 1909 of an Assistant Postmaster General with a role similar to a Parliamentary Secretary in other departments.[9] Opinion differed as to whether the Postmaster General deserved a seat in Cabinet: between 1835 and 1900 something under half of the holders of the post were included; from 1900 to 1915, it was the norm; between the wars it was exceptional. This reflected the uncertainty about the type of politician who should hold the office. Was it a reward for a worthy nonentity, an apprenticeship for a rising star, or an important position in its own right?

9.1 CABINET MEMBERSHIP OF POSTMASTERS GENERAL, 1835–1940

	Number of terms of office	In Cabinet
1835–1900	24	11*
1900–1915	6	6
1915–1940	14	2
Total	44	19

* including one PMG who spent a short part of his term in Cabinet.

Source: H. Robinson, *The British Post Office*, pp. 445–6.

'No office', argued Viscount Wolmer, 'is so foreign to a politician's previous training as is the Post Office.' The Postmasters General usually

Ally Sloper, the popular cartoon character, provides a less serious view of the role of the Postmaster General and the widening functions of the Post Office in the later nineteenth century. The cartoon dates from 1891.

came to the post without ministerial experience, and without business abilities. Political control, argued Wolmer, meant a cautious timidity in order to avoid overt failure. 'A business like the Post Office which involves long-distance planning and the taking of risks which, though of some magnitude, are the ordinary risks of industry – is essentially unsuited to control of this nature.'[10] Some Postmasters General were honest in their assessment of the office. Neville Chamberlain, on his appointment in 1922, described his new post as one of 'comfortable obscurity'.[11] He was not a member of Cabinet, but those who were might welcome the Post Office as a convenient base for a wider political involvement. Herbert Samuel, who was Postmaster General from 1910 to 1914 and again in 1915–16, remarked in his memoirs upon the work involved in attending Cabinet, reading various memoranda and Foreign Office papers, attending debates and nursing his constituency. The business of the Post Office had a low priority. Although there were deputations to receive, papers to read and conferences to attend, he concluded that:

> The office of Postmaster General is not one of the more onerous in the Government. The volume of work in the Department is of course enormous; but it is almost all of a routine or technical character, conducted by a highly skilled specialist staff. The Secretary of the Post Office, its permanent head, stands in somewhat the same relation to the Postmaster General as the manager of an industrial undertaking to the chairman of the company.[12]

Samuel did, for all of his denial of involvement, have some influence. This was both negative in preventing a solution to the vexed issue of devolution, and positive in the attempt to improve the position of boy messengers which connected with the wider social programme of the Liberal government. Chamberlain and Samuel were perhaps expressing the view of politicians with ministerial careers outside the Post Office who were unlikely to exaggerate the importance of an appointment which was, to them, merely a stepping-stone. Samuel became Home Secretary, Neville Chamberlain held a variety of posts culminating in the premiership, an office which was also attained by Attlee. Austen Chamberlain and Kingsley Wood rose to become Chancellor of the Exchequer, Canning was Governor-General of India and first Viceroy, and Hartington was appointed Secretary of State for War. More typical, however, were the Postmasters General who were rewarded for long and faithful service in the past, such as Arnold Morley, the former Liberal chief whip, or who were consoled for the frustration of their ambitions. It might be precisely such men who welcomed the opportunity to flex their political muscles within the Department. The autocratic rule of

Rowland Hill was countered by two Postmasters General under whom he served: the Earl of Hardwicke between 1852 and 1853; and Lord Stanley of Alderley between 1860 and 1864. S.A. Blackwood had a similar experience during his period of Secretary from 1880 and 1893. Henry Fawcett, the Postmaster General from 1880 to 1884 took a detailed interest in the administration of the Department, and in particular he overruled Blackwood's opposition to the payment of higher wages. H.C. Raikes, the Postmaster General from 1886 to 1891, also involved himself with the executive details of the Post Office, dedicating himself to winning power from the permanent officials. He insisted upon examining all questions 'minutely and laboriously', preventing the permanent officials from taking any action unless he was certain of its merits. Raikes set a 'very high standard as to the amount of attention to detail required from the responsible head of the office'. Raikes's political career had been limited by a failure to compromise and by his 'autocratic bent', and these traits of character resulted in a desire to dominate St Martin's le Grand. Blackwood himself was an autocrat who 'was indisposed to brook the slightest interference with his sway', and the result was a period of tension as these two self-willed men engaged upon a 'struggle for supremacy'. They might agree in rejecting Fawcett's policy of concession to the workforce, and adopt a stance of uncompromising hostility to unions in1890. But Raikes aimed to impose his will upon Blackwood as well as the postmen. 'All my department is in mutiny', he informed his mother, 'because I choose not to be a mere cypher, and act upon my own opinion when I have one. I hope, however, if all is well, to teach them that they have got a master at last.'[13]

It did not necessarily follow that the concern of a Postmaster General for his dignity and status resulted in any positive initiatives. The conflict between Hardwicke and Raikes on the one hand and Hill and Blackwood on the other was associated with the disruption of the deliberations of the Secretariat rather than with any new directions in policy; it was Herbert Samuel who, ironically, had a greater impact upon the history of the Department by frustrating reform of the administrative structure. The positive changes in policy which resulted from the personal initiative of Postmaster General were few: perhaps the most important was Lord Stanley's decision in 1865 to consider the nationalisation of the telegraphs.[14] The Postmaster General could hardly fail to be a negative influence, for the short tenure of the office meant that it is was usual to deal with decisions left by his predecessor, and to leave any new problems to be resolved by his successor.[15] The Secretaries certainly provided a greater element of continuity than the Postmasters General. There were twelve Secretaries between the introduction of the Penny Post and the Second World War, and they served

FIRMNESS WINS

Mr Raikes (the much abused). "There, Mr. Post Office, I think you're alright now"

H.C. Raikes was eager to impose his wishes upon the Post Office during his term as Postmaster General. The cartoon expresses one view: it would be more accurate to portray his period of office as one of tension forty-nine Postmasters General during forty-four terms of office. The longest term of office of a Postmaster General was Lord John Manners, who held office for a little under seven years; by contrast Evelyn Murray was the longest serving Secretary with a term of almost twenty years. The rapidly changing political headship of the Department could act as a source of disruption rather than provide effective leadership. Indeed, the same point might be made about the office of Postmaster General as about Treasury control: the immediate and direct influence on policy was less important than the indirect consequences of inflexibility and centralisation created by the need of the Secretary to refer business to the Postmaster General for approval, however nominal that might be.

Who were the Secretaries of the Post Office? The nine men who held the post between Rowland Hill and Evelyn Murray formed a diverse group. Hill, of course, had been a schoolmaster and a minor figure in the radical world of the 1830s before finding his mission in the Post Office. He was a self-made man who entered the public service when he was already in his forties. His successors all entered the public service at the start of their careers, although in somewhat different ways. Two passed their entire careers in the Post Office. John Tilley was born in 1813, the son of a London merchant, and he entered the Post Office as a clerk in 1829. He rose through the service and unlike any other Secretary acquired practical experience in the provinces, for in 1838 he was appointed Surveyor in the north of England. In 1848 he returned to St Martin's le Grand as assistant secretary, and in 1864 he was promoted to the secretaryship which he held until 1880. He was a close friend of Trollope, and married first his colleague's sister in 1839 and then his cousin in 1850. Tilley and Trollope held similarly sceptical views about the virtues of merit and competitive entry, and it would of course not have been possible for Tilley to have so successful a career under a system of literary examinations for entry into the secretariat. Although the major changes which occurred during his term of office were largely the work of others, and particularly of Scudamore, there is no doubt that Tilley was a competent administrator. He brought pragmatism to bear in place of the dogmatism of the Hill brothers, and he certainly had a firm grasp of the details and complexities of the Department.[16] The only other Secretary who spent his entire career in the Post Office was A.F.King, of whom it is difficult to say more than that he led a blameless life at St Martin's le Grand. He was born in 1851, the son of a clergyman in Essex, and he was successful in the competition for entry into the civil service in 1873. He joined the Post Office, and rose to assistant secretary in 1903, joint second secretary in 1905, second secretary in 1907, and finally Secretary between 1911 and 1914. He was a late developer in his personal life as well as his career, for he did not marry until 1927. When he was passed over for the secretaryship in 1909 he claimed that he was pleased, 'because I don't care for the chief post. I have no ambition and am naturally lazy; at any rate mentally.' This might, of course, have been intended to satisfy the new and inexperienced Secretary that his appointment would not be resented, but there is an ominous ring of truth in King's remarks. Success in competitive literary examination was certainly no guarantee of practical ability, as Trollope would have been the first to remark.[17]

The remaining six Secretaries had experience beyond the Post Office. Blackwood and Walpole were both products of the unreformed civil service, and had similar social backgrounds and connections. Blackwood was born in 1832, the son of a gentleman usher to William IV who was a civil servant in the Colonial Office. He was educated at Eton and Cambridge and in 1852 secured an appointment in the Treasury through his mother's influence with Lord John Russell. During the Crimean War he served with the commissariat and at this time he underwent a religious conversion which was to dominate the rest of his life, leading him into active involvement in such bodies as the National Temperance League, Band of Hope Union, the YMCA, Bible Society, and Dr Barnardo's homes. He was not only a leading Evangelical but also a figure in society, for in 1858 he married the dowager Duchess of Manchester. His connection with the Post Office started in 1874 when he was despatched from the Treasury to strengthen control over Departmental finances, although he had become an insider even before his promotion to the secretaryship in 1880.[18] His successor, Spencer Walpole, was less competent as an adminstrator and this was in many ways an eccentric appointment. He was born in 1839, the son of a barrister and grandson of Spencer Perceval, the assassinated prime minister. He was educated at Eton but, unlike Blackwood, did not attend university, instead entering the War Office as a clerk in 1857. His father had been Home Secretary briefly in 1852, and when he returned to the office in 1858 and 1866 he took Spencer with him as private secretary. In 1867 he was appointed, on his father's recommendation, to the post of inspector of fisheries at a salary of £700 a year, and he supplemented his official income by financial journalism, a task made necessary by the failure of his own investments. His personal fortune was restored when his biography of Spencer Perceval, which appeared in 1874, produced a legacy of £10,000 from the head of the family, and he could thereafter abandon journalism to concentrate upon writing a six-volume history of modern England which appeared between 1878 and 1890. Meanwhile, he was appointed governor of the Isle of Man in 1882, where he produced a steady stream of books. It might be wondered how far his career had fitted him for transfer to the secretaryship of the Post Office in 1893, but his new job did provide greater opportunity to participate in the literary life of London. His work as a historian is now forgotten and it cannot be said that he made any more impact at St Martin's le Grand than on the world of scholarship.[19]

Walpole was the last Secretary to have entered the civil service before the Northcote-Trevelyan reforms and the next two holders of the post were products of the examination system. This is not to say that they lacked connections, for both George Murray and Henry Babington-Smith came from a more elevated position than some of the pre-Northcote-Trevelyan officials such as Hill, Tilley or Scudamore. Murray was born in 1849, the son of a clergyman who was a fellow of All Souls. The family had aristocratic connections, and Murray was for part of his life heir presumptive to the Dukedom of Atholl. After an education at Harrow and Oxford, he entered the Foreign Office in 1873 through success in the limited competition. He transferred to the Treasury in 1880, and became chairman of the Inland Revenue in 1897 before his appointment as Secretary of the Post Office in 1899, where he remained until 1903 when he returned to the Treasury. He rose to the peak of the civil service as permanent secretary of the Treasury, and on his retirement in 1911 he became a director of the Westminster Bank and Southern Railway.[20] His successor, Babington-Smith, had an even greater measure of easy superiority. He was born in London in 1863, descended on his father's side from a successful Glasgow merchant who had become a Scottish landowner, and on his mother's side related to the 'intellectual aristocracy' of Victorian Britain. He was educated at Eton and Cambridge, where he joined the Apostles and won most of the available prizes. He was elected to a fellowship in 1889, but his career in the public service commenced in 1887 with an appointment at the Board of Education. He moved to the Treasury in 1891, and in 1894 travelled to India as secretary to the Viceroy, Lord Elgin, whose daughter he married. On the way home, he inspected the finances of Natal, and in 1900 he was sent to Turkey as British representative on the international committee of management of the Ottoman public debt. In 1903 he returned to England as Secretary of the Post Office, but in 1909 he resigned from the civil service to become director-general of the National Bank of Turkey. Other directorships followed, and he served on a wide range of important government committees up to his death in 1923.[21]

The Post Office at the turn of the century had settled down into a smoothly operating routine, and most of the forces for change came from outside rather than from within. The Secretaries who were appointed were experienced generalists rather than men with immediate knowledge of the Post Office, and they did not have the passionate dedication of Tilley or Scudamore to expand the work of the Department. The same point may be made of Matthew Nathan, the shortest-serving secretary, although in other respects he was remarkably different from Murray and Smith. He was a Jew, born in London in 1862 where his father was a manufacturer. He entered the Royal Engineers in 1880 after attending the Royal Military Academy, and in 1895 he first came to notice as secretary to the Colonial Defence Committee. In·1899 he entered colonial administration in Sierra Leone, and in the next few years he served as Governor of the Gold Coast, Hong Kong, and Natal. In 1910 he returned to England as Secretary of the Post Office, and in 1911 he was appointed Chairman of the Inland Revenue. His rise was, however, soon to meet a check. In 1914 he was appointed under-secretary for Ireland, and he was in sole charge at the time of the Easter Rising in 1916. His career went into an eclipse and he was recalled to safer fields as Secretary of the Ministry of Pensions and Governor of Queensland.[22] Although Nathan's successor, Alexander King, was the first Secretary since Tilley to spend his entire career in the Post Office, his appointment after thirty-seven years at St Martin's le Grand did not result in any fresh impetus. However, the arrival of Evelyn Murray in 1914, a young man of 34, did promise a greater sense of purpose.

Evelyn Murray was born in 1880, the son of George, and after Eton and Oxford he followed his father into the civil service. He joined the Board of Education in 1903, and rose at an exceptionally rapid rate to become Commissioner of the Customs and Excise in 1912 and Secretary of the Post Office in 1914, where he remained until 1934 when he returned to Customs and Excise as chairman. It was, of course, a difficult time to become Secretary, for the telephone system had scarcely been absorbed before the war led to serious disruptions. But even when allowance has been made for the unusual difficulties faced by Murray, the fact remains that he was, as he admitted, temperamentally conservative and, in the opinion of some, constitutionally lazy. Certainly, his working hours were unusual, from a little before noon until 8 p.m. and he had a somewhat distant and aloof manner. His private secretary D.O.Lumley, remarked that Murray 'said very little as a rule, his instructions were laconic and he disliked going into explanations or answering any but the most essential questions'. He did not discuss business with more than one or two officials at a time for he intensely disliked meetings, and consultations with the Postmaster General or Treasury were almost invariably made alone. On the other hand, he did delegate large areas of business to his deputies. He loathed publicity, and was opposed to the appointment of a public relations officer in the early 1930s. He had a reputation for being aloof, standoffish, and even rude, which Lumley more politely described as a sense of being 'born to command'. Essentially he was a partrican figure who was not inclined to change the established order, and his main contribution was to keep the cumbersome machinery of the Post Office running. 'Chinks in the palpably top-heavy structure of the Post Office', remarked Lumley, 'did not show themselves earlier, solely because of the immense administrative ability and experience which Murray brought to its management.'[23]

9.2 (a) SECRETARIES AND POSTMASTERS GENERAL, 1836–1946

Secretary	Term of office	Number of PMGs
Col. W.L. Maberly	1836–1854	6
Sir Rowland Hill	1854–1864	6
Sir John Tilley	1864–1880	6
Sir Stevenson Arthur Blackwood	1880–1893	8
Sir Spencer Walpole	1893–1899	2
Sir George Murray	1899–1903	3
Sir Henry Babington Smith	1903–1910	3
Sir Matthew Nathan	1910–1911	2
Sir Alexander King	1911–1914	2
Sir Evelyn Murray	1914–1934	14
Sir Donald Banks (Director-General)	1934–1936	2
Sir Thomas Gardiner (Director-General)	1936–1946	4

(b) TERMS OF OFFICE OF SECRETARIES AND POSTMASTERS GENERAL

	Secretaries 1836–1946	PMGs 1835–1947
under 2 years	1	21
above 2 years and under 5	3	17
above 5 years and under 10	3	6
above 10 years	5	nil
	12	44

Source: H. Robinson, *Britain's Post Office* (1953), pp. 281–2.

Note: 1 Hill's term of office is calculated from his assumption of the sole Secretaryship.
2 Two PMGs had two terms of office: Lord John Manners 1874–80 and 1885–6; and Herbert Samuel 1910–14 and 1915–16.

The autonomy of the Department was limited in a variety of ways apart from the concern of the Treasury for overall financial control and the political responsibility of the Postmaster General. The Post Office was bound by general civil service regulations on matters such as superannuation; contracts for uniforms were awarded by the War Office; stationery was supplied by the Stationery Office. Particularly

317

irksome was the fact that the Office of Works had responsibility for all buildings, so that 'we cannot put in a nail, or drive a screw, or hang a bell'. Any Member of Parliament was at liberty to question in the Commons the standard of service in his constituency, or to discuss postage rates and packet services.[24] The managers of a private business might need to consider the wishes of the shareholders, but were normally left to run the concern as they wished provided a reasonable dividend was paid. The Secretary of the Post Office was in a much more difficult position, and the range of forces which influenced the formulation of policy have already been discussed when considering particular issues. Here the emphasis will be upon the major debates over the autonomy of the Post Office from Treasury control and political influence which transcended the consideration of specific policies. One was the 'Scudamore scandal' and its aftermath in the 1870s; the other was the introduction of 'self-contained' finance in the 1930s.

The Scudamore scandal

Rowland and Frederic Hill had insisted upon the observance of strict financial standards, based upon the belief that each service should be self-supporting. So long as these views were accepted within the Post Office there could be a corresponding freedom from close Treasury control. However, in the 1860s there was a shift of perceptions within the Department, marked by the retirement of Rowland and the defeat of Frederic on the terms for the award of packet contracts. Financial considerations were given less weight, and more emphasis was placed upon the extension of the functions of the Post Office as a 'major instrument for social benefit'.[25] The scandal which arose in the early 1870s from Frank Scudamore's management of the purchase of the telegraph companies brought the issue into the open. He had acted without regard for the political authority of the Postmaster General or the financial control of the Treasury, and had been guided by considerations far removed from the Hills' strict attention to revenue and expenditure. Scudamore had won the internal debate in the 1860s; his victory was followed by nemesis in the 1870s.

The downfall of Scudamore was only possible because the internal financial administration of the Post Office had serious weaknesses. Until 1854, there were two major financial positions, the Accountant-General and the Receiver-General. The Accountant-General was appointed by the Postmaster General in order to keep an account of all revenue. The Receiver-General was an independent appointment designed to remove all responsibilities for cash from the hands of the Postmaster General; he took receipt of all money paid into the Department, and paid costs directly from these funds. The system of accounts was complex and confused, producing needless duplication without providing a real check or a real picture of financial performance. Although Rowland Hill had argued for reform in the 1840s, it was not until 1854 that the offices of Accountant-General and Receiver-General were amalgamated. At the same time, the revenue and expenditure accounts were separated so that instead of expenses being met from receipts, the entire gross revenue was paid into the Exchequer and expenditures were provided by an annual vote of Parliament. This made it impossible to incur any expenditure without the prior approval of the Commons, a procedure which had serious drawbacks. Both the gross expenditure and gross revenue appeared in the Budget and the result, it was claimed, was that

> Every increase is ascribed to government extravagance, and the critics seldom take the trouble to discriminate between expenditure which brings no tangible return and that which is more than balanced by the revenue it earns . . . The Chancellor of the Exchequer and the Treasury are naturally disposed to groan at the annual rise in the Post Office vote, even though it yields a more than equivalent return in revenue, and to urge the postponement of schemes which, though not essential, would be welcomed by a commercial undertaking as a profitable investment.

The financial structure created by the reforms of 1854 could therefore impose limits upon expansion of the Post Office, and it was precisely these constraints which Scudamore attempted to circumvent in order to complete the nationalisation of the telegraphs.[26]

The nationalisation of the telegraph system was approved by Parliament in 1868, and in 1869 £7m was voted to carry the decision into effect. Scudamore was appointed Second Secretary in 1868 with responsibility for the creation of this new public service, and he embarked upon a programme of rapid expansion after the formal transfer of the companies in 1870. The problems were immense, and both the Secretary (John Tilley) and the Postmaster General (William Monsell) allowed Scudamore to treat the telegraph service as his personal empire. Treasury control over the finances of the telegraph service was minimal, and between 1869 and 1872 every request for funds was approved, without Scudamore submitting any statistical justification. The vote of £7m had been exceeded by 1871 and a further £1m was voted, which was in turn exceeded in 1872; on this occasion the Treasury refused to accede to his claims for more money. Scudamore simply continued with his plans to extend the telegraph system despite the fact that no funds had been voted by Parliament. When Tilley enquired of George Chetwynd, the Receiver and Accountant-General, in January 1872 why payments to the Exchequer had fallen, Chetwynd gave an inconclusive reply and the matter was dropped. But in 1873 the real reason became apparent: the payment of gross revenue to the Exchequer was being diverted in order to provide funds for the telegraph system in excess of the Parliamentary vote. Chetwynd protested his innocence, insisting that 'most assuredly I kept nothing back that I knew, and to the best of my belief I knew all that I could have been expected to know at that time'. Tilley and Monsell accepted this 'complete disclaimer', but it was clear that Chetwynd's ability to monitor and control expenditure was minimal. It was also apparent that the Secretary was not in complete charge of all parts of the Department; permanent officials were not accountable to the Postmaster General; and the efficacy of Treasury control was questionable. The episode 'marked a milestone in Post Office–Treasury relations'.[27]

Scudamore was unrepentant. His assertion that the Treasury was aware of the financial position, and had therefore given implicit approval, could not really stand up to scrutiny. He was, however, prepared to move from defence to attack: Treasury approval, he claimed, was redundant and merely led to pettifogging delays. 'You might as well expect a canary to hatch a setting of ostrich eggs', he informed Gladstone in 1871, 'as to expect the Treasury to dry-nurse the telegraph system.'[28] He was impatient with the checks and delays of Treasury control, and he proclaimed the virtues of autonomy:

> If the Post Office were to submit every measure increasing or tending to increase directly or indirectly the public expenditure to the Treasury, the work of the Post Office, and the work also of the Treasury, would be enormously increased. No doubt the Post Office ought to submit large measures for sanction before carrying them out, but there should be some limit within which the Post Office could of its own mere notion increase expenditure.

Scudamore argued not only for freedom of the Post Office from Treasury control, but also for freedom of the permanent officials from political interference:

> Year by year as the Post Office had been brought more and more into direct contact with the public – year by year as it has been impelled by the requirements of the whole community to the utmost promptitude of action – it has become more and more necessary that the Secretaries should from time to time act spontaneously and on their own responsibility, and then seek a covering responsibility from the Postmaster General, – the Parliamentary Chief of the Department.

The principle upon which he operated was 'in matters which are essential to the carrying on of the Service and will not brook delay, provide for the business first: obtain authority afterwards'. There was an insistent public pressure for improved services which, he argued, could not have been satisfied 'unless I had committed the irregularities to which exception is now taken'. How else, he demanded, could the task laid upon him by Parliament have been fulfilled?[29]

There was widespread acceptance of Scudamore's case. Although Monsell was obliged to resign, Gladstone felt 'that the services of Mr Scudamore have in our opinion given him a high place in the annals of British administration and that we should regard as a serious loss either his removal from office or relations of confidence towards him'.[30] This did not mean that the administration of the Department could be left untouched. One necessity was much stricter rules to ensure effective Treasury control. 'The great point', remarked R.W. Welby in 1874, 'is to be able to point to a rule, . . . and when the offence happens, to be able to put one's finger on that rule, and say you have transgressed your duty – you knew it and must take the consequences. The trangression of duty at the Post Office last year was notorious, but there was no written rule to which we could point as broken.'[31] Procedures within the Post Office were also open to criticism. The Secretary and assistant secretaries had discretion on which papers were sumbitted to the Postmaster General, which meant that political control might be nominal. Furthermore, the Secretary and second secretary could submit minutes to the Postmaster General without consulting each other, but were at liberty when the papers were returned to urge him to reconsider the decision reached on the advice of their colleague. The result could be a conflict of advice and confusion. Internal financial control was no stricter that the external check by the Treasury, for the Receiver and Accountant-General did not have direct access to the Postmaster General and had to make any submission through the Secretaries whose behaviour he might be criticising. The Post Office had, it appeared to the Treasury, asserted its autonomy to an undesirable degree and escaped from the bounds of financial discipline.[32]

The imposition of Treasury control and the strengthening of internal financial checks commenced in 1873. Detailed statements were to be submitted to the Treasury in order to provide information on Departmental finances, and the Receiver and Accountant-General was to warn the Treasury directly of any suspicious features in Departmental accounts. When he was ordered to make a payment for which no funds were legally applicable, he should apply to the Treasury and inform the Postmaster General. Scudamore was alarmed by these 'really crude' measures, and in particular opposed the independent power given to the Receiver and Accountant-General by the creation of a direct line to the Treasury or Postmaster General. But the Treasury was adamant 'that the existing regulations of the Post Office have broken down, for they impose no sufficient check on the permanent officers of the Department, and they do not secure that complete subordination to Parliamentary chiefs, which is an axiom of Parliamentary Government'.[33] The Treasury pressed its power over the Post Office further in 1874. Although the War Office and Admiralty were incapable of financing operations from revenue independently of votes of Parliament, they nevertheless had officials with special responsibility for the financial implications of policy. By contrast, the Post Office could draw upon its considerable revenue, yet it had no officer with the power to inform the Treasury and Postmaster General of the financial consequences of any measure. The need for such an official was stressed by the Treasury, for 'it is hardly to be expected that the able and zealous officers, who are devoting their best energies to the conduct of a service in the success of which they feel so keen an interest, should at the same time exercise the vigilant control over its finance which an independent financial critic would do'. The answer was to create a permanent financial officer or Financial Secretary, appointed by the Treasury with the same rank as the second secretary. Any proposals involving expenditure would be submited to him for report before it was sanctioned by the Postmaster General, and the opinion of the Financial Secretary was also to be forwarded to the Treasury.

It is not surprising that John Tilley responded with alarm, for it seemed that the power of the secretariat would be superceded. Since most proposals involved expenditure, the new official would have wide powers with direct access to the Postmaster General and Treasury. The result, argued Tilley, could only be resentment from 'officers who have grown grey in the service', and consequent tension and disturbance within the Department. Tilley wished to reduce the Financial Secretary to the rank of assistant secretary with direct control over the accounting system which would allow him to check all items of expediture and draw attention to any cases of extravagance or breach of regulation. This would give the officer a defined departmental funciton, locating him firmly within the hierarchy in a position subordinate to the Secretary. A compromise was reached between the Treasury and Post Office by the end of 1874. The Financial Secretary was given a Departmental function as head of the office of Receiver and Accountant-General, and his opinions were to be submitted to the Secretary who would take them into account along with the advice of other subordinates in drafting recommendations to the Postmaster General. It was also agreed that the Secretary should have discretion on which cases were to be submitted to the Financial Secretary for his opinion, rather than being obliged to seek his views on all proposals which either involved expenditure above a certain limit or introduced new financial principles. Direct access to the Treasury was also curtailed. The general result was clear: the Financial Secretary had been downgraded and his capacity for independent action largely removed. The Financial Secretary did retain the power to read and comment upon the minutes which the Secretary submitted to the Postmaster General, and he could originate reports on financial questions for direct submission to the Postmaster General. At the end of 1874, S.A.Blackwood of the Treasury was appointed to the new office of Financial Secretary. The Treasury, remarked one cynic, 'having tried everything at the Post Office and found it incorrigible, had determined to test the efficacy of prayer'.[34]

There was, not surprisingly, considerable resentment against Blackwood as an intruder in the world of St Martin's le Grand. The immediate issue was whether Blackwood should take charge in the absence of Tilley and Scudamore, rather than the assistant secretary, Frederic Hill. Blackwood argued that it would be unprecedented for an assistant secretary to take charge when a secretary was present but Scudamore countered that 'it would be equally without precedent that a gentleman, who is wholly unacquainted with the general business of the Department and who is by the terms of his appointment restricted to one part only of that business, should take the entire charge of it'. The Financial Secretary, it was argued, did not understand the wider implications of policy, and the Postmaster General ruled that Hill should take charge. The matter degenerated into a bitter and personal exchange of minutes, as Scudamore attempted to exclude the Financial Secretary from the formulation of policy and control of the Department, and Blackwood sought to place himself at the centre of affairs. When detailed regulations were formulated at the suggestion of Blackwood in order to clarify the position, it was apparent that Scudamore's views had prevailed. The functions of the Financial Secretary were defined in a narrowly technical manner, and he was firmly excluded from full membership of the Secretariat:

The Financial Secretary will abstain from interfering in questions of policy, except in their financial bearings, or except so far as his own office (the office of Receiver and Accountant General) is concerned; and even in the case of the Receiver and Accountant General's office, he will, before recommending changes of importance, whether in point of numbers, salaries, or even of matters of account, confer with the Secretary.

The Financial Secretary, having been appointed in order that he may watch and check the financial bearings of the measures projected by the Secretaries, the object of his appointment would be defeated if he were himself to act as one of their number. In the possible but not very probable event, therefore, of all the Secretaries being absent at one and the same time, the charge of the Department . . . will devolve not upon the Financial Secretary, but upon one of the Assistant Under Secretaries; or, failing these, upon the senior officer of the Secretary's Office who may chance to be present.

The Treasury protested at this attempt to place the Financial Secretary in an inferior position when the intention had been to give him the rank of second secretary, complaining that the Post Office was 'treating him in fact as the Eton masters treated the French master who was neither to wear cap and gown nor to sit in the masters' seat at chapel'. The Treasury argued that Blackwood should be an integral part of the Secretariat with access to all minutes, which Tilley insisted was inconsistent: the Financial Secretary could not be both a member of the Secretariat and head of the office of Receiver and Accountant General. 'The Secretary's Office is the governing office of the Post Office throughout the United Kingdom. . . . The Receiver and Accountant General's Office is simply an office of account having no control beyond its own walls.' The Financial Secretary should, claimed Tilley, be removed from the office of Receiver and Accountant General and located in the Secretary's Office, where he would receive all minutes and comment on their financial bearing; as a result he would be denied a separate adminstrative base and take on the colouring of the Secretariat 'with whom he would be in constant and direct communication'. The Treasury was not impressed, and ruled that Blackwood was 'to take in the Department the position which the title of his office indicates that he was intended to hold': a Secretary entitled to all the papers, empowered to take charge of the Department, granted direct access to the Postmaster General, and permitted to call attention to financial matters even when his opinion was not specially sought. The Postmaster General accepted this in 1875. Scudamore had been defeated and he resigned to engage in the onerous task of organising the posts and telegraphs of the Ottoman Empire, where he died in 1884.[35]

'Machine for raising revenue' or 'instrument for social benefit'

The outcome of the Scudamore scandal would appear at first sight to suggest that the rigorous adherence to financial performance which had marked the Hill era and which had been overturned in the 1860s had been reasserted. The ethic of the Post Office had changed since the era of Hill, and the Treasury in the mid-1870s attempted to impose from outside the attention to financial perfomance which was lacking inside

324

the Department during Scudamore's ascendancy. But the attempt did not succeed, and by 1876–7 Blackwood was already in opposition to the Treasury. The Post Office, argued Blackwood, could not be guided by the Treasury's insistence that 'the Revenue must be taken on the whole as the measure and expression of the work'. This might be an 'obvious truth' in private business, but in Blackwood's opinion could not be applied to the Post Office where different considerations applied. Acceptance to the Treasury's principle would, Blackwood feared, mean that 'instead of the social and commercial interests of the country being considered as of paramount importance ... the Department is to be a mere machine for raising revenue, and is to be conducted as an ordinary mercantile establishment, profit and loss being the only guides'. This, he felt, was inappropriate.

The Post Office, Blackwood explained, was a monopoly which was obliged to provide services in areas where profit was impossible, and could not refuse to provide staff or buildings needed by the public service. Postage rates might be altered for the public benefit with the result that the work of the Department might be increased without raising the revenue in proportion. The Post Office could not control its expenditure in the same way as a private business, and its prices were similarly controlled by Acts, Treasury Warrants, postal conventions, and packet contracts, with the result that 'work is often imposed upon the Department which cannot be performed except at a loss, and sometimes at a very heavy loss'. The Post Office, claimed Blackwood, could in consequence not prevent costs from rising faster than revenue, for there was a basic difference from a private business:

> Unlike the transactions of ordinary commercial undertaking, where the work can be curtailed and the expenses reduced on the one hand, and the prices of the articles sold or of the services rendered can be raised or lowered on the other, (subject of course to the operations of the laws of supply and demand), at the discretion of the proprietors, the Post Office is bound on both sides by fixed limits.

Insistence upon strict attention to financial performance would change the whole character of Departmental policy, for

> Under such circumstances [the Postmaster General] would of course only establish branches of business under conditions which would afford good expectations of profitable results. We would never think of subsidizing ships for the advantage of the public, at a rate which must inevitably impose on him a heavy loss, or of carrying mail to outlying places at an expense with which the receipts derived from the service would be utterly incommensurate. But so long as he is in any

325

case compelled by the requirements of political necessity or public convenience to undertake services which must cost more than they bring in, it is, I submit impossible to ensure that his expenditure shall under no circumstances increase at a greater rate than Revenue.[36]

Blackwood, who had been appointed as the watchdog of the Treasury, had become the guardian of the Post Office. Indeed, in 1880 he was appointed Secretary and during his term of office the profit margin started to narrow, largely as a result of the Fawcett wage revisions of 1881 and the new postage rates of 1885. By 1888 the Select Committee on Revenue Department Estimates was expressing a 'natural feeling of disappointment' that expenses had grown faster than revenue, and Blackwood could not deny that this trend would 'exhibit the business, if looked at from the commercial point of view, as a losing concern'. His contention was that the Post Office should *not* be treated as a commercial undertaking for, unlike a private business, it could not close a branch office or discontinue a line of its wares. The evidence produced by the Committee

> may be very interesting as an arithmetical calculation, but, in my humble opinion, they must fail to produce a true view of the business of the Post Office, or to exercise any valuable effect upon its administration . . . [T]he Post Office is not conducted as a commercial business would be. There are many circumstances connected with the convenience and even the prosperity of particular localities which induce a Government entirely to disregard financial considerations, and to afford postal facilities which otherwise would not be regarded as absolutely necessary, where the revenue and the expenditure is wholly disproportionate.

The provision of packet services to the Scottish islands; the contracts with shipping companies to fulfil Admiralty or Foreign Office requirements; the introduction of a parcel post in response to the international service; the provision of a sample and pattern post, were all cases where financial considerations were neglected. The accounts of the Post Office were further distorted by the fact that capital expenditure on sites and buildings appeared against the revenue of the year.

Although he warned the Select Committee against 'erroneous conclusions' based upon revenue and expenditure figures which ignored such points, the Report nevertheless recommended

> that the Department of the Postmaster General, in all its branches, is a vast Government business, which is most likely to continue to be conducted satisfactorily, if it should also continue to be conducted

with a view to a profit, as one of the revenue yielding departments of
the State. Excessive expenditure appears . . . to be sooner or later
inevitable in a great Government business which is not administered
with a view to an ultimate profit to the State.

Your Committee are fully alive to the fact that in all its branches the
General Post Office cannot from time to time escape the necessity of
unremunerative outlay. But this consideration appears to them to
constitute an additional reason for keeping in mind the necessity of
working in the main upon business principles, and with a view to a
profit on the transaction of each year.

This stress upon financial measurement of the performance of the
Department did not have much influence. Blackwood had forewarned
the Committee that although it might denounce the existing state of
affairs, its recommendations 'could hardly affect practically the
administration of the service. . . . To regard the Post Office as a house of
business which ought to show, if it is wisely conducted, a net increase of
revenue upon the annual increase in business would be, in my opinion, a
very imperfect view to take of the matter.'[37]

By 1914 it was possible to extend Blackwood's list of occasions upon
which financial considerations had been rejected. The jubilee concessions of 1897 and the loss-making reduction of foreign postage rates;
the role of the War Office in requiring the employment of ex-soldiers
and of the Poor Law Commission in reducing the number of boy
messengers; the needs of the Admiralty in providing armed cruisers,
were just some of the external forces which made it impossible to treat
the Post Office simply as a commercial venture producing the largest
possible surplus. The Treasury in the 1870s and the Select Committee
of 1888 had been fighting a losing battle. Roland Wilkins of the Treasury admitted in 1910 that a great deal of the correspondence with the
Post Office was concerned with 'cases where criticism is practically
impossible' and merely produced delay which 'tends to encourage the
feeling that financial control, instead of being a real and useful thing, is a
kind of unintelligent fetish'. Routine applications were submitted in a
monthly schedule for so-called 'covering' authority after the event and
were not even looked at; the fortnightly schedule for 'precedent
sanction' before expenditure was incurred was 'pretty carefully considered . . . on certain rather rule-of-thumb principles, and queries are
fairly often raised' with the result that perhaps half-a-dozen reductions
were secured a year. These procedures might, it is true, force the Post
Office to consider financial implications when making a submission to
the Treasury, but it was widely accepted by the Treasury that the Post
Office could be delegated more powers. One Treasury clerk com-

Profit Margin on Postal Service (net revenue as a percentage of expenditure)

a Calculated on basis in use when Penny Postage introduced: excluding newspaper stamps; expenditure excluding packet service and stationary.

b Revenue including newspaper stamps, expenditure including packet service and stationary. In 1868 public departments ceased to be charged.

c Commercial accounts

1837: 240·4
1838: 241·6
1839: 215·8

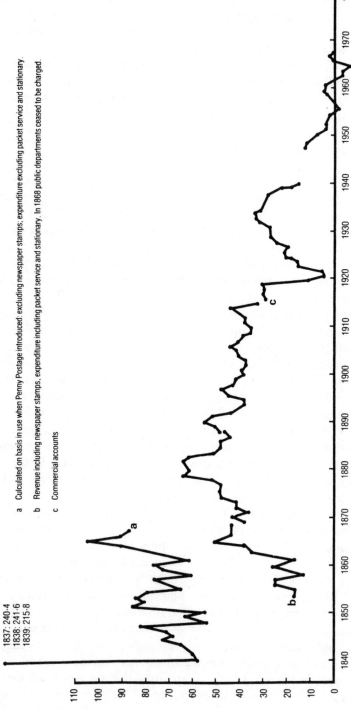

mented upon 'the expensiveness and uselessness of too close and centralised control over other Departments, who must know their own financial responsibility'; indeed, 'the old attitude of the Post Office in regard to the Treasury is dead, and cannot well be revived under present conditions'. Why, pondered the Postmaster General in 1902, was there any need for 'Treasury interference (to call it Treasury *control* is a misnomer)' provided that the total sum voted to the Department was not exceeded? It was, he felt, 'really rather absurd that we should have to write specially to the Treasury every time we want to add an established man to cope with increase of work'. The schedules were adjusted in the decade before the First World War in order to give more power to the Postmaster General, but in many ways the involvement of the Treasury in consideration of policy had been nominal with little impact on the main trends.[38]

What exactly did happen to the financial performance of the Post Office? Expenditure on transport fell sharply up the the First World War as a proportion of expenditure and revenue, and expenditure on labour rose. The fall in transport costs as a proportion of revenue was at first more marked than the increase in labour costs, so that the expenditure on these two items fell from 61.5 per cent of revenue in 1870/1 to 51.7 per cent in 1880/1. Thereafter, labour costs as a proportion of revenue rose faster than the fall in transport costs, and they were together responsible for 61.2 per cent of revenue in 1900/1. From the turn of the century until the First World War, there was a period of relative stability (see Table 9.3). These trends in large part explain the movement of the profit margin which may be expressed as net revenue as a percentage of expenditure (see Table 9.3 and graph). The profit margin improved markedly from 16.8 per cent in 1854 to 61.7 per cent in 1880/1, but then started to deteriorate as the cost of labour mounted: by 1900/1 the profit margin stood at 39.4 per cent. The net revenue was still considerable, for it had been £389,181 in 1854 and at the outbreak of the First World War it stood at £6,671,250. There was, up to the First World War, no contradiction between the Post Office as a 'machine for raising revenue' and an 'instrument for social benefit'. However, by the end of the First World War the picture was fundamentally different, for the profit margin had fallen to 4.1 per cent in 1920/1 (Table 9.4). Although tariffs had been increased during and after the war, the cost of labour had nevertheless risen from 47.0 per cent of revenue in 1913/14 to 68.1 per cent in 1920/1. This was the main reason for the precipitous fall in the profit margin, which meant that the surplus on the postal services could no longer cover the deficit on telegraphs and telephones. Indeed, the Post Office as a whole was in deficit from 1919/20 to 1921/2 (Table 9.5) and it is not surprising that in the interwar period more attention was paid to financial performance.

Lloyd George in 1919 set the tone when he informed the Postmaster General that

9.3 FINANCIAL PERFORMANCE OF THE POSTAL SERVICES, 1854–1913/14

	Cost of conveyance			Cost of labour			Expenditure on conveyance and labour as a percentage of revenue	net revenue	Net revenue as percentage of expenditure
	£	per cent of expenditure	per cent of revenue	£	per cent of expenditure	per cent of revenue			
1854	1,433,830	62.0	53.1	na	na	na	—	389,181	16.8
1870/1	1,993,289	52.4	36.7	1,347,630	35.4	24.8	61.5	1,628,237	42.8
1880/1	1,662,346	37.7	23.3	2,024,534	45.9	28.4	51.7	2,720,784	61.7
1890/1	1,980,030	29.8	19.6	3,600,306	54.2	35.7	55.3	3,451,173	52.0
1900/1	2,275,721	22.7	16.3	6,277,697	62.5	44.9	61.2	3,953,886	39.4
1910/11	2,534,754	17.8	12.8	9,398,886	65.9	47.6	60.4	5,473,531	38.4
1913/14	2,703,841	17.7	12.3	10,314,312	67.6	47.0	59.3	6,671,250	43.7

Source: PP 1864 XXX, *Tenth Report of the Postmaster General on the Post Office*; PP 1902 LV, *Return of Revenue and Expenditure of the Post Office*; PP 1912–13 XLIII, *Report of the Postmaster General on the Post Office, 1911–12*; PP 1916 XIV, *Report of the Postmaster General on the Post Office, 1915–16*.

9.4 FINANCIAL PERFORMANCE OF THE POSTAL SERVICES, 1920/1–1938/9

	Cost of conveyance			Cost of labour			Expenditure on conveyance and labour as a percentage of revenue	net revenue	Net revenue as percentage of expenditure
	£	per cent of expenditure	per cent of revenue	£	per cent of expenditure	per cent of revenue			
1920/1	6,707,590	15.9	15.3	29,896,666	70.9	68.1	83.4	1,714,238	4.1
1930/1	5,704,730	16.2	12.7	24,262,605	68.8	53.8	66.5	9,849,904	27.9
1938/9	6,186,635	14.7	11.7	28,400,574	67.6	53.8	65.4	10,808,259	25.7

Source: PP 1922 XI, *Post Office Commercial Accounts for the year ended 31 March 1921*; PP 1931–3 XIV, *Post Office Commercial Accounts 1930*; PP 1938–9 XVI, *Post Office Commercial Accounts 1938*.

The state of the national finances is such that only what is indispensable to sound administration ought to be maintained. Everything in excess of this must be ruthlessly cut down. In the interest of economy we must be willing to content outselves where the second best is too costly.

The initial Departmental response was that further retrenchment was impossible without endangering the efficiency of the service, particularly at a time when there was considerable pressure to restore prewar standards of service.[39] But the mounting deficit in 1920/1 indicated that the pressure had to be resisted. The level of services of 1914 was not restored; the Penny Post which had been temporarily abandoned became a permanent casualty of the war, and wages were kept under firm control. The profit margin on the postal services reached 34.5 per cent at its interwar peak in 1933/4, which was not too far removed from the level at the turn of the century. This could only be achieved by a greater sensitivity to financial criteria that had been normal before the First World War. Whereas Blackwood had some scope for concessions when net revenue stood at 61.7 per cent of expenditure in 1880/1, Evelyn Murray could not be so flexible: his policy was to increase the surplus and to defend it against the demands of the staff for higher wages and of the public for lower postage rates. The Post Office was by the end of the 1920s making a considerable contribution to the Exchequer, which exceeded £9m in 1928/9. But doubts were mounting as to the virtues of paying the entire surplus to the Exchequer. Might this not hinder the formulation of an investment programme, particularly in telephones, and create a narrow view of the development of services?

9.5 SURPLUS AND DEFICITS ON POST, TELEGRAPH AND TELEPHONE SERVICES 1913/14–1930/1

	1913/14 £	1920/1 £	1930/1 £
Post	+6,172,763	+1,714,238	+9,849,904
Telegraphs	−1,211,742	−3,728,779	−1,005,669
Telephones	+239,111	−4,721,970	+343,219
Total	+5,200,132	−6,736,511	+9,187,454

Source: PP 1933–4 XXVI, *Statistical Abstract for the United Kingdom*.

'Self-contained' finance

'Long ago', argued Clement Attlee in 1931, 'a bargain should have been made definitely limiting the amount of the contribution to be made to the

State by the Post Office.' The payment of the entire surplus was, he argued, an inequitable form of indirect taxation and this had a depressing effect on the officials of the Post Office, tending 'to slow down development and cramp initiative'. This danger was intensified by the Treasury control over expenditure: 'It is as if an experienced and intelligent businessman had to submit his plans for the development of his business and many of his day to day decisions to the veto of a signatory of the May Report. . . . I am quite clear that Treasury control as now exercised should be abolished'.[40] Viscount Wolmer agreed. 'A sound industrial concern would never distribute the whole of its annual surplus. It would carry forward part of it to reserve, with a view to utilising it as favourable opportunities arose in the further expansion of the business.'[41] This analysis was accepted by the Bridgeman Committee which felt that 'sound and progressive management' was hampered by the automatic payment of surpluses to the Exchequer. The relationship between Post Office and Treasury should, it was recommended, be changed by the introduction of 'self-contained' finance. Whereas the absorption of increased profit by the Exchequer resulted in inertia, the retention of surpluses would encourage enterprise:

> So long as the existing financial arrangements continue, so long will the tendency to regard the Post Office as a revenue-producing instrument obscure and impede its primary function, which is the service of the public. By self-contained finance we mean briefly a system under which the Post Office, after making a certain agreed annual contribution to the Exchequer would be allowed to use its surpluses, after making the necessary reserves, for the benefit of the public, the improvement of services and the development of its business. Self-contained finance would enable the management of the Post Office to concentrate upon the service of its public instead of being faced with dual and often conflicting objectives.

This proposal would have the additional advantage of allowing a relaxation of Treasury control 'which under a more autonomous system of finance might, we anticipate, be substantially reduced'. The Exchequer should, the Bridgeman Report recommended, receive a fixed contribution of £11.5m and half of any excess above that amount; the balance should be carried to a seperate Post Office fund for the development of facilities and services.[42]

The precise details of the scheme were finalised by an interdepartmental committee which reduced the Exchequer contribution to £10.75m and specified the powers to be delegated to the Post Office. The basic approach was that the relations between the Treasury and the Post Office should be designed so far as possible to reflect the principle that, while the Treasury is concerned with and should be consulted beforehand upon all questions of policy which have, or may have, financial implications, the Post Office will itself accept the fullest measure of responsibility for the execution of approved policy in the most economical way. It is impossible to define this relationship in terms of a precise delegation of financial powers. It must rest upon a general obligation on the part of the Post Office to consult the Treasury on all matters which raise novel or important issues, and upon a general understanding that, when the Treasury's concurrence is sought with regard to such matters, it will direct its criticism primarily to objective issues rather than to detailed points of administration.

The Post Office would, for example, have autonomy where a modification did not exceed £10,000 in the first year, introduce a new principle, or prejudice the revenue from other services, and the Department could conclude mail contracts up to a limit of £25,000. The new scheme was sanctioned by the Treasury in 1933. However, the extent of autonomy should not be exaggerated.[43] A manual was maintained which listed every power delegated by the Treasury and although this gave considerable freedom in the operation of services, a limit was still set to independent action: the Post Office could do something if it was mentioned in the manual but not otherwise, however trivial the cost. This convention was reversed in 1956, so that the Post Office might incur expenditure unless there was something in the list which implied that it should not. Whilst the changes in the 1930s certainly extended the scope of delegation, it was by no means true that the Department could do whatever its discretion suggested. In any case, after the Second World War the problem was not how to utilise the surplus but how to cover the deficit, and self-contained finance was to be more imaginary than real.[44]

The detailed history of the Post Office has so far stopped with the outbreak of the Second World War and it is time that some attempt should be made to bridge the gap between 1939 and the present, for major changes have clearly taken place. The recommendation of the 1830s that the office of Postmaster General should be abolished was finally implemented in 1969 when the Post Office ceased to be a department of the civil service and became a nationalised industry. What effect did this have on the financial and political position of the Post Office? The economics of postal services were also fundamentally affected by the emergence of full employment which placed consider-

333

able strain on such a labour-intensive operation. Large-scale mechanisation might be seen as the answer, which in turn created a new set of problems. The Bridgeman reforms had modified the administrative structure of the Department, marking the culmination of debates which went back to the nineteenth century. But no sooner had a settlement been reached than the Second World War and the changed postwar economic climate created a new set of strains and tensions. How did the new structure respond?

PART V

Epilogue:
The Postwar World

Retreat and Reform
in the Postwar World

The Post Office as an organisation is fast becoming a national disgrace. (*Guardian*, 8 October 1984)

... the Post Office has maintained the best postal service in Europe and, in recent years, made more than enough profits to finance itself. (*The Times*, 13 September 1984.)

Criticism of the Post Office is a national pastime, and never more so than in recent times. It would be remarkably easy to write an epilogue which gives a picture of postwar decline and inefficiency, and every customer of the Post Office surely has some grievance to relate. This is not surprising, for in a service of such magnitude even a small margin of error may effect millions of letters, and a few troublespots may disrupt the flow of mail to a wide area. The standard of service may still be better than in most countries, as *The Times* asserted; but it did go on to criticise the Post Office for its stultifying management and union traditions, failure to exploit the full benefit of new technology, inability to meet delivery targets and inadequate financial control. There is, of course, always a strain of hypocrisy in a newspaper accusing others of precisely its own failings, but there are many days when even a dispassionate historian of the Post Office would agree with some criticisms. But is this altogether fair? Certainly, the difficulties of the Post Office need to be appreciated so that criticisms are not based upon unrealistic standards, and it must always be remembered that many problems are common to the economy as a whole.

Problems in the era of full employment

The postwar financial performance of the postal services certainly presented a gloomy picture of decline. The profit margin has been defined in

337

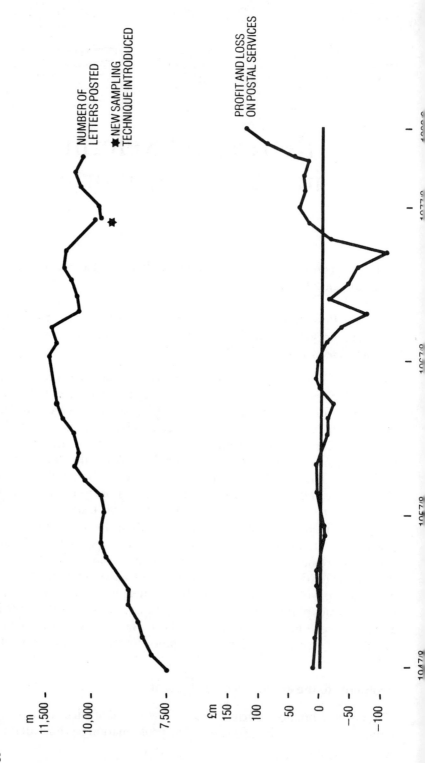

Traffic and financial performance since 1947/8

338

earlier chapters as the net revenue as a proportion of expenditure. It fell from 28.5 per cent in 1937/8 to 13.6 per cent in 1947/8, and then went on falling, moving for the first time into a deficit in 1955/6. Although a surplus returned in 1958/9, this was a short-lived phenomenon before the onset of larger deficits in the 1960s. It was not only the financial performance which gave cause for concern: the level of traffic also started to fall. In 1947/8, 7,600m letters were posted and twenty years later in 1967/8 the number had reached 11,500m. This subsequently fell to 9,458m in 1976/7, after which there was a tentative recovery. The Post Office seemed to be faced with an ominous future of mounting deficits and declining traffic.

The explanation of the financial problem is not far to seek: an increasing proportion of revenue was needed to pay wages and salaries. In 1937/8, wages and salaries accounted for 52.3 per cent of revenue; this proportion had increased to 59.7 per cent in 1947/8 and 66.0 per cent in 1955/6, and is now even higher, around 75 per cent. The postal services are, of course, labour-intensive and this put the Post Office at a great disadvantage in the period of full employment from 1945 to 1970. And it was not only the arrival of full employment which created problems. Historically, the postal service had rested upon the extensive use of part-time staff, and upon hours and conditions of work which were no longer acceptable, particularly when it was possible to move to better paid jobs in the booming industries. It became difficult for the Post Office to recruit enough staff to maintain services. Working for the Post Office was no longer such an attractive proposition as it had been up to the 1930s. It was less well paid than many other occupations, and the attractions of being 'on the establishment' had disappeared as welfare benefits were extended to the rest of the population. Security was less valued at a time of full employment, and the disadvantage of unsocial hours counted for much more. Changes in the educational system also had their effect. Before the war, the Post Office had been able to be highly selective in recruiting 14-year-old school leavers for outdoor work, and holders of school certificates for indoor work. The Education Act of 1944 changed this, and the brightest pupils increasingly stayed at school until 18 or went on to university. The calibre of the intake fell, yet the Post Office remained heavily reliant upon internal promotions from the basic grades rather than the direct recruitment as managers of those who had remained in full-time education to take A-levels or university degrees. The result, Michael Corby has argued, was a 'mass of mediocrity' in the middle range of management. There was, it might be argued, a problem not only of the quantity of recruits but also of quality.

The steady increase in wages throughout the economy during this period posed a serious dilemma. The Post Office did not have its own pay policy until it achieved corporation status in 1969, and it was tied by the so-called 'Tomlin formula' which set pay in the civil service in terms of general trends in the economy, and in any case it had to attempt to maintain its labour force. But it proved impossible to offset higher pay by gains in productivity, and the result was an erosion of profit which could only be checked by increases in postage rates. However, this might not be welcomed by governments anxious to curb inflation, with serious financial consequences for the Post Office. Indeed there was a period when the government had been so eager to hold down public-sector prices that they had compensated these services for the loss of profits which arose from their inability to adjust prices at their own discretion. This policy meant that the annual loss of the postal services rose until it exceeded £100m in 1974/5. Government policy then changed to demand that the postal service should break even by the end of the following financial year, within about eighteen months. There followed two increases in postage rates in one year, but this attempt to restore profit margins seriously endangered the volume of mail.

10.1 POSTAGE RATES, 1945–1984, FOR ORDINARY INLAND LETTERS

1940		$2\frac{1}{2}d$ for up to 2 oz
1957	$3d$ for up to 1 oz	$4\frac{1}{2}d$ for up to 2 oz
1965		$4d$ for up to 2 oz

	first class	*second class*
	for letters up to 2 oz	
1972	$3p$	$2\frac{1}{2}p$
1973	$3\frac{1}{2}p$	$3p$
1974	$4\frac{1}{2}p$	$3\frac{1}{2}p$
1975	$7p$	$5\frac{1}{2}p$
	for letters up to 60 gr	
1975	$8\frac{1}{2}p$	$6\frac{1}{2}p$
1977	$9p$	$7p$
1979	$10p$	$8p$
1980	$12p$	$10p$
1981	$14p$	$11\frac{1}{2}p$
1982	$15\frac{1}{2}p$	$12\frac{1}{2}p$
1983	$16p$	$12\frac{1}{2}p$
1984	$17p$	$13p$

Any fall in traffic would lead to a further decline in productivity. There was, therefore, the prospect of an alarming deterioration in the postal services unless some escape could be found from the vicious circle created by the insistent pressure of rising wages. This, of course, was not a problem which was confined to the Post Office, which nevertheless faced more formidable problems than most private businesses.

The need for higher wages was inescapable, but why was it not possible to increase productivity and cut the labour force in compensation? The pressure upon the Department in providing a labour-intensive service cannot be doubted, but it must remain an open question whether its response was adequate. At the end of the war, it is true, the major concern could not be the improvement of productivity, for greater emphasis had to be placed upon improving the conditions of the staff in line with the general ethos of postwar Britain. Split duties were no longer acceptable, nor was part-time employment on the prewar scale; both were to be curtailed. In the 1930s, the replacement of part-timers had rested upon the union's acceptance of split duties in order to cover the traffic peaks, but it was now decided to end split duties as well. Although the level of service after the war was lower than in the 1930s, the volume of traffic continued to increase, and the staff with it. The national shortage of manpower meant that by the late 1940s the Post Office was coming under increasing pressure from the government to economise in the use of labour, and this led to a 'slow dogged' process of attrition as staff was brought into line with traffic. By the early 1950s there was a much more imperative need to reduce the demand for labour, for the Department was facing serious difficulties in simply recruiting men to fill vacancies. These pressures combined to force the Post Office to economise in labour by tighter management control over the relation of traffic to staff, but it was felt that this process could only go so far, for the goodwill of the workforce was being strained as attitudes hardened and resistance grew. With hindsight, it does appear as if the system was overstaffed and there was a failure to develop reliable measures of productivity to adjust traffic and staff, but this was not how it appeared at the time. Much more obvious was the fact that the increase in wages to attract labour was resulting in an ominous erosion of the profit margin. It was clearly time to take more radical action.

At the same time as these major issues faced the Post Office, its constitutional status and administrative structure underwent radical changes. These continuing readjustments made it difficult to concentrate upon the fundamental problems of the postal services, and at the same time the criteria by which success was judged shifted. The response to the problems which arose in the era of full employment must be understood against the background of the changing administration of the Post Office.

341

Managing the Post Office

The management structure of the Post Office underwent considerable change, and part of the weakness of response to the problems facing the department must be explained by the continuing uncertainty surrounding the administrative framework. The Bridgeman Report supplied a satisfactory administrative structure which lasted until the late 1960s. However, the related self-contained finance was suspended during the war, and the high postwar surplus was admitted to be a form of taxation. The principle was revived in 1956. Although the whole surplus of the Post Office continued to be paid into the Exchequer, only a fixed sum of £5m a year was retained in lieu of taxes, from which the department was exempt, and any remaining surplus was available for the use of the Post Office. The White Paper on *The Status of the Post Office* in 1960 recommended a movement forward from the idea of self-contained finance: the practice of Parliament voting Post Office expenditure and of Post Office revenue being paid into the Exchequer was to cease. Instead, a Post Office Fund was created, under the management of the Postmaster General, and all Post Office income was paid into the fund and all expenditure met out of it. The aim was to run the Post Office as a self-contained business which used the criteria applied in the world of commerce for judging efficiency, and which had freedom to innovate and develop. The Post Office did not, however, become a nationalised industry, for it remained a government Department under a Minister who was answerable to Parliament for every detail of day-to-day business, and staffed by civil servants. In other respects, the Post Office was regarded as if it were a nationalised industry, with greater freedom to exercise its own judgement than earlier, and with the same kind of obligations as other nationalised industries to meet standards of performance.

Accordingly, when the government laid down financial targets for the nationalised industries in 1961, the Post Office was brought within this structure. It was expected to earn a return of 8 per cent on its assets in each of the five years from 1963/4, although in fact the return for posts over the five years was 0.7 per cent. From 1968, posts and telecommunications were to meet different targets: telecommunications, as a capital-intensive sector, was set a return on its capital; posts, as a labour-intensive sector, was set a target of an annual return of 2 per cent on expenditure over the five years 1968/9 to 1972/3. These targets were designed to generate about half the capital requirements of the services, and not even these distinctly modest expectations were attained in the postal services. During this period, therefore, the Post Office had a unique status as a government department which was treated as far as

342

practicable as if it were a nationalised industry. In 1966 the government decided that this interim situation should be resolved by turning the Post Office into a public corporation analogous with other nationalised industries. However, it was still felt that posts and telecommunications were complementary and should remain within a single organisation: common functions would be supplied on a joint basis and the two services would be managed separately within this overall framework. At the same time, activities which were not regarded as appropriate to a commercial organisation, such as national savings and the control of radio, were removed from the Post Office and retained under direct government control. In 1969, the Post Office became a public corporation, its staff ceased to be civil servants, and the office of Postmaster General disappeared.

The new structure was still unsatisfactory, for the attempts of the central headquarters to compromise between two competing services could produce results unacceptable to both. Certainly, the change in status did not produce an immediate transformation, and some complaints in the 1970s had a marked similarity with the criticisms of the 1920s and 1930s. The Post Office, claimed the Carter Committee in 1977, had a 'strongly centralised style of management', and still relied too heavily upon the civil service habit of defending established positions long after they ceased to be defensible, so that when change came it was too often forced by events. The management style was to react rather than to initiate, no doubt a reflection of civil service traditions, the desire to carry the unions in any change, and the new statutory obligation to consult the councils representing the users of Post Office services and the various boards and commissions created by government in attempts to exercise controls over prices and incomes. Specialisms such as finance and marketing were relatively unimportant in the new organisation, and only limited discretion was allowed to the regions. A recurring theme was the difficulty of one institution handling the two strongly contrasting businesses of posts and telecommunications, with their very different concerns of productivity, investment and future prospects. Both the Hardman Committee in 1971 and the Carter Committee in 1977 recommended the creation of two separate corporations. They came into being in 1981.

The chairmen of most of the nationalised industries have complained that their ability to respond to their economic problems has been hampered by the shifting requirements of governments and the rapid turnover of Ministers. The Post Office was no exception in this, and there was a lack of continuity in its administration which made it all the more difficult to cope with major issues. What strategies were adopted against this shifting administrative background, and how successful were they in resolving the dilemmas of the Department?

343

Mechanisation

The appearance of a deficit in the postal services in 1955/6 provided the spur to a serious effort to solve the problems facing the Post Office. Renewed efforts were directed to the schemes of mechanisation which had languished during the war and in the postwar period. The emphasis in research and development in the immediate postwar period had been placed upon telephones; this was perfectly understandable given the limited funds which were available, and the high demand for telephones. By the mid-1950s the needs of the postal service received more attention. The introduction of relatively simple labour-saving devices such as conveyors to move mail in sorting offices offered some scope for action, but in the long term the hopes of the Department were placed on the mechanisation of sorting itself. An inland letter was sorted on average three times up to its preparation for delivery, and if a machine-readable code could be inserted at the first sorting, this could automate subsequent stages with a consequent saving of labour. By the early 1960s a major programme of mechanisation of sorting offices had been formulated which would, it was hoped, overcome some of the problems faced by a labour-intensive service. The justification was not in the first place the financial rate of return; the Post Office felt that it had to mechanise because it could not foresee a time when it would be able to obtain all the staff it needed to handle increasing traffic. It was also expected that a reduction in the share of labour costs would lessen the vulnerability of the postal services to the upward movement of wages.

The benefits were certainly exaggerated in the contemporary enthusiasm for technology for its own sake, so characteristic of the 1960s. The mechanisation of sorting would, in fact, save only about 6,000 posts or 5.5 per cent of the letter-mail staff. Greater labour savings than this could have been made, as Michael Corby has argued, merely by 'good housekeeping' based on a more systematic adjustment of staff to traffic. Mechanisation had the allure of the fashionable. The programme has more recently come in for serious criticism in some quarters. The calculation of the expected return on the investment had always been suspect, depending upon the assumptions which were made. There was a temptation to produce self-justifying results, and there was cynicism in some quarters about the financial viability of the mechanisation programme. Corby has even gone so far as to claim that 'a miasma of ineptitude seems to pervade every area involved in mechanisation'. How fair is this assessment?

The introduction of machine sorting depended upon the reduction of the address to a machine-readable form by 'typing' a code on the letter

Post codes were introduced in Norwich in an experimental form in 1959; this slogan was used in 1962 to encourage their use.

in phosphor dots which could be 'sensed' by the sorting equipment. This could be done in a number of ways. 'Extract' coding relied upon the operator taking a sequence of letters from the address: a variety of permutations were tested and the technique was feasible if the first three and last two letters of the name of a town were used. This would, however, only permit 'outward' sorting to the post town; 'extract' coding could not be extended satisfactorily to allow 'inward' sorting to the level of the street. The operator would need to type at least ten characters, and there would be many cases in which it would either prove impossible or produce ambiguities; furthermore inward and outward extract coding would require two separate stages which would reduce the savings. The alternative was 'public' coding which relied upon mail users inserting a code in the address which the operator would merely copy. It was argued that a five or six character public code would remove any ambiguities and permit an increased rate of operation. The first public code was introduced at Norwich in 1959 but it was not as successful as had been anticipated, for senders put codes on fewer than half the letters. Doubts were expressed in some quarters about the virtues of extending public coding to the entire country, but it was decided in 1965 to proceed with a revised version of the 'alpha-numeric' codes used at Norwich. This permitted a very precise subdivision down to the level of a single premises or a small group of addresses on every postman's walk. The only other country which opted for codes of this form, permitting both outward and inward sorting right up to delivery by the postman, was Canada. Germany and the United States had by 1965 already introduced public codes which were less refined, permitting only outward sorting. The more sophisticated British and Canadian option, by allowing inward sorting, took the long-term view, and it is interesting to note that the Americans, for example, now admit that they may have been short-sighted in introducing the ZIP codes and have started to extend them to permit inward sorting.

Despite the enthusiasm for mechanisation, progress was much slower than had been anticipated. A touching faith was placed upon public co-operation, and it was assumed that 70 per cent of letters would be coded by their senders. In 1983 the level was still only 51 per cent although in other countries it had reached as much as 90 per cent. This was not necessarily because of the characteristics of the code, for the level of use in Canada is much higher. The root of the problem has been the delay in making the system fully operational, for until then there is little point in pressing the public to use codes. Implementation of the national Letter Post Plan started in 1969 and aimed to concentrate the sorting of the mail in 120 mechanised letter offices. There were twelve in operation by 1972, but then the UPW withdrew its co-operation. In 1975 a joint review of the plan reduced the number to eighty-three, of which sixty-four were in operation in 1984. The plan is due to be completed in 1985. There can be no denying the massive scale of the changes which have been involved. Traditional patterns of work in the existing network of 1,600 smaller sorting offices have been disrupted as a few large, mechanised centres have been introduced, which are more akin to factories. This centralisation might in future be carried further, for an 'optical character recognition' machine is already in use which will read the address and code on the letter, print the appropriate code on the envelope, and undertake a preliminary sorting. These machines handle letters at a much greater speed than can be coded by coding desk operators and clearly lead to the notion of greater centralisation of sorting work. This process of concentration in large offices has not, however, commanded universal assent. The Carter Committee of 1977 commented that some other postal administrations such as Australia saw virtues in a decentralised system, and concluded that 'we are apprehensive that the British plans have taken into account the immediate advantages of concentration, but not the more indirect disadvantages'. This debate will no doubt continue. The other major problem which the Post Office faced in introducing the new mechanised sorting offices was the question of grading of the coding-desk operators. This work is a version of typing, and it may seem puzzling that it is undertaken by men engaged for the different task of manual sorting. It has been argued by some that there should be a separate grade of machine operators and that women might be very suitable. However, this solution would have the disadvantage of reducing flexibility. The work is in fact paid for at the rate for Postman Higher Grade, a category which had been created in the 'reallocation' scheme of 1946 which had transferred sorting office work to postmen. The UPW was naturally eager to protect the position of the Postmen Higher Grade, and conflict over the rate of payment for coding-desk work led to the withdrawal of co-operation. It remains to be seen whether the system will in fact produce the anticipated financial savings when it becomes fully operational in 1985. The full benefits certainly cannot be obtained until the national network is complete.

Two-tier post

By the late 1960s there was another, and more urgent, debate within the Post Office concerning the deteriorating standard of the existing service. Reductions in the number of deliveries and collections and of counter hours were ways of paying for declining productivity. The most radical proposal, which was publicly discussed in 1970, was the abolition of the second delivery, and the spreading of the remaining delivery in towns over a period of six hours between 7 a.m. and 1 p.m. in two 'waves' for business areas and residential districts. People wishing to receive their mail earlier would be encouraged to use the private box system which allowed the collection of mail from post offices. This would not only cut the workforce by between 12,000 and 15,000 and so reduce the size and frequency of increases in the postage rate, but it would also give a later delivery to everybody in the second 'wave'. It is not surprising that it faced opposition from both the unions and the Post Office Users National Council, and it has not been proposed again.

The two-tier system of a higher-priced fast and lower-priced slow service which was introduced did not make a significant contribution to the financial and manpower problems, and it was primarily directed towards operational difficulties. The Post Office had, over the past forty years, reduced the evening peak by deferring the handling of basic-rate printed matter posted after a certain hour. However, the letter service was increasingly jeopardised by growth in the volume of mail and staff shortages. Many letters were, it was felt, not urgent and had to be sent by this service because they were excluded from the cheaper and sometimes slower printed paper service by the regulations which specified the content of the mail. Speed was, it was claimed, the relevant consideration, and the customer should be given the freedom to choose between a quick service or a slower service at a lower rate. The abolition of the printed paper service and the substitution of a two-tier service would both give the customer greater choice, and help to flatten the evening peak by reducing the proportion of urgent mail. The lessening of pressure would, it was hoped, assist in maintaining the quality of the first-class service which was threatened by staff shortages; resources might be redeployed to handle the reduced peak of priority mail more efficiently. It might also assist mechanisation which was then under consideration, by allowing a more regular flow of traffic to keep the expensive capital equipment fully occupied, for there was increased emphasis upon having the right quantity of work for the efficient use of machines. The financial implications of the scheme were, however, uncertain. It was not clear how much traffic would opt for the two services, and a miscalculation of the price differential might have serious consequences both for revenue, expenditure and quality. A high proportion of second-class mail would reduce income and make it expensive to maintain a full first-class distribution system; a high proportion of first-class mail would increase the revenue but do little to solve the operational problems.

The new service was introduced in 1968 when it was hailed as 'the biggest thing since Rowland Hill'. The claim was treated with some scepticism, for the view of the public was that it was merely a device to increase rates, and to foist a slower and less reliable service upon the customer. This was not fair, and the new service in fact allowed a greater freedom of choice for the mail-user. However, the timing of the change to coincide with an increase in postage rates, and the choice of name, was unfortunate. 'First-class' gave an expectation of a standard of performance which could not be achieved; 'second-class' was an unfortunate description, leading to a false notion of deliberate delays. Two-tier post, whatever its operational advantages, proved to be a serious blunder in customer relations.

The new system was something of a gamble, for it was far from certain how the public would choose between the first- and second-class rates. In the past, the division between the letter and printed paper posts had been 60:40, whereas the division between first- and second-class mail turned out to be 40:60, which was less favourable financially than the Post Office had expected from the soundings of customers, and also created an imbalance between the first and second deliveries.

Leaving aside these difficulties of implementation, was the decision to introduce a two-tier service sensible? Other postal administrations have not been quick to follow the example of Britain, which might lead to some doubt whether the correct decision was made. Care must, however, be taken in drawing conclusions from such comparisons, for the postal services in other countries are often heavily subsidised, which means that there is less need to change. Perhaps other administrations will move to a two-tier operation as they come under pressure to be financially viable. It is argued by the present management of the Post Office that this decision was correct, for there was no operational alternative: the distribution system was unable to handle traffic loads and the quality of service was falling. The two-tier service, we have seen, was not designed to solve the problems of productivity. What action was taken to tackle this issue directly?

Labour relations and productivity

Mechanisation, codes, a two-tier service and the introduction of new services, formed a package of reforms in the late 1960s. This package, however, did not reach the root of the problem: low productivity or, in other words, the inability to absorb rising costs. Even a moderate pay rise, which still did not maintain the relative position of postal workers in the hierarchy of earnings, produced a serious erosion of profit with the prospect of either a mounting deficit or higher postage rates. There was, indeed, a disinclination to confront this problem. In part, this was because the Post Office made unrealistic assumptions in the 1960s about the future growth of traffic, and so had no plans for coping with productivity falling with lower traffic volumes. More than this, there was a problem of management style. 'Fortunate as the Post Office is, at most times, in its industrial relations,' commented the Carter Committee, 'good relations may have been bought by an unwillingness to press the unions on matters of productivity.' Labour productivity actually deteriorated when improvements might have been expected from the early effects of mechanisation: between 1965/6 and 1975/6 productivity in the mail services fell by 11 per cent, and this does not take account of the decline in the service offered. Management explained the trend in part by the fact that the reduced volume of mail was delivered to an increased number of addresses; a postman had to complete his walk regardless of the number of letters so that it was difficult to reduce the costs in line with traffic. However, the importance of this factor should not be exaggerated, for delivery accounted for only 30 per cent of the cost of handling inland letters, and the increase in the number of addresses could only justify a small proportion of the decline in productivity. Criticism is even more pertinent of productivity in sorting, which accounted for 43 per cent of the cost of inland correspondence. There was a 12 per cent increase between 1965/6 and 1975/6 in the time taken to sort a given volume of mail and although a fall in the productivity of delivery might be excusable in part, there was no doubt that the slump in the productivity of sorting was alarming. Staff levels continued to be established by traditional methods rather than by objective measurement, and there was a reluctance to face the issue of productivity because of a disinclination to reach a breaking point with the unions, with the consequent disruption of services and the fear of an outcry from Parliament and the public. Consultation of unions had, in any case, become so firmly entrenched in the managerial procedures of the Post Office that it was difficult to contemplate a showdown on the issue of productivity.

In the 1920s and 1930s the Post Office had been willing to encourage secessionist unions, even at the expense of the disruption of the Whitley machinery. This policy was to change after 1945. There had been close co-operation with the UPW during the war, and the Attlee government adopted a policy of encouragement to civil service unions. In 1946 the so-called 'Listowel formula' laid down that a request for recognition by

349

any union would be considered if it represented at least 40 per cent of the organised staff in a grade; recognition would be granted for an initial period of three years, after which it might be withdrawn if membership fell below a third of the grade. There was no automatic right to recognition, for a claim would only be considered, and the view of the Department was increasingly that small unions were an irritant. Issues of individual freedom might be involved, but the acceptance of secessionist bodies led to fragmentation and confusion, making negotiations difficult and producing chaotic infighting between unions with the danger of leap-frogging claims. The attitude of the Post Office, as of other employers, changed in the late 1940s towards concentration in the hands of a few unions. This trend was continued by the Conservative government, and the Torrington Committee of 1951 recommended that only one union should be recognised for each grade in the Post Office, with a reduction in the number of associations from the existing thirty-one. In future, no encouragement should be given to secessionist unions by providing them with a target membership, and the Listowel formula was abolished. The Department should instead encourage groupings of grades in which unions might colloborate or amalgamate, and should take a positive role in keeping dissentients within the existing unions. 'We consider', concluded the committee, 'that an atmosphere of competing trade unionism is inimical to the long-term interests both of the staff and the Department.'

The management co-operated in the 1950s with the main unions' efforts to consolidate their strength, and the machinery for consultation was meanwhile extended from the existing Whitley councils with the addition of the Joint Production Councils in 1949 and the Joint Advisory Council in 1951, culminating in 1978 and 1979 with an experiment of union representation on the Board itself. This was very much a consequence of the general climate of opinion and the Post Office itself was to become increasingly concerned that managerial independence had been surrendered. The Monopolies and Mergers Commission in 1980 remarked that

> management is in danger of losing its will to take management decisions, and forgetting that it has a duty to do so. What started in Whitley Council days as a very proper policy of extending and formalising consultation with staff at all levels about postal operations and policy has gradually developed into a situation in which any management decision is a matter for negotiation with the UPW, and where failing agreement in such negotiation, management is reluctant to act for fear of disruption of postal business.

Such criticism must, of course, always be treated with care, for a failure by the Post Office to co-operate with unions after the war would have produced equally critical remarks about autocratic behaviour. The managers of the Post Office were following the policy of governments of the day and accepting the general ethos of labour relations, both of which have changed radically in the 1980s.

Consultation did indeed act to delay and frustrate adaptation rather than to assist it. It was difficult to get speedy decisions from the UPW; action was impossible as the lengthy processes of consultation ground on, and the union in any case often adopted a negative stance. The Post Office in the 1950s had pushed ahead with a policy of bringing the unions into the fullest consultation and by the 1960s it could be argued that managers had yielded too much initiative and were disinclined to give orders. Some who were active at the time now feel that their idealism was misplaced as the unions adopted militant attitudes, and they remark upon the failure of the strong unions encouraged by the Post Office to reciprocate. The Department took great care not to offend, limiting its own freedom of manoeuvre, without achieving the necessary changes by consultation.

One case in point was the UPW's opposition to the employment of women and part-timers. At the end of the war, it was agreed that part-time work should be curtailed, and the proportion of women in the workforce was also reduced from 47 per cent in 1945 to 30 per cent in 1948. Women were not needed when returning servicemen had to be absorbed. However, the continuation of full employment in the 1950s and 1960s, with competition from better-paid jobs, turned the attention of the Department towards the greater use of women and part-timers as a means of the maintaining mail services. This was opposed by the UPW which naturally wanted to keep up pressure on wages. Although a 'thermostat' was agreed in 1965 which allowed the employment of women and part-timers when vacancies rose above 5 per cent, this only applied in London. The Post Office had no similar agreement in areas such as the Midlands where vacancies were well above this level. The union's interest in maintaining the pressure on wages may be understood, but the failure of productivity to keep pace with rising labour costs was creating a crisis in the Department's financial performance which could ultimately only have harmful effects upon the staff.

This provides the background to the first national postal strike in 1971. Despite the existence of the elaborate machinery of consultation, unions found the initial phase of the corporation disturbing, for there appeared to be an attempt to win back managerial control by attempting to draw a clearer distinction between consultation and negotiation. These various strains provided the context for the dispute over wage rates. After the change to corporation status, the Post Office was no longer bound by the civil service requirement to take into account pay in comparable jobs. The old mechanistic principles were replaced by the concept of what the Post Office could afford, and therefore direct comparison with any other employment became of less relevance. There was certain to be discontent as members of the civil service moved ahead of their erstwhile colleagues in the Post Office. The staff felt that it should be no worse off than if it had remained in the civil service, but the Post Office could not accept that a very major part of its expenditure should be dictated by the civil service settlements over which it had no influence. The UPW pay claim of 1970 would have increased the wage bill for the grades concerned by 19½ per cent; the Post Office countered with an offer of 7 per cent which was subsequently raised to 8 per cent. This was below the rate of inflation and less than the general increase in wages, so that the union had a clear case that the standard of living and relative position of postal workers were deteriorating. However, the view of the Post Office was that it could not afford to pay more, for as a nationalised industry it was expected to meet certain financial targets which it was already failing to reach. An increase in wages would produce a serious shortfall unless postage rates were set at a higher level. There was a disinclination to do this, for rates were already increasing faster than the retail price index and there was a prospect of a drastic reduction in business. The Post Office was, as the Hardman Committee noted in 1971, caught in a dilemma in operating a labour-intensive service:

> unless productivity can be increased substantially, the prospect is a vicious circle of increases in charges at shorter and shorter intervals with accelerating decline in the volume of postal traffic. In face of rising labour costs the tariffs have to be increased. But the effect of increases on demand is to depress the volume of postal traffic. Unit costs are raised and productivity reduced. On the postal side the scope for raising productivity through raising capital investment, though important, is relatively limited. There can be no satisfactory way out of this dilemma through depression in the pay standards of postal workers.

The answer, in the opinion of the Committee, was not to allow the postal workers to fall behind, but to break the traditional pattern of low output per head by a new system of wage determination linking pay to productivity.

Escaping from decline

The vicious circle of increasing postage rates, declining traffic, and deteriorating productivity was in fact not broken in the 1970s. The cost of labour per unit of mail rose from an index of 100 in 1965/6 to 128 in 1969/70, 208 in 1973/4 and 390 in 1975/6. Although the union's more substantial demands were defeated in the strike of 1971, there was no real victor. Mechanisation and productivity measures were blocked by the union and management failed to press its advantage. The rate of increase of postal wages was below the level in the rest of the economy, which had the unfortunate effect of creating problems in recruiting labour of a reasonable standard, without solving the basic problem of productivity. The wage increases which were paid could not be absorbed and were passed to the consumer in higher prices, producing a fall in traffic and further deterioration in productivity. The result was that during the 1970s the Post Office paid wages which were low in comparison with outside industries while its charges were high in relation to the general movement of the retail price index.

What could be done to escape from the vicious circle of rising costs, increasing postage rates, falling traffic and deteriorating productivity? A two-pronged solution was decided. The first was the introduction of genuine productivity payments to move away from a workforce receiving low basic pay augmented by overtime, and to secure a high throughput over standard hours. The second was a vigorous marketing effort designed to extend services and attract more traffic. Both were easier said than done, for it meant breaking the restrictive practices which existed at many offices, and ultimately securing agreement to new methods of work measurement and pay determination. Management had to become more willing to tolerate disputes and less inclined to favour compromise to maintain the service. These policies are clearly having some success. Since 1980 productivity nationwide has increased by about 12 per cent. In consequence prices have been held below the movement in the retail price index whilst still maintaining profits, funding the whole of its own large capital investment programme, and making a contribution to other public-sector investments.

The second possible way of escaping from the vicious circle was by marketing to increase the volume of the mail. This was the recommendation of the Post Office Review Committee of 1977, which urged the introduction of 'short-run marginal cost pricing'. This rested upon the assumption that there was spare capacity in the system, and argued that the price charged to new business should reflect merely the extra costs it imposed, without covering the full cost of the system. The Post Office had hitherto operated on the basis of fully allocated costs, which took into account the entire cost of the postal service. This was not merely a change in an abstruse accounting practice, for it had wide implications for marketing: it entailed a positive attempt to find new sources of traffic such as direct mail advertising and the adoption of a

353

more flexible approach to contracts with large users. Direct mail grew by 101 per cent between 1975 and 1983, and is now the third largest advertising medium in the United Kingdom, with an expenditure of £299m in 1983. There has also been an extension of new services such as Datapost which have catered for particular needs. In general, there has been a change to a consumer-oriented approach.

This has been one of the major recent changes in the management of the Post Office. Although an Advisory Council including businessmen was appointed in 1921 to bring the Department into closer contact with its users, this did not change attitudes and it certainly did not entail a more dynamic policy of selling services. The Post Office had traditionally been production-oriented, starting from the product and its cost, setting the price on this basis, and only then approaching the consumer. The Post Office historically had not adopted an aggressive marketing policy, and in 1927 the union had commented that 'if we could see the old and short-sighted take-it-or-leave-it attitude entirely discredited and a make-the-fullest-use-of-me policy encouraged by the Post Office, the various services would become better known and more popular'. Neither the Postmaster General nor the Secretary had been enthusiastic in 1927, but in 1932 a new sales and publicity section was set up which in 1933 took over the Empire Marketing Board. Stephen Tallents, who joined the Post Office in this move, brought a more professional approach to bear upon publicity and public relations, most obviously through the work of John Grierson's film unit. The change must, however, be kept in perspective. The Treasury was alarmed at the increasing cost of publicity, with amounted to a decidedly modest £71,000 in 1935, and the concern so far was with the public image of the Department and not with the introduction of marketing considerations into the formulation of policy. This was still felt to be improper, a contradiction of Rowland Hill's principle of uniform pricing for the same service. Such attitudes already started to change before the introduction of a Postal Marketing Department in 1971 which gave the new approach a greater emphasis. Although there were initial uncertainties an aggressive marketing strategy has now been adopted. Despite the increasingly competitive environment created by new methods of communication, there has been a willingness to take the risk of introducing new services to maintain the market share.

The result is that there is now much more optimism about the future than seemed possible ten years ago. Productivity is improving, work practices are changing, overtime has been reduced, the programme of mechanisation largely completed, and a firmer managerial style has emerged. It is possible, looking back over the history of the Post Office, to see a number of turning points: the introduction of the Penny Post in

1840, the Treasury enquiry of 1854, the Scudamore scandal in the early 1870s, Fawcett's emphasis on social service, the reform of the administrative structure in the 1930s. The 1980s will surely be another of these crucial turning points. As the Monopoly and Mergers Commission pointed out in 1984, if the vicious circle is not broken then the customer will have to pay an unduly high price for the service, and the choice will be between a rapid contraction in the business or its maintenance at heavy cost to public funds. If the improvements of recent years continue then the Post Office will be able to offer an effective and financially viable contribution to communications.

Notes

Preface

1   H. Robinson, *Britain's Post Office: A History of Development from the Beginnings to the Present Day* (1953).
2   L. Hannah, *Electricity Before Nationalisation* (1979) and *Engineers, Managers and Politicians: Electricity Supply Industry in Britain from 1948 to the Present* (1982). The first volume of the NCB history has appeared: M. W. Flinn, *The History of the British Coal Industry, Volume 2: 1700–1830: The Industrial Revolution* (1984).
3   H. Robinson, *The British Post Office: A History* (1948) and *Carrying British Mails Overseas* (1964).
4   For example, C. Wilson, *History of Unilever* (2 vols, 1954); D. C. Coleman, *Courtaulds: An Economic and Social History* (3 vols, 1969 and 1980); W. J. Reader, *Imperial Chemical Industries: A History* (2 vols, 1970 and 1975); T. C. Barker, *Glass-makers: Pilkington: The Rise of an International Company, 1826–1976* (1977); R. W. Ferrier, *History of the British Petroleum Company, Volume 1, The Developing Years, 1901–32* (1982).
5   The Business History Unit at the London School of Economics, where L. Hannah holds the chair and from which *Business History* is edited. See his inaugural lecture, *Entrepreneurs and the Social Sciences* (1983).
6   This approach was inspired by the American writer A. D. Chandler in *Strategy and Structure: Chapters in the History of Industrial Enterprise* (1962) and *The Visible Hand: The Managerial Revolution in American Business* (1977).
7   L. Hannah, 'Mergers in British manufacturing industry, 1880–1918', *Oxford Economic Papers*, XXVI (1974).
8   A. V. Dicey, *Lectures on the Relation between Law and Public Opinion in England during the Nineteenth Century* (2nd edn, 1914).
9   J. B. Brebner, 'Laissez-faire and state intervention in nineteenth-century Britain', *Journal of Economic History*, VIII (1948); O. MacDonagh, 'The nineteenth-century revolution in government: a reappraisal', *Historical Journal*, I (1958); J. Hart, 'Nineteenth-century social reform: a Tory interpretation of history', *Past and Present*, 31 (1965).
10   The exception is the unpublished thesis of Charles Perry, 'The British Post Office, 1836–1914: a study in nationalisation and administrative expansion', PhD, Harvard, 1976.
11   Most notably E. P. Thompson, *The Making of the English Working Class* (1963).
12   For example, P. Joyce, *Work, Society and Politics: The Culture of the Factory in Later Victorian England* (1980); R. Price, *Masters, Unions and Men: Work Control in Building and the Rise of Labour, 1830–1914* (1980); C. R. Littler, *The Development of the Labour Process in Capitalist Societies* (1982).
13   A. Trollope, *An Autobiography* (1883; 1946 edn), pp. 250–1.

Chapter 1

1 University College London, Chadwick Mss, folder 1588, letter 118, 1 Dec. 1873. I owe this reference to Claire Gobbi.

2 Particularly R. and G. B. Hill, *The Life of Sir Rowland Hill and the History of Penny Postage* (2 volumes, 1880).

3 A. Trollope, *An Autobiography* (1883, 1946 edn), pp. 250–1.

4 I owe this riddle to Mr James McKay.

5 E. Yates, *His Recollections and Experiences* (1884), II, p. 225.

6 H. Robinson, *The British Post Office: A History* (1948), pp. 71–3, 304–5 and chapters 15 and 16; Post 17/21, *A List of Post Towns and Principal Places, with the Postage of a Single Letter to and from London . . .* (1836). The charge in London was raised from 1*d* to 2*d* in 1801: see Robinson, *British Post Office*, p. 194.

7 H. Parnell, *On Financial Reform* (3rd edn, 1831), pp. 1, 17, 38–47.

8 R. Hill, *Post Office Reform: Its Importance and Practicability* (2nd edn, 1837). A private edition was printed in January 1837 and a second public edition in February; it was published by Charles Knight.

9 Ibid., pp. 55–9; 'Rowland Hill and the Penny Post', *Economica*, ns VI (1939), pp. 430, 432; R. and G. B. Hill, *Life*, I, pp. 252–3.

10 (M. D. Hill), 'Post Office reform', *Edinburgh Review*, LXX (1839–40), p. 545.

11 R. and G. B. Hill, *Life*, II, p. 417.

12 R. D. Owen, *Threading My Way* (1874), pp. 307–8, quoted in W. A. C. Stewart and W. P. McCann, *The Educational Innovators, 1750–1880* (1967), p. 98.

13 D. Gorham, 'Victorian reform as a family business: the Hill family', in A. S. Wohl (ed.), *The Victorian Family: Structure and Stresses* (1978), p. 121. I owe this and other references on the Hills to Dr J.R. Dinwiddy.

14 *Remains of the Late Thomas Wright Hill together with Notices of his Life* (1859); R. and G. B. Hill, *Life*, I, chapter 1; F. Hill, *Frederic Hill. An Autobiography of Fifty Years in Times of Reform, edited, with additions, by his daughter, Constance Hill* (1894), pp. 19–20. The scientific writings of Thomas Hill were collected in *Selections from the Papers of the Late Thomas Wright Hill* (1860).

15 (M. D. Hill), *Public Education: Plans for the Government and Liberal Instruction of Boys in Large Numbers; as Practised at Hazelwood School* (2nd edn, 1825). The principles were largely the work of Rowland, although most of the book was written by Matthew.

16 Barham, 'Victorian reform', p. 128. The scheme is discussed in Stewart and McCann, *Educational Innovators*, pp. 98–123; and J. L. Dobson, 'The Hill family and educational change in the early nineteenth century. I: Thomas Wright Hill and the school at Hill Top, Birmingham', *Durham Research Review*, no 10 (1959), pp. 261–71, and 'The Hill family and educational change in the early nineteenth century. II: Hazelwood School: the achievement of Rowland Hill and his brothers', *Durham Research Review*, no 11 (1960), pp. 1–11.

17 R. and G. B. Hill, *Life*, I, chapter VII; R. and F. Davenport-Hill, *The Recorder of Birmingham: A Memoir of Matthew Davenport Hill, with Selections from his Correspondence* (1878), pp. 17, 51, 60–6, 74–91; Dobson, 'Hill family II', pp. 9–10. See also J. Bentham, *Chrestomathia* (ed. M. J. Smith and W. H. Burston, 1983), pp. xvii–xix.

18 Quoted in Dobson, 'Hill family II', p. 10.

19 Charles Knight, *Passages of a Working Life during Half a Century, with a Prelude of Early Reminiscences* (3 vols, 1864–5), I, pp. 256, 273; II, pp. 44–6, 55, 96, 122, 139, 180, 194–6, 249–50; III, pp. 67–8; J. L. Dobson, 'Bruce Castle School and the Hills' part in the work of the Society for the Diffusion of Useful Knowledge', *Durham Research Review*, no 12 (1961); F. Hill, *Frederic Hill*, pp. 77–100; Davenport-Hill, *Recorder*, pp. 103, 107, 110–1, 113–9; R. and G. B. Hill, *Life*, I, pp. 200-1.

20 Davenport-Hill, *Recorder*, pp. 139, 148, 234.
21 F. Hill, *Frederic Hill*, p. 115.
22 F. Hill, *Frederic Hill*, pp. 110–1; R. and G. B. Hill, *Life*, I, p. 392; Gorham, 'Victorian reform', p. 141.
23 R. and G. B. Hill, *Life*, I, pp. 202–4.
24 R. Hill, *Home Colonies. Sketch of a Plan for the Gradual Extinction of Pauperism and for the Diminution of Crime* (1832); R. and G. B. Hill, *Life*, I, pp. 202–4.
25 R. and G. B. Hill, *Life*, I, pp. 216–23, 365.
26 Hill, *Post Office Reform*, p. 8.
27 This interpretation differs from Gorham, 'Victorian reform', which suggests (p. 120) a change between the early 1820s when the Hills were radical reformers standing outside a society whose fundamental structure they criticised and the 1830s when they supported the prevailing structure. She claims that they moved from radical outsiders to conservative insiders (p. 128), abandoning libertarianism and embracing regulation (p. 129). The point which should be stressed is the continuity between the inventor of the 'Hazelwood system', the author of *Home Colonies* and the advocate of strict political economy at the Post Office.
28 Robinson, *British Post Office*, p. 248.
29 *Parliamentary Debates*, 3rd ser., XXIII, col. 743.
30 The contents of the reports are summarised in PP 1837–8 XLV, *A Return in Abstract of the Recommendations Contained in the Ten Reports of the Post Office Commissioners*, pp. 510–5.
31 Robinson, *British Post Office*, p. 255.
32 Wallace's evidence to the Sixth Report, quoted in Robinson, *British Post Office*, pp. 256, 272–3.
33 Robinson, *British Post Office*, pp. 256–7.
34 PP 1837 XXXIVi, *Ninth Report of the Commissioners appointed to inquire into the management of the Post-Office Department*. Hill gave his evidence in February 1837. Hill, *Post Office Reform*, pp. 103–4.
35 PP 1837–8 XXXV, *Tenth Report of the Commissioners appointed to inquire into the management of the Post-Office Department*, p. 187.
36 Robinson, *British Post Office*, p. 276.
37 'Post Office Reform', *Quarterly Review*, LXIV (1839), p. 518.
38 The criticism is in ibid., pp. 519, 533.
39 Robinson, *British Post Office*, pp. 278–91, 289–91. The secretary of the Mercantile Committee was Henry Cole: see H. Cole, *Fifty Years of Public Work*, I, (1884), pp. 34–69. The evidence to the Select Committee is in PP 1837–8 XXi and PP 1837–8 XXii, First and Second Reports from the Select Committee on Postage.
40 PP 1837–8 XXi, *Third Report from the Select Committee on Postage;* Robinson, *British Post Office*, pp. 261, 288.
41 Robinson, *British Post Office*, pp. 292–4, 297–9.
42 PP 1843 VIII, *Select Committee on Postage*, Qq 993, 1016, 1021–6.
43 Yates, *Recollections*, I, pp. 96–9.
44 *Dictionary of National Biography*, Vol XXXIV (1893), pp. 394–5.
45 Post 30/43, E721HH/1839, file V.
46 PP 1837–8 XXi, *First Report, Select Committee on Postage*, Qq 986, 2883–5; 1837–8 XXii, *Second Report, Select Committee on Postage*, Qq 10847–54.
47 *The Administration of the Post Office from the Introduction of Mr Rowland Hill's Plan of Penny Postage up to the Present Time* (1844), pp. 194–7.
48 PP 1837–8 XXii, *Second Report, Select Committee on Postage*, Qq 10908, 10911.
49 PP 1837–8 XXii, *Second Report, Select Committee on Postage*, Q 10921.
50 Post 30/43, E721HH/1839, file VI.
51 W.H. Ashurst, *Facts and Reasons in Support of Mr Rowland Hill's Plan for a Universal Penny Postage* (1838), pp. iv–vi.

52   R. Hill, *Results of the New Postage Arrangements* (1841), p. 9.
53   *Administration of the Post Office*, p. 178.
54   R. and G.B. Hill, *Life*, I, pp. 366–9.
55   This section relies, except where stated, upon Rowland Hill's Post Office Journals, Post 100/1–18.
56   R. and G.B. Hill, *Life*, I, pp. 364–70.
57   PP 1843 VIII, *Select Committee on Postage*, Qq 993–1016.
58   Ibid., Q 1803.
59   R. Hill, *Results*, p. 4.
60   PP 1843 VIII, *Select Committee on Postage*, Q 3018.
61   Post 100/22, Secretary's minutes to Postmaster General, December 1846; R. and G.B. Hill, *Life*, II, pp. 39–45 and chapters XVI, XVII, XIX, XXII.
62   Yates, *Recollections*, I, pp. 102–3; Lady Biddulph, *Charles Philip, Fourth Earl of Hardwicke: A Memoir* (1910), pp. 275–6; Constance Battersea, *Reminiscences* (1922), p. 152.
63   PP 1836 XXVIII, *Fourth Report of the Commissioners appointed to enquire into the management of the Post Office Department*, 23 July 1835, p. 35.
64   R. and G.B. Hill, *Life*, II, p. 405.
65   The clash between Hill and the committee is covered by Post 30/148, E4801/1861 and Post 14/232, reports and minutes on internal arrangements in the Circulation Department, 1860–1.
66   Trollope, *Autobiography*, p. 128.

Chapter 2

1   Quoted in Robinson, *British Post Office*, p. 366.
2   Ibid., p. 335.
3   PP 1843 VIII, *Select Committee on Postage*, Qq 3177–210.
4   Hill, *Post Office Reform*, contains the contradiction in two passages, on pp. 53–4 and 63.
5   PP 1843 VIII, *SC on Postage*, Qq 2961, 2968–9.
6   Hill, *Post Office Reform*, pp. 35–36, 95.
7   PP 1837 XXXIVi, *Ninth Report of the Commissioners appointed to inquire into the management of the Post Office Department*, examination no 3, pp. 456–64.
8   PP 1843 VIII, *SC on Postage*, Q 2900.
9   Hill, *Post Office Reform*, pp. 37–46.
10   Ibid., p. 100.
11   This topic greatly concerns the philatelist, and I hesitate to enter this specialised field. These brief comments are based upon Robinson, *British Post Office*, chapter 22; see also H. Wright and A.B. Creeke, *The History of the Adhesive Stamps of the British Isles for Postal and Telegraphic Purposes* (1899).
12   R. and G.B. Hill, *Life*, I, p. 392.
13   Robinson, *British Post Office*, pp. 358–60; Post 30/198, E1470/1870.
14   R. and G.B. Hill, *Life*, II, pp. 335–6; Robinson, *British Post Office*, pp. 359–60.
15   Post 30/129, E706/1859; J. Farrugia, *The Letter Box* (1969), pp. 25–32, 40–4.
16   PP 1900 XVIII, *46th Report of the Postmaster General on the Post Office*, p. 782.
17   A. Trollope, *He Knew He was Right* (1869), p. 58.
18   PP 1843 VIII, *SC on Postage*, appendix 17 (Treasury minute, 13 August 1841) pp.517–9, and Qq 1093–5. See, for example, the discussion in chapter xxxiv of Jane Austen, *Emma* (1816).
19   Hill, *Results of the New Postage Arrangements* (1841), p. 3.
20   PP 1843 VIII, *SC on Postage*, appendix 17, pp. 517–9.
21   Ibid., Qq 866–8, 2880–9.

22   Robinson, *British Post Office*, pp. 356–8; R. and G.B. Hill, *Life*, II, p. 270; PP 1854–5 XX, *First Report of the Postmaster General on the Post Office*, p. 574; PP 1898 XXI *44th Report of the Postmaster General on the Post Office*, pp. 702–9; *Historical Summary*, pp. 36–44.

23   Post 30/843, E2258/1899, files I, II, III; Post 30/636, E14348/1893, files I–VI, VIII, IX.

24   PP 1843 VIII, *SC on Postage*, Qq 1952, 1988, 1992–3, 2201, 2207–8, 2215–7, 2220, 2222, 2232, 2234.

25   Post 100/7, Rowland Hill's *Post Office Journal*, No. 4, 28 November 1846; Post 100/8, Rowland Hill's *Post Office Journal*, No 5, 12 May, 22 August 1848, 15 February, 30 November 1850, 7 March 1851.

26   PP 1856 XXXVII, *Second Report of the Postmaster General on the Post Office*, appendix A, Report by a Committee of Officers on the Question of Establishing District Sorting Offices and Hourly Deliveries in the Metropolis, pp. 105–9; PP 1857 (sess 1) IV, *Third Report*, p. 300 and *Second Report*, appendix A.

27   PP 1852–3 XCV, *Abstract of return of Post Office Receiving Houses in London, etc* pp. 116–7; *Post Office Guide for Birmingham and District, March 1903*.

28   PP 1898 XXI, *44th Report of the Postmaster General on the Post Office*, pp. 706, 708.

29   Post 33/2655–6, M8011/1929, file II.

30   Post 33/4056, E2671/1918, file III.

31   Post 30/3721, E12478/1916, files II–VI, VIII, IX.

32   Post 30/1377, M11284/1924; Post 33/777, M14099/1922, file I.

33   Post 33/824–5, M15508/1922, file I.

34   Post 33/4524, M14023/1934, files VI, VII, X, XII.

35   R. and G.B. Hill, *Life*, I, pp. 310–11.

36   R. and G.B. Hill, *Life*, II, pp. 405–6.

37   The monopoly was originally created in the seventeenth century.

38   Post 30/501–2, E5411/1887, files I–V.

39   Post 30/747, E13181/1896; Post 30/2264, E11241/1912; Post 30/1766, E27098/1909; Post 30/2133, E21908/1911; Post 30/2537–8, E14983/1913.

40   Post 30/1519, E7225/1908, files I, XII, XIII, XV, XVI; Post 30/235, E2433/1873; T.R. Nevett, *Advertising in Britain: A History* (1982), pp. 92–3.

41   Post 30/917–21, E15440/1900; Post 30/520, E5344/1888; Post 30/1228–9, E5442/1919.

42   Post 30/520, E5344/1888.

43   According to L. Stephen, *Life of Henry Fawcett* (1886), p. 438.

44   Post 30/1228–9, E5442/1919, file I.

45   R.H. Coase, 'The postal monopoly in Great Britain: an historical survey', in J.K. Eastham (ed.), *Economic Essays in Commemoration of the Dundee School of Economics 1931–55* (1955) pp. 25–37 and 'The British Post Office and the messenger companies', *Journal of Law and Economics*, IV (1961), pp. 12–65.

46   Robinson, *Britain's Post Office*, p. 164.

47   Post 30/166, E3764/1864, file I, PP 1854 XI, *Select Committee on Conveyance of Mails by Railways*, Q4219.

48   PP 1837 XXXIVi *Ninth Report of the Commissioners appointed to inquire into the management of the Post Office Department*, pp. 458–9; R. and G.B. Hill, *Life*, I, p. 336; PP 1843 VIII, *SC on Postage*, Q 82.

49   Post 30/112, E2035/1857, file II and A.D. Smith, *The Development of Rates of Postage* (1917), pp. 220–1.

50   Post 30/112, E2035/1857, files VII, VIII; Post 30/166, E3764/1864, file I; Smith, *Rates*, p.221; Robinson, *British Post Office*, pp. 355–6.

51   P.S. Bagwell, *The Railway Clearing House in the British Economy, 1843–1922* (1968), pp. 97–8; Post 30/166, E3764/1864, file I.

52   Post 30/166, E3764/1864, file I; Post 30/210, E7535/1871, file III; Post 30/172,

E703/1866, files I, II; Smith, *Rates*, p. 232.

53 Post 30/166, E3764/1864, files III, VI.

54 Post 30/166, E3764/1864, file I; Post 30/210, E7535/1871, files III, VI; Smith, *Rates*, pp. 31–2, 233, 340.

55 Post 30/210, E7535/1871, files VIII, X; Post 30/725, E6532/1896; Post 25/1, Parcel Post: Scudamore's plan, 1871.

56 PP 1854 XI, *Select Committee on Conveyance of Mails by Railways*, Qq 4194, 4206, 4209, 4219; Post 30/166, E3764/1864, file I; Post 30/210, E7535/1871, file I.

57 PP 1854 XI, *S.C. on Conveyance of Mails by Railways*, has evidence on the parcel service in the early 1850s; Bagwell, *Clearing House*, pp. 90–7, 100–8, 118.

58 Post 30/431–2, E1551/1883, files II, VI.

59 Ibid., files III, VII.

60 Ibid., files V, VI, VII–XIII, XV, XVI, XXIV, XXVII, XXIX, XXXI, XXXVII, XXXVIII, XL; Bagwell, *Clearing House*, p. 119.

61 Post 30/431–2, E1551/1883, files VII, XVI; Bagwell, *Clearing House*, pp. 113–4.

62 Post 30/431–2, E1551/1883, files VII, XII, XVI; Post 30/478–480, E12885/1885, file I; Post 30/427–8, E606/1883; Post 30/485, E3586/1886; Post 30/451, E15387/1883, file VI. The estimates vary because of the different assumptions made in commercial and parliamentary accounts.

63 Post 30/485, E3586/1886; Post 30/451, E15387/1883, file VI; Post 30/490, E7087/1886, files III–VIII, X, XI, XII, XVI, XVIII; Post 25/6, Parcels Post and Book and Letter Rates of Postage, Proposed Revision; Post 30/431–2, E1551/1883, file XXXVII.

64 Post 25/6, Parcels Post and Book and Letter Rates of Postage, Proposed Revision; Post 33/723, M12222/1922, file II.

65 Post 30/2384–5, E26265/1912, file I.

66 For example, Post 30/490, E7087/1886, The parcel post and letter and book posts: letter to Treasury, 9 February 1885; and Post 25/6, Parcels Post and Book and Letter Rates of Postage, Proposed Revision.

67 Post 30/2384–5, E26265/1912, files X, XI, XIII, XIV, XX, XXI; Post 30/3620, E6634/1916, files I–III.

68 Post 33/723, M12222/1922, files I–III, V.

69 Ibid., files XVII–XIX; Post 33/4165, M2077/1934, file II; Post 25/18, Report of the Parcels Post Facilities Committee; Post 33/4778, M9339/1935, file VI; Post 33/4131, M1376/1934, file I.

70 Post 33/723, M12222/1922, files XV, XVII; Post 33/4975, M8139/1926, files III, IX–L.

71 The standard account of postage rates is Smith, *Rates*, pp. 30–6; rates are given in Post Office Archives, Historical Summary, no 10.

72 Post 53/6, *Report of Postage Rates Committee on a Suggestion of Mr Walpole for amending the Scale of Postage on Inland Letters, 21 December 1895*; Post 30/703, E16980/1895.

73 Post 30/3532, E22832/1915, file X.

74 Post 30/210, E7535/1871, files VIII, X; Post 30/319, E4655/1877.

75 Post 30/431–2, E1551/1883, file II; Post 30/474, E8276/1885, files I, V, VI; Post 53/6, *Parcel Post and Letter Rates of Postage. Proposed Revision*.

76 Post 29/494, Pkt 120 Q/1890; Post 53/6, *Report of Inland Postage Committee*, 1890.

77 Post 53/6, *Report of Postage Rates Committee on a Suggestion of Mr Walpole*; Post 30/703, E16980/1895; Post 53/6, *Memorandum on inland rates*, January 1896.

78 Post 53/6, *Report of Postage Rates Committee on a suggestion of Mr Walpole; Enquiry into Inland Postage Rates, 1903*, and *Report of Committee on Suggested Alterations in the Scales for the Letter Post and Parcel Post, and on other Possible Postal Improvements*; Post 30/1311, E16781/1906.

79 Post 30/4447, E18667/1919, file I; Post 30/4140, E10833/1918, files I, III, V and unnumbered.

80 Post 30/4724, E24931/1920, files II, V; Post 30/4648, E18138/1920, files I, VI, XI; Post 33/195, M13233/1921, file II.
81 Post 33/4942, M20543/1935; Post 33/987, M4785/1923.
82 Post 33/4942, M20543/1935; Post 33/3465–6, M14920/1931.
83 A. Adburgham, *Shopping in Style: London from the Restoration to Edwardian Elegance* (1979), p. 154.
84 Hill, *Post Office Reform*, pp. 66–8.

Chapter 3

1 Post 30/63, E3841/1847.
2 These comments are based on J.B.Brebner, 'Laissez-faire and state intervention in nineteenth-century Britain', *Journal of Economic History*, VIII (1948); R.L. Crouch, 'Laissez-faire in nineteenth-century Britain', *Manchester School*, 35 (1967); O. MacDonagh, 'The nineteenth-century revolution in government: a reappraisal', *Historical Journal*, I (1958) and *A Pattern of Government Growth: The Passenger Acts and their Enforcement, 1800–60* (1961); H. Parris, 'The nineteenth-century revolution in government: a reappraisal reappraised', *Historical Journal*, III (1960); J. Hart, 'Nineteenth-century social reform: a Tory interpretation of history', *Past and Present*, 31 (1965); L.J. Hume, *Bentham and Bureaucracy* (1981), pp. 238–58. On the Post Office, see C.R. Perry, 'The British Post Office, 1836–1914: a study in nationalisation and administrative expansion', PhD Harvard, 1976.
3 Post 30/153–4, E2189/1862.
4 Post 30/34, E1047/1837.
5 Ibid.; Post 30/68–72, E5831a/1848; PP 1837–9 XXXV, *Tenth Report of the Commissioners appointed to Enquire into the Management of the Post Office Department*, pp. 189–90.
6 PP 1854–5 XX, *First Annual Report of the Postmaster General on the Post Office*, Appendix E, pp. 620–1; Post 30/63, E3841/1847; Post 30/74, E6163/1849; Post 30/68–72, E5831a/1848.
7 Post 30/63, E3841/1847; Post 30/68–72, E5831a/1848; Post 30/153–4, E2189/1862.
8 Post 30/656–8, E2526/1894; Post 30/153–4, E2189/1862.
9 Post 30/656–8, E2526/1894; Post 27/53, Postal Orders. Mr Chetwynd's suggestions for Issue of, 1874; Post 30/961–3, E21150/1901; Post 30/347, E1311/1879; Post 27/54, Report from the committee of Enquiry into the Money Order System of the Post Office, into the Proposed scheme for Post Office Notes, and as to Postal Drafts payable to order, 1876; Post 30/321, E6491/1877.
10 Post 30/321, E6491/1877; Post 30/656–8, E2526/1894; Post 30/762–3, E3937/1897. It should be noted that a large element of guess-work was involved in calculating the profitability of the money order service. Everything depended on the assumptions made in calculating the cost, which fell into two main parts: the chief office in London, on which expenditure could readily be determined; and the expense of issuing and paying orders in local post offices, which could only be estimated. In 1886, for example, the second item was put at £2 per 1,000 transactions but in 1893 at £4 per 1,000 issues and £3 per 1,000 payments. This changed the cost from 2.23*d* to 3.09*d* per order, which made all the difference between profit and loss. There was also the matter of postage. The letter of advice was sent to the paying office free of charge, and it was sometimes claimed that the service should be debited with one penny; and it might be wondered whether it should not equally be credited with the profit on the letter containing the order which the purchaser sent to the recipient. It is indeed difficult to talk with confidence about the profitability of the various parts of the Post Office, whether the parcel post or remittance services.

11 Post 33/457, M27074/1921; Post 27/61, Money Order and Postal Order Committee 1921–2, Report; Post 27/60, Report of Money Order Committee, 1920; Post 33/5408, M27310/1938.

12 These comments are based upon M. J. Daunton and M. Wagner, 'The people's money box: a profitable public enterprise?', paper presented to a colloquium on 'Vergleichende quantitative Unternehmensgeschichte', Munster, 13–15 October 1983.

13 These comments on the savings banks before the creation of the Post Office Savings Bank are based upon H.O. Horne, *A History of Saving Banks* (1947), pp. 1–167; the quotations from Nicholl and Attwood are on pages 71–2 and 101.

14 Horne, *Savings Bank*, pp. 168–74; C.W. Sikes, *Post Office Savings Banks. A Letter to the Rt Hon. W.E. Gladstone, M P, Chancellor of the Exchequer* (1859).

15 Post 30/150, E946/1862; Post 75/2, Post Office Savings Banks. Reports, Minutes and Memoranda explanatory of the Origin and Progress of the System of Post Office Savings Banks, 1871; Post 30/145, E2572/1861; Post 100/14, Rowland Hill's *Post Office Journal* no 10, 1861; Post 30/153–4, E2189/1862.

16 Horne, *Savings Banks*, pp. 177–81.

17 Ibid., appendices II and III; *Annual Reports of the Postmaster General*; Post 30/551, E1787/1890.

18 Post 30/178, E5983/1866; *Annual Reports of the Postmaster General*; Post 30/316, E4118/1877; Horne, *Savings Banks*, pp. 393, 221–5; Post 30/337, E6528/1878.

19 Post 30/704, E16988/1895; Post 33/4610, M17012/1934; PP 1902 IX, *Select Committee on Savings Bank Funds*, pp. 3–6.

20 *Annual Reports of Postmaster General*; Post 75/3, *Annual Reports of the Post Office Savings Bank*, 1871–94; Post 30/3525, E22380/1915; Post 33/4742, M6015/1935; P. Johnson, 'Credit and thrift and the British working class, 1870–1939', in J. Winter (ed.), *The Working Class in Modern British History* (1983).

21 Post 30/1699–1700, E14099/1909, file XIII; *Parliamentary Debates*, 3rd ser., vol. 173, cols. 478, 1580–1; A. Wilson and H. Levy, *Industrial Assurance: An Historical and Critical Study* (1937), pp. 39–44.

22 Post 30/469, E329/1885.

23 Post 30/192, E1457/1869; for a recent account of these various organisations, see P.H.J.H. Gosden, *Self-Help: Voluntary Associations in Nineteenth-Century Britain* (1973).

24 Post/169, E1788/1865; C.R. Perry, 'Frank Ives Scudamore and the Post Office telegraphs', *Albion* XII (1980), p. 366; G. Crossick, *An Artisan Elite in Victorian Society: Kentish London 1840–80* (1978), pp. 134–8 and ch. 9.

25 Post 30/1699–1700, E14099/1909; Post 30/4431, E17842/1919.

26 Post 30/1699–1700, E14099/1909, file XX.

27 PP 1882 XII, *Select Committee on Post Office (Annuities and Life Assurance Policies)*, pp. 385–90; Post 30/1350–1, E31480/1906; Post 30/1699–1700, E14099/1909; Post 30/4431, E17842/1919.

28 Post 30/211, E8977/1871; Post 30/534, E2025/1889; Post 33/675, M9555/1922; Post 30/4625, E15321/1920.

29 *Annual Reports of Postmaster General*; Post 75/3, *Annual Reports of Post Office Savings Bank, 1871–94*; Post 30/316, E4118/1877.

30 Post 30/2079, E19277/1911.

31 Post 29/1074, Packet 72/1911.

32 Post 75/32, Postal Cheque System. Report of a Committee of the Post Office Advisory Council, 1928; Daunton and Wagner, 'People's money box'.

Chapter 4

1 This account is from W. Lewins, *Her Majesty's Mails: A History of the Post Office, and an Industrial Account of its Present Condition* (2nd edn, 1865) pp. 263–301.

2   *Quarterly Review*, LXXXVII (1850), p. 69.
3   B. Austen, 'The impact of the mail coaches on public coach service in England and Wales, 1784–1840', *Journal of Transport History*, 3rd ser. II (1981).
4   Post 11/16, Conveyance of mail by rail, miscellaneous papers 1827–56.
5   Post 30/143–4, E2239/1861, files I, XVI, XVII.
6   Post 18/1, Travelling Post Office. Mail Bag Apparatus. Introduction. Correspondence with Railway Companies, 1832–9.
7   Post 30/172, E6058/1865.
8   Post 11/49, *Report of the Committee appointed by the Lords Commissioners of Her Majesty's Treasury to consider the principles upon which railway companies should be paid for the conveyance of letter mails 1894*. The relevant acts were:
    1838 Railway (Conveyance of Mails) Act. This gave the power to the Postmaster General to call on any company, on giving notice of at least 28 days, to carry mails and guards by ordinary or special trains running at such hours and speeds and making such stops as he directs.
    1847 Post Office (Duties) Act. This empowered the Post Office to send mail with or without a guard.
    1868 Regulation of Railways Act. The Postmaster General might call on a company to appropriate the whole of a special train to the Post Office.
    1873 Regulation of Railways Act. The companies were required to convey, without written notice, by any train, all mails which were tendered for conveyance, and to afford all reasonable facilities for the receipt and delivery of mail to any station without requiring the mail to be booked, etc.
    (Post 11/11, Conveyance of mails by railway. Memorandum on the Postmaster General's powers . . ., 1895–1911).
9   In his Presidential Address to the Institution of Civil Engineers: see PP 1856 XXXVII, *Second Report of the Postmaster General*, p. 110.
10 PP 1856 XXXVII, *Second Report of the Postmaster General*, appendix B, Report by Mr E. Page, Inspector General of Mails, on some points connected with the relations between the Post Office Department and Railway Companies, 29 February 1856, pp. 110–3; R. and G.B. Hill, *Life*, I, p. 411.
11 Page, 'Report', pp. 109–119; PP 1854–5 XX, *First Report of the Postmaster General*, p. 585; PP 1856 XXXVII, *Second Report of the Postmaster General*, pp. 78–9.
12 Post 11/16, Conveyance of mail by rail, miscellaneous papers, 1827–56; PP 1856 XXXVII, *Second Report of the Postmaster General*, pp. 113–15.
13 PP 1837–8 XLV, *Copy of Contract between the Postmaster General and the London and Birmingham Railway Co. in May 1838, and the award of the arbitrators*, pp. 576–7.
14 PP 1854 XI, *Select Committee on Conveyance of Mails by Railways*, Qq 3906–7, 3911–4.
15 Post 30/67, E4232/1848, file V.
16 PP 1854 XI, *SC on Conveyance of Mails*, Qq 3005–7, 3012, 3023, 3028, 3035, 3063, 3089.
17 Post 30/67, E4232/1848, files II, III, V, VII, VIII; Post 30/73, E7374/1848, file 1; PP 1854 XI, *SC on Conveyance of Mails*, Qq 3038–45, 3203, 3224, 3226, 3275, 3291, 3299, 3270–1, 3045, 3198, 3258.
18 Post 30/73, E7374/1848, file 1.
19 Post 30/61, E8385/1846, file 1.
20 R. and G.B. Hill, *Life*, I, pp. 411–3.
21 PP 1854 XI, *SC on Conveyance of Mails*, pp. 3–16.
22 Ibid., Qq 1621–3, 1779–82.
23 Ibid., Qq 269, 517.
24 Ibid., pp. 14–5.
25 Ibid., Qq 1524–7, 1779–82.
26 Ibid., Qq 4225, 4249.

27 Post 30/174–5, E2985/1866, file III.
28 Ibid., files IV and VII.
29 Post 30/174–5, E2985/1866, files XIV, XXI, XXVI; R. and G.B. Hill, *Life*, II, p. 230; G. Alderman, *The Railway Interest* (1973), p.25.
30 Post 30/174–5, E2985/1866, file XVII and see also R. and G.B. Hill, *Life*, II, p. 279 and appendix J.
31 Post 30/174–5, E2985/1866, file XLVIII; Post 30/138, E2324/1860.
32 Post 30/174–5, E2985/1866, file LII.
33 Post 30/521–2, E6766/1888, file II.
34 Post 11/11, Conveyance of mails by railway. Memorandum on Postmaster General's powers, 1895–1911; Post 30/623, E4098/1893.
35 Post 30/623, E4098/1893.
36 Post 30/673, E10994/1894, files I, X, XI.
37 Ibid., file I.
38 Ibid., file VIII; Post 11/49, Report of Committee appointed by the Lords Commissioners of Her Majesty's Treasury to consider the principles on which railway companies should be paid for the conveyance of letter mails, 1894.
39 Post 30/673, E10994/1894, file XV.
40 Post 30/521–2, E6766/1888, files I, IX, XII, XVIII, XX.
41 Post 30/1037, E17033/1903, files I, II, III, VI.
42 Post 11/32, GWR versus Postmaster General, 1903. Copy of award; Post 30/1037, E17033, file XII.
43 Post 30/3060–1, E16283/1914, files I, II, IV, VI.
44 Post 30/3305, E3396/1915; Post 33/3231, M2245/1931; Post 33/2409–10, M12053/1928; Post 33/3157–9, M16028/1930.
45 Post 30/3358, E7687/1915, files I, V, XI; Post 30/4682, E20978/1920, files I, II; Post 33/1994, M6454/1927, file I.
46 Post 30/4682, E20978/1920, files II, III; Post 33/2727, M1967/1929, files XI, XIII, and Report; Post 33/3033–4, M10047/1930, files I, II, IV, V, XV, XXI, XXIV.
47 Post 30/2289–90, E12768/1912, files I, II, XIV, XVI, XXIII, XXV, XXVIII; Post 30/3567, E2655/1916, files III, V, XI.
48 Post 33/1362, M9971/1924, files II, III; Post 33/1275, M4569/1924, file II.
49 Post 33/1362, M9971/1924, file II.
50 Ibid., file III.
51 Post 33/1275, M4569/1924, file IV.
52 Ibid., files V, VI; Post 33/1505, M4066/1925, files II, III, IV; Post 33/1272, M4388/1924, files I, II, IV; Post 33/2967, M7829/1930, file II.
53 Post 33/3863, M4351/1933, file V; Post 33/4670, M914/1935, files I, II, III, VI, VIII, XXIII, XXIV, XXV, XXXII.
54 Post 33/3382, M12198/1931; Post 33/1994, M6454/1927, files I, III; Post 33/2727, M11967/1929, file XIV.
55 Post 30/3358, E7687/1915; Post 30/4682, E20978/1920; Post 33/1994, M6454/1927, file III.
56 Post 30/4682, E20978/1920, file II; Post 33/1443–4, M1/1925, files I, V; Post 33/2727, M11967/1929, files II, V, VI, XVI; Post 33/3569, M3252/1932, files Bottom A, III, V, VI, VIII, IX, XI, XIII, XIV.

Chapter 5

1 Post 33/2369–70, M10015/1928, file IV.
2 PP 1851 XXXIV, *First Report of the Select Committee on Steam Communications with India*, Q 2107.
3 C.R. Perry, 'The General Post Office's Zanzibar shipping contracts, 1860–1914', *Mariner's Mirror*, 68 (1982).

4   R.G. Greenhill, 'The state under pressure: the West Indian mail contract, 1905', *Business History*, XI (1969).

5   PP 1860 XIV, *SC on Packet and Telegraphic Contracts*, Q4265.

6   Ibid., Q 4261; R. and G.B. Hill, *Life*, II, pp. 241–2.

7   Smith, *Rates*, pp. 263–72.

8   Mrs Adrian Potter, *The Life and Letters of Sir John Henniker Heaton* (1916), pp. 3–13, 198.

9   Post 29/430, Pkt 140N/1887; PP 1887 XLIX, *Copy of Letters addressed by the Hon. Member for Canterbury to the Postmaster General on the subject of an Imperial Penny Postage*, pp. 351–65.

10 Potter, *Heaton*, pp. 173–81; Post 29/633–4, Pkt 225Z/1899, files V, VII, VIII; Post 53/6, Mr Walpole's memorandum on the imperial penny postage question, 14 January 1896; PP 1907 LV *Papers laid before the Colonial Conference, 1907, Memorandum by GPO*, pp. 1198–1200.

11 Smith, *Rates*, pp. 272–6.

12 Potter, *Heaton*, pp. 182–95; PP 1907 LV *Papers laid before the Colonial Conference*; Post 29/1108–9, Pkt 23/1912; Post 29/945, Pkt 229H/1907; Post 29/924, Pkt 122H/1907; Post 29/1363–4, Pkt 29/1919; Post 29/1267–8, Pkt 95/1915.

13 P.S. Bagwell, *The Transport Revolution from 1770* (1984), p. 66 and 'The Post Office steam packets, 1821–36, and the development of shipping on the Irish Sea', *Maritime History*, 1 (1971).

14 PP 1836 XXVIII, *Sixth Report of the Commissioners appointed to Inquire into the Management of the Post Office Department, 30 April 1836*, pp. 147–8, 163.

15 Post 29/92, Pkt 447L/1860, file XXIII.

16 Post 51/13, P and O contracts to India; Post 29/26–7, Pkt 330P/1839; J.K. Sidebottom, *The Overland Mail: A Postal Historical Study of the Mail Route to India* (1948).

17 PP 1851 XXI *Second Report, SC on Steam Communications with India*, Q 4230.

18 Ibid., p. 661, Qq 3683, 3760, 3828, 3864–8, 3872, 4212–3, 4228, 4408, 4418, 5365.

19 PP 1851 XXI, *First Report, SC on Steam Communications with India*, appendix 4.

20 PP 1851 XXI, *Second Report, SC on Steam Communications with India*, pp. 660–1, 665.

21 Ibid., Qq 4529–31, 4592, 4629.

22 Ibid., Qq 4747, 4857, 4830.

23 Ibid., appendix 13.

24 Ibid., appendix 8 and evidence of G.T. Braine.

25 Post 51/13, P and O contracts to India; Robinson, *Carrying British Mails Overseas*, pp. 166–7.

26 Robinson, *Carrying British Mail Overseas*, pp. 132–4; PP 1846 XLV, *Halifax Mails. Halifax and United States Mail Contract*, pp. 197–231; F.E. Hyde, *Cunard and the North Atlantic, 1840–1973* (1975), pp. 1–9.

27 PP 1846 XLV, *A Copy of the memorials from the Great Western Steamship Co. in 1842 and 1846*, pp. 299–304: see also evidence of Capt C. Claxton to PP 1846 XV, *Select Committee on Halifax and Boston Mails*.

28 PP 1846 XV, *SC on Halifax and Boston Mails*, Qq 231–4.

29 Ibid., p. 27.

30 PP 1846 XLV, *Memorials from the Great Western Steamship Co.*

31 R. McCalmont, *Some Remarks on the Contract Packet System and on Ocean Penny Postage* (1851).

32 PP 1852–3 XCV, *Report of the Committee on Contract Packets*, pp. 139–45; the Treasury minute is appendix A, pp. 183–6.

33 R. and G.B. Hill, *Life*, II, p. 239.

34 PP 1859 (sess 1) XVII, *Copies of all applications, reports, papers, or communications*

made to any department of the government relating to proposals for new contracts to establish steam communication, for postal purposes, between Great Britain, or Ireland, and North America, since 1 Jan 1858; PP 1859 (sess 2) XXII, *Copies of all correspondence between Her Majesty's Government and the provincial government of Canada, in reference to the conveyance of mails . . .*, pp. 450–68. Post 29/97, Pkt 651L/1860; PP 1860 XIV, *Second Report from the Select Committee on Packet and Telegraphic Contracts*, pp 527–9; PP 1860 XIV, *First Report from the Select Committee on Packet and Telegraphic Contracts*, pp. 3–14.

35   PP 1860 XIV, *SC on Packet and Telegraphic Contracts*, p. 17; Post 29/94, Pkt 447L/1860, file XXVIII.
36   Post 29/94, Pkt 447L/1860, file XXXV.
37   PP 1868–9 VI, *Report from the Select Committee on Mail Contracts*, Q 106. The phrase is Pearson Hill's.
38   PP 1859 (sess 2) VI, *Select Committee on Packet and Telegraphic Contracts*, Qq 418–9, 432–3, 444–6, 464, 556, 732.
39   PP 1866 IX *SC on East India Communications*, Qq 65–8, 213.
40   Post 29/143, Pkt 10T/1868.
41   Post 29/147, Pkt 563T/1868.
42   Post 29/144, Pkt 162T/1868; Post 29/153–4, Pkt 145 U/1869.
43   Post 29/144, Pkt 162T/1868; Post 29/153–4, Pkt 145U/1869; PP 1868–9 VI, *SC on Mail Contracts*, p. 269, Qq 451, 454, 820–2; this contains the evidence on the sudden switch from competition to collusion: see Qq 1368–70.
44   Post 29/153–4, Pkt 145U/1869; Post 29/152, Pkt 949T/1868; Trollope, *Autobiography*, p. 269.
45   PP 1860 XIV, *First Report, SC on Packet and Telegraphic Contracts*, Qq 3273, 3281–7, 3292, 3302–3, 3322, 3474, 3581, 3572, 2656, 2686–7, 2879, 2881, 2734–46, 2876; PP 1868–9 VI, *SC on Mail Contracts*, Qq 1371–4, 1391, 1438; Hyde, *Cunard*, pp. 27–34, 58, 66–8.
46   PP 1866 IX, *SC on East India Communications*, p. 7.
47   *Postal Communications with India, China and Australia under the Tenders issued by the Government for New Contracts. Speeches delivered by R.W. Crawford and other members in the debate in the House of Commons on Thursday 1 August 1867* (1868), p. 69.
48   This section is based upon Post 29/143, Pkt 10T/1868.
49   Post 29/143, Pkt 10T/1868.
50   PP 1868–9 VI, *Report from the Select Committee on Mail Contracts*, Q 650.
51   Post 29/153–4, Pkt 145U/1869.
52   Post 29/297, Pkt 142G/1881.
53   Post 29/256, Pkt 128E/1879; Post 29/432–5, Pkt 158N/1887.
54   Post 29/432–5, Pkt 158N/1887.
55   Post 29/531, Pkt 55S/1892.
56   Post 29/669, Pkt 276Z/1899.
57   V. Vale, 'The government and the Cunard contract of 1903', *Journal of Transport History*, ns V (1979).
58   Post 29/832, Pkt 281E/1904.
59   Post 29/922, Pkt 79H/1907.
60   Post 33/2369–70, M10015/1928.
61   Ibid. and Post 33/4978, M8286/1936.
62   Post 29/272–4, Pkt 16F/1880; *Argument against the India and China Postal Contract for the Eight Years, 1880–1888* (1880?).
63   Post 29/462–3, Pkt 4080/1888; Post 29/636–7, Pkt 232Y/1898; Post 33/4984, M8343/1936; Post 29/934–5, Pkt 171H/1907.
64   National Maritime Museum, P & O/3/31.
65   Post 29/607–8, Pkt 65X/1897.
66   PP 1902 IX, *Select Committee on Steamship Subsidies*, pp. 321–7; Post 33/2901, M2931/1930.

67 Post 29/804–5, Pkt 87E/1904; Post 29/817–8, Pkt 134E/1904; PP 1904 XXIII, *Report on the Eastern Mail Service Committee*, pp. 542–9.
68 Post 29/934–5, Pkt 171H/1907.
69 Post 29/1117, Pkt 52/1912; Post 33/4984, M8343/1936.
70 *The Aeroplane*, 18 Feb. 1920.
71 Post 33/84, M5810/1921, evidence to Advisory Committee on Civil Aviation.
72 P.T David, *The Economics of Air Mail Transportation* (1934).
73 Post 33/679–80, M9868/1922, file IV; Post 33/84, M5810/1921, files X, XII, XXI.
74 Post 33/84, M5810/1921, file XIII; see also Post 30/3870–1, E5324/1917 and Post 29/1423–4, Pkt 79/1920.
75 Post 33/84, M5810/1921, file III.
76 Post 33/84, M5810/1921, file XII.
77 *St Martin's le Grand*, XXXIII (1923); Post 33/84, M5810/1921, file XXIII.
78 F. H. Williamson, *The Air Mail Service* (Post Office Green Paper no 1), p. 4; PP 1926 XVIII, *Agreement made with the British, Foreign and Colonial Corporation Ltd providing for the formation of a heavier-than-air transport company to be called the Imperial Air Transport Co. Ltd.*, pp. 277–96.
79 Post 33/84, M5810/1921, file XXVIII.
80 Ibid., file XXXIII.
81 Ibid.
82 Post 33/3221, M2006/1931, file 1.
83 Post 33/679–80, M9868/1922, file XIX.
84 Post 33/3221, M2006/1931, file VIII.
85 Post 33/5296, M20057/1938, file II.
86 Ibid., files IV, VI, VIII, IX, XI, XIX, XVI, XXI.
87 Ibid., file IX.
88 Ibid., file III.
89 Ibid., file XII.
90 Ibid., files XVI, XXI.
91 Ibid., file XXVI.
92 Ibid., files XXVI, XXVII, XXVIII, XXX: Post 33/5346, M23825/1938, files I, V, VIII.
93 Post 29/1425, Pkt 80/1920.
94 Williamson, *Air Mail Service*, pp. 4–6.
95 RAF Museum, Hendon AW/1/2752.
96 *Daily Telegraph*, 19 Sept. 1930.
97 PRO Avia 2/1897.
98 AW/1/2752.
99 Post 33/4108, M701/1934, file XIX.
100 Post 33/3221, M2006/1931, file VIII.
101 PRO Avia 2/1897.
102 Post 33/3223, M2025/1931, file I; Post 33/4949, M20550/1935, file VIII; PRO Avia 2/1897.
103 Post 33/4249A, M4006/1934, files V, VII, XXI.
104 Ibid., file XXI.
105 Air Ministry and GPO, *Empire Air Mail Scheme* (1937).
106 Post 33/5263, M21819/1937, files VI, II; AW/1/2758; *Empire Air Mail Scheme*.
107 PRO Avia 2/2791; Post 33/5263, M21819/1937, files II, XVII and unnumbered; AW/1/2752, 2753, 2767.
108 Post 33/5263, M21819/1937, files II, XIV and unnumbered.
109 Ibid., unnumbered file; Post 33/5189, M16106/1937, file V; *Empire Air Mail Scheme*.
110 Post 33/5263, M21819/1937, file XIV.

111 Post 33/5296, M20057/1938, file XXII.
112 AW/1/5077, 5076; PRO Avia 2/2498 and 2465 part I.

Chapter 6

1 E. Murray, *The Post Office* (1927) p. 190.
2 Staff figures up to the First World War are given in the Annual Reports of the Postmaster General on the Post Office; thereafter, see *Statistical Abstract for the United Kingdom*, and the returns in the papers of the Post Office Board from 1934 onwards.
3 On this, see M. Wagner, 'Wage structures in manufacturing industry and in public administration: Austria 1868–85', *Historical Social Research*, 26 (1983).
4 Post 33/2719–20, M11532/1929, files V, XXIV; Post 33/3163–5, M16055/1930, file II; Post 33/2905, M3296/1930, file III.
5 Post 30/276, E4392/1875; Post 30/938, E4060/1901, files II, IV; Post 60/91, *Postmen, their Duties and Pay, 1891*, p. 13; Post 30/221, E3762/1872.
6 Post 30/938, E4060/1901, file II; Post 30/276, E4392/1875; Post 60/15, Letter carriers' general revision, 1882.
7 Post 30/97, E2346/1855, files V, VII, VIII, IX; Post 30/938, E4060/1901, file V.
8 PP 1897 XLIV, *Report of Inter-departmental Committee on Post Office Establishments*, pp. 24–5; Post 30/938, E4060/1901, files VIII, IX. The grade of assistant postman was short-lived: see Post 33/3163–5, M16055/1930, file I.
9 Post 33/1235–7, M3864/1924, file XLIV; Post 30/2174, E3132/1912, file I; Post 33/1232–3, M3860/1924.
10 Post 33/2905, M3296/1930, files I, II; Post 33/1173, M257/1924, file II.
11 Post 33/3163–5, M16055/1930, file II; Post 33/1173, M257/1924, file I, II, VII, CX, XI, XVII; Post 33/2905, M3296/1930, files I, III.
12 Post 33/3163–5, M16055/1930, files I, II, III; Post 33/2719–20, M11532/1929, files V, VI, VII, XV, XVI, XX, XXX, XXXIV, XLIX.
13 These comments are based on R. H. Tawney, 'The economics of boy labour', *Economic Journal*, XIX (1909); R. Bray, 'The apprenticeship question', *Economic Journal*, XIX (1909); N. B. Dearle, *Industrial Training, with Special Reference to the Conditions Prevailing in London* (1914); PP 1909 XLIV, *Royal Commission on the Poor Laws and Relief of Distress. Appendix Volume XX, Report by Mr Cyril Jackson on Boy Labour*.
14 Post 30/1924, E1976/1911; Post 30/468, E15611/1884, file III; Post 30/1052, E22956/1903, file I; H. Montgomery Hyde, *The Other Love: A Historical and Contemporary Survey of Homosexuality* (1970), pp. 123–7.
15 C. Simpson, L. Chester, D. Leitch, *The Cleveland Street Affair* (1976).
16 Post 30/1052, E22956/1903, files I, II, IV, V; Post 30/598, E 18949/1891, file XI; Post 30/1924, E1976/1911; Post 30/1802–3, E2913/1910, file X.
17 Post 30/1802–3, E2913/1910, files II, III, IV, V, VII, X, XI; Post 30/1052, E22956/1903, files X, XI. The belief that London led to degeneration was a commonplace: see G. Stedman Jones, *Outcast London: a Study in the Relationship between Classes in Victorian Society* (1971), chapter 6.
18 Post 33/273–4, M17046/1921, files I, II, IX, XII, XXXVII; Post 30/3311, E4080/1915, file I.
19 Post 30/1762, E26973/1909, file I; Post 30/1052, E22956/1903, files XIX, XXII, XXV, XXVII.
20 Post 30/1802–3, E2913/1910, file XXXIV; Post 30/1925, E1977/1911, files II, VIII, IX; Post 30/2126, E21790/1911, files I, II, IV, V, XI.
21 Post 30/2126, E21790/1911, file V; Post 30/1762, E26973/1909, file I; PP 1909 XLIV, *Report by Mr Cyril Jackson . . .*, pp. 940–1, 1014, 1172.
22 Post 30/1924, E1976/1911; Post 30/1917, E26109/1910; Post 30/1762,

E26973/1909, files I, II, III, V, VI, IX; Dearle, *Industrial Training*, appendix 5, pp. 571–6; PP 1911 XXXIX, *First Annual Report of the Standing Committee on Boy Labour in the Post Office*, pp. 206, 208; PP 1911 XXXIX, *Second Report*, p. 224; PP 1914 XXLIV, *Fourth Report*, pp. 873, 875; PP 1914–16 XXXII, *Fifth Report* pp. 989–90, 995.

23 Post 33/1614–5, M11066/1925, files I, IX, X, XX, XXXI, XXXVII.

24 E. M. Spiers, *The Army and Society, 1815–1914* (1980), pp. 183–4; A. R. Skelly, *The Victorian Army at Home. The Recruitment, Terms and Conditions of the British Regular, 1859–99* (1977), pp. 236, 204–16, 251–61, 321; PRO, WO 33/70, *Civil Employment of Discharged Soldiers and Army Reserve Men*; PP 1895 XII, *Select Committee on Retired Soldiers and Sailors Employment*, p. 153.

25 Post 30/1802–3, E2913/1910, file III.

26 Ibid., files X, XX, XXI; Post 30/938, E4060/1901, file IX.

27 PP 1913 XLII, *Return of the number of persons holding on 31 March 1913 (1) established (2) unestablished appointments as messengers, postmen . . . in the several government departments*, pp. 272–3; PP 1897 XLIV, *Evidence taken before the Committee on Post Office Establishments*, Q 14872; Post 30/1802–3, E2913/1910, file XXII; Post 30/2830, E4856/1914, files VI, IX, XIIA; Post 30/2876, E6627/1914.

28 Post 33/1824, M9978/1926, files II, III, VIII, IX, X, XV.

29 Post 33/2174, M16683/1927, file I; Post 33/4818, M12657/1935, files I, III, IV, IX; Post 33/3963–5, M8677/1933; Post 33/1242, M3889/1924, file XVIII; Post 33/2719–20, M11532/1929, file V.

30 Post 30/464, E12710/1884, files 1, III.

31 Post 30/759, E2787/1897, file II.

32 Post 30/1174, E5234/1905.

33 Post 60/89, Report of Proceedings of Committee appointed to consider the Pay, Duties and Prospects of Promotion of Town Letter Carriers, etc., other than those employed in London, 1881.

34 PP 1914 LXXI, *Return showing the changes in the wages and conditions of service of Post Office servants . . .*, pp. 732–72; PP 1907 VII, *Report from the Select Committee on Post Office Servants*, p. 338; PP 1913 X, *Report from the Select Committee on Post Office Servants*, pp. 339–41; Post 30/1021–2 E9992/1913 files I, VIII, X, XI, XVI, XVIII, XXVI.

35 Post 60/91, Postmen, their Duties and Pay, 1891, and PP 1914 LXXI, *Return . . .*

36 Post 30/2179, E3593/1912; Post 30/1734–5, E21664/1909, files I, XV, XIX, XX, XXII; Post 30/3005–6, E13421/1914, files IV, VI.

37 Post 30/405, E5639/1881; Post 30/680, E4/1895, files I, III: Post 57/13, Indoor Force. Reports of Committees, etc on Methods of Recruiting, Training, etc.

38 Post 30/408, E8787/1881; Post 30/2831, E4870/1914, files I, II, III, V, VIII, XV; Post 30/603, E4370/1892; Post 30/1821, E5941/1910, files I, II: Post 33/91, M6369/1921.

39 Post 33/1041, M7219/1923, file I; Post 33/3142–4, M15650/1930, file I; Post 30/2831, E4870/1914, files XV, XXIII; Post 33/1693, M1652/1926, file III: Post 33/3892, M6011/1933, files II, VII; Post 33/1097, M9132/1923.

40 Post 33/2951, M6033/1930, file XIV.

41 Post 30/1536, E12171/1908, file I; Post 30/2489, E11951/1913, file 1.

42 Post 30/2489, E11951/1913, files VI, IX, XI; Post 30/1536, E12171/1908; Post 30/4083, E4764/1918, file I; Post 30/3411, E11913/1915; Post 30/4382–3, E14132/1919; Post 30/4243–4, E3221/1919.

43 Post 33/2142, M15635/1927, file XXVIII; Post 30/3020, M14324/1914, files I, IV, X, XIV, XV, XVII, XVIII, XIX.

44 Post 33/329–30, M20612/1921, files I, VI, VII, IX, X, XV, XVIII, XXXI; Post Office circular no 3954, 30 Oct. 1946.

45   Post 33/3213, M1756/1931, file I, bottom A; Post 33/2951, M6033/1930, files I, V, VII, VIII, XIII, XIV.

46   See above, chapter 1; Post 30/114–5, E4472/1857.

47   Post 30/148, E4801/1861, files II, III, IV, VI, VII, VIII; Post 14/232, Minute by Sir Rowland Hill on the Report of the late committee upon the Circulation Department of the GPO, 1861, and Observations of the Committee on the Minute by Sir Rowland Hill.

48   Post 30/227, E7564/1872; Post 30/425, E12429/1882; Post 30/255, E3975/1874; Post 30/221, E3763/1872; Post 30/276, E4392/1875; Post 30/243, E7630/1873.

49   Post 30/305, E7827/1876.

50   Post 30/468, E15611/1884; *Some Records of the Life of Stevenson Arthur Blackwood KGB, compiled by a Friend and edited by his Widow* (1896), pp. 346–7.

51   Post 30/468, E15611/1884; Post 60/15 Letter Carriers' General Revision, 1882 and 60/88 Report from the Postmaster General to the Treasury, 1881; Post 30/405, E5639/1881; L. Stephen, *Life of Henry Fawcett* (1886), pp. 442–3.

52   Post 30/598, E18949/1891; Post 60/91, *Postmen, Their Duties and Pay, 1891*.

53   PP 1897 XLIV, *Report of the Interdepartmental Committee on Post Office Establishments*; Post 30/1185, E6980/1905 PP 1907 VII, *Report from the Select Committee on Post Office Servants*; PP 1913 X, *Report from the Select Committee on Post Office Servants*; Post 65/5 Memorandum. Discontent in the Post Office.

54   Parliamentary Debates, 5th series, 1914, vol. LXIII, cols. 321, 327, 382–3, 420, 425, 428–30.

55   Post 33/1164–6, M14012/1923; Post 33/2275, M4047/1928.

56   Post 33/2019–21, M8031/1927; Post 60/42 Post Office Manipulative Classes. Wage claim and evidence submitted by the UPW to the Industrial Court, 1927; Post 33/3767, M13303/1932; Post 33/3893–4, M6020/1933.

57   Post 30/280–1, M17758/1921; Post 33/3893–4, M6020/1933.

58   For the indices of wages and prices, see B. R. Mitchell and P. Deane, *Abstract of British Historical Statistics* (1962).

59   G. Routh, 'Civil service pay, 1875–1950', *Economic*, n.s. 21 (1954).

60   Post 60/7, *Return of salaries, wages and allowances of the Post Office department generally . . . 1835–51*; PP 1857 IV, *Return of letters carried . . .; Annual Reports of the Postmaster General*.

61   Post 33/1675, M1200/1926; Post 33/1196–8, M2095/1924; Post 30/722, E6306/1896.

62   Post 30/3113, E25112/1914; Post Office Board Paper 25, 1946.

63   Post Office Board Papers 25, 1946 and 38, 1948; Post 30/4188, E13317/1918; Post 33/4481, M12031/1934; Post 33/4941, M20540/1935; Post 33/5281, M18982/1938; Post 33/5395, M27249/1938; Post 33/5417, M27319/1938; *Statistical Abstract for the United Kingdom; Post Office Accounts*.

Chapter 7

1   PP 1914 LXXI, *Return showing the changes in wages and conditions of service of Post Office servants . . .* pp. 768–71.

2   C. R. Littler, *The Development of the Labour Process in Capitalist Societies* (1982), pp. 15–17, 70–2.

3   On this process, see W. Rubinstein, 'The end of "old corruption" in England, 1780–1860', *Past and Present*, 101 (1983).

4   Post 30/34, E1047/1837; Post 30/68–72, E5831a/1848, file VIII; PP 1837–8 XXXV, *Tenth Report of the Commissioners appointed to enquire into the management of the Post Office departments*, pp. 187–90.

5   Post 30/116, E4768/1857; Post 30/62, E2977/1847.
6   Max Weber, *The Theory of Social and Economic Organisation* (English edn, New York, 1947), pp. 331, 334–5.
7   Post 33/1642, M12437/1925, file I; Post 30/743–6, E12655/1896, files VI, XI; PP 1860 IX, *Select Committee on Civil Service Appointments*, Qq 1622, 1808, 1816, 1937, 1951.
8   See below, chapter 8.
9   Post 60/89, Memorandum on the Wages of the Minor Establishment in the Post Office, 1874.
10 PP 1854 XXVII, *Report upon the Post Office*, p. 406.
11 PP 1854 XXVII, *Report on the Organisation of the Permanent Civil Service*; PP 1860 IX, *SC on Civil Service Appointments*, pp. 3–15; PP 1872 XIX, *Seventeenth Report of Her Majesty's Civil Service Commissioners*, pp. 3–55; J. Pellew, *The Home Office, 1898–1914: From Clerks to Bureaucrats* (1982), chapter 2 provides a case-study of another Department; on the background to the Northcote-Trevelyan Report, see J. Hart, 'The genesis of the Northcote-Trevelyan Report', in G. Sutherland (ed.) *Studies in the Growth of Nineteenth-Century Government* (1972), pp. 63–81.
12 A. Trollope, *An Autobiography* (1883; 1946 edn), pp. 44, 48–50; *The Three Clerks* (1858).
13 J. Pellew, 'Reform in the Post Office, 1850–85', MA dissertation, Queen Mary College, University of London, 1970/1; R. and G. B. Hill, *Life*, II, p. 250; PP 1860 IX, *SC on Civil Service Appointments*, Qq 1708, 1717, 1725, 1775, 1787, 1817; PP 1888 XXVII, *Second Report, Royal Commission on Civil Establishments*, Qq 17754–5; PP 1856 XXII, *First Report of Civil Service Commission*, pp. 392–405, 472–3; PP 1860 XXIV, *Fifth Report of Civil Service Commission*, pp. 443–9; PP 1867–8 XXII, *Thirteenth Report of Civil Service Commission*, pp. 250–9; C. R. Perry, 'The British Post Office, 1836–1914: a study in nationalisation and administrative expansion', PhD Harvard, 1976; L. Woolf, *Sowing* (1960), p. 211.
14 PP 1860 IX, *SC on Civil Service Appointments*, Qq 1601–2, 1645–6, 1675, 1712–3, 1746–7; PP 1888 XXVII, *RC on Civil Establishments*, Qq 17808–9; Post 30/743–6, E12655/1896, files VII, XXVIII, LII, LIV; Post 30/1821, E5941/1910, files I, II; Post 30/344, E770/1879.
15 Post 30/2898, E8424/1914, files I, III: Post 30/2526–7, E14352/1913; Post 30/2799, E3087/1914, files I, III; Post 30/4670–2, E19413/1920, file I; Post 30/4682, E20975/1920, file I; Post 30/2831, E4870/1914, files I, II, III, V, VIII, XV, XXIII.
16 The details of benefits are, unless otherwise stated, from PP 1914 LXXI, *Return showing the changes in wages and conditions of service of Post Office servants . . .*, pp. 768–71.
17 C. Booth, *Pauperism, a Picture, and the Endowment of Old Age, an Argument* (1892); D. Collins, 'The introduction of old age pensions in Great Britain', *Historical Journal*, VIII (1965); J. Roebuck. 'When does old age begin? The evolution of the English definition', *Journal of Social History*, XII (1979); B. B. Gilbert, *The Evolution of National Insurance in Great Britain* (1966), chapter 4; on occupational pension schemes, see L. Hannah's forthcoming book.
18 M. Wright, *Treasury Control of the Civil Service, 1854–74* (1969), chapter 14; Post 30/240, E6071/1873.
19 Gilbert, *Evolution of National Insurance*, chapter 5 and p. 166.
20 On entitlement to holidays, see J. A. R. Pimlott, *The Englishman's Holiday: A Social History* (1947).
21 Post 60/77, *Correspondence relating to promotion from class to class in the General Post Office*, p. 28.
22 PP 1854 XXVII, *Report upon the Post Office*, pp. 404–5.
23 PP 1854–5 XX, *First Report of the Postmaster General on the Post Office*, pp. 587–8.

24 Post 60/77, *Correspondence*, pp. 3–4.
25 Ibid., pp. 26–8.
26 Ibid., pp. 13–26. This volume is a printed version of Post 30/164, E3849/1863.
27 Post 30/4256, E4368/1919, files II, III; Post 60/77, *Correspondence*, p. 6.
28 Post 30/598, E18949/1891, file I; PP 1897 XLIV, *Report of the Interdepartmental Committee on Post Office Establishments*, p. 9.
29 PP 1907 VII, *Report from the Select Committee on Post Office Servants*, pp. 316–7; Post 30/1535, E12126/1908.
30 PP 1913 X, *Select Committee on Post Office Servants*, pp. 301–14, 353, 397; E. Murray, *The Post Office* (1927), pp. 190–1. Careers are taken from Post 1/463, Treasury Letters, November 1913, which gives the requests for pensions and gratuities for each officer on retirement; *List of Officers in the General Post Offices of London, Edinburgh and Dublin* (1910); and *St Martin's le Grand* XXIII (1913), lists of retirements.
31 Post 1/463, Treasury Letters, November 1913.
32 Post 60/91, *Postmen. Their Duties and Pay*, pp. 9–10.
33 Post 30/385, E6804/1880, file XII.
34 Post 60/73, *History of Good Conduct Stripes*; Post 60/74, Good Conduct Stripes, memoranda; Post 30/385, E6804/1880, files XII, XIV, XVII.
35 Post 30/385, E6804/1880, files IX, XVII, XXII.
36 Ibid., file XXIV; Post 30/468, E5611/1884, file VIII; Post 60/15, Letter Carriers General Revision, 1882.
37 Post 30/598, E18949/1891, files I, VI, VII, IX; Post 60/91, *Postmen. Their Duties and Pay. Report*, pp. 17–19; Post 60/70, *Good Conduct Stripes, Method of Award in Connection with the Report of the Tweedmouth Committee*.
38 PP 1913 X, *Report from the Select Committee on Post Office Servants (Wages and Conditions of Employment)*, pp. 307–8; Post 30/2892, E7435/1914; Post 30/385, E6804/1880, file XXIV.
39 PP 1897 XLIV, *Report of the Interdepartmental Committee on Post Office Establishments*, p. 20.
40 PP 1863 XXXI, *Return of the several rates of wages paid weekly . . .*, pp. 171–2.
41 PP 1890–1 LXIII, *Return relating to postmen's pay, etc in the year 1885, and as fixed in August 1891*, pp. 737–9.
42 Post 60/15, *Letter Carriers' General Revision 1882*.
43 PP 1914 LXXI, *Return showing the changes in the wages and conditions of service of Post Office servants*, pp. 732–72.
44 This section is based, unless otherwise stated, upon Post 65/3–5, *Discontent in the Post Office. Its Rise with Special Reference to the Causes which Led up to the Formation of Associations for the Furtherance of the Same, and the Attitude Adopted by Successive Postmasters General towards such Associations* (1905).
45 Post 30/832–3, E300/1899; Post 60/18, Postman Deputation to the Postmaster General, 11–24 July 1890; H. St J. Raikes, *The Life and Letters of Henry Cecil Raikes, late Her Majesty's Postmaster General* (1898), pp. 329–62.
46 Post 65/2, Joint Committee of Postal and Telegraph Associations, interview, 1901.
47 Post 65/6, Staff Association Memorials, Treatment, 1906–10.
48 PP 1917–18 XVIII, *Reconstruction Committee. Sub-committee on relations between employers and employed. Interim report on Joint Standing Industrial Councils*, pp. 415–22; K. Middlemas, *Politics in Industrial Society. The Experience of the British System since 1911* (1979), pp. 137–8; H. Parris, *Staff Relations in the Civil Service: Fifty Years of Whitleyism* (1973); L. D. White, *Whitley Councils in the British Civil Service. A Study in Conciliation and Arbitration* (1933), pp. 70–85; Post 33/5203, M17048/1937, files V and bottom.
49 Post 33/5203, M17408/1937, files VIII and bottom; S. D. Spero, *Labour Relations in British Nationalised Industry* (1955), pp. 69–70.

50   *The Post*, 9 August 1918.
51   Post 33/58, M3544/1921; Post 33/1985–6, M6082/1927, files I, II, III, VI, VII, XIII, XIV, XVI, XX, XXIV, XXIX; *The Post*, 9 April and 11 August 1927; Parris, *Staff Relations*, pp. 124–6.
52   Post 33/1985–6, M6082/1927, file XX.

Chapter 8

1   PP 1930–1 X, *Report of the Royal Commission on the Civil Service*, pp. 587–8.
2   Viscount Wolmer, *Post Office Reform. Its Importance and Practicability* (1932), p. 249.
3   Post 30/1422, E16592/1907, file II; Post 73, *Report of the Decentralisation Committee*, 1909; H. J. Hanham, 'Political patronage at the Treasury, 1870–1912', *Historical Journal*, III (1960), pp. 80–2.
4   Post 30/1422, E16592/1907, file II; see also Post 73, *Report of the Decentralisation Committee*, 1909.
5   Post 73, *Report of the Decentralisation Committee*, 1909.
6   Ibid.
7   Quoted in Wolmer, *Post Office Reform*, pp. 228–9.
8   PP 1931–2 XII, *Report of the Committee of Enquiry on the Post Office*, pp. 768–9.
9   PP 1907 VII, *Select Committee on Postal Servants*, p. 390.
10   Post 30/1422, E16592/1907, file II.
11   Post 73, *Report of the Decentralisation Committee*, 1909.
12   PP 1931–2 XII, *Report of the Committee of Enquiry on the Post Office*, pp. 768–70.
13   Post 73, *Report of the Decentralisation Committee, 1909*; see also Post 30/1422, E16592/1907, file II; PP 1931–2 XII, *Report of the Committee of Enquiry on the Post Office*, p. 769; *List of Officers in the General Post Office of London, Edinburgh and Dublin . . .* (1910); Perry, 'British Post Office', chapter 1 provides brief biographies of leading officials.
14   *Annual Reports of the Postmaster General*.
15   PP 1860 IX, *Select Committee on Civil Service Appointments*, Qq 1696–8; Hanham, 'Political patronage'.
16   W. Lewins, *Her Majesty's Mails*, p. 292.
17   Post 30/3062, E16286/1914, files I, III, IV, VI, XI, XIV, Post Office Buildings: provision and maintenance, and Report of Committee on Post Office Buildings.
18   PP 1907 VII, *Select Committee on Post Office Servants*, pp. 382–8; Post 30/348, E1504/1879; Post 30/408, E8935/1881, files I, III, IV; Post 30/426, E587/1883, files I–V; Post 30/819, E13240/1898, files X, XVII; Post 30/1099, E12956/1904, files I, II; Post 30/5000, M10838/1936, files I, VI, IX; Post 30/1372, E3058/1907.
19   Murray, *Post Office*, pp. 184–5.
20   PP 1854 XXVII, *Report upon the Post Office*, pp. 403–4.
21   Murray, *Post Office*, p. 184.
22   PP 1911 XLIX, *Estimates, Revenue Departments, for the Year ending 31 March 1912*, pp. 794–7, 844–5.
23   *List of Officers. . .*, p. 147.
24   PP 1854 XXVII, *Report upon the Post Office*, p. 428.
25   Ibid., pp. 400–1, 429–30.
26   Post 30/1918, E26128/1910.
27   *List of Officers. . .*, p. 329.
28   Post 30/121, E2835/1858; Post 30/304, E7430/1876, file I.
29   Post 30/304, E7430/1876, files VI, XIV.
30   Ibid., files I, XIV; Post 30/295, E2756/1876.
31   Post 30/95, E71/1855, file III; Post 30/507, E9038/1887, file VI.

32   Post 30/295, E2756/1876; Post 30/507, E9038/1887, file VI; Post 73, Committee on Surveying Staff; Post 30/1500, E2894/1908; Post 30/676, E14162/1894.
33   Post 33/858–60, M473/1923, files XVIII, XXXIV, XLIX, LIII.
34   PP 1907 VII, *Select Committee on Post Office Servants*, p. 390.
35   Post 30/1422, E16592/1907, file II.
36   Post 73, *Report of the Decentralisation Committee*, 1909, etc.
37   Post 30/1422, E16592/1907, file IV.
38   Post 73, *Report of the Decentralisation Committee*, 1909, etc.
39   Ibid.
40   Post 30/1953–4, E5692/1911, file XIX.
41   Post 30/1918, E26128/1910, file IIIa.
42   Post 30/1953–4, E5692/1911, file XXI.
43   Post 30/1918, E26128/1910, file IX.
44   Ibid., files X, XIII.
45   Post 30/1953–4, E5692/1911, file XXI.
46   Post 30/1918, E26128/1920, file XVIa.
47   PRO, T1/11424/10406/1912.
48   PP 1922 VI, *Select Committee on the Telephone Service*, pp. 202–4; Post 33/461, M27114/1921; Post 33/1597, M9915/1925.
49   C. R. Attlee, 'Post Office reform', *New Statesman and Nation*, 7 November 1931, pp. 565–6.
50   Wolmer, *Post Office Reform*, pp. 249–50.
51   PP 1931–2 XII, *Report of Committee of Enquiry on the Post Office*, pp. 771, 773–5.
52   Post 33/5529, M8566/1940.
53   Ibid.
54   Post 33/5529 M8566/1940.
55   Post 33/5034, M13005/1936, file II; Post 33/5530, P8567/1940, files I, IX; Post 33/4741, M6010/1935, file II; Post 33/5529, M8566/1940.
56   Post 73, *First Report of the Committee on Metropolitan and Regional Organisation*, 1934, p. 17.
57   Post 33/5092, M18112/1936.
58   Post 73, *First Report of the Committee on Metropolitan and Regional Organisation*, 1934.
59   Post 73, *Report of the Postal Services Department Devolution Committee*, 1935.
60   Post 33/4979, M8308/1936.
61   Post 73, *Report on the Present System of Regionalisation in the Post Office* (1951); Post Office Board 1938, volume 2, POB 2 (38) and 3 (38), BP 16 (38); Post 33/5352, M23919/1938, files VIII, XIV, XV, XVI.
62   PP 1931–2 XII, *Report of Committee of Enquiry on the Post Office*, p. 772.
63   Post 33/4314, M6019/1934.
64   A. D. Chandler, *Strategy and Structure: Chapters in the History of The American Industrial Enterprise* (1962), pp. 41–2; L. Hannah, *The Rise of the Corporate Economy* (1976), chapter 6, 'Management and the limits to growth'.

Chapter 9

1   PP 1888 XXVII, *Second Report of the Royal Commission on Civil Establishments*, Q 10,623.
2   PP 1887 XIX, *First Report of the Royal Commission on Civil Establishments*, Qq 8–9.
3   H. Roseveare, *The Treasury: The Evolution of a British Institution* (1969), pp. 205–6.
4   M. Wright, 'Treasury controls, 1854–1914', in G. Sutherland (ed.), *Studies in the Growth of Nineteenth-Century Government* (1972), pp. 195–226.

5   PP 1829 XI, *18th Report of the Commissioners of Revenue Inquiry*, pp. 11–12.
6   PP 1834 XLIX, *23rd Report of the Commissioners of Revenue Inquiry*, pp. 482–5.
7   PP 1836 XXVIII, *4th Report of the Commissioners appointed to inquire into the management of the Post Office Department, 23 July 1835*, pp. 35–6.
8   *Parliamentary Debates*, 3rd series, vol. CLXXXII, col. 1079, 11 April 1866.
9   Murray, *Post Office*, p. 179.
10 Wolmer, *Post Office Reform*, pp. 223–6, 236–7.
11 K. Feiling, *The Life of Neville Chamberlain* (1946), p. 102.
12 H. Samuel, *Memoirs* (1945), p. 77.
13 Raikes, *The Life and Letters of Henry Cecil Raikes* pp. 3–6, 254–5, 273–80, 292–3.
14 C. R. Perry, 'Frank Ives Scudamore and the Post Office telegraphs', *Albion*, XII (1980), p. 353.
15 Wolmer, *Post Office Reform*, p. 236; Attlee, 'Post Office reform', pp. 565–6.
16 See the entry in the *Dictionary of Business Biography*.
17 *The Times*, 9 May 1942; *Who Was Who, vol. IV, 1941–50*; letter from King to M. Nathan, 4 Dec. 1909 in the Nathan Papers, Bodleian Library, quoted by Perry, 'British Post Office'.
18 *Some Records of the Life of Stevenson Arthur Blackwood compiled by a friend and edited by his widow* (1896).
19 *Dictionary of National Biography, second supplement*, vol. III (1912).
20 *Dictionary of National Biography, 1931–40*.
21 *Dictionary of National Biography, 1922–30*; G. H. Bushnell, *Sir Henry Babington-Smith, 1863–1923, Civil Servant and Financier* (1942).
22 *Dictionary of National Biography, 1931–40*.
23 *Dictionary of National Biography 1941–50; The Times*, 31 March 1947; D. O. Lumley, 'The last Secretary to the Post Office', typescript in Post Office Archives.
24 See the complaints in PP 1888 XVIII, *Select Committee on Revenue Department Estimates*, Qq 54–71, 184, 247; also Raikes, *Henry Cecil Raikes*, pp. 363–5.
25 The phrase is Perry's, 'Frank Ives Scudamore', p. 352. This provides an excellent account of the scandal, and has been used for much of what follows.
26 Post 8/34, Post Office accounts – a description; Post 30/82–3, E5196/1852; PP 1854 XXVII, *Report upon the Post Office*, pp. 400, 410–21; Post 30/105, E4364/1856; Murray, *Post Office*, pp. 31-2.
27 Perry, 'Frank Ives Scudamore', p. 363; Post 30/239, E5707/1873.
28 Quoted in Perry, 'Frank Ives Scudamore', p. 362.
29 Post 30/290, E1075/1876.
30 Quoted in Perry, 'Frank Ives Scudamore', p. 364.
31 PRO, T1/7425B/1630 in Perry, 'Frank Ives Scudamore', p. 363.
32 Post 30/290, E1075/1876.
33 Post 30/274, E2620/1875.
34 Post 30/269, E663A/1875; H. Buxton Forman, *A Few Words About the Late Sir Arthur Blackwood, Secretary of the Post Office* (1894), p. 15.
35 Post 30/269, E663A/1875, 'Frank Ives Scudamore', p. 364.
36 Post 30/305, E7827/1876.
37 PP 1888 XVIII, *Select Commitee on Revenue Department Estimates*, pp. 7–8 and Qq 271–5, 295, 325, 349, 369, 398, 400, 710, 712, 767, 948, 950–1.
38 PRO, T1/11424/10406/1912; Post 30/1665, E8368/1909; C. R. Perry, 'The British Post Office, 1836–1914'.
39 Post 30/4610, E13933/1920.
40 Attlee, 'Post Office reform', p. 565.
41 Wolmer, *Post Office Reform*, pp. 218–19.
42 PP 1931-2 XII, *Report of Committee of Enquiry on the Post Office*, pp. 743, 757–62.
43 Post 33/4614, M17026/1934.
44 Comment of Mr Henry Tilling.

Chapter 10

The epilogue differs from the preceding chapters in that it cannot be based on detailed archival research. To a very large extent, it is based on conversation with present and past employees of the Post Office at all levels, from postman to director. The following were also used:

Post 33/3588, M4097/1932 and Post 33/3576, M4004/1932 on the Advisory Council and public relations.

Post Office Board, Minutes and Papers from 1945 to 1953.

Report of a Committee appointed by the Post Office and Union of Post Office Workers to enquire into the circumstances of a dispute arising out of the Union's claim for pay increases and shortening of incremental scales, 1971.

Report of the Post Office Review Committee, 1977.

Monopolies and Mergers Commission, *The Inner London Letter Post: A Report on the Letter Post Service in the Area comprising the Numbered London Postal Districts, 1980.*

Monopolies and Mergers Commission, *The Post Office Letter Post Service: A Report on the Letter Post Service in the Head Post Office Areas of Glasgow, Belfast and Cardff and in the Numbered London Postal Districts, 1984.*

Reallocation of Indoor Postal and Telegraph Duties: Effect on Rank and File Grades, May 1946.

PP 1951–2 XVIII, *Report of the Post Office (Departmental Classes) Recognition Committee.*

PP 1955–6 XXVI, *Report on Post Office Development and Finance.*

PP 1959–60 XXVII, *The Status of the Post Office.*

PP 1966–7 XVII, *First Report from Select Committee on Nationalised Industries. The Post Office. Volume 1. Report and Proceedings of the Committee.*

PP 1966–7 XVIII, *First Special Report from the Select Committee on Nationalised Industries: The Post Office (Observations of the Post Office).*

PP 1966–7 LIX, *Reorganisation of the Post Office.*

PP 1967–8 XXVII, *National Board for Prices and Incomes Report No. 58, Post Office Charges.*

PP 1967–8 XXXIX, *Nationalised Industries: A Review of Economic and Financial Objectives.*

M. E. Corby, *The Postal Business, 1969–79: A Study in Public Sector Management* (1979).

R. Pryke, *The Nationalised Industries: Policies and Performance since 1968* (1981).

Index

387

226, 227, 229, 231, 235, 243, 244, 251,
253, 256, 260, 268, 272
Treasury Committee to investigate
responsibility for building work
(1912), 277–8
Trevelyan, Sir Charles, 241; *see also*
Report on the organisation of the
Permanent Civil Service
Trollope, Anthony, xiii, xviii, 3, 5, 35,
40–1, 165–6, 238, 241–3, 248, 249,
250, 313, 314
trustee savings banks, 93, 94, 95, 97–102,
106, 115
Turnor, P. V., 286
Tweedmouth, Lord, 200, 220, 228, 257
Twopenny Post *see under* London
two-tier post, 347–8

Union Générale des Postes, 150
Union of Post Office Workers
(UPW), 114, 139, 144–5, 201, 205,
266, 267, 268, 346, 349–54
Union Postale Universelle (UPU), 80, 81,
150, 151, 152; rates, 173, 175, 176, 178
United Kingdom Postal Clerks'
Association, 113
United States, 80, 81, 149, 152, 153,
157, 158, 163, 165, 172, 174–5, 180,
189, 235, 303, 345
unsealed post *see* open post

wages and salaries *see under* employees

Waghorn, Thomas, 154
Wallace, Robert, 16, 17–18, 19, 35; *see
also* Select Committee on postage
Walpole, Sir Spencer, 314–15, 317
War Office, 205, 209, 210, 211, 212,
304, 317, 322, 327
Warrington, 224
war tax, 76
Welby, Ralph W., 109–10, 305–6, 321
Wellington, Duke of, 19
West Indies, 27, 147, 159, 171
White Star line, 172, 173–4, 175
Whitley Councils, 265–8, 349, 350
Wilkins, Roland, 327, 329
Willcocks, E., 252
Williamson, F. H., 137, 175, 185
Wilson, Captain, J. H., 156
Winslow, 276–7
Wolmer, Viscount, 270, 272, 295–6, 305,
308, 310, 332
women *see* employees, female
Wood, Sir Kingsley, 310
Woolf, Leonard, 244
Wooster, H. S., 283
World War I, 48, 49, 64, 72, 76, 79, 137,
138, 201, 207, 231, 232, 265, 316, 329
World War II, 143, 188, 236, 349

Yates, Edmund, 5, 21, 30

Zanzibar, 147, 171

With the Night Mail from Euston Station
(from *The Graphic*, 21 December 1889)